Showdown at Big Sandy

ALSO BY GREG DOUDNA

Redating the Dead Sea Scrolls Found at Qumran

4Q Pesher Nahum: A Critical Edition

Showdown at Big Sandy: Youthful Creativity Confronts Bureaucratic Inertia at an Unconventional Bible College in East Texas*

*(Ambassador College, Big Sandy, Texas, 1972-75)

Greg Doudna

2006

Published by The Scrollery, PO Box 4395, Bellingham, WA 98227 USA (www.scrollery.com).
Email: showdown@scrollery.com

First edition 1989
Revised edition 2006   h

Copyright © 1989, 2006 by Greg Doudna.
All rights reserved. No part of this book may be republished without written permission, except in the case of brief quotations embodied in critical articles or reviews.

Printed in the United States

ISBN 978-0-9789-8380-2
Library of Congress Control Number: 2006910786

PREFACE

The polished, portly, dignified, slow-speaking evangelist paused as he prepared to read the next question. It was a Friday evening Bible Study in the Auditorium of Ambassador College, Pasadena, late 1970s. Several hundred Worldwide Church of God members had gathered to hear the scripture expounded by whichever minister was scheduled for that evening. As was customary, the minister in charge read and answered written questions submitted from the audience. The evangelist cleared his throat and began reading.

"Is it possible for God to reveal a New Truth to a member in an outlying church area?"

The Worldwide Church of God was a church which taught and practiced government from "the top down." The pyramid was the preferred analogy to the divine will of hierarchical obedience. God was on top of the pyramid. Under God was Christ, and under Christ was Herbert W. Armstrong. Under Herbert Armstrong were the headquarters evangelists and department heads. Under them were the pastors and elders in the field ministry. Under the ministry were the local deacons. On the bottom, learning humility and obedience in this life and thereby proving worthiness to be given rule over cities in the millennium, were the church members.

New Truth was revealed to the church in the same way, following all the proper channels. God through Christ would reveal New Truth to Herbert Armstrong. Herbert Armstrong was ably assisted by the headquarters evangelists. They would aid him in studying into matters needing attention. Together headquarters would come to discern God's Truth. Once Herbert Armstrong understood New Truth as Truth, he would adopt it as church doctrine. The role of the church member was to support Herbert Armstrong in his tireless task of preaching the true gospel to the world as an end-time witness. The members' job was to pray for and financially support the Work with an attitude of dedication, zealousness, and humility. The whole church was to pull together in unity behind Herbert Armstrong and his headquarters team, to help get the job done.

"Is it possible for God to reveal New Truth to a church member in an outlying area?"

The immaculately dressed and groomed evangelist, carefully styled hair in place, looked out over the audience from under his bushy eyebrows which strangely always reminded me of Leonid Brezhnev.[1] Although he was a long-time administrator not known for being overly innovative, he was not, however, completely the unbending conservative. He was not one to dogmatically crush a new way of looking at old truths, within limits of course.

"Well ...," he answered in his deep rolling voice, "I suppose it's *possible*." The evangelist was nothing if not magnanimous. As if considering a new idea that until this moment had never before occurred to him, the evangelist weighed the theoretical possibility that God could reveal a New Truth to a local church member.

"I suppose God could if He *wanted* to," he continued.

"Of course He never has in the *past*, and He isn't doing so *now*"—the evangelist paused, peering intently out over the audience as if daring anyone to disagree—"but I suppose God could if He *wanted* to." With this, the dignified evangelist dismissed the matter, satisfied that it had been thoroughly and definitively answered, and went on to the next question. And so it went.

---

[1] Ruler of the Soviet Union 1964-1982.

Preface

~ ~ ~

The occasion above was one of the last services of the Worldwide Church of God I attended. So much had happened. I thought back to how it all started.

I recalled my early years in a home of mainstream American values, of conservative Protestant orientation, in Akron, Ohio. I had been raised on two basic truths. The first was that the Bible was the Word of God. The second was that it was important to do what is right regardless of whether "everyone else does it." As I entered my teenage years I read some literature my father was studying. From this I learned that the Ten Commandments said to keep the seventh day as the Sabbath. And, I learned that the seventh day was Saturday, not Sunday. I realized that if keeping the Ten Commandments was right, then this included the seventh-day Sabbath and this is what I must do.

This is how the message of Herbert Armstrong's Radio Church of God (as it was then called) first struck home to me. But more than that, literature from the Radio Church of God opened up exciting things in the Bible and promised a better world. (The name was changed to Worldwide Church of God in 1968.)

Even more, I learned there existed a college campus which was an oasis of tranquility in the midst of this troubled world. Here there were no drugs or student demonstrations. Here happy students learned true values—not just how to make a living but how to live. I decided I wanted to go to Ambassador College more than anything on earth.

This is my story of what happened when that dream came true. I was a student at Ambassador College in Big Sandy, Texas from 1972-75. This was a branch campus of the headquarters Ambassador College at Pasadena, California. Today the Ambassador Colleges are gone. I was there when it flourished, during a pivotal time in its history, a time of turmoil, scandal, and intrigue. I use narrative and humor as a means of telling this

Preface

story. I invite you to walk with me some of the steps of the way, like going to a strange land and back again. I will show you what it is like to be inside a sect—an unconventional group which believes it alone has the truth of human existence. It will be an odyssey through sectarian interpretations of the Bible, with strange sights and creatures along the way. There will be plenty of youthful creativity running into bureaucratic obstruction. And you will gain a window of insight into an unusual chapter in American religious history.

And finally, if it is not obvious already, this book is very *American*. International readers should realize that this book follows a time-honored tradition of American writing in which what happens in America is obviously the most interesting and important subject for discussion. It is not that I mean to ignore you. But this is an American story. There is no land on earth which can produce unusual biblical fundamentalisms like America. It is one of our claims to fame, being an upstart country of recent origins compared to ancient civilizations of Europe, Africa, and Asia. Unanchored in so much tradition, we are free to reinvent plenty of wheels. The idiosyncratics and cranks and colorful figures which populate our land are an American heritage, especially so in the world of religion.

~ ~ ~

A first edition of this book in 1989 received very limited circulation and is out of print. The present revision was prepared in the aftermath of a 30th year reunion of my Ambassador College, Big Sandy classmates, held at Winter Park, Colorado on August 4-6, 2006.

Sylvia "Bobby" Clark, Russ Gmirkin, Mike Heffley, Earl Smith, Karen Stevens, and the late Lillian Cantleberry gave valuable reading/critiquing of the original manuscript of 1989. I am grateful for additional reading/critiquing from my wife, Anne Caroline Doudna, and again Bobby Clark and Earl Smith as I

Preface

prepared the 2006 edition. Many others played a part in this book, too many to name here. In particular, I think of every faculty member, student, and employee at Ambassador College, Big Sandy 1972-75, without whom this book would not have come about. This book is dedicated to all of those people from those bygone days, as well as the unseen, unknown people of those years who gave financial support to Ambassador College, often at personal costs that no one will ever know. Everyone in this book is a real person, everything narrated happened, and no names have been changed. I sincerely hope this book will be helpful to others.

Greg Doudna
Bellingham, Washington
Oct. 16, 2006

TABLE OF CONTENTS

Preface   v

PART ONE: INNOCENT IN PARADISE

1. Big Sandy Oasis: Ambassador College   3
2. The Story of the Worldwide Church of God   29
3. The 7000-Year Plan   67
4. The Doctrine Against Interracial Marriage   109
5. Big Sandy School Days: 1974   145

PART TWO: CREATIVITY

6. How I Tried to Prove the United States is Ephraim, not Manasseh   173
7. Afterward on Anglo-Israelism, Part I   199
8. Afterward on Anglo-Israelism, Part II   223
9. The Further Adventures of the Ephraim/U.S. Theory: Chaos Theory in Action   259
10. Is God Reproducing?   279
11. Desert Romance   303
12. Meat Offered to Idols   307
13. Letter of the Law and Spirit of the Law   319
14. Quest for Immortality   325
15. Key Events in the 1973-74 Sacred Calendar (And Other Timely Topics)   335
16. Headquarters in Prophecy   355
17. The Most Important Holy Day   369
18. Faith Healing and Doctors   381
19. Creation and Origins   409
20. Tithing   425
21. Big Sandy School Days: 1975   453

PART THREE: DENOUEMENT

22. Ambassador College, Pasadena: 1976	469
23. The Return Home	483
24. Letters and Reflections	491
25. Big Sandy Voices: the Song of the Quest	509
Addendum: The Demise and End of Ambassador College, Big Sandy	517
Entering freshman class of 1972-73 at Ambassador College, Big Sandy	519
Index of Persons	521

PART ONE

INNOCENT IN PARADISE

CHAPTER 1

BIG SANDY OASIS: AMBASSADOR COLLEGE

To get to the Big Sandy campus of Ambassador College in the early 1970s, you would go about a hundred miles east from booming Dallas on Highway 80. After you journeyed beyond the effects of Dallas's wealth and sprawl, Highway 80 gradually turned into long stretches of sometimes rolling but mostly flat, rural countryside. You would see cows by the side of the road, oil derricks here and there, lean old men in ten-gallon hats who waved, women in faded print dresses, children playing. Your drive would be punctuated by passing through sleepy, old-timey towns. After feeling that civilization had been left behind and the clock turned back, you would finally come to the site—former site, now—of Ambassador College on the left two miles after passing through the bustling metropolis of Big Sandy (population 1600). If you continued further on Highway 80, you would come to the larger cities of Gladewater and Longview. The city of Tyler, meanwhile, is nearby to the southwest. This is east Texas, the atmosphere of which is portrayed so well in the Sam Shepard movie, *Paris, Texas*.

The name "Big Sandy" did not come from soil type (though cotton growing of earlier times had depleted the soil, requiring heavy fertilization to restore it), and the nearest beach is hundreds of miles away. Nor did the name come from any local misconception of the town's size or degree of importance.

4
Big Sandy Oasis: Ambassador College

Rather, the town received its name from its first sheriff, a big man named Sandy, hence "Big Sandy." It was an area of Texas where the custom of openly carrying guns on downtown streets had survived well into the twentieth century. Now (early 1970s), Big Sandy consisted of a drug store, a bank, a Dairy Queen, Howard Clifton's barber shop, a general store, miscellaneous other shops and offices, a couple of filling stations, a disreputable hotel, and a cantankerous and atrociously printed Big Sandy weekly gazette with all-capitals, badly-misspelled, smudgily printed headlines and articles.

To the oasis-like Ambassador College campus, tucked away in a setting of lakes, woods, and acreage in this unlikely locale, I had come for the purpose of obtaining an education over the next four years: a liberal arts college education with emphasis on learning true values unavailable in worldly universities.

Chancellor Herbert Armstrong frequently said all three of his Ambassador Colleges "mutually excel one another." (His other two campuses were at his headquarters in Pasadena, California, and in Bricket Wood, England.) But it was well-known that Herbert had a particular fondness for his Bricket Wood campus in England. The Big Sandy campus, however, the youngest of the three, was the favorite of Herbert Armstrong's son Garner Ted. Garner Ted Armstrong was the voice of the "World Tomorrow" radio broadcast heard across America and, to repeat an over-used expression, Herbert Armstrong's "heir-apparent."

Here, at Big Sandy in the early 1950s, Garner Ted had met his wife Shirley. She was the sister of a landowner named Buck Hammer. Hammer had donated his land to Herbert Armstrong for Feast of Tabernacles use. Then, starting in 1964, the third campus of Ambassador College was opened on the site. Garner Ted, an outdoors person at heart, frequently came to Big Sandy for a few days at a time. Sometimes he would play his banjo and sing with the student body. Big Sandy might be likened to the rural and unlearned "Galilee" of the Work compared to the more sophisticated "Jerusalem" of headquarters at Pasadena.

5
Big Sandy Oasis: Ambassador College

~ ~ ~

None of the Ambassador Colleges were accredited. Church membership or belief was not a requirement for attendance, but at least ninety-five percent of the student body were there because of background or interest in the church. My entering freshman class in 1972 numbered 120, with the total student body about 400.

Only about one in five applicants was accepted. Selection of applicants was based on high school grades (or previous college), Scholastic Aptitude Test (SAT) scores, and a character reference from the local Worldwide Church of God pastor. Tuition was kept reasonable and student jobs were provided, so that costs were affordable to most motivated and qualified aspiring students. (I do not recall any federal or state funds being available to students, except for veterans.) Out of our class of 120, there were nearly a dozen veterans, several older married students, and a high number (something like forty percent) of transfer students from other institutions. One of our number came from West Point. Another, Joe Cochran, had played football under famous Coach "Bear" Bryant at the University of Alabama. About twenty entering freshmen had degrees from other institutions. By some kind of astonishing coincidence, a fellow freshman, Mary Slider from Michigan, turned out to be the daughter of my mother's best friend in high school—though neither of our mothers had prior knowledge of the other's offspring's involvement in Herbert Armstrong's church or their respective applications to the same small, unaccredited college in east Texas.

On a somber note, one of our number, Randy Gregory, an unassuming, decent, universally well-regarded fellow student whom I knew well, became a focus of national news in the United States in March 2005 when he was the tragic victim of a horrific mass shooting in Brookfield, Illinois. (Gregory, who was pastoring a small church congregation, and ten others were gunned down as they met for their sabbath services.

6
Big Sandy Oasis: Ambassador College

Gregory and one of his sons were killed; his wife, the former Marjean Strommen, a later Big Sandy student, was also shot but survived.)

Our freshman class was the brightest Big Sandy had ever accepted, as measured by academic standings and SAT scores. There were a number of high school valedictorians. Later, certain administrators were overheard remarking that it had been a mistake to take in such a bright freshman class. Bright minds too easily fell prey to "intellectualism" and "independent thinking."

Freshman orientation

Chancellor Herbert Armstrong flew in to Big Sandy to greet the incoming freshmen and to give an orientation address. Though he had just turned eighty, he was filled with energy and humor. He warmly welcomed us. Then he launched into practicalities: There was to be No Necking.

This was in keeping with a book Armstrong had written, *The Missing Dimension in Sex*. Armstrong explained that amorous kissing or necking is the first stage of lovemaking and belongs only in marriage, not before. Socializing between the sexes was encouraged at Ambassador College, but was to be chaste. Chaste meant non-contact, except at dances where contact was compulsory. The elder Armstrong's rule against premarital necking was enforced on campus. Students were responsible for self-enforcement of the no-necking rule when they went off-campus on dates. College officials often did not inquire too closely on the matter of forbidden kissing in cases of engaged students or those imminently expected to become engaged. The college administrators did not have hearts entirely of stone. But no college official could admit this openly.

After his prohibition of Student Necking, our chancellor then asked a trick question. "How many of you men here want to become ministers?" Two hands were innocently raised by young men obviously unfamiliar with Worldwide Church of God cult-

7
Big Sandy Oasis: Ambassador College

ural mores. This was not the right response to give to Chancellor Armstrong's question.

"Well, you two men probably won't become ministers," Armstrong replied. God *called* men to the ministry. It was not something that someone could just *choose* to be on one's *own*.

Actually, at least half of the young men present, by conservative estimate, did hope to become ministers. And a good number of the young women hoped, secretly or otherwise, to marry ministers. Being selected as a ministerial trainee after graduation and then becoming ordained meant status and material perquisites in the Worldwide Church of God. The ministry was the privileged elite. But it was not considered becoming or appropriate to *say* one wanted to become a minister. That was supposed to come four years later, as it were, as a complete surprise. It was supposed to be God's doing, not one's own.

(The fact that not more than two men expressed a desire to become ministers would also have come as a surprise to some draft boards. For purposes of the draft, all male students were certified as in training for the ministry and were able to receive exemptions from their local draft boards on this basis.)

After Herbert Armstrong had finished orienting us, there was a formal reception. I shook hands with Chancellor Armstrong, as well as with a mysterious figure by his side in dark sunglasses who accompanied him everywhere. It was to be my only personal contact with Herbert W. Armstrong and legal counsel Stanley R. Rader.

Nine-hole golf courses, racquetball courts, and "George"

The setting of the Big Sandy Ambassador College campus was beautiful. There were landscaped valleys, tasteful bridges, and fountains and sculptures between the buildings. About half the students lived in well-designed student dormitories. Each thirty-two person dormitory would have four to a room, with separate eight-desk study rooms, a lounge out front with a fireplace and piano, and a large number of "prayer closets." These "prayer closets" gave accessible privacy and quiet at a moment's notice.

Since there were not enough dormitories to house everyone, the other half of the students lived in air-conditioned, carpeted, compact but efficient two-person living units which collectively comprised "Booth City." In "Booth City," men's and women's residence areas were divided by what students called the "Berlin Wall" (over which there was to be no crossing). Surprisingly, living in "Booth City" was favored over the dormitories by students.

The campus had a nine-hole golf course. It was kept green year-round under the blazing Texas sun through an extensive water sprinkler system consuming countless thousands of gallons of water and an inordinate number of hours of student labor. There was also a brand-new racquetball courts building. Unfortunately, after paying for watering the golf course and installing the new racquetball courts, there just wasn't much money left over for classrooms. The classrooms were temporary metal structures still in use nine years after the college had begun.

There was a lighted airstrip and a hanger with several church-owned aircraft. There was a ranch, a campgrounds area in the "Piney Woods," and a convention center headquarters for the Church's annual fall Festival of Tabernacles. Last but not least, there was the wonderful little library in the Redwood Building with its woefully inadequate collection of archaic theological titles which seemed mostly to have been picked up in dusty second-hand bookstores sometime in the 1950s.

Funny-looking, dinosaur-like fat little armadillos occasionally could be seen at night trying to run out of the way when surprised by a car's headlights. (They usually ran in the wrong direction—they weren't too bright.) The most unusual resident wildlife, however, was "George," a six-foot alligator. George somehow had washed into the sewage lagoon as a three-foot baby during a flood, decided to call it home, became a favorite tourist attraction, and continued growing. We would often see him sunning himself beside the lagoon. To many, he seemed to

Big Sandy Oasis: Ambassador College

slowly grin whenever he saw anyone looking at him, but that may have been due to overactive imaginations. (Sadly, the sewage treatment facility broke down one night. Raw, untreated sewage poured directly into the lagoon. This proved a bit too strong even for George. He perambulated over the campus grounds, wandered around and finally came to rest in an ornamental pond below the library under a footbridge. Two coeds taking an early-morning walk discovered him. George's grin may have been real that morning; in those few hours he had happily munched up most of the pond's expensive, imported foot-long goldfish. He wasn't permitted to set up permanent housekeeping in his new chosen location. Poor George was captured and transported for release in more native surroundings before anyone else became a snack. Many students mourned his departure.)

The student dining hall featured excellent food with home-grown vegetables, fresh whole milk, and beef from college-owned cattle. Mealtimes also involved an assistant cook whose sour disposition was legendary (and often our first sight for the day at breakfast)—but he was so predictable in his sourness that it made him beloved by students, almost as if there was a competition to see who could get the acerbic so-and-so to crack a smile. This was reinforced by the occasional instances in which someone did.

The head cook, Carlton Green, on the other hand, was the complete opposite—he always had a welcoming nature and cheery demeanor, in addition to being highly competent in running the kitchen. Green, an African-American, would probably have been named the single best-liked individual on the entire campus if students were polled—simply because *everyone* knew Carlton Green going through the meal lines, and he made *every* student coming through feel special and accepted.

After growing up in a northern Midwestern industrial city, I enjoyed the feeling of open space, wide skies and fresh air. I brought a used motorcycle my freshman year, and I remember many carefree hours riding it on back roads, on trails in the woods around Lake Loma, and into nearby towns. I was glad I had come to Big Sandy. I loved the setting, the sunsets, the sounds of the crickets in the evening, and the other students and faculty members. It really was an oasis hidden away from the rest of the world.

I loved the informal atmosphere. At Big Sandy, it was actually possible to wear blue jeans to classes. This would have been unthinkable at the other two Ambassador campuses. The administration at Big Sandy wasn't too keen on blue jeans either, and periodically expressed passing displeasure. But they never launched the pitched battle in earnest which would have been necessary to enforce a complete ban on them. As a result, men students, I among others, often wore jeans. (This freedom to wear jeans did not, however, apply to women. Eighty-year old Chancellor Armstrong, a thousand miles away, decided that women should wear dresses at all times.)

Friday nights there would be Bible study. It was the most normal thing in the world after Bible study to stay up with other students all hours of the night discussing and studying the Bible while downing cheese and a six-pack of beer. Deputy Chancellor Mr. Dart once questioned in a sermon how much of value got accomplished in conversations after midnight. But speaking from experience, I can say that was when the most interesting stuff got talked about and biblical speculations ran the most freely, unhindered by normal inhibitions somehow connected with conventional daylight hours.

Student employment

It was believed beneficial for students to work for part of their college expenses. All students were therefore employed eighteen to twenty hours a week at various jobs on campus. My student job during my freshman year was servicing ranch vehicles and ministers' cars in the Transportation Department. Two full-time mechanics and church members working at the Transportation Department, Steve Prociw and Dick Cowan, happened also to be

11
Big Sandy Oasis: Ambassador College

the mayor and fire chief of Big Sandy, respectively, in their off hours. This was something of an anomaly since the church had a strict doctrine against both voting and holding political office. But no one seemed to notice or mind. Also employed at this department were ex-National Security Agency agent (that's like CIA) and future Worldwide Church of God minister Larry Moluf; fellow freshman Tom Melzer, who excelled at hanging from rafters and making monkey sounds; flute player Creighton Miller from Toledo; Corvette aficionado and fellow Akronite Tim Sobitz, Jr.; Ron "You lika my pizza?" Smith; likeable Bob Overstreet; Jim "Omar" Share; Robert Robinson "man of few words"; easy-going Service Department head Larry Haines, and assorted other memorable characters. Rarely have cars been washed, lubed, and serviced by more distinguished personnel.

Our supervisor was David Robinson, a conservative long-time minister. One day one of the Conscientious Objector employees and I set off an M-80 firecracker behind the Transportation Department building just after closing time at 5:00 p.m. It sounded like a cannon. People came running out of buildings from all around to see what had blown up and how many ambulances were needed. In the midst of everyone running *toward* the sound of the explosion, two figures could be seen running *away* from the explosion—the other employee and me. Unknown to us, Mr. Robinson had not yet left. By noting the trajectories of running directions and exercising elementary logic, he correctly deduced who the culprits were. I was called to report to Mr. Robinson's office over the shop loudspeaker. (Hearing your name called over this loudspeaker was like hearing God calling.) I went prepared for the Last Judgment. But since this was a first offense and I was suitably contrite, my dressing-down was unexpectedly mild. Mr. Robinson's reprimand consisted mostly of elementary safety instruction, and actually was the occasion for getting to know each other better. (I never gave him cause for a second reprimand.) A few years later, Mr. Robinson set off his own explosion in the church of a different nature when he wrote a book in which he portrayed Herbert Armstrong in less than flattering terms.[2] Worldwide Church of God officials unsuccessfully tried to legally suppress Robinson's book.

Early in my sophomore year, the fall of 1973, I applied for and got what to me was an absolutely dream job—night switchboard. The hours were unconventional—midnight to 3:00 a.m. six nights a week. But I had all this *time* in quiet and stillness to read, study, think and write, in between the occasional phone call and radio contact with the patrolling campus security vehicle. This job enabled me to have the time to study and think up things.

Faculty reminiscences: "No! That's 'N'-'O'!"

The resident administrator at Big Sandy during most of my freshman year, under the absent Herbert Armstrong, was Deputy Chancellor Les McCullough. Dignified Mr. McCullough was not one to be tangled with. He had a distinctive way of answering submitted written questions during Bible Studies. If a submitted question asked something he didn't like, he would read the question with rising, restrained fury in his voice. Then he would put down the slip of paper and GLARE at the audience, as if every member sitting out there was somehow complicit in the affront. (It was not questions on theological topics which would produce this reaction. He would handle those in stride. The questions which irritated him would be along lines of: "Is it OK to jump on a freight train hobo-style as a means of travel to Mexico City?"—in that case sent up by a concerned coed after learning of her male friends' intentions—or something similar.) After everyone in the audience was thoroughly intimidated, McCullough would rip forth with his answer. It would be a model of diplomacy: "NO! That's 'N'—'O.' Absolutely not!" (Silence. Long pause for the words to sink in.) Then, that settled,

---

[2] David Robinson, *Herbert Armstrong's Tangled Web* (Tulsa, OK: John Hadden Publishers, 1980).

Big Sandy Oasis: Ambassador College

without further comment he would go on to the next question on a totally different subject.

Or he might answer the question in this way: "Mr. Herbert Armstrong wouldn't do it. Mr. Garner Ted Armstrong wouldn't do it. Mr. Kelly wouldn't do it. *I* wouldn't do it. But if *you* want to ... (dramatic pause) ... GO AHEAD!!!" (The rafters would shake.) Somehow this answer was, if anything, even clearer in communicating his view than his straightforward "NO."

But perhaps the deputy chancellor's favorite expression, always uttered with utmost solemnity, was: "At Ambassador College, the door swings both ways." This meant students could be kicked out as easily as they had been admitted. No students could ever complain about not knowing where they stood with Mr. McCullough. Privately, students' quotation to each other of this expression would bring a smile. But no one laughed when Mr. McCullough said these words. You didn't mess with Mr. McCullough.

Deputy Chancellor McCullough provided the commanding presence, the image of authority, and the flashiest sports car on campus. But most of the actual work of running the college seemed to be done by McCullough's faithful assistant, Dean of Students Ronald Kelly. It is amazing to me to recall that Kelly then was so young—in his early thirties. Perhaps it is amazing to me because I remember his hair was rapidly going completely white at his early age. With the prodigious quantity of work he did and his involvement in never-ending student affairs, maybe it is no wonder his hair went white.

Mr. Kelly was a hard-working "company man" if ever there was one. In one memorable Feast of Tabernacles sermon he proclaimed himself proud to be a "company man" or one of many "yellow pencils" cut from the same mold. If you got involved in all the social activities, went to the basketball games, and did not show too much proclivity for intellectual pursuits, this fit in with Mr. Kelly's vision of a true Ambassador education. If you stood out as nonconformist in any away (i.e. reading books), then you were likely to be viewed with suspicion. Mr. Kelly (who also acted as dean of faculty one year) did not try to disguise his lack of interest in things intellectual. During my freshman year he guaranteed in a public forum that there would never be a class in psychology or philosophy at Ambassador College. There was no point, he explained, in studying the history of man's ideas when we already had all we needed to know in the Bible. (The next year there were classes offered in both psychology and philosophy.)

Mr. Kelly was always good-hearted toward me whenever our paths crossed. I never created the kind of problems that would have brought me more to his attention. (I never, for example, smoked dope, skinny-dipped in Lake Loma, got drunk, dated a black girl, or went to a meeting of dissidents.) Mr. Kelly was a visiting speaker at the Akron, Ohio church once for the spring holy days. When my father introduced himself, Mr. Kelly said diplomatically, "I think of Greg as an Original Thinker." This hugely pleased my Dad, who always loved to hear compliments about his son. Knowing what Mr. Kelly thought of most original thinkers made the reference more cryptic to me.

Like fading memories I remember: fascinating Jewish and medieval traditions from young, intense Hebrew instructor Mark Kaplan ... first-year speech class from reflective Daryl Reedy ... the biological basis of evolution theory from sage Donald Deakins ... ancient Mayan and Egyptian calendar and eclipse cycles from guest lecturer and retired registrar from Pasadena, Ken Herrmann ... Old Testament Survey and exhortations to build character from hard-working Richard Ames ... a fascinating ecosystem explanation for why Lake Loma had no big fish from biologist Richard Wakefield ... astronomical phenomena from long-timer Sidney Hegvold ... ways in which ancient myths and history were linked to biblical history, from discoverer-of-old-books Allen Manteufel ... French class from irreverent Berlin Guillory ... how language is related to thinking, from new faculty member Don Ward ... graphic arts class from Alan Heath ... speech instruction from new deputy chancellor Ronald Dart, and so on. There were many others, but these are

Big Sandy Oasis: Ambassador College

representative of the portrait which was, to me, Ambassador College at Big Sandy.

Then there were my fellow students. So many stories that could be told. My assigned roommates my freshman year in Men's Dorm 1 were two juniors, Woody Coston and Tony Prettyman, and one senior, Michael Billingsley. Billingsley was from Georgia, tall, clean, strong, dignified, the first in his family to attend college. He always wore a fresh, spotless, long-sleeved white shirt and blue jeans. He would play a soulful, beautiful vocal rendition of "Dixie" and get real quiet. It was as if he was far away and tears deep inside were not far below the surface. He explained to me he knew slavery was wrong and that he knew it was in God's will that the Confederacy be defeated, but that he still got emotional about the invasion of his homeland that the Civil War involved. When Billingsley was listening to "Dixie," that was not the time to laugh or joke.

Woody Coston, also quiet and dignified, was heavy-set, receding hairline, walrus moustache, dressed Western, grew up ranching and worked on the Ag crew at the farm. He played lots of Johnny Rivers music, songs like "Poor Side of Town" and "Memphis." He played Johnny Rivers so much that for years after I knew the words to many Johnny Rivers' songs practically by heart.

Good-natured Tony Prettyman was from Toledo. He and I went to Colorado Springs, Colorado during spring break of my freshman year to take a camping trip up Pike's Peak. We made it partway up before turning back and staying at my cousin Marilyn's place in Colorado Springs. We attended Sabbath services in Colorado Springs and I remember a striking, sincere 16-year old girl named Tammy Hall introducing herself and talking with us; later she came to Big Sandy and went on to become Mrs. Joseph Tkach, Jr., wife of the pastor-general of the Worldwide Church of God since 1995 and editor of women's ministry publications.

I could go on for another hundred pages describing the students I remember so well, who have scattered to the four corners of the earth now. Things like the Colorado Springs trip were adventures that never would have happened if I had stayed in Akron.

Women at Ambassador College

Women were expected to fit a certain ideal—attractive, modest, charming, funny, not too intellectual. Women with inquiring minds typically had problems, unless they learned to disguise or dumb down their intelligence. There was just no place for intellectual brilliance in a woman at Ambassador College. Women were to learn home economics and how to be a hostess for their future husband. It was repeatedly advised by the male ministers that while a woman should have *some* intellectual capabilities so that she could be an interesting conversationist with her husband, she should not *exceed* him in intellectual abilities. An anonymous blogger called "neotherm" wrote this in 2006:

> I recall that at Ambassador College, Big Sandy the most important qualification for a woman to have was physical beauty and maybe some musical talent. For women students it was really kind of a "meat market." So the Overall Women's Club Monitor or whatever she was called tended to be a very attractive young woman. And of course, all kinds of evil come about in a little closed society where a woman's worth is defined solely by her appearance. For attractive young ladies with little other merit, it was paradise. Their market value was extraordinary. All manner of opportunities would open up. I have witnessed this.

A lot of women chafed at this, of course. One incident stands out. Second year speech class was required for all men. It made waves on campus when at the first weekly combined speech class meeting the start of my sophomore year (fall 1973), among the sixty or so sophomore men, I among them, there was a lone woman, courageous Trish Willhoite, calmly at her seat waiting for class to begin. No woman had ever taken men's second year speech class before, and everyone was surprised that that was

Big Sandy Oasis: Ambassador College

even possible. However, Trish had simply registered for it and nothing in the bureaucratic process had prevented her, so there she was, bright and ready to learn second year speech along with all the men. She stayed in the class throughout the year too.

Another student, outspoken Linda Moll (now Linda Moll Smith) from Kansas, a transfer student to Big Sandy from the English campus at Bricket Wood, recalled:

> Late in my junior year [1974-75] I was so outraged by a forum in which Ron Dart spent the entire time telling the men students ONLY how important it was for them to plan their futures, careers, etc. and not even mentioning the women that I wrote him a long, fiery letter telling him just how crazy and short-sighted that was. As a direct result of that letter, the next year, Fourth Year Bible (which was considered a ministerial training class, read "for men only") was open to "selected" junior and senior women. And, second year speech for "the ladies" as well.

Women were such commodities that the Conscientious Objector employees, young men of good character the same age as the students, were strictly forbidden to date the AC coeds (they were reserved for AC males). And so it was at God's College.

Howard Clark

No portrait of Big Sandy of those years would be complete without mention of Howard Clark (1930-2002), charismatic and colorful speech instructor and thorn in the side to established norms in thinking. Howard Clark was a real character. He was highly popular with students, encouraged independent thinking, and was ultimately fired. Heavy-set with a booming voice, his cheery "Howdy!" would resonate into all corners of the library whenever he entered, as he greeted anyone and everyone on his way to his office.

Clark had been disabled after having been shot up in the Korean War in 1950. He came into the church in California in the 1950s, with a family and almost completely paralyzed.

Big Sandy Oasis: Ambassador College

Herbert Armstrong's oldest son, Richard David Armstrong (who died following a tragic automobile accident in 1958) privately anointed Clark and prayed for him. In one of the most astonishing miraculous healings in the church, Clark recovered the use of his arms and legs and never needed the wheelchair again. The memory of this remarkable event kept Clark with the church long after he saw many outrageous foibles in it. (Later, he came to distinguish between personal faith and human organizations.) Clark enrolled in Ambassador College and—through some breakdown in the system, some headquarters officials would later conclude—went on to be ordained as a minister.

I was not among the fortunate students assigned to Clark's freshman speech class sections. (His were always the most popular.) But at the weekly combined speech class I would hear him talk of interesting things ranging from the mechanics of voice production to Alfred Korzybski's General Semantics (with emphasis upon "put a comma after what you know, not a period"), to readings from Richard Bach's classic, *Jonathan Livingston Seagull* about soaring free from the flock. Clark also saw to it that Eric Hoffer's *The True Believer* was in the bookstore and read by students. This classic by Hoffer describes "true believers" who seek to latch on to movements which promise group meaning greater than individual existence.

Although he had a reputation for being one of the best speakers in the church, Clark was not assigned further Sabbath speaking at Big Sandy after one sermonette my freshman year which I missed but certainly heard about. (Sermonettes lasted about twenty minutes, and preceded the special music and hour-and-a-quarter main sermon.) Clark said he had a simple message that morning. Then he proceeded to slowly and eloquently read the "Beatitudes" portion of Christ's Sermon on the Mount directly. Then he sat down! Combined with rumors that in classes he was making comments like, "Jesus Christ would probably be thrown off this campus if he walked in one day in person," not a few persons wondered what Clark was "getting at" reading the Sermon on the Mount like that, without comment.

Big Sandy Oasis: Ambassador College

Clark usually ate in the student dining hall with the students rather than in the more plush faculty dining room. Clark also didn't bother to use the privileged reserved seating or parking lots for ministers. He just parked his car where the members parked and sat with the rest of the members. Considering how important most ministers considered such status symbols and trappings of position, Clark's behavior stood out like a sore thumb. Clark's thumbing of privileged status was humorous at times. For example, on Saturday nights there were basketball games. Howard Clark and his family would take their seats in the student bleachers. Students would crowd around and the Clark section of the stands would have a blast. Meanwhile, more than once I saw faculty and ministers sitting huddled in their own privileged special bleachers on the other side of the court all by themselves looking on in stony silence. Another thing that stood out: all six kids of Howard and Beverly Clark went to public schools—not to the church-run Imperial Schools for grades 1-12.

Clark would regale students with tales of headquarters from his years in Pasadena. Clark's job at Pasadena in the 1960s was putting out the *Envoy*, the Ambassador College yearbook, which was a showpiece for the church. Clark said working conditions were less than ideal. Every stage of the *Envoy* had to be approved personally by Herbert Armstrong. Herbert would find things he didn't like and get enraged. He would grow livid, his jowls would shake, and he would say, "Howard, we've just got to *break* you!" Herbert would spend hours going over the page proofs with a gold ruler and magnifying glass, measuring the sizes of people's heads in the photographs to make sure no one of lower rank was bigger in the photograph than the higher ranks. One time, to show his displeasure for Clark's camera work, Herbert intentionally poured a glass of tomato juice on the completed page signatures. Then some of the tomato juice fell on the carpet and Herbert chewed out Clark for causing that. Another time Herbert expressed himself by throwing Clark's page proofs on the floor and stomping on them with his feet. Herbert would just wear himself out from being so enraged, then take time out for a nap to recover his energy while Clark waited in his office. After taking his nap, Herbert would come back refreshed and resume blasting away where he left off. One day Herbert chewed out Clark for nine hours, taking time out only for lunch. As Clark dryly put it, it was "difficult working conditions." Clark said he was fired a record twenty-one times in 1965 by Herbert Armstrong and others. (They would always calm down and let Clark have his job back.) "Herbert spent a lot of time firing me that year," Clark reminisced.

Clark was pretty forgiving. He made allowances for Herbert's temper, thinking, "Well, God uses all kinds of people."

Crisis of faith and resolution

As one who wished to believe the best, it was perplexing to me to hear two versions of the same church—the official one from the church, and another unofficial picture whispered here and there by students. Our student handbook said, "Students are encouraged to question their instructors." But some restive students were saying there was no room for individual thought and creativity within the church's organizational structure. They said the bureaucracy put down opposition in ruthless ways, crushing dissenting voices. What was the real nature of the church? Was it God's Church, founded and led by His appointed authorities? Or was it an institution gone power mad?

During the second semester of my freshman year, in the spring of 1973, I underwent a crisis of faith. Was the Bible really trustworthy? If not, what hope was there? This resolved in a personal conversion that seemed at the time like something out of William James' *Varieties of Religious Experience*—I *prayed* to be given eyes to *see* that the plan of God was true, and like a miracle, the scales lifted and I *saw*, in a way that was beyond reason ...

I can reconstruct some of the content of this crisis of faith and its resolution from notebooks and journal entries I kept as I was in the midst of it.

21
Big Sandy Oasis: Ambassador College

A junior student, Jerry Hanisko, told me of some of the findings of scholarship on the late canonization of certain books of the New Testament. This did not mesh with the idea that the apostles canonized the New Testament as we were taught in our classes. Hanisko was too intelligent and reasonable for me to write off. He said, "This scholarship cannot be ignored. That isn't being *honest*." Then, James Ribb, Big Sandy's brilliant instructor in German, told me he had experienced a "counter-conversion" when he went to graduate school after graduating from Ambassador College. (Ribb left teaching at Big Sandy at the end of my freshman year; he went on to study philosophy in Vienna.) Ribb gave me a book to read by Hugh Schonfield entitled *Those Incredible Christians*. Schonfield's book was an eye-opener, with its portrayal of an early James versus Paul conflict among the earliest Christians underneath the version written in the Book of Acts. (This is the same Schonfield who became famous in the 1960s for his "Passover Plot" theory. Schonfield, who was Jewish, believed Jesus was the Messiah but was not divine. In 1985 I visited Schonfield, then age 83, at his home in London.)

At the same time, a favorite cousin, Paul Doudna of St. Louis, too kind to say he thought I was crazy for going to Herbert Armstrong's college for an education, had written a letter to me in which he made two salient points. First, he cited certain parallel accounts in Kings and Chronicles in which armies are numbered. In one account it will read "hundreds," but in the identical, parallel account, it will read "thousands" (e.g. 1 Chron 18:4 and 2 Sam 8:4; 2 Sam 10:18 and 1 Chron 19:18; 1 Kgs 4:26 and 2 Chron 9:25). If I really believed the scriptures are without error, what did I make of these discrepancies, he asked. His second point was that the very nature of language itself argues against "biblical inerrancy." Either the Bible was written in normal language subject to the various limitations and imperfections of all human language, or else it was written in a language only superficially resembling human language and not subject to normal flaws.

22
Big Sandy Oasis: Ambassador College

I looked up the verses in Kings and Chronicles and sure enough, the numbers did disagree. (I had never noticed that before.) I took the troubling verses to a nearby senior student who was already experienced as a ministerial trainee, Briscoe Ellett. Briscoe gave a fiery counterpoint to all of the rationalism I was being confronted with. Men attempted to use *human reason* to refute God's truth because of unwillingness to *face themselves.* They are closed-minded and don't *want* to see plain evidences before them of the truth. As for the Kings and Chronicles numerical discrepancies, those were probably just scribal errors but that didn't affect the accuracy of the text, which the Masorete scribes were scrupulous to maintain. I don't know that I've ever heard anyone hold forth more colorfully for what he believed in than Briscoe Ellett. I shudder to think what verdicts juries would come up with if Briscoe had become a trial attorney.

Next I went to talk with Mr. Richard Ames, minister and speech instructor. I wanted to know in particular about Paul being wrong on expecting Jesus's return in his lifetime. Mr. Ames gave three answers: First, Paul was right in that Christ's return is now imminent for us. Second, Paul later corrected his error. Finally, it's a minor point. Mr. Ames said the evidence that the Worldwide Church of God was the true church was a love between God's people which went beyond human affection, and he saw it in the church. This was in addition to the signs of having the Sabbath, the holy days, and knowledge of the true plan of God.

Then I had a long talk with Howard Clark. Clark said not to think in terms of self-contained "proofs" banging around in a box. That is missing the mark. His faith, he said, was not based on a package of proofs or the workings of an organization but rather on a spiritual relationship by the Holy Spirit. He took this spiritual relationship to the Bible and understood the Bible in its light. Clark said he wasn't afraid of "these other guys" (the worldly philosophers and thinkers). They stimulated his thinking. Clark emphasized, "Don't see God through the eyes of

Big Sandy Oasis: Ambassador College

the organization." Your relationship with God, he said, must be direct, through the Holy Spirit, not through the filter of an organization. But still, Clark said, even with all the problems in the organization, where else can the truth be found? He assured me that if I kept seeking and praying, before long a light would dawn and I'd begin to see things clearer.

Finally I talked with junior Bill Meyer, intellectual, widely read, a true gentleman, not the least bit afflicted with dogmatism, and one who believed the church was right. (Coincidentally, he had also grown up about two blocks away from me in Akron, Ohio, though I didn't get to know him until I came to Big Sandy.) Meyer took a different approach than the "proof of the Bible" approach. He said the evidence for God was in the relationship with God that works. Things worked in his life, he said, that he did not believe could be attributed to human causes alone. He admitted others would say it was psychology and he was biased, but nevertheless he stood by what he had experienced. To ask for logical "proofs" of God may be missing the point, said Meyer, just as the love of a husband for his wife, or vice versa, isn't proven through syllogistic reasoning. The evidence is in knowing the other through the relationship, not through logical points built on top of one another.

All of these persons, in their various ways, showed caring and compassion. None responded by becoming defensive, perturbed, or angry at the questions I asked. I prayed that I be given eyes to see as true the plan of God which I saw as so beautiful if it were true. To my amazement this prayer was answered. I experienced the transition from wishing to believe to believing.

As for the original intellectual questions, it is difficult to describe. Somehow I saw things in a new light and was at rest, knowing that for every question there was an answer out there waiting to be discovered, and I was no longer anxious. My eyes were opened. I experienced the reality of "grace." It transformed how I saw the most mundane of things. Everything seemed cast in an aura of God's love. I've never experienced anything like it since.

Big Sandy Oasis: Ambassador College

Baptism and new life

Chastened and humbled, having experienced the answer of God, I counseled with and was baptized by evangelist Dean Blackwell on May 7, 1973. The first thing I did following this was begin reading the whole Bible. I started with the first chapter of Genesis and read straight through to Revelation. Along the way I would pause to reflect upon, think about, underline, and seek to understand what I was reading. This occupied the next four months or so. Out of that basic familiarization began the process of emerging creative insight, as I examined, broke down, worked and reworked the history and archetypical imagery with which the Bible is filled.

In purity of soul I sought to know the will of God. Some of the prophets' language was so eloquent and beautiful it made me weep for its expressiveness. I saw that the Hebrew prophets, with their calls for justice to the poor and stranger, were ancient social prophets. I came to the New Testament. I saw the richness of Jesus's parables fused with his life's events-as-parable. Themes and images and language from former scripture, separated by hundreds of years in time, seemed to weave in and out among each other in multi-dimensioned ways like the work of some dramatist writing fiction in history. I read through to Revelation. I saw paradise restored, the return to Eden, all tears wiped away and all things made new. I saw the triumph of Christ fulfilling, in a way no one could have planned or coordinated in advance, the promises and dreams spoken by the former prophets of the Bible.

The Bible was living and real. It explained the meaning of things personal and macrocosmic. I engaged it with heart, soul, and mind. I saw how I had come out of my own Egypt, crossed over my own Red Sea, went through wilderness aloneness, and experienced entry into the Promised Land of comprehension and truth. I hungered to know all I could. I sought out faculty members from whom I could learn more. I attended and sat in on interesting classes whether I was registered for them or not. The

Big Sandy Oasis: Ambassador College

universe unfolded in its grandeur and I learned and grew as a neophyte child of God with eternity ahead, learning priceless truths hidden from the world's wisest.

Out of this immersion into the meaning of scripture, ideas would flash and burst in my mind like electric lightning in a cloud chamber. I saw the best in the church. I believed that only here on earth was a comprehension of the true gospel, which like an open secret through all the ages had been hidden until now. Only here, it seemed, was there understanding of truths of scripture which inexplicably had been missed by the rest of Christianity. I believed in the sincerity and goodwill of the men at the top of the church. Although I knew that humans are fallible and make mistakes (for that is what goes along with God working through clay containers), I believed ... wanted to believe ... the best, with all the innocence of first love.

And so when others around me became dissidents, I did not. My conversion was too recent, too real. What did dissidents have to offer except criticism? Were any dissidents preaching the gospel to the world? The church was doing the work of preaching the gospel to the world as an end-time witness. I was swept with gratitude for the miracle of my conversion and the privilege of being at Big Sandy.

Going through channels

I had passed through the temptation to doubt, to become cynical, to go the path of dissidents. I rejected the dissidents' criticisms that the church was a closed system that refused to listen to the people on the bottom. If I learned some new insight from the Bible, would I argue with church authorities and ultimately leave like some of those around me? Would I leave just because I saw something in a novel way that headquarters didn't yet see? No—that wasn't right. I would not be like those dissidents who became impatient and ended up rejecting the organized Work of God.

As I would be struck with insights, I would write papers and submit them to the church to contribute what I had discovered. I wasn't sure precisely *how* one was supposed to submit something new to the church. I would take guesses at the correct people up the line to whom to submit my papers. In this way I tried to share my efforts with the church.

Herbert Armstrong himself was the final authority on decisions regarding church teachings. He relied on those around him at headquarters for advice and input. We were told that matters of value should be submitted to the ministry. If it was deemed of value, it would progressively rise up the pyramid until it was shown to Herbert Armstrong. He would pray about it. If God showed him it was true, he would change the doctrine for the church. This was the established system for the processing of New Truth. This was the way God worked. Members were cautioned not to "get ahead of God" in their studies.

I would do it the right way. I would be humble before God who had been merciful to me. Jesus had said, "The truth will make you free." The motto of Ambassador College was "Recapture True Values." I would trust in God's appointed channels. I had faith those channels would work. The church was receptive to new ideas if they were *properly* submitted. If one had faith in God and remained patient *in a right attitude*, truth would win out. I believed it all.

About my papers (or, "Rescued from the circular file")

This book continues with stories surrounding some papers I produced during those youthful days as a student at Big Sandy. These particular papers illustrate how one creative youth's mind interacted with the theology taught at Ambassador College.

College officials emphasized the importance of having a "good attitude." That meant being teachable, patient, and compliant to those over one in authority. All of these papers were submitted in the best attitude in the world. Naively, I thought my submissions to the proper channels higher in authority would

Big Sandy Oasis: Ambassador College

result in contributions to church understanding and growth. Some of the papers I produced during my Big Sandy student days were:

"Evidences for the 7000-Year Plan" (Jan 7, 1974)

> ... in which I showed through charts and graphs that the return of Christ must be very near

"The Bible and Interracial Marriage" (Jan 23, 1974)

> ... in which I showed there is not the slightest biblical justification for forbidding interracial marriage among Christians, and cited examples such as Moses marrying a black woman to prove it

"The United States in Prophecy" (Sept 30, 1974)

> ... in which I set about to conclusively prove that the United States is Ephraim, and Britain is Manasseh, not vice versa

"Meat Offered to Idols: did Paul Permit what James Forbade?" (Nov 2, 1974)

> ... in which I attempted to reconcile apparently conflicting statements in the New Testament concerning this burning issue

"The Servant and the Woman" (Nov 15, 1974)

> ... in which I likened the course of the church to a lovely lass being taken across a blazing desert by a dashing Arab sheikh

"Are We Missing Out on the Most Important Holy Day of All?" (March 13, 1975)

> ... in which I showed why the day of the "Wave Sheaf" may be the most important annual holy day in the sacred calendar

"Key Events and the 1973-1974 Sacred Calendar" (March 1975)

> ... in which I thought I found significant correlations between the travels of Herbert Armstrong and Stanley Rader and the meaning of the holy days of that year

Big Sandy Oasis: Ambassador College

"Will the 'Beast' of Revelation Come Out of the True Church?" (May 2, 1975)

> ... after reading this, *no* church will rest easy

"Healing in a New Light" (May 3, 1975)

> ... in which I showed that miracle healing without medical treatment is not biblically promised

"Why Must We Die?" (May 4, 1975)

> ... in which I reflected on this puzzling question, and concluded that physical mortality is inherited from Adam's sin, not God's design

"Tithing" (Aug 17, 1975)

> ... in which I showed that tithing is supposed to go to poor and homeless, not church leaders

I wrote these papers as an idealistic nineteen to twenty-one year old Ambassador College student. That is a past era for me now. These papers are like artifacts from an archaeological stratum of a past life. The story of these papers from student days will provide a case history of a "systems theory" phenomenon: when one is inside a system of belief, coincidences abound and the belief *itself* makes the system work. But this story will also show how I came out of it, so it is a story of hope as well.

In the next chapter I will tell what the Worldwide Church of God of those days was like and how I came to be at Ambassador College. Then I will return to Big Sandy and the stories of these papers and associated creative interactions thereof, and how it all turned out.

Join with me in reentering that world (I promise you we'll come back out again!). Strap on your seatbelts and get ready for a ride ...

CHAPTER 2

THE STORY OF THE WORLDWIDE CHURCH OF GOD

Like all Doudnas, my origins go back to Conservative Friends (Quakers) of Barnesville, Ohio. The Quakers do not have the most conventional heritage.

They called themselves "Friends in Truth"; then, "Religious Society of Friends." But others called them "Quakers,"[3] and the name stuck. Emerging in a time of social ferment in 1600s England, the Quakers developed testimonies of plainness and simplicity. Out of this emphasis upon plain-speaking and simplicity, they rejected ceremonies and vain words.

My Quaker ancestors took simplicity seriously. They had no paid pastors, steeples, altars, holidays, baptisms, prepared messages, or hymns. Instead of listening to sermons from hired ministers (whom they unkindly referred to as "hirelings"), they met for worship in silence, sitting on wooden benches in plain, unadorned meetinghouses. Out of this meeting in silence, the unrehearsed Word of God came forth—spoken messages through whoever felt a leading to speak. Quakers had the astonishing idea that God could speak through any person.

Quakers had an unusual way of decision-making. In Quaker meetings, decisions are made neither by authority of office nor by majority vote. Instead, decision making comes about through a "sense of the meeting" (arrived at in an orderly manner). If

---

[3] Because some would "tremble before the Lord," i.e. physically tremble or "quake" when speaking or praying and overcome with the Spirit. (This is not done today.)

Quakers cannot come to unity upon a matter, it is simply shelved until next time. To do otherwise would be regarded as "rushing the Spirit." This process sometimes takes longer, but Quakers have done it this way for over three hundred years.

Also deep in the Quaker heritage is an elemental equality of all persons. Thousands of Quakers went to prison in seventeenth century England for the shocking crime of impudently refusing to remove their hats and bow before nobles. To add even further outrage, Quakers would not even address their betters with titles such as "Sir" or "Lord" or even "Mister." It was all vanity, these Quakers thought. They had a simple rule for addressing their fellow human beings. Whatever was a person's first name, that was how that person was addressed, without title, no matter who they were. This applied to kings as well as servants, men and women, old and young, nobles and working stiffs—everyone was addressed the same.

Quakers combined inner, religious experience with practical action. They were in the forefront of the abolitionist movement against slavery, reforms for better treatment of the insane, and ideas of religious liberty. Some of America's earliest feminists were Quaker women.[4] The influence of Quakers is recognized as being far out of proportion to their relatively small numbers.

I returned to learn of my Quaker roots in later years. But I took a slight detour first. My detour was my involvement in a church built by an ex-Quaker named Herbert Armstrong.

~ ~ ~

Herbert Armstrong (1892-1986) came from Quaker upbringing and ancestry. In his youth he learned Quaker virtues of trust, honesty, humility, and faithful dealing. But somewhere along the line, something seems to have gone haywire. For Herbert Armstrong did not remain in the simple Quaker ways. As a

---

[4] Margaret Hope Bacon, *Mothers of Feminism: The Story of Quaker Women in America* (San Francisco: Harper and Row, 1986).

young man Herbert Armstrong was ambitious, a salesman of tremendous ego determined to make it big. From humble origins, Herbert Armstrong succeeded in building a worldwide organization which billed itself as God's earthly arbiter of truth.

Whereas Quakers originated in vigorous opposition to a paid ministry, Herbert Armstrong believed in ministers being paid, and paid very well. (At the end of his life he was reported to jet around the world with six-figure cashier's checks on his person.) In Herbert Armstrong's church meetings there was no such thing as group silence, inner listening, or the possibility for any member to speak. Herbert Armstrong made himself and a selected circle of subordinate ministers into a new privileged class—just like the nobles of old. Like the English upper crust in the days of the first Quakers, the ministers of Herbert Armstrong's church were entitled to financial support, deference, special parking, and chief seats, courtesy of the hard-working, obedient membership. Members were told this was the divine will. Unlike the meetings of Quakers where, from the beginning, both men and women alike are equally free to speak, Herbert Armstrong's church was run by men. No speaking of women was allowed.

In his youth, Herbert Armstrong learned the bedrock Quaker truth that there is "that of God in every person." But Herbert Armstrong fell away from his Quaker upbringing. The crowning symbol of Herbert Armstrong's dream come true was a costly, ornate structure of glass and concrete, seven stories high, completed in 1974, in Pasadena, California. In full symbolic apostasy from his Quaker heritage, Herbert Armstrong called this building made of human hands: "God's House."

~ ~ ~

By a strange, further coincidence, Richard Nixon, President of the United States during the time I was at Herbert Armstrong's Bible college, came from Quaker origins too. But like Herbert Armstrong, Richard Nixon also departed from Quaker ways in his adult life—ending his term in the White House in a swirl of conspiracy and paranoia, surrounded by enemies. Herbert Armstrong felt a special affinity for Richard Nixon. He thought Nixon was the best President America ever had. The Watergate scandal only heightened Armstrong's regard for Nixon. (For Herbert Armstrong knew that Nixon, like he himself, was being skewered by a spiteful, satanic press bent solely on stirring up strife and destroying people's trust in their leaders.) Herbert Armstrong's admiration for Richard Nixon went further than simple kinship of spirit. Though the two figures never met, Herbert Armstrong always believed Nixon was really a relative of his.[5]

How did Herbert Armstrong build a church so opposite from his heritage? How did I come to be in a church so opposite from my heritage?

~ ~ ~

My father, David Doudna (1914-), was raised in a Conservative Friends or Quaker home, near Columbiana, Ohio. He went to school his first seven grades in a one-room Quaker country

---

[5] Herbert Armstrong claimed that Richard Nixon's middle name "Milhous" was in his, Herbert's, ancestry, though he never provided details. (Was this a reference to Richard Nixon's maternal grandfather Franklin Milhous's marriage to a Sarah Emily Armstrong?) Whether or not there was a close connection there was certainly a distant one. Herbert Armstrong's mother was a third cousin of Herbert Hoover, America's other president of Quaker heritage, according to Neil Earle, *Herbert Armstrong: A Developmental Study*, 2004 ed. (http://www.glendorachurch.org/Armstrong/Chapter2.htm), whereas Richard Nixon was either a seventh cousin or eighth cousin once removed from Herbert Hoover according to standard references (http://users.legacyfamilytree.com/USPresidents/nix_hoov.htm). At a Scottish festival in Oberlin, Ohio in June 1988 I saw a table for "The Armstrong Clan." A brochure of this organization said full membership was open to all Armstrongs by descent or marriage, and "associate registration is open to Kinmonts, Fairbairns, *Nixons*, and Croziers" (emphasis mine). A woman at the table named Armstrong cheerfully told me of two expressions which came into the English language from the Armstrongs: "blackmail" and "caught red-handed."

schoolhouse. When he was fourteen, his mother died. He and his younger sister went to live with his Quaker grandparents. (His brokenhearted father worked nearby.) Like other Quaker children during the Depression, my father chafed at the restrictiveness of rural plainness and farming life with its limited opportunities, and did not remain with the Quakers after his teenage years. He was working as a draftsman when, in 1941, the Japanese attack on Pearl Harbor changed things. He enlisted in the Army Air Corps and said goodby to his tearful relatives. His old-fashioned grandfather pondered this gross violation of Quaker principles. Finally he said to his beloved grandson, "David, thee knows I believe fighting in war is wrong, and that I could never go to war myself. But if thee is going, I want thee to be the best soldier thee can be."

My father saw active duty on bombing missions from New Guinea as a radio operator and gunner. The casualties were high. Within the first six weeks, half of his training crew were dead. Over his period of active combat, eighty percent of his outfit never came back home. But he completed sixty-six missions and returned to the States thirteen months later without a scratch. Then came the atomic bombings of Hiroshima and Nagasaki and the end of the war. My father soon came to believe the Bomb should never have been dropped on these cities. Demoralized and looking for direction, he took a job in Louisville, Kentucky. There he found a changed life through a movement called Moral Re-Armament.

~ ~ ~

Moral Re-Armament groups consisted of often professional and well-to-do people who continued in their respective faiths. They would meet in each other's homes for periods of silence. During these "quiet times" they would listen for "guidance." This would be followed by "sharing" with the others of convictions they had received. This in turn would be followed by "checking" attitudes and motives against the Four Moral Standards—Absolute

Honesty, Absolute Purity, Absolute Unselfishness, and Absolute Love. Moral Re-Armament founder Frank Buchman said these Four Moral Standards were derived from Christ's Sermon on the Mount.

The Moral Re-Armament movement particularly claimed influence in the lives of world leaders. Today Moral Re-Armament is little known. It greatly declined after the death of its founder, Buchman, in 1961, though the "Up With People" singers were a later legacy. There was also involvement of Moral Re-Armament, or "the Oxford Group" as it was then called, in the origins of Alcoholics Anonymous, which started in Akron, Ohio in the 1930s.

My father held in high esteem the white-haired, Philadelphia-educated founder of Moral Re-Armament, Frank Buchman. Buchman claimed friendships with a whole range of notables, from Gandhi in India to Adenauer in West Germany. Jomo Kenyatta, the first President of independent Kenya, praised the work of Moral Re-Armament and one summer sent his daughter to Caux, Switzerland, to the Moral Re-Armament center there. Moral Re-Armament even had advocates among members of the Japanese Diet.

After Buchman's death and Moral Re-Armament's demise in the 1960s, another white-haired man who visited world leaders would enter my father's life, claim his loyalty, and have a profound effect on me: Herbert Armstrong.

~~~

Moral Re-Armament brought my parents together. My mother, the former Phyllis Murphy (1918-2005), was a bank officer and then a high school teacher. She was raised in a small town in Michigan as part of a large, closely-knit family whose lives centered around the Congregational Church. My father and mother met in 1948 when she journeyed to Louisville for a Thanksgiving visit with an aunt and uncle. Her aunt and uncle happened to be active in Moral Re-Armament and close friends with my father, who was their guest. A romance blossomed and they married in 1951. Their new home became Akron, Ohio, where my father was employed as an electrical engineer. From this happy union I was born in 1954. Three years later my brother Shawn was born. I spent the first eighteen years of my life in Akron.

I learned to read on my father's lap before I entered school, with my father pointing to the next strange word in a story and saying "sound it out, Greg ... sound it out"—and I would slowly sound each letter and then, to my delight, learn a new word, and in this way learned to read. I remember countless talks with my father for hours at a time as a small child, my asking questions, his answering, my asking more questions, his answering. My parents also refused to have a television in the home as policy. These two things (knowing how to read, and no TV) gave me a flying head start when I started school. Then there was an illustrated book of mathematics history that my cousin Paul Doudna sent me as a birthday present once that was my most loved book of all. It told the history of different scientific ideas and how they developed anciently in a way that was incredibly interesting. And I would spend hours at a time browsing through the *Compton's Encyclopedia* that my parents had bought, learning all sorts of things.

My parents joined a Methodist Church shortly after their marriage. This church, the North Hill United Methodist Church, with its conservative pastor who taught that God's views were pretty much identical to those of the Republican Party, whose ideal of an upstanding American was FBI director J. Edgar Hoover, and who warned in his sermons that the civil rights movement was tainted with communism, was an important part of my early life. Then the message of Herbert Armstrong changed things.

In the early 1960s, in the wake of a failed business venture, my father started studying something called the Ambassador College Bible Correspondence Course. He had heard it offered over the radio along with other literature, all without charge. In his studies of this Bible course, my father learned that a number of teachings of Sunday-keeping churches were wrong. Among other things, this Bible Correspondence Course opened up the meaning of the Hebrew holy days. My father learned that these annual celebrations picture the true plan of salvation.

This true plan of God, sadly, cannot be understood by the false churches of the world (a designation to which, my father was disconcerted to realize, the Methodist Church he was attending was judged to belong). The churches of the world cannot understand the true plan of God for a simple reason: they keep false, pagan holidays instead of the festival seasons God ordained, and they switched God's Sabbath to Sunday. By rejecting the teachings of God's Word, the world's churches made themselves blind. For a long time my prayerful father studied quietly on his own rather than cause upheaval with my mother and friends in the Methodist Church. But inside, he was troubled.

The Ambassador College Bible Correspondence Course and the radio ministry were the impact of Herbert Armstrong in the home in which I was growing up. At this point it is appropriate to ask ...

Who was Herbert Armstrong and where did he come from?

Worldwide Church of God founder Herbert Armstrong was born in Des Moines, Iowa, on July 31, 1892, the oldest son of Horace and Eva Armstrong. His Quaker family roots went back to Philadelphia settlers with William Penn. He attended a Quaker church, the First Friends Church of Des Moines, the first eighteen years of his life. As a child in school, he "rarely cracked a book or completed an assignment and almost never contributed to discussions," yet, "at exam time, he almost invariably scored close to 100 percent."[6] But he never completed high school. In his *Autobiography*, Armstrong recounts that at age sixteen, the desire kindled within him to "climb the ladder of success—to become an important SOMEBODY." A successful uncle advised him to choose self-education and practical experience over armchair study in college classrooms.

Armstrong sold newspaper want ads, then progressed to sales and writing ads for trade journals. During two years as a representative for a retail merchants journal, young Armstrong traveled throughout the Midwest. Along the way he originated (so he believed) modern opinion poll research.[7] In 1917, just as he was about to be drafted and could well have ended up as cannon fodder on some forgotten battlefield in Europe, he married a second cousin.[8] She was the former Loma Dillon (1892-1967). (The marriage exempted Herbert from the draft.) Loma and Herbert settled in Chicago and joined a Methodist church, the River Forest Methodist Church of Maywood. But now poor Herbert began to be plagued with, as he later reported, a series of humbling business reserves due to depressions in the economy and his refusal to be dishonest in business.[9]

In the early 1920s the young family, with their growing children, moved to Salem, Oregon, where Herbert's parents had moved earlier. Here, Armstrong went into partnership with a man

---

[6] Stanley Rader, *Against the Gates of Hell* (New York: Everest House, 1980), 30.

[7] "On one of these trips, a challenge from an angry merchant resulted in what I believe was the *pioneer* experience in all these surveys and samplings of public opinion. So far as I know, I was the originator of such polls" (Herbert Armstrong, *Autobiography* [Pasadena, Calif.: Worldwide Church of God, 1986], I, 71, 107-111). This was Richmond, Kentucky, 1915. Armstrong surveyed shoppers and reported his findings to the local retail merchants.

[8] Herbert Armstrong himself said Loma was his third cousin (*Autobiography*, I, 185, 188, 191). But Herbert Armstrong elsewhere said that Loma's father was his mother's first cousin (*Autobiography*, I, 185) which makes Herbert and Loma second cousins.

[9] "I was ambitious to make money. But not by falsification or dishonesty! I was *sincere!*" (*Autobiography*, I, 240).

who knew the laundry business and had a better soap. They started a merchandising and advertising service for laundries. Armstrong wrote the advertising. At first business boomed as leading laundries signed up in Oregon and Washington. But, Armstrong later recounted, the Laundry Owners National Association wiped out the growing business in one fell swoop. They required their members to pay dues toward a national advertising campaign. When this happened all but one of Armstrong's clients cancelled.

Meanwhile, in the midst of this economic turmoil and abrupt downward mobility, a lady in Salem, Mrs. Ora Runcorn, showed Loma Armstrong that Saturday, the seventh day of the week, was the proper day to be kept as the Christian Sabbath. This idea angered Herbert. As he later told it, he plunged into a six-month night and day study of the Bible and evolution, intent on disproving his wife's "fanaticism." Instead, in 1927 Herbert emerged a convinced seventh-day Sabbatarian and creationist. Now at financial rock bottom, Armstrong turned his life over to God. He wrote:

> I threw myself on God's mercy. I said to God that I knew, now, that I was nothing but a burned-out hunk of junk. My life was worth nothing more to ME ... but if he would forgive me—if He could have any use whatsoever for such a worthless dreg of humanity, that He could have my life ... I wanted to accept Jesus Christ as personal Saviour![10]

Herbert Armstrong and Loma were baptized by a Baptist minister—the pastor of the Hinson Memorial Baptist Church in Portland.[11] But Herbert and Loma did not become Baptists. They began fellowshipping with the Church of God (Seventh Day). The Church of God (Seventh Day) was a small, mostly rural denomination which had split off from the Seventh-Day Adventists in the 1860s because its members would not accept

---

[10] Armstrong, *Autobiography*, I, 308.
[11] Armstrong, *Autobiography*, I, 315.

Story of the Worldwide Church of God

the authority of Ellen G. White (whose writings are considered inspired by Adventists).

Herbert Armstrong's contributions rejected by an unheeding headquarters bureaucracy

Out of his studies of the Bible, Armstrong typed a number of papers and submitted them to various ministers and church leaders. One of his papers proved, for example, that the crucifixion of Jesus was on Wednesday instead of Friday. Another proved that the Anglo-Saxons were the lost Israelites in prophecy. There were others. Herbert Armstrong was painfully disappointed when these ministers and church leaders refused to accept and preach these new Bible truths which he had presented in such crystal clear style. Nevertheless, Armstrong's zeal for the Bible and public speaking abilities were recognized when in 1931 he was ordained a minister by the Oregon Conference of the Church of God.

According to J. Gordon Melton, editor of the *Encyclopedia of American Religion*, the Oregon Conference of the Church of God was formed in 1930 in response to the Depression in order to keep money at home rather than sending it to national headquarters in Stanberry, Missouri. Melton says there were only about fifty members in this Oregon Conference, and that Herbert Armstrong led in their breaking off and independent incorporation.[12] According to his *Autobiography*, Armstrong acted as secretary at this business meeting, was looked to as the group's leader, and was asked at the close of this meeting—to his surprise, claimed Armstrong—to conduct an evangelistic campaign. The separate incorporation enabled the Oregon Conference to finance Armstrong's evangelistic efforts and, soon, to employ him as a minister. "From the time of this business meeting, the

---

[12] J. Gordon Melton, *Encyclopedic Handbook of Cults in America* (New York: Garland Publishing Inc., 1986), 97-98.

brethren in Oregon looked to me for the leadership."[13] This tiny lay group led by Herbert Armstrong and founded upon his advice and urging was the source of his ministerial ordination.

Armstrong recounts other, more experienced ministers being brought in from outside by the lay member-controlled Oregon Conference. In 1933 Armstrong was edged out. According to Armstrong, the Oregon Conference voted to require Armstrong to teach new converts about "unclean meats"—i.e. not to eat pork—before baptizing them, but Armstrong refused to do this and resigned his salary.[14] Armstrong led converts loyal to him in forming a new independent local church. About twenty persons pledged support to Armstrong's plans for preaching the gospel via radio, print, and personal campaigns. Armstrong's July 1933 campaign in the Firbutte County schoolhouse which produced these converts is therefore when Herbert Armstrong dated the beginning of the "present era" of the true Church of God.

Armstrong started a regular broadcast on a tiny 100-watt radio station, KORE in Eugene, Oregon, in January 1934. One month later the *Plain Truth* magazine was born. The first issue was in simple mimeographed form, mailed to 106 radio listeners. Armstrong broadcast teachings such as British-Israelism or Anglo-Israelism (the belief that white, English-speaking people are descendants of the Lost Ten Tribes of Israel) and observance of the Hebrew holy days. He began picking up supporters and tithe-payers and established his own ministry called "The Radio Church of God." Herbert Armstrong had found his calling. He would preach the truth over the air waves in power.

Meanwhile in 1933, a leading church of God (Seventh Day) figure, Andrew Dugger, led in the formation of a new "Bible-based" manner of reorganization for the fractured Church of God (Seventh Day). This alternative organization was headquartered in Salem, West Virginia. Dugger's idea was that twelve apostles and seventy evangelists should be chosen by lot. Herbert

---

[13] Armstrong, *Autobiography*, I, 414.
[14] Armstrong, *Autobiography*, I, 522-24.

Story of the Worldwide Church of God

Armstrong's name was the fortieth drawn of the Seventy. This was later seen as significant since, as Herbert Armstrong explained, forty is "God's number for organized beginnings." For several years Herbert Armstrong and the members supporting his ministry in Oregon were part of the new Salem, West Virginia organization. Herbert Armstrong had articles published in the Church of God (Seventh Day) publication, the *Bible Advocate* in Stanberry, Missouri, and as late as 1937 the *Bible Advocate* continued to carry reports on Armstrong's evangelistic tent meetings in Eugene.

In 1937 the Salem, West Virginia organization revoked Herbert Armstrong's ministerial credentials after a dispute over Armstrong's teaching of Anglo-Israelism and the holy days. Frank Walker, a Church of God (Seventh Day) evangelist, met Herbert Armstrong at a camp meeting in 1940. Armstrong told Walker the Salem, West Virginia group had wanted to take over his radio work. Referring to his own work, Armstrong told Walker, "I don't want a tight organization, but I can see it coming."[15]

Armstrong's former Church of God associates claimed he would not cooperate or be subject to higher authority. Armstrong, on the other hand, claimed the church leadership refused to accept new truths which were being revealed to him. He denounced all organizations claiming authority. He passionately proclaimed the only authority was Christ, not earthly headquarters of men.[16] And so the defrocked Herbert Armstrong was on his own.

---

[15] Richard Nickels, *Herbert Armstrong: 1892-1986* (http://www.servantsnews.com/PDF/litlst10.pdf).

[16] Herbert Armstrong expounded on this theme in February 1939 in an article entitled "Did Christ Reorganize the Church?" published in the *Good News* (in the single issue of this publication issued by Armstrong at that time). In it, Armstrong wrote, "[T]here is *no Bible authority* for any super-government, or organization with authority over the local congregations! ... And thus the very *principle* of *church government* becomes *the image to the Beast!* ... Those who are *in*, and *members* of such an organized church

Growth of "the Work"

Herbert Armstrong's work, faithfully assisted by his wife Loma, grew at an average rate of twenty-five to thirty percent a year. His radio program went out over more stations, including powerful stations reaching across much of the continent. The *Plain Truth* magazine's circulation rose. From the beginning, Armstrong made no request for money in either his radio broadcasts or in his free literature offered to the public. But among those who wrote in for further information, some went on to become baptized, tithe-paying members of Armstrong's church. Other listeners, though not members, became regular financial supporters called "co-workers."

There were lean years of struggle and hardship. But the "Work," as it became called, prospered. In 1940, *Plain Truth* circulation was 3000. By 1944, circulation was 35,000. In 1946, Armstrong moved to Pasadena, California, explaining to his loyal co-workers that this would enable him to be near better broadcasting facilities. The following year, 1947, Armstrong founded Ambassador College as a four-year, coeducational, liberal arts institution. It began its first year with eight faculty members and four students. As the college grew, it provided

---

government ... are *in Babylon*, and actually worshippers of the *image of the Beast!*" (And Herbert Armstrong repeatedly wrote similarly in his church bulletin in those years in the 1930s.) Clandestinely circulated copies of the 1939 *Good News* article caused quite a stir at Big Sandy in 1974 when I was a student. Referring to the 1939 article in the 1970s, Herbert Armstrong said he had written it before coming into a fuller knowledge of the truth. But see the reporting of John Robinson concerning a witnessed conversation in 1975 in which Herbert Armstrong spoke candidly to a young minister he had just ordained, Marc Segall, and told him that "the New Testament reflected a collegial approach to church government and that what he wrote in 1939 was the ideal" and that "if he had had more faith he would have continued that practice, but he 'was afraid of losing control'" (J. Robinson, "WCG Church Government up to Tkach Era, Part II," *In Transition* 3/1 [Jan. 1997], at http://www.thejournal.org/in-transition/main.html).

trained personnel for Armstrong's expanding work and ministry. Male students and graduates were sent out on "baptizing tours" across the United States. Local church congregations were established, meeting in rented halls under the care of pastors sent from headquarters. In January 1953, Armstrong's broadcast began reaching European countries and the British Isles via Radio Luxembourg. By now his vision had become clearly identified. The Work was to become truly worldwide. Herbert Armstrong was personally destined to fulfill Christ's commission: "This gospel of the kingdom will be preached throughout the whole world, as a testimony to all nations; and then the end will come" (Matt 24:14).

It was sometime in the 1950s that God revealed to Herbert Armstrong that New Truth only came, after all, through headquarters. That is, God's words came to earth only through headquarters of the church being built under divine direction by Herbert Armstrong. This became church doctrine. Articles were written instructing outlying followers not to assemble without a minister sent from headquarters. Experience had shown, it was explained, that when such unauthorized meetings occurred, too often greedy local personalities would rise up, sever the helpless people's connection with headquarters, and start stuffing the people's tithes into their own pockets. The new God-inspired rule against unapproved meetings would prevent such a traumatic event from happening.[17]

This prohibition of unauthorized assembly and discouragement of lay members from expounding on spiritual subjects continued as the church grew. Evangelism and outreach were done from headquarters via broadcast and print media. Interested persons from the public wrote to Pasadena requesting a visit from a Pasadena-appointed minister. If the interest was genuine, the minister extended invitation to attend local church services. The church services were held in rented locations and were not

---

[17] H.L. Hoeh, "Should You Assemble Without a Minister?", October 1957 *Good News*.

advertised or listed in phone books. The headquarters monopoly on preaching the gospel—that is, headquarters control over who does it and how—was believed to be necessary. Otherwise, church leaders were convinced, there would not be oneness in the church, and the preaching of the gospel would not get done in an organized manner on a worldwide scale.

In the mid-1950s, Herbert Armstrong began turning over some of the broadcasting to his son Garner Ted Armstrong (1930-2003). Garner Ted was talented, quick-witted, and, some would say, "silver-tongued." Garner Ted had, however, gotten off to a slow start at an earlier age. As a baby he hadn't spoken a word until he was two. When he finally did begin saying words, his overjoyed father and mother considered little Ted's voice to have been a divine gift miraculously given for a great purpose. After rejecting his "Dad's religion" and spending four years in the Navy, Garner Ted returned home, entered Ambassador College, and shortly thereafter became converted. Handsome, articulate Garner Ted took to radio and television like a duck to water.

By 1948, *Plain Truth* circulation reached 175,000. Church offices were opening in many parts of the world. The Ambassador College Correspondence Course was developed which was a means of conversion for many new members, including my father. In 1960 a second Ambassador College was opened at Bricket Wood, England. In 1962, *Plain Truth* circulation hit 400,000. In 1964, a third Ambassador College was opened at Big Sandy, Texas. In 1965, *Plain Truth* circulation passed 600,000. The next year, 1966, it reached 775,000. The year after that, 1967, circulation topped one million. In 1968 Herbert Armstrong changed the name of the church to Worldwide Church of God.

As the decade of the 1960s drew to a close, *Plain Truth* circulation soared past two million. The daily "World Tomorrow" radio broadcasts were well-known and could be heard across America, most commonly on country-western music stations. (This resulted in Worldwide Church of God

Story of the Worldwide Church of God

membership consisting of a high percentage of country-western music lovers.)

One of the growing number of avid readers of the *Plain Truth* was an Australian named Dennis Rohan. In 1969 Rohan brought upon the church some decidedly unfavorable publicity. Herbert Armstrong had written an article saying there must be a Jewish Temple rebuilt before the return of Christ. But the site of the Temple is now occupied by the Dome of the Rock and the Al-Aksa Mosque. Armstrong therefore wondered if the Mosque would be destroyed. Rohan, eager to do whatever would help expedite the return of Christ, traveled to Jerusalem, went into the Al-Aksa Mosque and set it on fire. When he was arrested, Rohan waved a copy of the *Plain Truth* into news cameras, and photos of this went into wire services around the world. Of course the church had nothing to do with Rohan's action, and Rohan was not even a member. Nevertheless, the Israeli government was none too pleased. The *Plain Truth* hurriedly published clarifications, saying that when they urged people to take the Bible prophecies seriously, they didn't quite have *that* in mind.

"Who's in charge?"

Following the assassination of Robert Kennedy in June 1968, my father became convinced our violent world could be saved only by the return of Christ. He became convinced that he must act on what he knew, no matter how unpopular the Worldwide Church of God was to the outside world. He left the Methodist church and counseled with the Worldwide Church of God pastor of the Akron church, David Antion. I began attending Sabbath services with my father and younger brother at this time by choice. I was thirteen. (I was already sending in tithes from my paper route earnings and trying to keep the Sabbath at this point.) In August 1968 my father was baptized by Antion as a member, at the same time as a young African-American woman, Faye Odie, who later became a student at Ambassador College, Big Sandy after African-Americans were allowed to attend (see chapter 4).

My mother never joined. She almost became interested at one point and accompanied my father to the Feast of Tabernacles, the Worldwide Church of God's main fall convention. There she heard Herbert Armstrong speak in person for the first time. His sermon topic was on the theme, idiomatically put, of "I'm in charge." My mother decided she would prefer Herbert Armstrong not be in charge of her, and returned to a mainline evangelical church (Assemblies of God). My sensible brother Shawn, three years younger than I, quit attending Worldwide Church of God services when he was sixteen. Thankfully religion did not break my parents apart. But it was stressful on my mother. She told her story in an article entitled "Religion Divides our Home," in the August 1985 issue of *Home Life* (a Baptist magazine).

By now my father was no longer employed as an electrical engineer. He had left his job to go into a business venture which hadn't turned out to be so lucrative. He eventually returned to his childhood love of beautiful woodworking and marquetry, and my mother returned to secretarial work and teaching. I worked a lot during my high school years and was responsible for my own college savings.

Distinctive beliefs and practices of the Worldwide Church of God

Saturday, not Sunday, of course, was the Sabbath. The Sabbath began on sunset Friday and ended sunset Saturday. This ruined most sports, music, and drama activities for church kids in public schools. In my case, it ruled out the debate team, in which I had shown promise in class.

Standard Christian holidays such as Christmas and Easter, as well as Halloween and Valentine's Day, were not observed due to their pagan origins. (Thanksgiving and Fourth of July were OK.) Instead of conventional Christian holidays, the Hebrew festivals were celebrated—seven annual Sabbaths or holy days described in the Bible. These were believed to picture, in type, the plan of salvation being worked out by God. The Feast of

Tabernacles, for eight days in the fall each year, was the main church convention and was the high point of the year. Children missed those days in school and arranged to make up their schoolwork when they returned.

The dietary laws given to Israel in Leviticus 11 regarding "clean" and "unclean" meats were believed to be divine health principles no less applicable today. Therefore no pork, shellfish, shrimp or lobster were eaten. During the days of Unleavened Bread in the spring, all leavened products were put out of the house for seven days (usually given to neighbors). Everything was vacuumed and the toaster thoroughly shaken to get rid of the hidden crumbs. This was supposed to symbolize the effort necessary to get sin out of our lives. During these seven days, Jewish matzos were eaten instead of bread. Wheat Thins were a popular second choice. I found matzos were so tasty I came to prefer them over normal bread any time of year.

Once a year, on the Day of Atonement in the fall (the Jewish Yom Kippur), church members fasted from sunset to sunset. Most people think fasting merely means not eating. The Worldwide Church of God said fasting also meant no drinking any water or liquids the whole time—nothing at all (based on Deut 9:18). Few members were aware that Herbert Armstrong considered himself exempt from the strict no-liquids rule on the Day of Atonement. (A staff aide, Robert Fahey, came upon Herbert Armstrong drinking a cup of coffee on the Day of Atonement. When Fahey expressed surprise, Armstrong explained that he personally had never believed that liquids were forbidden—that teaching, he said, had been brought into the church by others.[18]) When I was a freshman at Big Sandy, student pranksters in my dorm went around putting Tabasco hot sauce on the lips of sleeping fellow students on the Day of Atonement. They claimed it was a helpful test of principle on the injunction not to drink water. But this behavior was not typical. The Day of Atonement was a solemn day in the Worldwide Church of God.

---

[18] *Ambassador Report*, June 1985.

The only occasion more solemn was the annual Passover ceremony of matzos, wine, and ritual footwashing which reenacted the Last Supper of Jesus.

Baptism was by immersion and for adults only. Counseling for baptism happened only by request and there was no set age, but there were few baptisms under the age of eighteen. While there was no infant baptism, there was a custom called "the blessing of the children" every year after the Feast of Tabernacles. Infants of ages two and under were brought forward, prayed for, and blessed.

There were no pictures of Jesus allowed in members' homes. The removal of a picture of Jesus over the fireplace in our living room made my mother especially sad. This prohibition was based on the second of the Ten Commandments forbidding "graven images" for religious worship. In addition, artists' portrayals of Jesus were believed to err in picturing him with long hair. Jesus clearly had short hair, church literature explained, based on 1 Corinthians 11:14 and hair styles of the Roman empire of the time. It was reluctantly allowed that Jesus had a beard, but it was always quickly added that the beard of Jesus was "neatly trimmed." (How that was ascertained was always beyond me, particularly in light of the biblical command not to trim beards of Leviticus 19:27.)

Women were to be subservient to their husbands, just as their husbands were subservient to the ministers and the ministers to Christ. I heard some wives in the Akron church actually call their husbands "sir" (since 1 Peter 3:6 says Sarah called her husband Abraham "lord"). Ministers were to be addressed as "Mister," not by their first names. (It was OK for wives to address their husbands by their first names, however.) Twenty-two year old "elders" would be addressed as "Sir" and "Mister" by men and women three and four times their age. Ministers were not called "Reverend" because only God is revered. Ministers were *respected* but not *revered*. Women wore dresses, and men neckties, to Sabbath services, because, as Herbert Armstrong would frequently emphasize, God *does* care how one presents oneself in appearing before Him, and God, like Herbert Armstrong, did not care for casual dress. Herbert Armstrong definitively explained this in his 1979 article, "How You Dress for Church—Could it Keep You Out of the Kingdom?"

Herbert Armstrong was opposed to the use of doctors and drugs. They weren't natural. In cases of illness members would call for anointing with oil from a minister and trust in divine healing through prayer. Naturopathic healers and special diets were often used, but conventional medical treatment was regarded as ungodly and to be avoided. Doctors were allowed to clean wounds and set broken bones, but not much beyond that. Sometimes people got better and sometimes they died. (Herbert Armstrong's successor, Joseph Tkach, Sr., ended that doctrine in 1987.)

Smoking was prohibited but alcohol was accepted. Church literature showed that wine was used all through the Bible; making wine was Jesus's first miracle; the accusation that Jesus was a "winebibber" proved they weren't simply drinking grape juice; and the Bible condemns drunkenness but not alcoholic consumption in moderation. From this Bible foundation came the irony that, as one observer put it, "This is the only church I've ever heard of where you have to quit smoking and start drinking," referring to the ubiquitous beer and wine at social and religious functions which were part of Worldwide Church of God culture of those days. (Unfortunately, this abundance of alcohol in moderation resulted in some immoderation, including, according to some reports, in Herbert Armstrong himself.)

Military service and bearing firearms as part of a job were not to be done. In practice, a tithe-paying U.S. federal marshal whose job involved carrying a firearm was allowed to attend the Akron church indefinitely without problem; he just was not allowed to be baptized. I remember one sincere young man in the Akron church in 1968 had come into the Worldwide Church of God after he had already been classified 1-A, subject to the draft. His application to be reclassified as a conscientious objector was refused, despite the best efforts of a lawyer. He was ordered to report for induction to active duty. He appeared as ordered but refused to step across the line and take the oath. He was charged, it went to trial, and he was convicted and sentenced to prison. The night before he was to report to prison he fled to Canada. I heard a few members whisper criticisms that he had not stayed and gone to prison, but most members supported him and many sent letters and packages to assist him. (The ministers, who had tried to help him, did not condemn him.) Later when it was legal to do so he returned.

There were three tithes on family income. All were paid on gross income before taxes. The first tenth was mailed into Pasadena to do the Work and pay for the ministers. The second tenth was saved at home in bank accounts for family expenses in going to the Feast of Tabernacles. The third tenth was only paid every third year. It was sent in to headquarters for a fund supporting church widows and the destitute. In addition to the three tithes, there were Building Fund pledges and holy day offerings. In addition to these, there were usually a couple of budget crises every year which, according to Herbert Armstrong, threatened "the very livelihood of the Work." These crises required additional, urgent, special offerings to be airmailed into headquarters.

In its theology the Worldwide Church of God agreed in some things with fundamentalist Christianity and differed in others. There was belief in biblical inerrancy (the Bible is infallible), miracles, and the virgin birth. Visions, tongues-speakings, and charismatic phenomena for today were not accepted. (Theoretically, a true gift of tongues was considered possible; however, it had never happened in modern times.) There was no added scripture to the Bible. It was taught, however, that God had elected, for reasons known only to Himself, to work specially through Herbert Armstrong as His chosen apostle to whom important biblical truths were revealed.

The Worldwide Church of God believed Jesus Christ is divine Lord and Savior and that Christ eternally preexisted with God the Father. But the Holy Spirit was believed to be a force, not a person. (Hence, the Trinity was denied. Instead, God the Father and Jesus Christ are the first two members of a future universe-ruling "God family" into which true Christians in our age will be born.) Human beings do not have an immortal soul. Instead, immortality was only for the righteous ('the saved"). Everyone went unconscious at death and remained that way until the resurrection. At the resurrection, the righteous will be changed into glorified spiritual form the same as Christ and will be born into the "God family." The wicked will be brought back to life for a final and painful roasting, but then, mercifully, will be allowed to go extinct again. Nobody goes to heaven (except Christ). Instead, Christians will rule with Christ on earth after the resurrection. However, the earth itself is only a training ground for the universe beyond. Every human who has ever lived will be given a fair chance at salvation—if not now, then in a future resurrection.

Heaven, the place where God sits on a throne with angels in attendance, was believed to be a real place somewhere in space to the north (Job 26:7; Ps 48:2; Ezek 1:4). (Though being spiritual, it is of course invisible to telescopes.) Originally, before the creation of man, the created archangel Lucifer had been placed on earth with his angels for the purpose of making earth beautiful and habitable for man. But Lucifer rebelled and ascended toward heaven to attack God in the *north* (Isa 14:13). God smashed him back down to earth, leaving a lot of debris in space as a result (comets and asteroids and whatnot). As for Lucifer, he's still down here, now known as Satan the devil, stirring up trouble everywhere until Christ returns and has him cast into a bottomless pit with a big lock on the top of it.

Divorce and remarriage doctrine

One of the most controversial doctrines was the doctrine on divorce and remarriage. Herbert Armstrong taught that all first marriages on earth were bound by God for life. Jesus had said, "What God has joined together, let not man put asunder." The way Herbert Armstrong interpreted it, Jesus's injunction was logically meaningless. It was impossible, said Armstrong, for man to put a marriage asunder even if he was hell-bent on doing so. There could be no divorce in the sight of God if both partners were still living, no matter what human courts said, no matter how long ago a divorce had occurred, and no matter what had transpired since then. There were no legitimate grounds for divorces at all in the divine record books. (The "adultery exception" mentioned by Jesus in the Gospel of Matthew was interpreted to mean unfaithfulness or fraud before the marriage only. Armstrong cited the example of Joseph and Mary as precedent for this interpretation.)

What this meant was that any remarriage after a divorce was considered an adulterous union and must be ended if a first mate was still living anywhere on earth. Persons remarried after divorce were required to sever their new marriages even if children were involved. Hundreds of happy marriages and families were cruelly ripped apart based on the devastating impact of this doctrine. Nearby Cleveland, Ohio, was the scene of a major legal case in 1968 brought about by this doctrine. An angry husband sued Akron pastor David Antion, the Worldwide Church of God, and Herbert Armstrong for advising his wife that their marriage was "adulterous" and causing her to divorce him based on this advice. A jury awarded the aggrieved husband financial damages. Because of the legal implications of this precedent, the "Bradescu case" made national news. This happened a couple months before I began attending church, but I read the headlines the case made when I delivered my paper route every afternoon. (The jury's judgment was overturned on appeal.)

In 1970 an Akron reporter interviewed Garner Ted Armstrong by phone.[19] The younger Armstrong was quoted in the Akron newspaper as saying that the doctrine on divorce and remarriage

---

[19] Peter Geiger, "Underground Sect Training to Rule at Christ's Return," *Akron Beacon Journal*, Aug. 16, 1970, p. A-1.

had been changed and the booklet on the subject recalled. The new Akron Worldwide Church of God pastor, Bryce Clark, told the Akron church that the reporter was completely wrong and the doctrine was still the same. It turned out later the reporter had not quoted wrong. Garner Ted Armstrong had, in fact, been opposed to his father's doctrine on divorce and remarriage all along. But at that point, the statement that the doctrine had been changed was no more than Garner Ted's wishful thinking.

The postscript to both the doctrine and Akron pastor David Antion is instructive. Antion, who also happened to be Garner Ted Armstrong's brother-in-law, was transferred to Pasadena in 1969. In 1971, Antion was made superintendent of United States ministers for the Worldwide Church of God. This was the highest position in the church under the Armstrongs. Antion, who by now had become a reforming liberal by Worldwide Church of God standards, held the post until 1974. In that year a wide-ranging rebellion of pastors broke out. Prominently featured in this rebellion was these pastors' refusal to further enforce the hated doctrine on divorce and remarriage. Antion, who was sympathetic to the plight of the dissident pastors, refused to join Herbert Armstrong in condemning them. Instead, Antion resigned his position and in a press conference pleaded with Herbert Armstrong to listen to the dissidents' grievances.

Herbert Armstrong was not one to listen to rebels against his authority. But as pressure from dissidents became even more severe and threatened to bust the church wide open, God inspired Herbert Armstrong to change the doctrine on divorce and remarriage. This milestone occurred in May 1974. Henceforth, the aged Armstrong announced, remarriages after divorce before conversion would no longer be broken up. Armstrong decided that God began dealing directly with the lives and marriages of converted Christians at the point they became converted, not before. (Herbert Armstrong also later denied that his courting of a younger divorced woman, whom he later married, beginning about this time, had anything to do with his 180-degree turnaround on the subject of divorce.)

Attending Worldwide Church of God services in Akron

The Akron church met in a rented hall on the third floor of an old downtown building. An elevator, operated by my father, would take up the elderly, while younger members would walk up the stairs. There were no external signs or public notices announcing the weekly church meeting every Saturday. Only members knew about it. Crews of members set up the folding chairs and did the cleaning. The old building was a firetrap. Fortunately, no one smoked.

Attendance averaged about four hundred each week when I first began coming to services. People would drive into town from up to a hundred miles away. Services lasted two hours. There was no separate children's program. Children were expected to sit quietly through the service with their parents, including the hour-and-a-quarter sermon. It was as hot as blazes in the summer. Fans would blow hot air out the windows while adults sweated, children fidgeted, toddlers slept peacefully in their mothers' arms, and the truths of eternal life were preached from the pulpit.

The hymnal featured Psalms set to music by the Armstrong family composer, Dwight Armstrong. Dwight Armstrong was Herbert's younger brother. Kind music critics said the music lacked excitement or depth. Nevertheless, repetition of these simple Psalms set to music, replacing traditional Protestant "old favorites," soon became everyone's new "old favorites."

Everyone brought briefcases filled with Bibles and notebooks for their families, and everyone took notes. There was much socializing after church services. Wednesday nights were Bible Studies. These lasted one and a half hours. When the pastor finished his subject or chapters in the Bible for that evening, a young ministerial trainee would read excerpts from the "Ambassador College News Report," which always scared the daylights out of me. The Ambassador College News Bureau collected wire-service stories about famines, disasters, predictions of imminent nuclear war, ecological collapse, disease epidemics, and worse. The purpose of these reports was to prove how far gone the world was, which meant that Christ's return and the millennium were logically that much closer. After Bible Study, some of the farmers in the congregation would sell fresh farm eggs, milk, or Trail bologna from their car trunks or pickup trucks—produce which was always superior to what was available in supermarkets.

Being shy at first, I spent time in a tiny library room maintained by volunteer members. There I discovered, to my delight, Herman L. Hoeh's *Compendium of World History*, published by Ambassador College. This was a two-volume sweep through ancient history showing how dates of ancient kings and empires harmonized with biblical chronology and Bible figures. I learned that pagan gods of mythology were actually real persons named in Genesis. Their exploits had caused them to become remembered as pagan mythological figures. I had never read anything like it before. I was totally fascinated by the *Compendium* and I devoured its pages.

Another fascination for me was one of Herbert Armstrong's early converts from his Oregon days, a famous comic book illustrator named Basil Wolverton. Wolverton was the Worldwide Church of God's answer to the Jehovah's Witnesses' Mickey Spillane (author of the "Mike Hammer" detective series). Wolverton, a first-rate storyteller, wrote and illustrated *The Bible Story*. This multi-volume series was published and distributed by the church and was present in most members' homes. The way Wolverton wrote it made spellbinding reading. He also drew hilarious illustrations for the men's "Spokesman's Club" speech manual. These included caricatures of persons giving the "get the facts" speech, the "attack" speech, and so on. Wolverton also drew graphic depictions of tormented people suffering under the plagues of the Great Tribulation about to afflict earth in a few short years. These unsettling illustrations added visual punch to Herbert Armstrong's popular booklets *1975 in Prophecy!* and *The Book of Revelation Unveiled at Last!*

Hearing Gerald Waterhouse

Every year or two there would be a visit from a roving evangelist named Gerald Waterhouse (1926-2002). A special weekday evening meeting would be called and we would go down to the hall, not forgetting to take seat cushions. The seat cushions were a necessity because Gerald Waterhouse did not pay any attention to normal one and a quarter hour time limitations on speaking. He averaged about two and a half or three hours, nonstop.

But not one bit was dull to me. Speaking in rapid-fire, exclamatory, anecdotal, used-car-salesman style (and using no notes), he would expound on all sorts of things—number synchronisms, the inspired role of Herbert Armstrong, the detailed sequence of events leading up to Christ's return, the meanings of names, how the Two Witnesses of Revelation were going to be Herbert and Garner Ted Armstrong, what life would be like at "Petra" where the church would miraculously go to live for three and half years starting in 1972, the wickedness of "evil-ution," how the three Ambassador Colleges were like Elijah's three colleges (2 Kgs 2:3, 5: 4:38), and so on.

Some church members would dread Waterhouse's arrival due to his speaking so long and concerns over getting their small children to bed at a reasonable hour. But not me. It was all new to me. I was riveted in wide-eyed wonder by Waterhouse's creativity in interpreting prophecy and the humor he wove into his nonstop talking.

"Bad news is good news"

One of the most basic messages was the idea that, as one friend put it, "bad news is good news." The worse the disasters in the news—earthquakes, plagues, threat of nuclear war—the more likely the world was to being in the beginning stages of the Great Tribulation and the closer the world was to the end of the age. This was good news because it meant the time of Christ's return

Story of the Worldwide Church of God

and intervention which will end all human suffering was that much closer. Thus, bad news was good news.

In those years the war in Vietnam was the leading issue in the United States. There were debates in the halls of Congress and riots in the streets. (The famous shootings at Kent State University of May 1970, in which National Guardsmen fired into a crowd of protesting students and killed four, happened only ten miles away during my junior year of high school.) The Worldwide Church of God did not participate in voting and political campaigns. This did not, however, prevent opinions from being expressed on political matters. In 1971 Herbert Armstrong went to United States ambassador to South Vietnam Ellsworth Bunker, to get the "real truth" about why America was in Vietnam. Ambassador Bunker explained to the elderly Armstrong the basics of the "domino theory." The "domino theory" went like this: if the U.S.-propped-up Democratic Republic of South Vietnam fell, the rest of southeast Asia would not be far behind. Then Australia would go under. Before we knew it, they'd be crossing the ocean and invading Long Beach, California. It was important to stop the Viet Cong in their tracks *there*. Herbert Armstrong emblazoned this standard government line (which had been the White House rationale for about a decade by then) in the *Plain Truth* as being inside truth he had just newly learned in 1971.

The Worldwide Church of God presented the paradox of a church which had a doctrine against military service but which held "hawkish" right-wing views on Vietnam at the same time. Articles decrying losses of United States military power appeared regularly in the *Plain Truth* and *Worldwide News*. I do not recall a *Plain Truth* or *Worldwide News* article going beyond reporting on, say, the plight of refugees or homeless families to urging practical involvement in organizations doing something about these problems. In fact although the *Plain Truth* featured coverage of environmental issues such as air and water pollution and effects on the biosphere, there were pointed instructions from the pulpit discouraging church members from getting any ideas about joining environmental or other groups actually doing something about such problems. That would be participating in futile *human* efforts which are doomed to fail (man is *incapable* of solving these problems on his own). Such activities would cause one to lose focus on the preaching of the gospel of the coming kingdom of God, which was the *true* solution to these problems.

Meeting Garner Ted Armstrong in person at age fourteen

In the spring of 1969, when I was fourteen, Garner Ted Armstrong came to Akron during the days of Unleavened Bread. I had listened almost nightly to Garner Ted on the radio as a child. During his half-hour broadcasts Garner Ted would discuss world politics and troubles in the Middle East, disprove evolution, debunk popular misconceptions about the Bible, report on world ecological crises, and cover a range of topics of current interest, always ending with an offer of free literature. No radio program was more interesting to me. I sent in generous offerings from my paper route earnings to enable the "World Tomorrow" broadcast to spread even further. Now Garner Ted Armstrong was coming to Akron in person! I could hardly contain myself with anticipation. Three area congregations combined services for the big occasion—over a thousand people. Before the services began I saw others going up to shake Garner Ted Armstrong's hand. With temerity, I was bold enough to go up to shake his hand myself. I had actually met Garner Ted Armstrong in person! Returning to my father and brother, I waited eagerly for his sermon, for Garner Ted was always an interesting speaker.

Garner Ted Armstrong's words held my attention that day, but in a way I could never have dreamed when I got up that morning. For being new to the church, I had not the slightest hint that there was something wrong with my hairstyle. I knew the church said long hair was wrong, and I was as anxious to please as any kid in the church could be. But unwittingly, I was breaking another important rule forbidding hair on the forehead. However, this rule had never appeared in any printed literature nor had anyone told me about it. In keeping with normal 1960s style of my classmates in junior high school, I wore my hair combed sideways across the front of my forehead.

An obviously upset Garner Ted Armstrong hardly got into his prepared sermon topic at all. A young kid, he said, had come up to shake his hand, smiled and peered out from *under the hair over his forehead*. Garner Ted used this example (that is, me) as the launch pad for an extended tirade against youthful rebellion, willful rotten attitudes among church youth, hippies, long hair, and the deteriorating state of the world this reflected. I shriveled as Garner Ted blasted away with all his power and rhetoric. I didn't have a single rebellious thought in my heart at all. It was only in hearing Garner Ted's views on the matter that I learned that hair over the forehead was even objectionable to anyone. (His reasoning had something to do with the forehead being where the cortex or thinking portion of the brain is located. He mentioned Paul referring to "with unveiled face, beholding the glory of the Lord" [2 Cor 3:18]. A reference to the mark of the beast on the forehead was also thrown in, though I can't recall the precise logical connection.) It was like being rebuked by the psychological equivalent of a twenty-megaton thermonuclear blast (when a whisper in the ear would have sufficed). Of course, the first thing I did the next day was get my thoroughly traumatized self to a barber shop to get my hair cut and combed God's way.

~ ~ ~

I received more favorable attention from my hero Garner Ted Armstrong two years later. In 1970, when I was sixteen, I wrote a letter to Garner Ted in response to one of his broadcasts. Garner Ted had been reporting on environmental issues (from an environmentalist point of view). At one point he had made a comment conceding the impractibility of giving up all autos for bicycles. In my handwritten letter I praised bicycling (I was taking extended cycling trips around Ohio on my own at this point), and urged the practical advantages of this mode of transportation. Garner Ted made my youthful letter the subject of one of his thirty-minute radio broadcasts heard across the nation. I missed hearing that particular broadcast, but church members who did hear it told me Garner Ted read my whole letter, praised it, and credited my letter with inspiring his own use of a bicycle for transportation (and then he gave a few humorous anecdotes of his experiences as a bicycle commuter). I was on cloud nine.

Summer camp (SEP)

In the summer of 1969 I went to the church's four-week summer camp, the Imperial Schools Summer Educational Program (SEP) at Orr, Minnesota. We lived in bunk beds in barracks-like cabins with military-style inspections every morning. Everywhere we went as a group we were *marched* (not simply walked). There were activities such as canoeing, sailing, horseback riding, rifle range, archery, and so on. Garner Ted Armstrong was there the first weekend to welcome the campers. There was a sing-along with Garner Ted and his wife sitting on a porch watching. I remember all the campers standing in the open singing, and 15-year old girls dreamily looking at Garner Ted as they were singing, perhaps wondering if they might be so lucky to marry a husband so handsome and talented and good one day.

Mostly I remembered a huge emphasis on swats. They were big on that. Any little infraction, you'd get called into Counselor Koehler's room, sternly informed the reason for the punishment, and then voluntarily submit to being whacked hard on the butt (while clothed) with a wooden paddle. The number of swats at a time ranged from one to four depending on the counselor's assessment of the infraction's severity. Outside, the other campers would all be quiet and eagerly listen through the thin walls with stifled giggling at what was transpiring inside to their unfortunate fellow camper. Everyone kept a running count of

Story of the Worldwide Church of God

how many swats they got during the course of the four weeks. It was a common conversation opener with campers from the other cabins: "How many swats are you up to so far?" (And then trade stories of how they were obtained.) I received four during the four weeks, which was at the low end (I was well-behaved). The high in our cabin was something like 34, meted out to one poor kid who was hard of hearing. He would not hear some instructions, then get whacked by an increasingly irritated Counselor Koehler for not complying with instructions he had not heard or had misheard.

Although painful, Counselor Koehler's swats were not unbearable. His paddle was fortunately rather wide (the wider the paddle, the less the sting). But there was one case involving a different counselor that seemed like borderline sadism. It happened when six or eight of us had been temporarily left by ourselves by the lake with some canoes one time while our canoe instructor left us to get something. While he was gone a couple of the campers, bored, began to sit in the canoes and float them out into the lake a few feet, as well as wading in the water close to shore. Pretty soon everyone was doing it, including me. I didn't know there was anything wrong (since everyone else was doing it). We all were in swimming trunks and all were wet.

When the canoe instructor and another counselor came back and saw us wading in the water with the canoes, there was hell to pay. We all had to line up and one by one step into a designated area, then lean down and grab our ankles to receive the blows as the others looked on and waited their turn, like standing in line for execution. These were no ordinary swats. This counselor's wooden paddle was solid with a flat edge of narrow width, and even more to the point, we all had wet swimming trunks. He put his full strength into the blows. The pain was practically unbearable. (I am a little surprised that no one passed out from the pain.) This was no swats from Koehler in which afterward one could smile with the other campers and forget about it. I took mine without crying out (barely), but one kid, hit very hard on his wet swimming trunks, just groaned and collapsed to the ground unable to get back up. We each had a bright red spot on our skin in the shape of the paddle for a while afterward, and the kid who had fallen to the ground had a blister which as I recall required medical attention.

The Worldwide Church of God of those days was big into the benefits of corporal punishment. This was recommended in the booklet *The Plain Truth about Child Rearing*, which went into great detail on the importance and mechanics of introducing small children to the wonderful benefits of pain. (After all, Hebrews 12:6 clearly says God "chastens and scourges every son whom He receives," thus showing irrefutably the divine example for human parents to follow with their children.) In later years the Worldwide Church of God encountered legal problems with distributing church literature recommending physical punishment of children in Scandinavian countries, where such behavior on the part of parents is considered abuse and is illegal. Church officials, faced with this assault of godless laws of man on this important matter of God's truth (the benefits children receive from physical pain), nevertheless backed down and edited their literature in those countries in accord with the law.[20]

---

[20] In 1979 Sweden became the first country in the world to ban all corporal punishment of children. Finland followed in 1984, Denmark in 1986, and Norway in 1987 (and about a dozen more countries up to 2006). The landmark Swedish law states: "Children are entitled to care, security and a good upbringing. Children are to be treated with respect for their person and individuality and may not be subjected to corporal punishment or any other humiliating punishment." In 1979 the Swedish government sent a booklet to every family in Sweden entitled *Can you bring up children successfully without smacking and spanking?* It discussed how to bring up children with other methods, and emphasized that corporal punishment can cause both physical and psychological harm. The booklet pointed out that adults who were given corporal punishment as children are more likely to be depressed or violent themselves; that corporal punishment most often produces in its victims anger, resentment, and low self-esteem; and that children who are spanked regularly are more likely to lie, be disobedient at school, bully others, and show less remorse for wrongdoing. Many studies since then have reinforced all of these points. In all of the Nordic countries (Sweden, Denmark, Norway, Iceland, Finland) children have their own adult

Coming of age in the Worldwide Church of God:
courtship rituals

The Feast of Tabernacles was the major social time of the year. It was a chance for unmarried men and women to make new friends from among the thousands in attendance, without the normal feeling of being alone among the unconverted out in "the world." (Church members were supposed to marry in the church.) In addition to this, the Akron church hosted an annual regional "Eligibles Dance" every winter. It was a big deal. Single church men and women would travel to attend this dance from hundreds of miles away. Young women would plan for months ahead, get their hair done and dress to the hilt, except for makeup which was not allowed.

    I was shy when I first started attending church services. During my last two years of high school I finally learned to carry on a conversation with a young woman my age without expecting the floor to open up at any moment. In my junior year of high school, I won a statewide essay contest on conservation and became the "Ohio Conservation King." The reward was an airplane flight for several hours viewing Ohio strip mining areas, a small monetary award, and being honored at the annual banquet of the Ohio Conservation Congress along with the "Ohio Conservation Queen." The queen was a pretty, long-haired high school junior from Cincinnati, very sweet, daughter of a Methodist minister. When I saw her, talked with her, or even thought about her, my heart just flip-flopped. She liked me too, then she wrote and invited me to journey to Cincinnati to be her date for her high school prom. I almost did. But a conflict with

---

Ombudsman. In 1989 the United Nations approved the UN Convention on the Rights of the Child. As of 2006 Somalia and the United States remain the only two nations on earth not to sign. Highly recommended: Jordan Riak, "Plain Talk About Spanking," http://www.naturalchild.com/guest/plain_talk.pdf. Also: "It is Never Right to Hit a Child," an interview with Alice Miller, http://www.naturalchild.com/alice_miller/never_right.html.

the Sabbath and her not being in the church caused me to write back and decline. She went on to a Quaker college, became a teacher, and married happily. There was my chance for a more normal life.

High drama in the Worldwide Church of God

In 1971 and 1972 the course of the Worldwide Church of God was forever changed by a scandal involving Garner Ted Armstrong.

In mid-1971 Herbert Armstrong wrote a letter to the membership in which he said Garner Ted had asked for a rest and was being relieved of all duties for a couple of months. Apparently Garner Ted's need for rest required that he be removed from the board of directors of the church. Herbert Armstrong urged members to pray for Garner Ted.

Garner Ted promptly vanished so far as the outside world and the church members could tell. Wherever he was resting, he apparently didn't want the outside world dropping in to visit. Urgent letters came from Herbert Armstrong to the membership saying there were lying rumors going around. The elder Armstrong commanded that the rumor-mongering cease. Naturally, most of us had no idea what the rumors were which weren't supposed to be true.

Garner Ted appeared briefly to speak at the Feast of Tabernacles that fall. He gave no clue to what was going on. I was one of about 10,000 who heard him in Mount Pocono, Pennsylvania. His sermon was one of the most moving he had ever given. During his sermon he played a song which was popular at the time: "What the world needs now is love, sweet love." After playing this song several days later at another Feast site, church officials learned, he spent the night with a young woman other than his wife. He was stopped from further preaching. Members were told Garner Ted had become tired again. Garner Ted again disappeared. Back in the Akron church we were told, "Garner

Ted is under attack from Satan and needs our prayers." The mystery continued.

Early in 1972 the Akron pastor, Bryce Clark, read a special letter to the congregation from Herbert Armstrong one Sabbath. We were told the letter was being read simultaneously in all congregations across America. Members were told not to take notes and were enjoined to strict secrecy. With a touch of high drama, the letter said pastors were instructed to burn the letter after reading. This was supposed to keep the contents of Herbert Armstrong's letter out of the press. Of course, such "burn after reading" instructions did not keep the news out of the press and only added sizzle to the news stories.

In the letter, Herbert Armstrong said his son had been put out of the church for grave spiritual problems. The letter said that members should pray for Garner Ted to prevail against this attack of Satan. However traumatic this was to the church, the letter said, it was evidence that church discipline exempted no one, not even Herbert's own son. Garner Ted was quoted as saying he had become spiritually vulnerable when he drifted away from prayer and spent too much time in pursuits such as painting. (During my years at Big Sandy, a large painting done by Garner Ted Armstrong graced a wall in the student lounge. It was a mountain scene.) Herbert Armstrong said the period of Garner Ted's exile might be eight months before he could return.

The news media had a field day. *Time* magazine ran an article entitled, "Garner Ted Armstrong, Where Are You?"[21] (The answer to this question, it later turned out, was: in New York City getting advanced pilot's training.) Herbert Armstrong gave the reporters for *Time* a letter he had received from Garner Ted in which Garner Ted confessed to sinning "against the wife of my youth." But the elder Armstrong denied that handsome Garner Ted's sin was one of the flesh. Herbert Armstrong described his son's sin as "spiritual, not carnal."

---

[21] *Time*, May 15, 1972.

Income was dropping from Garner Ted's being off the radio program. In June 1972 Herbert Armstrong announced that Garner Ted had fully repented and was back. Garner Ted resumed his broadcasting duties, members rejoiced, income returned to normal, and the church was considered stronger than ever.

The true story behind Garner Ted's exile and Hebert Armstrong's attempt to cover it up unraveled later in 1974 during the dissident ministers' revolts. But even after the scandal came out, most of the church supported Herbert's rehabilitation of Garner Ted. Just as the Lord had used David who was a man of many sins, the thinking went, so He would likewise again use Garner Ted Armstrong.

Big Sandy: a dream come true

Throughout my school years, my goal was to go to Ambassador College, proclaimed as a "foretaste of the World Tomorrow." In the middle of a racially tense, high-crime, big-city public high school (forty percent white, sixty percent black, near the scene of race riots in the late 1960s), the dream of Ambassador College was the promise of a better world. Here was an oasis of tranquility in the midst of a troubled world. Here there were no drugs or student demonstrations. Here happy students learned true values—not just how to make a living but how to live. I wanted to go to Ambassador College more than anything on earth. I looked forward to the day when this could become reality. I prayed at night to God in heaven to allow me this.

I applied to the Big Sandy campus instead of Pasadena because Big Sandy's open, rural, Texas atmosphere appealed to me. It was a joyful day when I received a letter of acceptance. In August of 1972 I hugged my father, mother, and brother goodbye and flew south to this new land where I'd never been ... Texas. Now I return to the story at Big Sandy.

CHAPTER 3

THE 7000-YEAR PLAN

In sociologists' language, the *Plain Truth* magazine and the "World Tomorrow" radio broadcast of those days reflected an "eschatological" way of thinking, that is, a concern with last things or the end of the age. Groups which see the world through such eyes believe the world is in its last throes. By being inside the group, one is uniquely situated to personally witness and participate in an imminent, apocalyptic transition from the present sinful order to a shining new, millennial era. This becomes the fundamental truth upon which all else is based and finds its meaning.

There was nothing more basic to the message of Herbert Armstrong than that the end of the age was near at hand. The return of Christ was always no more than a few short years away, or, as Herbert Armstrong would constantly say, "Sooner than we think!"

How soon did Herbert Armstrong think? Throughout my three years at Big Sandy (1972-75), Herbert Armstrong's estimates in his sermons and writings remained consistent. He believed there were about two to three years left before the start of the Great Tribulation. There was some leeway allowed on this. Other evangelists in the church gave more liberal estimates in the four- to eight-year range.

~ ~ ~

Herbert Armstrong was not modest about what the True Church was destined to accomplish in the few short years before Christ's return. Starting in 1969 Herbert Armstrong approved an arrangement by which Ambassador College would supply fifty students' volunteer labor every summer on excavations in the Old City of Jerusalem conducted by Hebrew University professor Benjamin Mazar. In exchange for being allowed to provide this volunteer labor, Herbert donated $100,000 a year to the dig. Students from all three campuses, including Big Sandy, went over every summer (paying their own way) throughout my years at Big Sandy, and it was a major life experience for many students.

These were no ordinary excavations. According to Herbert they were "the most important archaeological excavation of our time" and "one of the most important scientific projects under way anywhere on earth today."[22] The reason? Herbert believed these excavations would uncover the throne of David, "the very spot where prophecy says the returning messiah—Jesus Christ—is to *rule the whole world*."[23] Herbert wrote the members and co-workers that the Ambassador College students volunteering their labor on this dig were hard at work clearing away the rubble from the throne on which Jesus Christ would sit and rule after his return to earth, and in this way were preparing the way for Christ's coming.[24]

Now lest you smile, I ask you to consider for a moment. Christ has to sit somewhere when he comes back, doesn't he? Maybe Herbert shouldn't be faulted for trying to be helpful.

Finding David's throne never was a stated goal of Mazar conducting the excavation. There was a very good, if trivial, reason for that. As Mazar repeatedly tried to tell Herbert Armstrong, the site of David's throne was about 200 yards to the

---

[22] Herbert Armstrong, Co-worker letter, Dec. 10, 1968, cited in *Ambassador Report* (which is also the source for some of the details in the preceding and following paragraphs).
[23] Herbert Armstrong, Co-worker letter, May 28, 1971.
[24] "Jesus is to sit on David's throne! Where was David's throne? It was on this very spot where we are now cleaning up and hauling off the rubble of century after century of accumulation! ... So there is a physical preparing, as well as [a] spiritual, in preparing the way for Messiah's coming!" (Herbert Armstrong, Co-worker letter, Dec. 10, 1968).

south of their dig area. It was not underneath where they were digging. But it did no good. Herbert preferred to believe they were directly over David's throne and would eventually reach it, no matter what Mazar the excavator might think. Maybe for $100,000 a year plus fifty bodies' free labor every summer they decided Herbert could have David's throne located wherever made him happy. Who knows. In any case, neither Mazar's excavations which ended in 1976 nor any other excavation has turned up David's throne. It seems Christ will have to make other janitorial arrangements.

~ ~ ~

It was also believed that the return of Christ would be preceded by a 3-1/2 year period. For the world, this would be the "Great Tribulation." But for the faithful, it would be a physical place of safety on earth. This place was identified as Petra, the ancient capital of the Nabataean kingdom, in modern-day Jordan. Today it is a desolate area of caves and desert. The church membership—those who heeded the call when the word came to go, that is—would be taken to a "place of safety" (based on Isa 26:20-21; Zeph 2:3; Luke 21:36; Rev 3:10; 12:14). Where this "place of safety" would be located was theoretically left open, but it was widely understood that it would be Petra. This came from references to finding salvation and safety in the "rocks" (a frequent biblical metaphor, e.g. Isa 2:10; 16:1-5; 33:16; 42:11). "Petra" means "Rock" in Greek. Therefore, Petra.

Herbert Armstrong had several meetings with Jordan's King Hussein, and told the membership more than once that he felt his friendship with King Hussein would enable him to make arrangements to relocate the church membership safely to Petra when the time came. (Whether King Hussein was aware of Herbert Armstrong's ideas on this matter, or what he thought about them if he was, is unknown.) No evidence ever came forth of actual preparations to relocate church members. Nevertheless, the notion of a future mass movement to a place of safety was the belief, with the timing of its activation being left "up to God."

Throughout the 1960s the belief was that the "time to flee" would be January 1972 (the first week of January, to be specific). However, in 1970 and 1971, with the moment of truth approaching, there was some serious effort on the part of headquarters to defuse expectations on this. Some pastors did a better job than others of defusing the expectations. Herbert Armstrong wrote letters to the members saying that the timing of when to flee was not certain. But he wrote in mid-1971 that he thought there was still a 50 percent chance that there would be a fleeing in January 1972.

With bated breath the members waited as 1971 drew to a close and became 1972. To the disappointment of many in the hinterlands, the first week of January 1972 just came and went without the "word to go" that had been awaited. Herbert Armstrong wrote the members that the first week of January 1972 indeed *had* been special, because in that very week *Reader's Digest* had agreed to run some ads that the church had requested. This was God's signal, said Herbert Armstrong, that the Work was to continue a bit longer. The time is still close, don't think the Lord delays his coming, don't let down, its time to *redouble* our efforts (postage-paid envelope provided), *thank you* brethren—was the message now.

But no amount of spin could take away the disappointment a lot of members felt over this. Some members had waited years for this, postponed buying homes, sent in retirement money to headquarters that they thought would not be needed, consoled themselves in the midst of sacrifice and struggle that there were only X number of years or months left (as they checked their mental calendar). But now—no end of the world, no fleeing to Petra, the distasteful present would go on a little longer. Then a strange thing happened. We began to hear sermons blaming *the members* for having had this belief, as if the members on their own had come up with it. The line from headquarters was, "We always said it was uncertain. But members just ran away with it and put more stock in it than we ever intended."

In any case, there was a clear resolve at headquarters not to repeat the error. While the time was always "very short," it was always from that time forward kept nonspecific and any estimates couched in terms of "maybe," while reminding the brethren that Jesus himself had said no one would know the day or hour. It was as if there was now a very strong, unspoken rule: "Don't even speculate an exact date." No way did headquarters want another 1972 fiasco.

Just to be clear, the "Petra" expectation was not *quite* formal doctrine, not *quite* mandatory to believe, and, in fact, not everyone did. The "place of safety" was a firm belief, but Petra as the place *where* that would be was in principle not quite certain. But it depended on which minister you talked to. Many ministers talked of it like it was a sure thing, others as if it was only a very meaningful "maybe" (said with pregnant pause after delivering the exciting speculation), while other ministers didn't talk about it much at all because they thought it was questionable or even, in a few cases, way out in la-la land. (There was always a tiny minority within the church, both ministers and members, who held to a "spiritual place of safety" alternative view—that true Christians would not be physically spared the tribulation to come, because preservation of physical bodies wasn't the point.)

~ ~ ~

What is it like to live in expectation that the return of Christ is just around the corner? A class paper I did, entitled "Evidences for the 7000-Year Plan" (January 7, 1974), shows how I and those around me at Big Sandy at the time, viewed the world. I wrote this paper as a class assignment for Mr. Richard Ames's Old Testament Survey class. This was my second research paper on a biblical topic written at Big Sandy. My first paper on a biblical topic (now lost) reconstructed events in the life of Abraham as occurring on holy days. (It was submitted earlier in the term to the same class.) But that one was merely a warm-up. It was not one-tenth as creative as my paper on the 7000-year plan, which in any case is my first Big Sandy paper of which a copy survives.

Mr. Ames had asked for a ten to fifteen page paper; mine turned out to be over sixty pages. (Fortunately, he took my exuberance for my subject matter in good spirits.) In this paper, I took an existing doctrinal basis and creatively sought to argue the case for it—more creatively, I was told, than had ever been done before. Since it was well received and was returned with a grade of "95," it may be considered the first and only of the papers I wrote at Big Sandy described in this book to have accomplished its purpose.

In this paper I first established by quoting current authorities that the world is in a very serious crisis without prior precedent, with human survival itself at risk. I didn't have to go far for documentation for this, since this was standard fare in church publications. I quoted, for example, scientist Gordon Rattray Taylor, author of *The Doomsday Book*: "By and large, men do not conduct their affairs as if this planet were on the verge of becoming uninhabitable. The threat is too serious to take seriously." And Isaac Asimov, "Man is carelessly altering his environment and (if he does not change his ways) heedlessly bringing doom upon himself ... we face the overriding crisis of human history *now*," and quite a few more like that.

Then I turned to biblical chronology. I showed that there is a chain of genealogies and generations going back to Adam, and that although there are disagreements over the exact count, nevertheless all agree our time is about 6000 years after the creation of Adam (according to the Masoretic text). I hammered at this "coincidence." The coincidence is that there is a good biblical case for a 7000-year plan, with 6000 years followed by a 1000-year millennium which would be a millennial "Sabbath." The 1000-year millennium is in Revelation. The 6000 years preceding the 1000-year millennium are logical by analogy with the seven-day week. And we are right at the end of that 6000

7000-Year Plan

years, with the world looking like it is about to end. I said, this is too much to be coincidence.

Then I quoted from ancient Jewish and early Christian authorities who spoke of a 7000-year plan, with an expectation that Christ would return (or in the case of Jews, the Messiah would come the first time) 6000 years after the creation of Adam. This was an idea in the early centuries AD among both Jews and Christians. And now the time of crisis was happening, right when Jewish and Christian exegetes from nearly two thousand years ago *had said*.

Up to this point this was basic church teaching, although the quotes I found from ancient Jewish and Christian authorities were an added feature. It was at this point that I started adding things that, I argued, further confirmed this scheme. In outline form, here are the key further points I made in that paper:

(1) It was believed in the church that Christ was killed at the end of a Wednesday evening (not Friday) of "Passion Week." What I noticed (I don't think this point had been made before) was a parallel between Christ being killed at the end of the fourth day of the week and at the end of the fourth "millennial day," that is at the end of 4000 years. (Jesus's death was not *exactly* at the end of 4000 years of course, but it was close enough for me to see an analogy.) Then after three days Christ rose on Saturday evening, at the end of the seven-day week, and that too had a parallel in the general resurrection at the end of the millennium, the end of the seventh millennial day.

(2) I noted a sabbatical year dating that had been done by a Big Sandy senior, soon to become faculty member, Dennis Dietz. Dietz had written a research paper dating the sabbatical and Jubilee years (the church up to then had said the exact years were lost and unknown). According to Dietz's study the next Jubilee year was scheduled for 1987-88, which Dietz noted would be the fortieth Jubilee from when, Dietz argued, Jesus started his ministry by proclaiming the Jubilee of 27-28 AD, according to Luke 4:16-21. Dietz simply noted that 1987-88 would be the 40th Jubilee from Christ, without making much point of it. But I made

a point of it. I also found things which went beyond Dietz's paper. I found that when Dietz's Jubilee count was extended backward, the upcoming 1987-88 Jubilee was also the *seventieth* Jubilee from the first Jubilee after the Israelites entered the Promised Land in 1444 BC (according to Hoeh's date). That was *forty* Jubilees (from Jesus) and *seventy* Jubilees (from entry to the Promised Land) ending in 1987-88, which was approximately when 6000 years were ending. Again, I argued, this was an awful lot to call coincidence. (More on Dietz's paper later.)

(3) Why was there a 2000-year gap between Christ's first and second comings? I tackled this conundrum. I cited a few things like "after much delay" of the parable of the women and the lamps of Matthew 25, God's patience and mercy cited in 2 Peter 3:9, and so on, as predictions of and reasons for delay of the return of Christ. But I also found a scripture which I thought alluded more directly to the 2000-year delay. Hosea 6:2 reads: "After two days he will revive us; on the third day he will raise us up, that we may live before Him." I argued the 2000 years from Jesus until the resurrection of believers at Christ's coming was the "two" days, which would be followed by the "third" day, the millennium when we would "live before Him."

(4) I noted already-existing church calculations concerning the "seven times" punishment on Israel from their going into captivity anciently at 722-718 BC to the revival of Israel 2520 (360 x 7) years later with the Louisiana Purchase making America great in 1804. There was a parallel 2520 year calculation from the time of Judah's fall in 604 BC to 1917, the Balfour Declaration promising the Jews a restored homeland. The fulfillments of these confirmed the "seven times" interpretations, and the end could not be before these were fulfilled (and both came about shortly before the end of 6000 years). (Nothing original on this point—the church already said this.)

(5) My next point was a real gem, and seemed not to have been noticed by anyone before, i.e. it was truly original. I discovered it the previous summer. I had been reading the story

7000-Year Plan

of Joseph in Genesis, the part where there are seven years of famine in Egypt and his brothers visit him after two years of the famine (45:11). I noticed that if you take those seven years in the story of Joseph, and compare it to the "seven times" of Israel's captivity starting 722 BC, you get 2 x 360, two times = 720 or 2 BC, corresponding to the visit to Joseph of his brothers, which was when *the Magi visited Jesus.* The church had articles proving that the Magi were Israelites of the lost tribes of Israel. This correspondence seemed just startling. (I could hardly contain myself when I saw it.) As I wrote in this term paper for Mr. Ames:

> Thirty-year old Joseph rose to prominence in Egypt after predicting a seven-year famine to Pharaoh. Exactly two years into this famine, Joseph's brothers, led by Judah, journeyed to Egypt for their historic meeting with Joseph (Gen 45:6). Joseph is a clear type of Christ ... this seven-year famine involving Joseph can be regarded as a parallel to the "seven times" punishment on Joseph's descendants—the house of Israel ... If "seven times" is 2520 years, then "two times" is 720 years. Beginning with 722 BC and going forward 720 years, we come to 2 BC. What happened in 2 BC? That was the very year the Magi visited Christ! The Magi have been identified as Israelites. They visited Christ two years after His birth in 4 BC (Matt 2:16). The Magi's visit to Christ *exactly parallels* the journey of Joseph's brothers to see Joseph, to the year. In the one case, Israel led by Judah visits Joseph. In the other, Israel led by Joseph (the leading tribe of the house of Israel) visits the King of the Jews ... Coincidence?

(6) Finally, I noted that "if the interval from Passover to Pentecost is drawn to scale to equal the interval from Israel leaving Egypt—which occurred on a Passover—to the founding of the New Testament church—which occurred on a Pentecost—then the same scale interval from Pentecost to Trumpets equals Israel leaving Egypt to just before the year 2000." This too was original. As you can see, I *was* creative in finding and seeing correspondences and patterns.

I closed by returning to the basic point that external world conditions show that the end-time is now, and at the same time we are about 6000 years after Adam, exactly when ancient Jewish and Christian exegetes, as well as argument from biblical typology, lead us to expect the end-time. This was supported by the other corroborations I had tabulated. My term paper had graphs and timelines. I saw elegance in my paper's important calculations. Clearly from these calculations we were right at the end of 6000 years, on the threshold of the Second Coming of Jesus Christ and the transformation of everything.

Jubilee years, or, how to go about setting a date for the Second Coming: a case history

My paper for Mr. Ames included references to datings of sabbatical and Jubilee years. That part of the paper did not come from church teaching. Rather, as noted above, that came from research by a new member of the faculty, Dennis Dietz. A year earlier intelligent, urbane Dietz had been in his senior year at Big Sandy. Dietz was a little unusual in that he had come to Big Sandy as a student after earning a PhD in physics at Pennsylvania State University. After he graduated from Ambassador he was hired at Big Sandy to teach courses in physics and chemistry. Dietz had submitted a paper to a class taught by Mr. Dart in the fall of 1973. Dietz's paper dated the sabbatical year cycle historically and suggested benefits to reclaiming knowledge and practice of the sabbatical year for today.

The church's position was that knowledge of the correct sabbatical year, unlike the weekly Sabbath, was lost. In contrast to the weekly Sabbath, which was believed to matter very much which day it was, church leaders inconsistently decided it did not matter which year out of seven one kept as the sabbatical year. The sabbatical year was in any case believed to apply only to farmers (only a fraction of the church's membership). Church members who were farmers were told to let their land lie fallow any one year out of seven. This would be counted the seventh

7000-Year Plan

year after baptism, or if the farmer preferred it would be OK to let a different one-seventh of their land lie fallow each year. Dietz's paper, entitled "Land Sabbaths in History," argued that the sabbatical year was not lost but was dateable.

I came to know Dietz well and would visit him in his tiny, tin-can-like office, one in a row of aluminum "booths" by the side of a road (air-conditioned and quite comfortable). Dietz was widely read, easy to talk to, and he could make science *really interesting*. Our talks covered topics ranging from physics and philosophy of science to his interest in the ideas of E.F. Schumacher, *Small is Beautiful: Economics as if People Mattered* (this was about sustainable local economies as preferable to giant corporations), and on to the economic and social meaning land-sabbaths and the Jubilee year could mean in today's world.

Dietz pointed out to me that there was far more to the sabbatical year than simply farmers letting fields lie fallow. The sabbatical year cycle had meaning integrally related to family health and preservation, fresh starts from debt, business cycles, the benefits of "the sabbatical" already in use today in some professions, and increased ecological awareness. Lenders would not lose money because loans would have built-in, planned expiration dates in the sabbatical years. There would be a rhythm in the economy, a periodic clearing of debt, fresh starts. And the Jubilee—that meant that once every generation every family would get a *fresh start*, would get their land back (if their parents or grandparents had screwed up and lost it). No more the vast differences between inherited fortunes and poor with no hope. The Jubilee was the great equalizer—every forty-nine years every family got their share of the land back and could make of it what they would again—through hard work, good luck, speculation, stupidity, whatever—for the next forty-nine years, when there would be a new *fresh start*.

Dietz pointed out that the specific reason the kingdom of Judah went into captivity anciently from the point of view of the prophet Jeremiah—the final straw—was violation of the sabbatical year injunction to release slaves and debt (Jer

34:8-22). Historians say it is doubtful that any Jubilee ever was implemented in Israel (it was an ideal never put into practice). But Dietz argued that Jesus's first proclamation of the gospel at Nazareth—the occasion for his first rejection—was specifically a proclamation of a Jubilee year (Luke 4:16-21). Jesus's announcement of the Jubilee year was a social justice message, Dietz told me. It had real economic meaning, and that is why some of those at Nazareth who heard Jesus's message sought to kill him (they were probably the landowners and creditors, Dietz thought). That was how incendiary the Jubilee was, how powerful the sabbatical and Jubilee might be today in America. The sabbatical years are linked with the weekly sabbath in the Pentateuch and in the prophets. If we as a church knew the seventh-day sabbath mattered, Dietz argued, logically the sabbatical year probably mattered as well.

~ ~ ~

Dietz's paper held much vision and promise. But like practically all other submissions of new understanding, though it attracted some interest among individuals, it went nowhere institutionally.

Dietz told me that he had written the paper for a course taught by Mr. Dart, the new deputy chancellor and resident administrator at Big Sandy. Oddly, this paper had come back to Dietz with a surprisingly mediocre grade of "C" from Mr. Dart (instead of the "A" that one would have thought Dietz's well-researched paper would have received). It seems Mr. Dart had not liked the paper. Dietz and Mr. Dart seemed to get along well otherwise so far as I could see, but that came later and was not because of this paper. Mr. Dart supported the church position, which was that the sabbatical year dating could not be known and therefore church officials had made a judgment as to what to do. Dietz's paper differed from the church conclusion on this matter, and the "C" appeared to reflect Dart's dissatisfaction with Dietz's paper challenging a church position.

7000-Year Plan

Mr. Dart may not have liked Dietz's paper, but Dr. Hoeh at Pasadena did. But first let me review some of Dietz's actual argument.

As noted, Dietz's paper dealt with establishing the correct dating of the sabbatical year, which had been thought to be "lost." According to Dietz's research, which drew on the first-century Jewish historian Josephus and other historical references, several sabbatical years had been kept by the Jews on known years, and a study of these showed clearly that the sabbatical years occurred every seventh year in unbroken succession (just like the weekly sabbath)—and the Jubilees occurred 49, not 50, years apart.

Most people—this is what you would hear in Worldwide Church of God sermons whenever the subject came up—thought there were seven sabbatical years every 50 years rather than every 49 years. By this way of looking at it, the Jubilee would break the recurring seventh-year sequence, once every 50 years. There would be seven sabbatical years, followed by a 50th year, the Jubilee, and then the *next* sabbatical year would happen eight years after the last sabbatical year. The Jubilee years would be fifty years apart, seven sabbatical year cycles plus one. That is what church literature at Pasadena had always said, and what I had always assumed.

But Dietz's research had convinced him that that was not how it was counted. Instead, the Jubilee years were 49 years apart. The sabbatical years occurred every seven years without ever breaking the recurring seven-year cycle. The Jubilee year, which was to occur every "fiftieth" year (following every seventh sabbatical year), would not break the succession of sabbatical years. Instead, each Jubilee or "fiftieth year" was itself the first of the fifty-year count to the *next* Jubilee year. That meant the Jubilee years are 49, not 50, years apart. This coincidentally harmonized with the church recognizing (in the spring of 1974) that Pentecost—an annual spring holy day—was on a Sunday, not a Monday. Pentecost is the "fiftieth day" following the seventh weekly sabbath from Passover. But Pentecost does not interrupt the unbroken succession of weekly sabbaths. By analogy, it was the same with the Jubilee.

So there were actually two chronological issues Dietz dealt with. The first was whether to count the Jubilee/ sabbatical year cycles in 50s or 49s. Dietz's paper argued it was 49s. The second was fixing the correct years in history once the right way of counting the cycle was established. But once it was realized the sabbatical year cycle was never broken, then in principle it was as simple as this: securely identify any land-sabbath year observed by the Jews anciently, and that identifies them all throughout history (given the unbroken sequence). What followed was almost trivial. For in fact there are at least a half-dozen or so land-sabbath years recorded in Jewish history of known date, and these "anchor points" agree in reflecting a single, unbroken seven-year repeating cycle (an appendix in Whiston's *Josephus* discusses this). By simple extrapolation Dietz listed all the sabbatical years coming down 2000 years to the present. The year 1972-1973, which had just passed, had been the most recent sabbatical year, according to Dietz's extrapolation.

The farm at Ambassador College, Big Sandy, was run by Dale Schurter, head of the Agriculture Department, some full-time staff, and a group of student employees of notorious reputation and high morale called the "Ag Crew" who gloried in their hard work and scruffy looks (and sometimes smells to match). The farm at Big Sandy had just finished observing a sabbatical year in 1972-73 (fall to fall), on the very year Dietz's paper had calculated was the correct one (and in the same year Orthodox Jews in Israel were keeping it). Although the farm at A.C. Big Sandy had not grown crops that year (1972-73), some on faculty row had grown home gardens that year. It seems some of the vegetables in those home gardens had not turned out so well—possibly a message there, some thought. Some involved with the farm were quite interested in and receptive to Dietz's paper on the land-sabbath year dating, although there could be no actual changes in policy unless instructed by headquarters. (That would

7000-Year Plan

be a long wait, since nothing ever happened, and there is no sign that headquarters, with the exception of Dr. Hoeh's interest in the historical chronology aspects, ever knew or cared about the topic.)

~ ~ ~

After reading Dietz's paper and talking with him about it, I had done some further thinking. Although it was a peripheral point in Dietz's paper, according to Dietz's research the next Jubilee year was scheduled for 1987-88 (fall to fall), and this would be the fortieth Jubilee since Jesus proclaimed the Jubilee year of 27-28 AD at Nazareth of Luke 4:16-21. I found this dating intensely interesting—"Would Christ return on the fortieth Jubilee?"—and took off with it.

I took Dietz's Jubilee year datings and worked backward to BC. I compared my results with Dr. Hoeh's dates for events in Genesis. Dr. Hoeh had worked out a chronology for world history that had Adam's creation dated to the exact year, in 4024 BC. On my midnight to 3 a.m. night switchboard job I counted, calculated, and compared calendars and chronologies. I worked and reworked the numbers ... and was *astounded* at the synchronisms I discovered. Surely these could not be mere COINCIDENCE. Another paper emerged, with numbers and graphs showing Jubilee year synchronisms. This went well beyond my 7000-year plan paper.

~ ~ ~

I mentioned earlier that this was a time in the Worldwide Church of God when matters of chronology and "setting dates" were definitely suspect. As noted earlier, it had been widely believed that in the first week of January 1972 the church would be taken to a "place of safety" (Petra), where the favored chosen ones would safely sit out the Great Tribulation which would afflict the earth for three and a half years before Christ's return in 1975.

Now, I know it is a burning question to you: how did they arrive at those dates? Well, in the following ways. First, 1975 was 6000 years after the creation of Adam in 4025 BC (according to an earlier dating by Dr. Hoeh). Second, the "seven times" of the Gentiles (Dan 4:25, 32; Luke 21:24), at the end of which it was believed Christ would return, were believed to be counted 2520 years (7 x 360) after the fall of Babylon in 539 BC. There was a minor problem there since calculation showed that should come out to 1982, not 1975. But Dr. Hoeh resolved this trifling discrepancy by proposing that Nebuchadnezzar's seven years of insanity (Dan 7:33-37) could be subtracted from the total years. This conveniently brought the date back where it should be, to 1975. Finally, 1975 was confirmed by a belief in the significance of nineteen-year time cycles.

Nineteen years is the cyclic basis of the Hebrew calendar, when the intercalations come into line. Now I hope you are sitting down. The start of Herbert Armstrong's radio ministry in Oregon in January 7, 1934, to the start of the expansion of Herbert Armstrong's radio ministry to Europe, which occurred in the first week of January 1953, was *exactly nineteen years*. It corresponded to nineteen years from 31 AD, when the apostles' ministry began, to 50 AD, when Paul first went to Europe (Macedonia). (Dr. Hoeh's dates here again.)

It was then deduced that a second nineteen-year time cycle from January 1953 to January 1972 would be allotted for the gospel to go to the whole world, after the first nineteen years having gone to Israel only. This would correspond to the early church having been allotted a second nineteen years from 50 AD to 69 AD, at the end of which the church went underground and the preaching of the gospel in power went silent in the first century AD. (There was a flight to a "place of safety" at about that time—the Nazarene Christians' flight from Jerusalem to Pella, a city in the Greek Decapolis across the Jordan, at the time of the Jewish War according to an early tradition.) The end of the Work in 1972 would be followed by the three-and-a-half-year

7000-Year Plan

Great Tribulation and then Christ's return in 1975 at the end of 6000 years.

Unfortunately, as I related earlier, expectations had been dashed when January of 1972 came and went without the call to leave the present evil society for the place of safety. Sadly, the promised Great Tribulation wiping out most of the world failed to materialize on schedule. The aftermath of this letdown was to attempt to keep in check any speculation that smacked of setting dates. Nevertheless, it seems that no amount of falsified past dates for Christ's return will prevent creative minds from coming up with new future ones, backed up by charts, numbers, graphs, scriptures, and unexplained coincidences, and I was no exception.

If Christ was indeed returning in our generation—in a few years (we continually believed the time was "very short")—then it was only natural for me to look to every clue available to try to decipher precisely when this event of the ages might take place. After all, God was mathematical as seen in astronomy and physics, and the Bible is filled with significant numbers, so perhaps somewhere underneath it all lay hidden The Truth, which I made it my purpose to attempt to discover.

The dating of the Jubilee year could be the key, I thought. In light of the significance of the Jubilee as a picture of the millennial reign of God, the upcoming fortieth Jubilee, scheduled for 1987-88, could be IT. No one in the church had put this together before, since Dr. Dietz's research on the Jubilee year dating was new.

No one knows the day or the hour

I must interject a word here about Jesus's words, "But of that day and hour no one knows, not even the angels of heaven, nor the Son, but the Father only" (Matt 24:36). I knew these words well, and they were frequently emphasized from the pulpit to the church members. How was this to be reconciled with my calculations? There were a couple of ways. First, if you read

Jesus's words closely, he said no one would know the *day* or the *hour*. He didn't say no one would know the "year," now did he? But if that sounds like splitting hairs, there was another explanation that I liked better. I learned this from a church member named Don Bivens. It was that at the time of the return of Christ, the heavens will be shaken, the earth thrown out of orbit, and we would *not* know day from night, or what hour it was, for that reason (Zech 14:7; Amos 8:9; Isa 24:19-20; Isa 13:13).

Don Bivens was unusual. Only a couple of years older than me, he was from the same home church in Oklahoma as a fellow student in my dorm my freshman year named Curtis Borman. I met Bivens when Bivens visited Big Sandy one weekend and came over to the dorm to see his friend Borman. I hit it off with Bivens, mainly because of his *extreme* energy and knowledge of the Bible. He could quote and turn to scriptures with lightning speed and *explain* them. Over the next couple of years he came down to Big Sandy for weekend visits several more times. I stayed up late out in the dorm lounge talking with him about prophecy and such things into the early morning hours more than once. He had notes from an old Bible study series on prophecy given by a minister in his home area and he related what he knew to me, some of which was far-out stuff (WCG-compatible but not necessarily WCG-endorsed).

It was Bivens who showed me the scriptures about the earth being thrown out its orbit when Christ returned. Among his many comments and asides, Bivens suggested that this could relate to Jesus saying no one would know the day or hour of his coming. No one would know the day or hour, because there wouldn't *be* normal days or hours then. There were a lot of scriptures that talked about this distortion of time and earth's equilibrium, if you were alert to them. In addition to the ones noted above, Bivens showed me Isa 13:10; 24:19-20; 30:26; 34:4; 60:19; Matt 24:29; Rev 6:12-14, and 8:12. (I took notes.) In any case Jesus didn't say one couldn't come *close* to knowing the time of his return, even if cataclysmic events (smashing comets and asteroids and planets out of orbit) might make normal clocks and calendars go haywire at the last moment.

Bivens' energy was contagious. He always called me and everyone else, "old buddy," as in, "How's it going ol' buddy?" He was a walking fountain of energy and good spirits, cracking jokes, full of life and spontaneous consideration for other people. He could cheer up anyone.

~ ~ ~

There is a sad outcome to the story of Don Bivens, and I am not joking here. I was shaken to hear it announced from the pulpit at Big Sandy one sabbath in 1975 that Donald Bivens, a church member in Ardmore, Oklahoma known to some in Big Sandy, had died tragically in an automobile accident. He was only in his early twenties. Members sorrowed over the news. It hit me hard, because I had spent hours talking with Bivens and liked him (as did everyone). And now he was cut off just like that, lifeless and dead? It just seemed *so wrong*. It was one of those things that stays with you. But this is a digression, and getting ahead of the story.

Jubilee years, or, how to go about setting a date for
the Second Coming: a case history (continued)

Returning to my studies of Jubilee years, there was a problem to someone like me who sought exactness, not approximation, in these important calculations. According to Dr. Hoeh's revised date for the creation of Adam, 4024 BC, the end of the present age, 6000 years after the creation of Adam, should come about in 1977, not 1987. At the time, this was the major problem I saw in the 1987 theory. (The major objection from others was that 1987 was way too far out in the future. Any fool could see that with the critical state of world conditions, it was hardly likely the world would last *that* long.)

I wrote a paper on some of the implications of the Jubilee year chronology that I saw. In my paper I attempted to resolve the troubling discrepancy between 1977 and 1987. That is, I sought to reconcile Dr. Hoeh's date for Adam with a 1987 Jubilee occurring 6000 years later. I did so in a creative way. I argued that the 6000 year period began not with Adam's *creation* in innocence in 4024 BC. Rather, the allotted 6000 years began with the *expulsion* of Adam and Even from the garden of Eden on the occasion of the first sin, the "Fall." I then postulated a ten-year gap between these two events!

How did I get that? Well, Jewish tradition says Adam's creation occurred on a Day of Trumpets (Rosh Hashanah). And the expulsion of Adam and Even from Eden, I argued on independent grounds, occurred on a Day of Atonement (Yom Kippur). There are ten days from Trumpets to Atonement in the Jewish calendar (Tishri 1 to Tishri 10) which, I argued, correspond to ten *years* from the creation of Adam to the unfortunate incident with Eve and the serpent which has caused so much distress in the world ever since.

(The point about the expulsion from Eden happening on a day of Atonement grew out of another paper I wrote entitled "Did the Temptation of Christ Occur on a Day of Atonement" [July 28, 1974]. In that paper I argued that every time Satan appears before God in the Bible these not only have Atonement day themes but, I argued, occurred on days of Atonement.)

I saw a correspondence in the ten-*day* interval between Trumpets and Atonement in the Jewish calendar (Tishri 1 to Tishri 10) and a postulated ten-*year* interval between Adam's creation in 4024 and his expulsion in 4014. And if the expulsion from Eden actually happened in 4014, then 6000 years later would come to 1987. (Remember, I *said* I was creative.)

My proposed date for the expulsion, 4014 BC, ten years after Adam's creation, was also, by a fortuitous coincidence according to Dietz's sabbatical year sequence extended backward, a sabbatical year (4014-4013). I suggested the curse on the ground at the time of Adam's sin (Gen 3:17-19) was related to violation

7000-Year Plan

of the land sabbath at the end of Adam's first complete land-sabbath cycle. Finally, to add even more elegance, I noted that 120 years plus 120 Jubilees equals exactly 6000 years, and that the Bible seemed to demarcate two periods of time in these categories.

I explained these discoveries in a paper dated June 26, 1974, modestly entitled "Jubilees are No Joke! The incredible story of God's hand in history: amazing patterns of Jubilee years." I submitted it to Big Sandy's deputy chancellor Ronald Dart, as well as giving copies to interested faculty and student friends. Probably because it was my original copy, Mr. Dart later had it mailed back to me. Perhaps mercifully, it came back without comment. I revised it and wrote an improved version of the paper dated November 15, 1974. The title of this one was now toned down to simply: "The 1987-1988 Jubilee Year." Following are excerpts.

> Continuing back 80 Jubilees before Christ's appearance brings us to the exact year of the birth of Seth, dated at 3894 BC by Dr. Hoeh. (Seth was born 130 years after Adam was created, Gen 5:3). Commentators recognize that Genesis 4:25 indicates Seth was born at the same time Abel was killed, as a replacement for him. Therefore, when Cain and Abel brought sacrifices before the Lord, and Cain murdered Abel, these events all occurred on the 80th Jubilee before Christ. Cain brought fruit of the ground and was cursed for it (Gen 4:2-5). No crops were to be grown on sabbatical or Jubilee years (Lev 25:3-11). Violation brings a curse on the land (Lev 26:34-35). Cain's punishment was a curse on the land wherever he tilled it (Gen 4:12).
>
> These events happened, as the margin of the King James Version of Genesis 4:3 has it, "at the end of days." A comparison with Leviticus 16 shows remarkable similarities between these events and the Atonement Day ceremony. Cain is a type of Satan and Abel is a type of Christ. Just as the one goat representing Christ was killed on the Day of Atonement, Abel was killed. Just as the other "Azazel" or "Scapegoat" was sent into the wilderness, Cain was sent into the wilderness.
>
> It is therefore likely that the events of Genesis 4 occurred on a Day of Atonement—which began the Jubilee of that year. "At the end of days," then, would refer to it being the end of the years preceding the

beginning of the Jubilee. Other scriptures also indicate these events were a "beginning" (Luke 11:50-51; John 8:44; 1 Jn 3:11-12; Luke 1:70). This Jubilee was the 80th Jubilee before Christ, and the 120th before our time. Dr. Dietz was unaware of this when he submitted his paper, and Dr. Hoeh's date for Adam was arrived at quite independently.

Many commentators think Cain and Abel were twins (since Eve is said to have conceived once, but bore two sons), and that they were born immediately after the expulsion (since there is no indication of time between Gen 3:24 and 4:1). If the expulsion occurred in 4014, then Cain and Abel would each have been 120 years old when they brought their offerings in Genesis 4. 120 years plus 120 Jubilees (5880 years) comes to 6000 years, the exact time allotted before the restoration as it was in the garden of Eden.

Israel wandered 40 years in the wilderness (Num 14:33-34). Will the New Testament church have to wander 40 Jubilees in the world? Isaac was 40 years old when he married Rebekah (Gen 15:20). Will Christ marry the church after 40 Jubilees? Joseph, another type of Christ, was 40 years old when he gave his brethren inheritance in Egypt, in "the best of the land" (Gen 47:11; 41:46-47; 45:6). Will Christ give us, His brethren, our land inheritance (Matt 5:5; Heb 2:8-10; Gal 3:29) on the 40th Jubilee? Christ was tempted of Satan 40 days in the wilderness. Will the body of Christ be tempted 40 Jubilees in the wilderness of this world? Christ was with His disciples after His resurrection for 40 days before *going to* heaven (Acts 1:3). Will Christ be in heaven for 40 Jubilees before *returning* in the same manner that He ascended?

Moses lived 120 years, and his life was divided into three 40s (Acts 7:23, 30), just as seem to be the Jubilees. Moses is a type of Christ (Acts 3:22). At 80 years old Moses met Pharaoh and led the Israelites out of Egypt. After 80 Jubilees Christ appeared, met and defeated Satan, and called spiritual Israel out of sin.

The coming Jubilee will *also* be the 70th Jubilee from the entrance of the Israelites into the Promised Land. Christ was 30 years old when He began preaching (Luke 3:23). David, another type of Christ, began to reign at age 30, reigned 40 years, and died at age 70 (2 Sam 5:4).

The first Englishman to land on the North American continent did so in late summer, 1497 AD (John Cabot). This was the 60th Jubilee from the first Jubilee observed by the Israelites in the Promised Land. Has God allotted a "sabbath" of 10 Jubilees for modern Israel in North America?

7000-Year Plan

> In the prophecy of Daniel 9, the "70 Weeks" was a time period of 490 years or 10 Jubilees. Jubilee time-periods were used to predict Christ's *first* coming. Could they be used likewise with His *second* coming?
>
> Christ promised that He would return within one generation of the Jews' reestablishment in Palestine (Matt 24:32-34). The Jewish nation became reality in May 1948. Many Bible students and scholars feel Christ will return within 40 years of this.
>
> There have been two major dates set for the return of Christ in modern times. The Adventists, the largest sabbath-keeping Protestant body, predicted 1844, and were wrong. Seventy years later the Jehovah's Witnesses predicted 1914 and they were wrong too. In Luke 12:38, Christ seems to refer to a first, second, and *third* watch for his return. Another 70 years later comes to 1984, perhaps the time of advent of the *false* Christ. Was Orwell prophetic? Will something significant happen in 1987-88, the 40th Jubilee from Christ, the 70th from the entrance into Canaan, and the 120th from the birth of Seth? We will not have to wait long to find out.

Pretty creative, eh? In all humility, I thought it was a *very* good case for 1987-88 as the indicated time for the end of this age. At the time, this was intoxicating stuff.

Dr. Hoeh is intrigued and visits Big Sandy

Word of Dietz's research on the dating of the land-sabbath reached Herman Hoeh in Pasadena. One of Ambassador College's original four students in 1947 at Pasadena, Herman Hoeh (1928-2004) (the name is pronounced *"hay"*) was the leading theoretician in the development of church doctrine, beliefs, and interpretations of history, which Herbert Armstrong would adopt for the church as a whole.

Hoeh had completed his two-volume *Compendium of World History* in 1963. He had written it for his Ambassador College doctoral degree in theology. Since Ambassador College was unaccredited, Hoeh was aware that his "Dr." title was questionable as a legitimate academic credential, and at various times Hoeh attempted to have people switch over from calling him "Dr." to "Mr." Hoeh. But it was hopeless; everyone, including I, could not think of him as other than Dr. Hoeh, and that is how he remains forever known.

Dr. Hoeh retreated on some of his positions a few years after the in-house publication of *The Compendium*. He said it had mistakes (without ever really specifying what they were) and he restricted the volumes' distribution. He never at any time allowed them to be available to the public, and after the late 1960s even regular church members were not supposed to obtain personal copies. But it was still used in classes at Ambassador College. (I had church members in Akron, Ohio, paying me to buy bootleg copies of the *Compendium* on their behalf from juniors and seniors at Big Sandy who no longer needed theirs for a class. There was a thriving black market in the church in copies of the hard-to-get *Compendium*.)

Ironically, by this time, 1974, although Dr. Hoeh was still on the payroll at Pasadena, he had no discernible job, nor, as I discovered when I later visited him in Pasadena, did he have an office. Yet he was still widely respected in the church and participated in various headquarters doctrinal investigations.

Mr. Dart may have found Dietz's paper unconvincing and of only "C" value (and perhaps hoped it would go away). Dr. Hoeh, on the other hand, reacted to Dietz's paper much more favorably. In fact, Dietz's dating argument was so convincing to Dr. Hoeh that he embraced it enthusiastically. Formerly Dr. Hoeh had held to the count in which Jubilees were 50 years apart. After reading Dietz's paper Hoeh now realized that wasn't right. A multi-paged handwritten letter arrived back to Big Sandy from Dr. Hoeh, written by Hoeh at home one Sabbath. Hoeh's letter worked Dietz's new, corrected dates for the sabbatical years into his own dates. I saw this letter; it included long handwritten lists of corrected dates.

Not only that, but Dr. Hoeh was so intrigued by what was going on at Big Sandy in this area that he made a trip to Big Sandy near the end of the summer of 1974 to check out these developments in person (in addition to visiting his old friend Kenneth Herrmann).

7000-Year Plan

Here is where this story intersects with me in a personal way. For one of the developments at Big Sandy of interest to Hoeh was my paper on the Jubilee years, which developed from Dietz's paper. As you can see from the excerpts above, I had argued that the Jubilee datings, if extended backward in time, corresponded in startling ways with key dates in Dr. Hoeh's chronology. I was, in a sense, independently "proving" Dr. Hoeh's dates. I had not sent my paper to Dr. Hoeh, and did not know it had gotten to him. But it had.

And so it was that I was surprised one day in August 1974 to hear that Dr. Hoeh was on campus and wanted to see me. For a student who had almost idolized the legendary Hoeh and his wide-ranging researches in ancient history, this was heady.

I was directed into a conference room. Dr. Hoeh and several other faculty members were seated there. There was a copy of my Jubilees paper spread out on the table in front of Hoeh. Dr. Hoeh courteously expressed interest in my research and asked me to explain my case to him in a nutshell, which I did. Hoeh listened intently and did not interrupt. When I was finished, Hoeh responded. He explained that formerly he had believed the Jubilee year cycle occurred in fifty-year cycles (i.e. the Jubilee year interrupts the sabbatical year sequence). But Dietz's research had now persuaded him, he said, that the forty-nine year cycle was indeed correct—but only for the time *after* the return from the Babylonian captivity in the fifth century BC. Before then (the way it had begun originally from the time of Moses and Joshua), Dr. Hoeh now believed, the Jubilees should still be numbered in fifty-year cycles. (Though I did not argue the point with Dr. Hoeh, this theory of a switch from a fifty-year to a forty-nine year cycle hardly seemed logical to me for a consistent God to approve. But it was not a theory invented by Dr. Hoeh. That is a standard Jewish rabbinical explanation, which Hoeh was now adopting.)

In other words, Dr. Hoeh accepted as legitimate the historical evidences after the fifth century BC of an unbroken sabbatical year cycle (the 49-year Jubilee cycle) to which Dietz had called attention. But Hoeh disagreed with sabbatical/Jubilee datings on the 49-year basis *prior* to the exile, which would negate my own attempted confirmations of some of Dr. Hoeh's own earlier chronology. (Dr. Hoeh sure was impressed with my attempt though.) This was the beginning of several occasions over the following year, in Big Sandy and Pasadena, during which I was able to spend time with Dr. Hoeh. He always treated me kindly and I felt a respect and liking for him as a person.

Redating Ezra and Nehemiah and the incredible Russell Gmirkin

It is not often that one discovers the date of the end of the age. But I thought I had. Always I said it was "not certain" (and in fact did simultaneously consider another competing system which could end in 1977; more on that later). But inside, I thought it looked pretty good, too good *not* to be indicating *something big* was up for 1987-88.

There was one troubling remaining key chronological indicator which did not quite mesh with 1987-88, however. This was the seven "times of the Gentiles," or period of 2520 years. If these 2520 years began at the fall of Babylon in 539 BC (as the church taught), this would end in 1982, five years short of 1987-88. But even this troubling discrepancy found an independent, synchronously arrived at solution.

A Pasadena student who was to become one of my best friends, Russell Gmirkin, independently and without knowledge of these sabbatical/Jubilee discoveries going on at Big Sandy, had written a freshman treatise as a class paper toward the end of his freshman school year in Pasadena in the spring of 1973. In his paper, Russ redated the rebuilding of the temple at Jerusalem from 515 BC, the conventional date, to 534 BC. This was shocking enough, but the intrepid freshman did not stop there. While he was at it, he also moved the biblical figures of Ezra and Nehemiah over a hundred years earlier to be contemporary with this temple rebuilding in 534 BC. (Historians have Ezra and Nehemiah in the 400s BC.) Russ's paper did not deal with the

7000-Year Plan

"times of the Gentiles" prophetic time period. But when I learned of Russ's redating I wondered if the "times of the Gentiles" ought to be considered as beginning from 534. That was when Judea was restored as a sovereign province according to Russ's reconstruction. Russ said this was the true end of Jeremiah's prophecy of Judah's seventy-year subjection to the king of Babylon (604-534 BC), rather than five years earlier in 539 (Jer 25:11). The addition of 2520 years forward from 534 BC came to ... AD 1987!—*precisely* coinciding with the fortieth Jubilee year from Jesus, to the very year!

~ ~ ~

Russ Gmirkin was probably one of the brightest and most unusual students ever to attend Ambassador College in terms of sheer genius and range of intellectual inquiry. Unfortunately, poor Russ had a problem dealing with classes he found boring. He simply ceased to attend them and show up for exams, without regard for such unimportant details as effect on final grades. This caused an unheeding bureaucracy at Pasadena to do the indignity of rudely flunking him out of school midway through his sophomore year. Shaken at this unseemly turn of events, he applied for readmission. In a classic example of administrative failure to comprehend the real problem, Russ was told he should go to Big Sandy and successfully pass a few even more elementary summer courses in order to "prove he was college material."

Well, Russ did so, and this is how I met him in the summer of 1974. From new interpretations of scripture and theology to insightful theories of psychology, to breakthroughs in mathematics and gravity theory—Russ explained to me a fascinating non-Einsteinian mechanism he had worked out for why and how gravitational attraction exists (as distinguished from the simple assertion that it does exist according to formula) [it was a version of Le Sage gravity theory, I later realized]—Russ's analytical mind saw everything, it seemed, in new and fresh ways. We hit if off, and talked for countless hours on my night switchboard job, iron sharpening iron as we compared our respective researches and analyzed the scriptures, discerning and working out the overarching subtleties of God's plan for the universe.

Russ's freshman treatise at Pasadena on redating the Ezra-Nehemiah period was originally written for a class in Ancient History. As I review the notes I took on Russ's description of his case, I am struck even today by the originality and range of his *tour de force*, even if it *was* wrong. (I can say this, having some personal knowledge of amazing *tour de force*s which later turn out to be wrong.)

At first, Russ's paper looked to some observers like it could be the most promising breakthrough in ancient history since Herbert Armstrong surmised that Job built the Great Pyramid. One headquarters researcher told Russ, "If this is right, then the entire history of that period will have to be rewritten." Russ's history instructor had nothing but high praise for the paper and recommended Russ submit it to Dr. Hoeh. Russ did so. Alas—or rather, fortunately—Dr. Hoeh's experienced eyes saw through the errors that the innocent freshman had made and saved the day, before things got completely out of control, such as maybe ending up in one of the church booklets with millions of readers or something.

At the next Friday night church Bible study, Russ and his paper became the featured topic when Dr. Hoeh made disparaging remarks about freshman students exceeding the range of what they were capable of studying. Referring to Russ's paper as an example of misdirected energies, Hoeh said it contained conclusions which "could easily be shown wrong by anyone knowledgeable in history." Needless to say, the reputation of Russ's paper took a precipitous nosedive after Dr. Hoeh got through with it. That was the end of Russ's short-lived attempt at rewriting conventional history books as an Ambassador College freshman—though paradoxically (the way these things often work), Russ's reputation and notoriety among his fellow students were significantly enhanced by the events of that evening. Here is what happened in Russ's own words:

7000-Year Plan

Being curious about Ezra-Nehemiah, this being an area of biblical history about which I was ignorant, I made this the subject of the required assignment for Ancient World History under Mr. Schultz. When he read my paper he was extremely impressed, said that he couldn't come up with something like this in ten years' time, and said I should bring it to the attention of Dr. Hoeh. So I accosted Dr. Hoeh on the sidewalk, and told him Mr. Schultz had asked me to give this to him. He was in a hurry so he took it and rushed off with no further conversation. I was really interested in the feedback I might receive.

That night I got my feedback, which was an entire Bible Study blasting the author of a paper that had just been given to Dr. Hoeh. In the midst of this scathing attack on the lack of intellectual humility of *freshmen*, he gave the author of the paper some pointed advice. Rather than continue research in this subject, as the author of the paper indicated he was going to do, Dr. Hoeh recommended the author put the paper aside, forget about it, and after six months bring it to someone educated in ancient history who could easily explain the obvious errors in the paper. This was fairly intimidating, but not very informative. (I didn't realize at the time that that was the whole point.)

So, following the inspired advice from the pulpit to the letter, and with a humble and sincere attitude, I dutifully put the paper aside for six months, at the end of which I called Dr. Hoeh and asked whether he could explain for me the historical problems with my paper. He said that would be fine, and to come to his office at such-and-such a time, and he would do exactly that.

When I arrived at his office, excited at the prospect of finally finding out where my paper went wrong, Dr. Hoeh told me in a sentence or two to go have a talk with the Dean and *then* he would explain where my paper was wrong.

So I went down to the first floor, and dutifully had a chat with Dean of Students Mr. Dickerson. I told him Dr. Hoeh told me to talk to him. Mr. Dickerson was friendly enough, as always. He said fine, what about? I said I didn't know—I thought he knew. Mr. Dickerson said he didn't know anything about it. So we both said it was nice talking with each other, shook hands, and I left.

Somewhat mystified, I proceeded back up to Dr. Hoeh's office where his secretary let me in a second time. Finally, I would get an explanation! I told Dr. Hoeh that I had gone down to talk to the Dean, and I was back now, so I was ready to hear what was wrong with my paper.

Remarkably, the explanation for which I had patiently waited six months took only two sentences. He explained to me that I had a bad attitude, and that the conversation was at an end.[25]

Unfortunately Russ loaned out the original of his paper, without making a copy, to a Pasadena friend. Sadly, this friend mistook Russ's treatise for trash paper and irresponsibly destroyed it. So there are probably no copies of Russ's notorious Ezra-Nehemiah paper in existence (unless the one turned in to Hoeh survives).

I mention this background of Russ's paper not simply for anecdotal interest but also to try to convey the excitement I felt at the time. The last missing link to the 1987 Jubilee theory for Christ's return seemed to become independently resolved by Russ's earlier research. (That is, the 2520 years "times of the Gentiles," thought to end in 1982, would be rescheduled for 1987.) I had no idea whether Russ's revisionism was actually true or not. But since it coincidentally provided the last missing link I needed, I decided it *must* be true. The prophetic time period could end in 1987 after all! My heart leaped. *Everything* was synchronizing and falling into place.

An excursus on Gmirkin's argument

I noted above that no copies are known to survive of Russ's paper on redating Ezra and Nehemiah. I did, however, preserve detailed notes of Russ's argument in that paper, and those notes survive. For purposes of historical interest I give below Gmirkin's argument, reconstructed as accurately as I can from these notes. It is important to note that both Gmirkin and I today are in agreement that the argument of Gmirkin then was incorrect. But just for fun I am going to pull a Dr. Hoeh and also *not say why*. If you have an interest in this sort of thing, see if *you* can figure out where Gmirkin's argument was mistaken.

---

[25] Letter, Russ Gmirkin to Greg Doudna, June 26, 1988.

7000-Year Plan

On the other hand, if this is too technical for your taste, no harm done, just skip over it. (You won't miss out on any of the story, I promise.) But if you *are* interested in what no one on the Ambassador College faculty at Pasadena in 1973 appeared capable of answering, here it is:

Russ Gmirkin's original Ezra-Nehemiah redating argument as an Ambassador College Pasadena freshman in 1973, blasted by Dr. Hoeh publicly as "easily shown wrong" (without saying why)

Gmirkin's argument. A comparison of names in Neh 10:1-9 and Neh 12:1-8 shows that Ezra and Nehemiah (supposedly active in 457 and 454 BC) were contemporary with Zerubbabel (conventionally dated to 521 BC). Other references also seem to confirm Ezra and Nehemiah were active in the time of Zerubbabel and Joshua (Ezra 2:2; Neh 7:7; 12:1). Ezra himself is said to be son of the high priest Seraiah who was executed by Nebuchadnezzar in 587 BC (Neh 11:11; 1 Chron 9:11; Ezra 7:1-5; 2 Kgs 25:18-21). This is inconsistent with the conventional dating of Ezra, and argues for the proposed earlier dating.

Joshua the high priest is said to have dedicated the altar in "the seventh month" (Ezra 3:1-2). Neh 7:73-8:9 refer to Ezra and Nehemiah leading a dedication in "the seventh month." Since the two accounts each follow identical preceding narrative, Russ proposed this was the same dedication.

Artaxerxes who made the decree permitting a Jewish return from Babylon under Ezra and Nehemiah to rebuild the temple (Ezra 7:11-26) becomes not Artaxerxes I Longimanus (464-424 BC) as conventionally thought, but rather one of the three presidents said to have ruled areas of the Persian empire under Cyrus the Great (Dan 6:2). These three subordinates under Cyrus were the biblical Artaxerxes (otherwise unknown to history), Daniel himself, and a Darius the Persian (different from the later Persian ruler Darius Hystaspes who ruled 522-486). The first year of Cyrus (Ezra 1:1), 539 BC, was therefore also the first year of Darius, the first year of Daniel, and the first year of Artaxerxes, all beginning with Cyrus's new administration. In support of this, note that a "Mithredath the treasurer" under Cyrus (Ezra 1:8) is also found under Artaxerxes (Ezra 4:7).

Other references seem to speak of the various returns of the Jews in Ezra and Nehemiah as contemporary with Cyrus (Ezra 1:1-2:2;

4:3-5; 6:14). The temple was begun in the second year of the Jews' return to Judea (Ezra 3:8; 1 Esdras 5:56-57), which was known as the second year of Darius (Ezra 4:24; Haggai 1:1)—which would be 538 BC. The building of the temple finished in the sixth year of Darius (Ezra 6:15) would then be 534 BC.

All of these figures—Ezra, Nehemiah, Haggai, Zechariah, Zerubbabel, the high priest Joshua—are therefore to be dated at this same time. The progressively increasing numerical sequence in datings in the book of Ezra tells one narrative story over a single seven-year period, i.e. "the first year of Cyrus" (1:1), "the second year" of the Jews' return (3:8), "the sixth year of the reign of Darius" (6:15), "the seventh year of Artaxerxes" (7:7).

It may be proposed that the biblical Darius took over direct rule for Cyrus in the area including Palestine when Cyrus went off to war, and that the biblical Artaxerxes, already ruling another territory, succeeded Darius in ruling the Jews' territory in his and Darius's sixth year. When Neh 2:1 refers to Nehemiah in "the twentieth year of King Artaxerxes" whereas Ezra is dated in the "seventh year of Artaxerxes" (Ezra 7:7), this may be explained as Nehemiah counting Artaxerxes' total reign including in his own land (Artaxerxes possibly was Assyrian, based on Ezra 4:15 and 6:22), before Cyrus took over and Artaxerxes became one of Cyrus's presidents. But Ezra (by this proposal) reckons Artaxerxes' reign only from how long he has been king since Cyrus's takeover, just as this is the way Ezra counts Cyrus's own reign (Ezra 1:1; 4:7; 7:1). In this way Ezra and Nehemiah are simultaneous, not thirteen years apart. *End of Gmirkin's argument.*

My own comment, looking at it from this distance, is that this was pretty darn good for an Ambassador College freshman (even if the argument *was* incorrect). Too bad no one on the Ambassador College faculty was capable of answering the freshman with a response addressing the substance of the argument, instead of the public excoriation and condemnation he was given for having committed the crime of original thinking.[26]

---

[26] Still stumped? See Diana Edelman, "Redating the Building of the 'Second' Temple," on the *Bible and Interpretation* website (http://www.bibleinterp.com/articles/Edelman_Redating_Second_Temple.htm) and A.L.A. Hogeterp, review of D. Edelman, *The Origins of the 'Second' Temple:*

7000-Year Plan

Return to the story at Big Sandy

The theory of the 6000 years and when they ended that I had worked out at Big Sandy seemed far too logical to be coincidental. It all seemed so persuasive at the time. It was the feeling of seeing Design and Plan where the world saw only chance and accident. It was the adrenalin rush of seeing the appointed time approach for the ending of an age, with the dawn of a shining new world sure to follow. This fortieth Jubilee just a few years away and its relationships with history and numbers seemed *far* superior to the church's earlier 1972 theory. (Or 1914 or 1844 before that.) If you ignore the trifling fact that the right year has now passed, it was a *beautiful* theory.

But if you appreciate correlations and interweaving of numbers, you haven't seen anything yet. No words I can use can do justice to one of my most beloved memories of all from my Big Sandy years: the incomparable Mr. Ken Herrmann (1924-2006).

Mayan calendar eclipse cycles and the amazing Mr. Herrmann

As you can tell by now, my analyses focused much attention on Dr. Hoeh's date of 4024 BC for the creation of Adam. This date of Dr. Hoeh was based on chronological numbers in the Jewish Masoretic text used by all English translations of the Bible. (The numbers differ in the Greek Septuagint version and in the Samaritan Pentateuch.)

Of course there are a number of points at which chronologies based on the Masoretic text can be questioned. Are the numbers precisely accurate? Are some of the numbers round figures? There are difficulties. For example, Terah fathers Abraham at 130 years of age (Gen 11:32; 12:4; Acts 7:4), whereas his son

---

Persian Imperial Policy and the Rebuilding of Jerusalem, Review of Biblical Literature 07/2006 (http://www.bookreviews.org).

Abraham wonders at the impossibility of having a son when he is only 99 (Gen 17:17, 24). But conundrums such as this are beyond the scope of analysis here. If the biblical numbers of the Masoretic text are taken as correct and without omissions (if one accepts that), a chronological line indeed can be traced back to Adam. Here is how Dr. Hoeh arrived at 4024 BC.[27]

4024 BC Creation of Adam

1656	Adam to the Flood
451	Flood to Abraham's 99th year
430	Abraham's 99th year to Exodus (Ex 12:40-41; Gen 17:1-13; Gal 3:15-17)
479	Exodus to 4th year of Solomon (1 Kgs 6:1)
36	4th year of Solomon to Jeroboam's start (1 Kgs 1:42-43)
387	Start of Jeroboam to fall of Jerusalem (adding dates of Judah's kings' reigns in Kings and Chronicles). Jerusalem's fall dated 585 BC.

But had Dr. Hoeh got it right? Was the 4024 date for Adam's creation correct?

Fortunately, there was an independent confirmation at Big Sandy, or so it seemed, of Hoeh's 4024 Adam-creation date. This came from work in eclipse cycles, astronomy, and calendar numbers by Ken Herrmann.

Like Dr. Hoeh, Herrmann had also been one of the earliest students at Ambassador College in Pasadena. He had arrived as a freshman in Ambassador College's second year in 1949. He had

---

[27] From a classroom handout used in an early 1970s Ancient World History class at Ambassador College, Big Sandy, summarizing from Herman L. Hoeh's *Compendium of World History*, 2 vols. rev. ed. (Pasadena: Ambassador College, 1967).

gone on to become the college registrar at Pasadena. He was a long-time friend of Dr. Hoeh's, and had recently retired with his family to live near the Big Sandy campus. Though not formally on the faculty at Big Sandy, Mr. Herrmann occasionally would be a guest instructor in various classes, presenting information in his areas of interest. I would often see him and talk with him in the library.

I liked Mr. Herrmann. He always conveyed a quiet humility and humor, always seemed to have a twinkle in his eye. I loved hearing what he was working on. During this time at Big Sandy he devoted much study to the Mayan calendar, as well as ancient weights and measures, developing further on work he had done in a 1967 thesis entitled "Calendar and Eclipse Interrelationships." Mr. Herrmann believed he had found evidence that the Mayan calendar originated in a widespread ancient apostasy from the original, divinely revealed Hebrew calendar. He saw a reference to this apostasy in Genesis 4:26. According to an interpretation of this verse going back to the medieval Jewish historian Maimonides, men called not *on* the name of the Lord, but called *themselves* by the name of God. (And in Dr. Hoeh's reconstruction of history, the figures in the early chapters of Genesis came to be revered as the gods of pagan mythology.) Mr. Herrmann devoted much research to reconstructing how ancient calendars, with particular focus on the Mayan calendar, could have derived from observation and worship of planetary bodies in the heavens, which these rebellious peoples substituted for the sacred, original calendar of God (the Jewish calendar).

These calendar and eclipse cycle calculations could not exactly be considered church teaching, i.e. Mr. Herrmann was freelancing these on his own, but they were interesting.

Mr. Herrmann did not confine himself to eclipse cycles and numerical coincidences. His quiet, iconoclastic asides in his guest lectures ranged from comment on the Worldwide Church of God insistence that ministers always be addressed as "Mister" ("Did Peter's letters go by the name, 'First Epistle of Mister Simon Johnson'?"), to a questioning of the origins of competitive athletics as a pagan and ungodly glorification of muscle, might, and war, and so on.

The Mayan calendar system, Herrmann pointed out in his lectures, destroys the sabbath, holy days, Jubilee and land sabbath cycles of the Hebrew calendar. There is no lunar month or seven-day week in the Mayan calendar. This calendar, Herrmann explained, started when men began worshipping planetary bodies instead of the Creator.

Mr. Herrmann found it significant that the beginning of the Mayan calendar, which is dated at 3113 BC, was 912 years after the date of Adam's creation fixed by Dr. Hoeh at 4025-24. The significance of this is that 912 is 48 x 19. (Nineteen-year cycles, remember, are the basis for the Hebrew calendar.) Furthermore, 912 years is also the lifespan of Seth, the son of Adam and Eve given to replace their murdered son Abel (Gen 5:8). And, 912 is (60 x 60)/4 years plus (60 x 60) days plus a year at each end. Finally, 912 is 12 x 76.

"So what?" you ask? Well, 76 years is an important eclipse cycle with a whole number of days. (To avoid making the subject more complex, I am rounding all numbers to the nearest whole figure. In his lectures Mr. Herrmann would cite both the exact decimal fraction and nearest whole number.) Mr. Herrmann suggested this 76-year eclipse cycle may have been the basis for the Hebrew calendar's division of each hour into 1080 "parts" and each part into 76 "moments."

~ ~ ~

The 912-year cycle is both a calendar cycle and a highly unusual eclipse cycle, Mr. Herrmann went on, with "a full number of anomalistic months and a whole number of tropical years." In other words, he said, 912 years later at the same location and on the same day, you will see the same eclipse. The period of 912 years prior to the beginning of the Mayan calendar in 3113 was, Mr. Herrmann believed, an independent, coincidental confirmation of Dr. Hoeh's date for Adam's creation in 4024. Mr.

7000-Year Plan

Herrmann pointed out that Dr. Hoeh's dates were set with no knowledge of these coincidences.

Care for more? The Mayan calendar goes back by 52s to 3113 BC. The Chinese calendar goes back by 60s to 2697 BC. The Hebrew calendar goes back by 19s to 3761 BC. From the Mayan start at 3113 to the Chinese start at 2697 is 8 x 52. From the Mayan start at 3113 to the beginning of Noah's warning of the Flood is 12 x 52.

Jupiter orbits the sun every 12 years. The pattern of Jupiter in the sky from earth's point of view is 1/12 of a loop in the sky per year, meaning Jupiter moves over one sign of the zodiac each year. Saturn orbits the sun every 30 years. This means Jupiter overtakes Saturn every 20 years. In three such overtakes Jupiter and Saturn are back to their original positions. Jupiter and Saturn therefore come together in the same place every 60 years. Herrmann suggested this might have been the basis for the 60-year count in the Chinese calendar.

Mr. Herrmann further explained that the perihelion of earth's orbit and the autumn equinox, as extended outward upon a map of the night sky, are currently 100 degrees apart. The two are moving away from each other at the rate of one degree every 60 years. This means 6000 years ago they were together at the time of Adam's creation. Also, the Milky Way crosses at this point. This seemed to be, said Mr. Herrmann, another supporting indication that we were near the end of 6000 allotted years. He also suggested that earth may be the only place in the universe where the moon is the same apparent size as the sun in the sky.

Mr. Herrmann also pointed out interesting numerical properties of the number 365, the number of days in a year: $10^2 + 11^2 + 12^2 = 365$. And, $13^2 + 14^2 = 365$. Or how about this on the 2300 days of Daniel 8:14? $2300 = 1260 + 1040$. Then, $1260 = 3\text{-}1/2 \times 360$. And, $1040 = 52 \times 20$. There are 52 years in a Mayan "Great Year." The Mayan year had 260 days. Consider that $260/365 = 52/73 = 1040/1460$. There were 1460 years in the famous Sirius-based Sothic cycle, the basis for the ancient Egyptian calendar. Consider that $1460/1461 = 365/365\text{-}1/4$. And,

360/365 = 72/73. Now will anyone claim all these are *coincidence*??

The Hebrew calendar begins in 3761 BC, which was exactly one-fourth of the way (264 years, or 12 x 22) from the year of Adam's creation to the birth of Noah. Then, from Noah's birth there were 600 (10 x 60) years to the Flood (Gen 7:6), and 120 (2 x 60) years of warning (Gen 6:3). Now, 60 x 60 = 10 x 360 = 16 x 225, and 225 days is the sidereal period of Venus. Mr. Herrmann observed the chance of all this happening by accident was probably one in several billion. It certainly seemed that way to me. I took detailed notes on these things at the time, thinking this must surely be the only place on earth where this information was being discovered.

Bolstered with what seemed to be all these supporting confirmations for a 4024 date for the creation of Adam, the evidence appeared all the stronger that the end of 6000 years would be scheduled for 1977 or 1987. If you were living in 1974, 3-1/2 years earlier, and believed the end of the world as we know it would be preceded by 3-1/2 year time periods described in Revelation, you might have found these numbers of interest too.

What happened?

But with all of this seeming evidence, what happened?

The additional fact—the slight detail—that stands out most is that both 1977 and 1987 came and went without a noticeable transformation to millennial paradise. Logically, this falsifies either that the end of 6000 years are *significant*, or that 6000 years ended in *1977* or *1987*.

This is ruling out an Adventist style solution, immortalized when a predicted date of 1844 came and went without the return of Christ. The numbers were believed to have been just too accurate to have been wrong. Therefore, reality was reinterpreted. The appointed date in 1844 was redefined, after the fact, as the occasion of "the cleansing of the heavenly sanctuary." (To this, one faculty member at Big Sandy remarked: "But what I want to know is—how did heaven become polluted?")

The Jehovah's Witnesses reinterpreted reality in a similar manner after a predicted date of 1914 came and went without—so far as anyone could see—the return of Christ. Again, the numbers were believed to have been just too accurate to have been wrong. This date was defined retroactively as when Christ *did* in fact return—invisibly, that is.

What is to be made of Mr. Herrmann's astronomical coincidences? Of course there are certain minor discrepancies that, in the excitement of the times, tend to be overlooked. Small perturbations in the orbits of all heavenly bodies tend to pull alignments out of phase. These accumulate over time and work to destroy eclipse phases and other cyclic phenomena, while other new cyclic phenomena, of course, will come into being. (The universe is not a "perfect clock.") Yet even so, what Mr. Herrmann put together *is* interesting—if for no other reason than as an illustration of the extent to which design and coincidence can be discovered with sufficient creativity.

Years later, seeking a second opinion, I showed Mr. Herrmann's thesis ("Calendar and Eclipse Interrelationships") to a friend of mine who writes astronomy articles for publication. While my astronomer friend didn't buy the thesis's remarkable conclusions, he conceded it was "the most amazing, in-depth treatment of eclipses" he'd ever seen. He added with a touch of awe, "And that's an understatement—this thesis contains information which you will not find in any university or library in the world." It was irreplaceable gems like Mr. Herrmann who are among my fondest memories of my Big Sandy years.

And somehow, if I had not thought that we were at about the end of 6000 years from the time Adam was created according to biblical chronology, I think I would not have been half as creative. Living on the threshold of history about to transform into eternity does wonders in concentrating the spirit and heightening the drama and romance of life.

Dr. Hoeh recalculates the end

Here is how Dr. Hoeh dealt with time moving past 1977 without Christ's return. In a sermon at Pasadena during the Feast of Tabernacles in 1977 Dr. Hoeh announced a recalculation of his dates. In this sermon Dr. Hoeh cited the work of Edwin Thiele on the chronology of the kings of Israel and Judah, added a couple of minor modifications of his own, and informed church members that this lowered his, Dr. Hoeh's, date for the creation of Adam by "about 41 years." That is, instead of Adam being created in 4024 BC, Dr. Hoeh now changed his date for Adam's creation to 3983 BC. The end of 6000 years no longer was 1977, but now—after recalculation—would be about 2018 AD. According to the sermon notes, Hoeh said, "we are not at the very end of 6000 years of history [but] this does not mean that Jesus must wait till the time is up till He returns."[28]

And then, according to these notes, Dr. Hoeh added this: "If we had thought that the end would not come till 2020 during these past two decades, it would have greatly changed the nature of this Work."

He sure got that right.

In retrospect

Today, I regard these Big Sandy chronological speculations as hallucinatory. I have converted, in the years since, to prevailing methods used in the sciences in establishing what is true. Such an orientation finds little place for numerical predictions or oracles influencing future physical reality apart from the meanings we invest in them.

---

[28] "Notes of Dr. Hoeh Sermon at Feast in Pasadena, 1977." According to the notetaker, Craig White, Dr. Hoeh later updated his redating from a lowering of the date for Adam by "about 41 years" to a "firmly fixed" 44 years (http://www.friendsofsabbath.org/~surfer/HL%20Hoeh/Hoeh_changes.pdf).

7000-Year Plan

When one is *within* a hallucinatory system, outside reality becomes interpreted and filtered. Coincidences are seen everywhere which seem to prove the validity of the model beyond doubt. What is overlooked is that a hundred other models and hallucinatory systems furnish ground equally fertile for believers finding meaning and multiplying points of coincidental contact within *them*. Looked at from the outside, these systems look like someone else's hallucination. But when one is inside or *within* such a system of belief, it seems so convincing, so *real*.

But it is also true that we all, even the irreligious, live by myth and metaphor. And so ancient prophecies may powerfully influence how we think, what we believe, and what we expect. In some cases ancient prophecies may even come to be their own agency in bringing about their own fulfillment. Such is the power of the words we speak into the world. Examples of this are all around us.

A different way of reading: a Jewish point of view

There are other ways to read the Bible. I close this chapter with a formative event for me when I was at Big Sandy which seems the right note upon which to end this discussion of the end of the age. It was a talk entitled "The Future of Mankind." This was not sponsored by Ambassador College. Rather, it was an address given by a James Allen Wharton, Professor of Old Testament at Austin Theological Seminary, to a Jewish audience at a synagogue in Tyler on January 20, 1975. I was invited by Mark Kaplan, Ambassador College's instructor in Hebrew, to accompany him on this occasion, a kindness for which I will always be grateful. I look back on Wharton's simple, direct message, and the way I have remembered these poignant words ever since, as one of the highlights of my Big Sandy years. The following is verbatim from my notes of Dr. Wharton's address, written on my program brochure as he was speaking that evening.

7000-Year Plan

Abraham Joshua Heschel said, "Guilt is never a proper motive for doing anything." The measure of our humanity is the grandeur and realism of our hope.

The Bible shows this life must be taken seriously. The God of the Bible cares about human life on earth. The Bible is about "living in the future in the present tense."

Notice the peculiarity of the Bible's way of talking about God. It does so by telling a very real human story, one year to the next, a narrative. This is the most profound way of telling a point, the most human: the story. We need to understand the biblical story of real people with a lot more depth. There is no way to reduce it to a system of structured ideas.

What do we learn? We learn that people matter to God, daily actions matter, that all people matter, ordinary people. There is candor—where is the saint found in the Bible? Who is 100% holy and spotless? The figures in the Bible are never wholly positive or wholly evil. They are shepherds, not gurus, practical, not idealistic. Yet it is not a cynical candor. The stories show concrete issues in human life, and give God's viewpoint. The Bible shows not only that human beings are accountable to God—we know that—but also that God is accountable to man. This is seen in Moses's prayer, when he argued with God on Israel's behalf.

The story of the Bible is *not yet over*. Heschel spoke of promise, vision, and anticipation—of the universal order of peace under law. Heschel said, "I just hope the young people haven't given up on the world before the Lord has." Our actions now are important. Live God's plan in *your* life. Christians are great on theology but Judaism is something you do, you live.

No human life is so insignificant that it is not important to God. Those of us who have the hope of God are very important to the world. The greatest moral barometer is the ability to be outraged. Jewish humor is based on human realism. The Hebrew prophets were morally maladjusted. They couldn't adapt to the way society was.

Don't quite settle for the present.

CHAPTER 4

THE DOCTRINE AGAINST INTERRACIAL MARRIAGE

Ambassador College was begun by founder Herbert Armstrong in 1947 for white Israelites only. He spelled this out in his original California articles of incorporation for Ambassador College. By "Israelites," Armstrong explained, he meant white Anglo-Saxons.

The Worldwide Church of God has not had a history of anti-Semitism (speaking institutionally and of the leadership). Prevailing sentiments have been favorable toward Jews. But the story of attitudes toward African-Americans in the Worldwide Church of God ("Radio Church of God") is an ignoble and shameful one. Attitudes towards African-Americans in God's True Church in the 1950s and 1960s sometimes were explained as reflecting white, conservative, anti-civil rights thinking of the larger society. But it went far beyond that. Herbert Armstrong and many of the top ministers held to a white southern ideology of segregation of the races. (In the southern states up to the 1960s, segregation was the law, "separate but equal." Whites in the front of the bus, blacks in the back—separate but equal.)

Herbert Armstrong wrote lead articles in the *Plain Truth* in the early 1960s condemning the attempts in America to end racial segregation. He made clear that God's divine will of segregation had nothing to do with *superiority* of one race over another. Rather, it was that God made the races *different* from each other, each with specialized talents, to the glory of God. The God-ordained way was "separate but equal."

For some strange reason, however, Herbert Armstrong's emphasis seemed a lot more on the "separate" than the "equal" part of the aphorism. African-Americans were strictly separated out of Ambassador College because of their skin color. But Herbert Armstrong and his headquarters support team oddly never got around to any serious consideration of the logical corollary of the perceived mandate for racial separation in God's True Church: providing an "equal" college for black church members' kids. Blacks were just left out in the cold on this one. The tithe rates of black members were not even proportionately discounted to reflect this inequity. Any budding complaint from the occasional black church member who objected to being expected to subsidize white kids' educations when his own kids were prohibited was dealt with by a very simple argument: "Look how much worse off blacks in Africa are right now."

But God's Church could not uphold the inspired no-blacks rule forever against social pressures from a secular society. As the Ambassador College whites-only admissions policy became increasingly untenable in light of changing attitudes in America, blacks were reluctantly admitted to Ambassador ... *but only if they were married*. The reasoning for this was very logical. Single students date. If black single students were allowed to mix with white students on campus, that carried the horrifying risk of *interracial dating and marriage*. Therefore the solution was completely logical: just prohibit single African-Americans from Ambassador College. That would prevent such a dreadful spectre from becoming reality. Thus for years faithful, loyal, tithe-paying single young African-American men and women church members continued to be denied admission to the college because of their race.

Finally in 1971, just one year before I arrived at Big Sandy, policy was changed to at last admit *single* black students to God's Colleges at Pasadena and Big Sandy for the first time (at Bricket Wood single blacks never were admitted) ... but with

Interracial Marriage

careful attention that equal numbers of single black men and women were admitted, and a strict rule that there was to be no interracial dating.

At Ambassador College, "dating" in which young men accompanied young women to things like Friday night Bible studies and Sabbath brunch, as well as Ambassador Club "Ladies' Nights" and dances, was encouraged and part of the way in which students came to know each other. No one tried to segregate other hyphenated American ethnic types from going to Sabbath brunches, etc. with their fellow students of the opposite sex. But African-Americans were supposed to "date" only from among the few other African-Americans of the opposite gender—from week one upon arrival for the next four years until graduation.

Curiously, I do not recall a single sermon or student forum at Big Sandy directly explaining the campus policy on race and dating. It was enforced by college officials in private conferences but, to my memory, never explained publicly in any official college venue. Nor was the policy explained to students in anything written issued by the college.

(I suspect certain intelligent administrators perceived it was best not to have their fingerprints on this if possible. Dean of Students Ronald Kelly and Director of Admissions Lynn Torrance were the major operational enforcement, but at least at Torrance's end there was care to not admit in writing the race-based reasons involved in admissions exclusions. Sometimes it seemed young Dean Kelly was tasked to announce and enforce sensitive policies and decisions, with wiser invisible ones above him giving signals, but not in writing, as to what was to be done.)

In practice all students, including African-Americans, mixed freely in the student dining hall at meals, work, group activities, classes, and living areas (there was no segregation in roommate or housing assignments). But there was this *barrier*, applicable only to African-Americans and no other ethnic group, against participation in "dating" other than with the handful of other African-Americans. In this way there was an exclusion of

African-American students at Big Sandy from part of the college experience of every other student. The rationale supposedly was the doctrine against interracial marriage, which was believed to be biblically objectionable.

And Ambassador College, of course, was based on *the Bible*, "the foundation of knowledge." That was engraved in stone (at the Pasadena campus, literally).

How I came to research interracial marriage

The summer after my freshman year (the summer of 1973), in company with a couple dozen other Big Sandy students, I set off bright-eyed and excited to make big money and gain great experience selling student handbooks door-to-door in southern Ohio for the Southwestern Company. First there was a week of sales school in Nashville where they cut the hot water off from the showers in the morning, made you memorize sales pitches for twelve hours a day, and didn't let you take naps or use the swimming pool. This was followed by driving to strange towns in southern Ohio and looking for neighborhoods with white frame houses (prime selling territory, working poor with lots of kids), not brick houses (people in brick houses, usually a little better off, don't buy). We would quickly rent rooms and go to work. The daily routine consisted of getting up at 6:00 a.m. to the sounds of loud rock music (to get the blood moving) and success tapes (to increase motivation to "WIN!"). Then there would be thirteen hours of grueling door-to-door entertaining and selling. We would joke with the people at the door and some would buy (the product did help kids in school—that part was for real). When we got in at night we would fill out our sales reports and mail in the day's money to Mac (our sales manager in Nashville), then drop asleep exhausted until 6:00 a.m. the next morning. These days would be punctuated by such exciting events as getting chased by dogs, being run out of town by angry sheriffs enforcing no-soliciting ordinances, and hearing more small-town

Interracial Marriage

gossip than could be imagined. I decided not to make a career of it.

During the first half of the summer I roomed and sold with fellow student Rex Sexton in a sleepy, impoverished southern Ohio town called Washington Courthouse, where we stayed in a rundown rooming house that turned into a funeral home after we left. During the second half of the summer I sold in Columbus, Ohio. There I stayed with two black fellow student salesmen a year ahead of me at Big Sandy, one of whom was the illustrious John James Griffin III. During the school year Griffin was a saxophonist on Garner Ted Armstrong's Personal Appearance Campaigns held in various cities in the United States and Canada. Griffin was widely read, bright and witty, and I had many interesting conversations with him. There were adventures as well. One weekend, I persuaded Griffin to accompany me hitchhiking from Columbus to Indianapolis, Indiana, to visit a fellow student, Jamie Rush. Unexpectedly, at one point during our rides a knife was pulled on us for no reason by two guys who looked like something out of the movie *Deliverance*. Griffin responded with a joke, there was laughter, and the knife was put away. I was glad I had invited Griffin along.

Griffin sensitized me to the complete lack of biblical basis for the church rule against interracial dating and marriage. He had read books by anthropologist Ashley Montagu and conducted a wealth of other research including things like corresponding with presidents of leading Jewish universities. Griffin showed me that common conceptions of race were completely out of keeping with the most basic findings in anthropology. Naturally I plied him with questions. He responded with more information than I dreamed possible. (I had not heard one clue to the existence of this information in classes at Big Sandy. It used to amaze me how much of my education during my Big Sandy years kept happening outside of classes.)

Griffin quoted chapter and verse of unimpeachable authorities who refuted some of the most widespread beliefs people have about race. After what Griffin showed me, I came to appreciate with him that in few fields is the gap between scientific knowledge and popular thinking more disparate than the subject of race—or more damaging in its social consequences. I saw clearly that there were unfounded, harmful, and unbiblical racial attitudes in the Worldwide Church of God. These were not just isolated attitudes in some individuals. These attitudes were grounded in the church's very structure and makeup.

I wrote a paper on the subject, entitled "The Bible and Interracial Marriage" (Jan 23, 1974). I had no personal stake in the matter. I wrote the paper simply because I saw clearly a point which ought to be changed because it was wrong. It was quite simple to me. The truth of the gospel was incompatible with racism. I would write a paper and show this to the church.

A controversial topic

One friend commented on it in retrospect this way. Writing a paper on any other topic, he said, could ruffle feathers, challenge cherished beliefs, maybe even bring charges of heresy. But in the other cases (like discussing 7000-year plans or who was Melchizedek) these were still mostly in the realm of academic or theological dispute. For a real Fourth-of-July fireworks *showdown*, my friend sympathetically explained, there could be no surer-fire recipe than writing a paper explaining to church leaders that there is nothing in Holy Writ which can be quoted to forbid, as my friend put it, "their daughters from dating a You Know What."

Complicating matters was the location of the Big Sandy campus. In the midst of the rural, peaceful beauty of east Texas and the hospitality and friendliness of the people of the region, there were also pockets of people with attitudes on racial matters which could fairly be described as something less than fully enlightened. Even the presence of black students on campus at all was cause for unkind comments from some quarters.

But I was oblivious to these practical exigencies. I forged ahead, so convinced was I of the utter rightness of the case I was presenting in my paper. The issue was to get straight what the Bible *said*, as a factual matter. My paper showed that there was no *biblical* justification for forbidding marriage between Christians on grounds of race (contrary to what the church insisted was the command of the Creator of the universe).

I wrote this paper on interracial marriage just three weeks after I had turned in the term paper, "Evidences for the 7000-Year Plan." That paper agreed with church doctrine and sought to make it more compelling. Now I felt bold enough to submit a paper which would take issue with a church teaching. After all, I had just received a "95" for my paper on the 7000-year plan. (I was quite proud of that "95.") And, I was now fully a sophomore. The new deputy chancellor and resident administrator at Big Sandy, Ronald Dart, communicated intelligence. He seemed to be someone to whom a reasonable argument would be judged on its merits and would get results. Most important of all, I knew what I had to say was on firm ground biblically. I was ready to take on all comers on that. I was ready to go into the ring, knock out all opposition, and emerge victorious (all in a completely submissive attitude, of course). This would culminate in Herbert Armstrong announcing a complete change to the whole church. My efforts would contribute to a better church, growing in truth.

With trepidation, but convinced of the rightness of my cause, I submitted my paper to Mr. Dart with a brief cover note. It was the only submission of numerous ones to follow in which Mr. Dart returned to me a response.

I will tell the response this paper received, but first here is a condensed version of the paper itself if you're interested. (If not, just skip over it and continue reading.)

"The Bible and Interracial Marriage"
Greg Doudna
January 23, 1974

Does the Bible prohibit marriage between the races? It is a common conception that the Bible does. The purpose of this paper is to show that this assumption is in error.

Interracial Marriage

Why does the Church of God teach against interracial marriage? It is difficult to know where to begin since various reasons are put forth by different individuals. The Church has published nothing on the subject since 1963 and there is some confusion as to exactly what the Church doctrine is on the subject. If nothing else, perhaps this memorandum could prompt some kind of statement setting forth the teaching of the Church and reasons behind it on this subject.

It should be noted that nowhere does the Bible define "race" or tell us which races are not to mix. It would be another subject in itself to dispel the popular and deeply-ingrained misconceptions that prevail about race. Race is to many people an emotionally loaded subject, something that Ashley Montagu calls "man's most dangerous myth."

There seem to be almost as many opinions on the doctrine concerning interracial marriage as there are ministers. For the purposes of this discussion, the definition of interracial marriage is accepted as being marriage between the modern-day descendants of Shem, Ham, and Japheth. This seems to be the church teaching, although a few would carry the restriction down the line to nationalities of the same race.

It has been proven that no differences in blood or blood types exist racially. Yet we often hear of racial mixing referred to as "mixing blood." Paul said God "hath made of *one blood* all nations of men" (Acts 17:26, KJV).

Deuteronomy 22:9-11 speaks of not plowing with an ox and ass together, not mixing linen and wool, and not sowing different kinds of seeds. This is supposed to demonstrate the principle of keeping the varieties separate. But the ox and ass are two distinct "kinds." Human beings are all *one* man*kind*. All races of men can mix and produce offspring. Deuteronomy 22 is speaking of *kinds*, not *varieties*. It does not speak of mixing for purposes of reproduction in any case.

Leviticus 19:19 is the *premise* for the doctrine forbidding interracial marriage, in the final analysis. It is the one scripture used to show that God intends varieties to be kept separate. "You shall not let your cattle breed with a different kind: you shall not sow your field with two kinds of seed: neither shall there come upon you a garment of cloth made of two kinds of stuff [KJV, "mingled of linen and woolen"]" (Lev 19:19). It is pointed out that there is only one Hebrew word for both "kind" and "variety," and that since cattle can reproduce only with cattle, this proves God doesn't want cattle bred with different *varieties of cattle*. Now it is a long jump from cattle to humans, but it seems that this statute here in Leviticus regarding

Interracial Marriage

cattle is the basis for prohibiting whites, Spanish-Americans, and blacks from dating each other at Ambassador College.

This is a misunderstanding of Leviticus 19:19. It is not even talking about mixing cattle, let alone humans. Any concordance will confirm that it is talking about unnatural breeding of cattle with different *kinds* of animals [i.e. cattle with non-cattle]. The commentaries confirm this is the correct understanding of this verse. Yet this verse is the basis—the trunk of the tree—for the entire doctrine against interracial marriage. A few verses later we read: *"The stranger who sojourns with you shall be to you as the native among you, and you shall love him as yourself; for you were strangers in the land of Egypt: I am the Lord your God"* (Lev 19:33-34). Nothing here about keeping separate. Nowhere, absolutely nowhere in God's Word do we find a single statement forbidding marriage for racial reasons *alone*.

This should be simple enough to show that the "trunk of the tree" is without foundation. However, other reasons are given to show that God frowns on interracial marriage, some of the more common ones being: (1) "common sense," (2) God divided the nations, (3) God commanded the Israelites not to intermarry with the Canaanites, (4) the examples of Solomon, Ezra, and Nehemiah, and (5) the Flood. Let us examine each in turn.

Common sense. This memorandum is concerned with biblical revelation on the subject, not "common sense." Factors such as "common sense," tradition, social pressures, effect on the children of such a union, genetics and so forth are factors that need to be considered by individuals contemplating marriage, but since when are these factors for *establishing doctrine*? Isn't dating and the final decision on marriage a personal thing between the individuals and families involved? Where in the New Testament does it say Christians must get permission from a minister to marry? *Is* racial separation really "common sense" after all? Much that passes for "common sense," especially on the subject of race, is pure *non*sense. Let's recognize that "common sense," in itself, is not grounds for establishing church doctrine or policy. And of course we know that partisan prejudices should play no part.

God divided the nations. Didn't God "divide to the nations their inheritances" (Deut 32:8; Gen 10; Acts 17:26)? God also gave inheritances to tribes and individuals within the tribes of Israel. But that did not mean the various families and tribes of Israel could not intermarry. The laws of inheritance do not forbid intermarriage.

The Canaanites. The Israelites were told to stay away from seven specific Canaanite nations (Ex 34; Deut 7; Joshua 23). All examples of mixed marriages are condemned because of *idolatry*, not *race*, and this is stated as such in the context of each reference. The Israelites were also told to destroy these peoples. Are we also to obey this part of the command today and be consistent? The New Testament also tells us not to marry heathens (1 Cor 7:39; 2 Cor 6:14)—the *only* restriction on marriage in the New Testament. Race was not the issue. Religion was the issue.

Proof that God allowed interracial marriage. Deut 21:10-13: "When you go forth to war against your enemies, and the Lord your God gives them into your hands, and you take them captive, and see among the captives a beautiful woman, and you have a desire for her and would take her for yourself as a wife, then you shall bring her home to your house, and she shall shave her head and pare her nails. And she shall put off her captive's garb, and shall remain in your house and bewail her father and her mother a full month; after that you may go in to her, and be her husband, and she shall be her wife."

Here, plainly, God specifically allows interracial marriage.

Well, someone is sure to say, just because God allows something doesn't mean He intends it. God also allowed war and polygamy in the Old Testament but Christ showed us better. Quite true. But where is the New Testament teaching countermanding or setting us straight on Deuteronomy 21? Christ was *silent* on the subject. If God forbids interracial marriage why would He specifically allow it in this case and never say differently anywhere else—either in the Old Testament *or* the New Testament? If this is the exception to the rule, where is the rule?

Solomon, Ezra, Nehemiah. Solomon sinned because his wives were pagan and idolatrous, not because they were of a different race. 1 Kgs 11:3-6 shows Solomon's sin was letting his wives turn his heart to other gods. Race was not the issue. Verse one speaks of Solomon sinning by marrying strange women and lists who they were—Moabites, Ammonites, Edomites, Zidonians, and Hittites. Yet Moab, Ammon, and Edom are from Shem—these were not interracial marriages! Marrying a Moabitess in itself is no sin—the Book of Ruth holds out as an example to us the beautiful love story and marriage of Boaz and Ruth. Ruth was a Moabitess, and Christ was descended from them. A whole book of the Bible devoted to glorifying an Israelite-Gentile marriage! There is nothing indicating this was an "exception." Probably some would condemn Boaz and Ruth if they lived today. The cases of Ezra and Nehemiah are similar. The Bible compares them with Solomon's (Neh 13:26). These also involved marriages of Jews with pagan foreign wives including Moabites and Ammonites (Neh 13:24), which were not interracial or

Interracial Marriage

outside of descendants of Shem. It is historical fact that any Gentile who embraced Israel's religion was accorded full citizenship in Israel's society.

The Flood. Did the Flood come on the world because of interracial marriage? Nowhere do we find a clear-cut statement that a Race A was marrying Race B, let alone that this is why God sent the Flood. "The sons of God saw that the daughters of men were fair; and they took to wife such of them as they chose" (Gen 6:2). It is reading into this verse what it does not say to insist it has to mean marriage between races. Some claim Genesis 6:9 refers to Noah being racially "pure." This is highly debatable—this view is in a minority among commentators. In any case, is racial purity something God looks upon with special favor? Christ Himself was not racially pure! Marriage between the races is not mentioned by Christ. If God destroyed all humanity in the flood totally or in part because of a make-believe rule not part of the Ten Commandments let alone even so much as *stated* in Genesis, would not one be justified in wondering at the rationality of this fickle God?

No command of God forbids marriage on racial grounds alone. Deuteronomy 21:10-13, on the contrary, makes specific provision for it. If any question remains on the subject let us now examine actual case histories of interracial marriages recorded in God's Word. *Rachab* the Canaanite harlot married directly into Israelite society and the line of Christ (Josh 2:1; Matt 1:5). Rachab is spoken of very highly by James and Paul (Heb 11:31; James 2:25). No mention is made of any so-called "sin" of intermarriage. *Uriah*, one of David's most loyal men, was a Hittite who was married to Bathsheba (2 Sam 11:3). David later married Bathsheba after Uriah was killed. One of them interracially married. *Joseph* married the daughter of an Egyptian priest (Gen 41:42-52). *Judah* took a Canaanite wife, Genesis 38, with no expression of God's disapproval. The *tribe of Benjamin* in Judges 21 took foreign wives when all their own women had been destroyed in war. Six hundred Israelite-Gentile marriages. *Moses* married an Ethiopian woman (Num 12:1). Was this sin? Aaron and Miriam thought so. God told Aaron and Miriam that Moses had *not* sinned! "My servant Moses ... *who is faithful* in *all* my house" (Num 12:7). "Man looks on the outward appearance, but God looks on the heart" (1 Sam 16:7).

Full and complete integration was practiced in Israel. Doesn't the Fourth Commandment itself, as well as many other scriptures, plainly speak of the "stranger within thy gates" (Ex 20:10)? The Israelites were to have one law for the strangers and themselves, and the strangers were to be treated the same as native Israelites (Ex

Interracial Marriage

12:49; Lev 19:34; Num 9:14). The Israelites were repeatedly warned not to oppress the strangers, fatherless, and widows. Many "strangers" did live within the land of Israel. It was definitely not an apartheid arrangement. The doctrine of separate schools, separate ghettos, separate restaurants, and separate living quarters for different races living in the same nation is nowhere found in God's Word.

What does all this have to do with interracial marriage? Simply this. Integration and interracial marriage stand or fall together. Segregation and racial "purity" stand or fall together. There is no way an integrated society can prevent some mixing of the races. Segregation discourages interracial marriage. Integration will sooner or later make cases of it inevitable, for how do you stop young people from falling in love?

Ambassador College is integrated.

Yet College policy forbids dating between the races.

Why is this?

The New Testament contains absolutely no restriction of marriage on racial grounds. Israel was the church in the wilderness (Acts 7:38), and not to marry heathen idolaters is saying don't marry outside the church. This is the Bible interpreting the Bible. No one in God's church today is a heathen (Gal 2:29). In Christ, "there cannot be Greek and Jew, circumcised and uncircumcised, barbarian, Scythian, slave, free man, but Christ is all, and in all" (Col 3:11). Paul said all nations are "from one" (Acts 17:26). Paul rebuked Peter for his segregationist tendencies (Gal 2:11-12). See also Acts 2:10; 2:44; 10:28; 1 Cor 1:10; James 2:1; and 2:9. Neither Christ nor the apostles taught racial separation. It is not part of the gospel. It is not part of the doctrines of the church given in Hebrews 6:1-2. This doctrine is not from God. Why then is God's church teaching it? "Every word of God proves true ... Do not add to his words, lest he rebuke you, and you be found a liar" (Prov 30:5-6).

Questions that need to be asked. What defines a race, in God's sight? What about those of mixed ancestry—or are they not allowed to marry anyone? Who is to decide? Many American blacks are actually over fifty percent white. Should they be required to marry a white person, to be consistent? How could such a rule be applied today even if it existed (which it doesn't)? Doesn't the application of such a rule depend on identification of the races—who is from Shem, who is from Ham and Japheth, and so on, which carry no guarantee of infallibility—indeed, some of which are nothing more than speculation? Isn't doctrine supposed to be established from clear scripture? What possible spiritual antitype is there for racial separation in God's Church? No matter how alien to us personally interracial marriage may be, God nowhere reveals Himself as condemning of it. If two individuals of different races, both converted Christians, wish to date, *what is their sin*, in the sight of God? Is the doctrine or policy being taught and enforced among Church members in foreign lands? If Italians are Chaldeans from Ham why was an Italian Student Body President of Ambassador College allowed to marry an English-American? Is this not inconsistent? What would be the crime in letting the decision on who is to marry whom rest with the individuals and families involved? How much needless trauma and tragedy has been caused in the past by the church policy on race? How much is continuing still today?

Conclusion. Whatever the reasons one may cite for considering interracial marriage inadvisable in today's society, scriptural principle is not one of them, and should not be claimed as such. It is not the purpose of this paper to set forth evidence showing that over thirty million whites in the United States have some Negro ancestry; that leading anthropologists have noted that all great civilizations have been built by mixed races; that a correlation has been found between racial purity and cultural inferiority; that in the United States the purest whites are white Southern mountaineers—and this is also the most culturally deprived group in the U.S.; that it is a fallacy that interracial marriage is genetically harmful (it simply is *not true* scientifically)—but inbreeding is, and so on. The sole purpose of this paper has been to examine the biblical revelation regarding interracial marriage. It is easy to attach God's name to our own viewpoints. If we look to the Word of God, however, the doctrine against interracial marriage cannot be found. [END]

A favorable response

Mr. Dart, the still-new deputy chancellor who had not previously had a significant personal interaction with me, sent me a very respectful memo in response to this paper. Mr. Dart's memo said he had read my paper. He said he could offer me considerable credit for it as my required term paper for his Old Testament Survey class (in which I was enrolled). And, he said, he intended to take up the matter with the Doctrinal Committee in Pasadena. After these favorable comments, he cautioned that it was necessary to be aware that "some slowness of change is necessary for stability" (or words to that effect). His memo asked if my paper reflected the views of most of the black students on campus. I wrote back that I believed it did, but I had written the paper on my own initiative and it was my own work. I mentioned the talks I had had with John Griffin on the subject when I roomed with him in Ohio the previous summer.

~ ~ ~

It is difficult to describe how elated I felt. I was heartened! I felt Mr. Dart's answer was a completely fair response. My paper was on its way! One of the most powerful men in the church was sufficiently impressed with the merits of what I wrote that he had promised to take up the matter with the Doctrinal Committee! I knew there could not help but be serious clashes further down the road. But the issue was going to be discussed. I was confident that truth would win out.

At the end of the semester Mr. Dart, otherwise a notoriously tough grader, gave me an "A" for his course based on this paper. I didn't care much about that. I was interested in the reaction my paper would receive from headquarters.

This paper alone could have been my showdown at Big Sandy. Unfortunately, this one never made it to high noon. It got derailed before the first rays of dawn.

Bad timing

Unfortunately, I had the misfortune to submit my paper approximately one week before the most threatening crisis in the history of the Worldwide Church of God up to that time exploded in full-blown fury (a dissident uprising). When it hit, Big Sandy looked, spiritually speaking, like a shootout at the OK Corral. When the smoke and carnage cleared over the following weeks (speaking metaphorically), the uprising was quelled and the dissidents defeated and in disarray. But a number of leading ministers and a couple thousand members across the United States were gone.

There was a real showdown all right, but it passed right over my head. It left my humble paper on interracial marriage abandoned in the swirling dust way off to one side of the road.

The battle raged between the True Church and the deceitful dissidents who were inspired by Satan the Devil himself, as Herbert Armstrong evenhandedly characterized it. The dissidents, of course, put it in slightly different words. They thought of it as a clash between a corrupt, controlling organization and courageous individual responsibility. A classmate friend of mine used more colloquial terms. He just said to me (with a philosophical smile as he packed his bags to leave): "I've been sold a bill of goods by an ad-man."

In the midst of this raging battle, I was an insignificant gnat. My unsung paper with its examination of ancient scriptures showing Moses married a black woman, and so on, was just pretty small stuff compared to this cosmic battle between Good and Evil. I watched sadly as my paper became completely sidelined and forgotten in the midst of (again, speaking metaphorically) the shootout and crops and houses set ablaze.

I waited patiently over the following months, but I never heard anything further regarding my paper. College policy was not changed. The church doctrine remained the same for another sixteen years. (In 1990 the Worldwide Church of God finally put an end to its Jim Crow biblical exegesis.) Thereafter, as the rest of this book illustrates, I had extreme difficulty even getting my papers acknowledged at all, let alone arranging for a fair and equitable showdown.

~ ~ ~

As for the Doctrinal Committee at Pasadena, it was abolished by Herbert Armstrong the first time it disagreed with him. Years later, Herbert Armstrong still rankled over the nerve of the Doctrinal Committee to suggest that he, Herbert Armstrong, had possibly been wrong on major points. He made this clear in 1985 in his book *Mystery of the Ages*. In the midst of a rhapsodic description of the glories of the millennial World Tomorrow, he interjected: "One thing there will not be in the millennial Headquarters Church is a doctrinal committee of intellectual 'scholars' to decide whether Christ's teachings are true doctrines" (p. 350).

John Griffin

The following is from an unpublished manuscript by a fellow student from those days, Peter Leschak. Leschak's diary-like manuscript was entitled *A Dissident's Viewpoint: A Chronicle of the Hassle* and was written October 1974. Leschak was two years ahead of me at Ambassador College, Big Sandy (his years: 1970-1974). During his Big Sandy years Leschak worked with E.C. Phillips at the water treatment plant, occasionally helping Mr. Bailey who handled Ambassador College's sewage treatment. (That later furnished a rich source of metaphor when he wrote about . . . oh, never mind.) Leschak went on to become an acclaimed writer.[29]

Of interest is Leschak's report of a Nov. 18, 1973 Ambassador Club meeting featuring John Griffin and the topic of interracial marriage. Unknown to me at the time, this occurred

---

[29] Peter Leschak, *Letters from Side Lake: A Chronicle of Life in the North Woods* (New York: Harper and Row, 1987); *The Bear Guardian: Northwoods Tales and Meditations* (St. Cloud, Minn.: North Star Press, 1990); *Brimming with the Furies Out on the Trail of Experience* (St. Cloud, Minn.: North Star Press of St. Cloud, 1993); *Seeing the Raven: A Narrative of Renewal* (Minneapolis: U. of Minnesota Press, 1994); *Hellroaring: the Life and Times of a Fire Bum* (St. Cloud, Minn.: North Star Press, 1995); *The Snow Lotus: Exploring the Eternal Moment* (Minnesota: U. of Minnesota Press, 1996); *Trials by Wildfire: In Search of the New Warrior Spirit* (Minneapolis: U. of Minnesota Press, 1999); *Rogues and Toads: A Poetry Collection* (St. Cloud, Minn.: North Star Press, 1999); and *Ghosts of the Firegrounds: Echoes of the Great Peshtigo Fire and the Calling of a Wildland Firefighter* (San Francisco: HarperSanFrancisco, 2003). The last named, *Ghosts of the Fireground*, has stories of Leschak's Big Sandy days drawn from the unpublished 1974 manuscript named above.

Interracial Marriage

only two months before Mr. Dart received my paper on the topic and follow-up note bringing to his attention again the name of John Griffin. Here are the relevant passages from Leschak's 1974 account:

> April 30, 1973.
>
> It was my turn for table topics in [Ambassador] club, and man, I was prepared. My show-stopper for the evening was going to be a baited question on interracial marriage. Here was the plan:
>
> I presented a little story to the club about these two young people, John and Mary, [who] were ideally suited for marriage. They had dated for years, had similar backgrounds, parental approval, etc., the whole works, except for one detail: John was white and Mary was black or vice versa. I then asked, "Would it be a sin in God's sight for them to marry?"
>
> Of course the idea was for some confident, but only semi-informed (as are most AC students) dude to jump up in holy righteousness, thump his Bible and loudly declare "NO!" Then I, having done extensive homework, and poised for the kill, would ask him to prove it from the Bible. Then, even if he did happen to know where to turn, I would demolish his arguments one by one. My point would then be to urge the men to be careful of dogmatism and to be sure they knew what they were talking about when they brandished their Bibles.
>
> Just for the record at this point, let me explain that I do not in any way advocate interracial marriage. That is from purely social considerations, however, and I don't believe God would consider it a sin.
>
> Anyway, back to the topics session. It went beautifully. I threw out the bait and was a bit surprized at first because three or four of the men rose and said they didn't think it would be a sin, but wouldn't recommend it for social reasons. I was afraid the plan was going to fall flat, but then a sophomore got up and gave the dogmatic "no." I asked him to prove it. He stammered for a few seconds, turned red and sat down. A junior then rose and gave the coup de grace. He informed the unfortunate sophomore that the point could not be proved from the Bible. I then gave my warning against unenlightened dogmatism. It was a real high. I had even better results with the same topic the next year.
>
> [...snip...]

Interracial Marriage

November 18, 1973.

It was six months since I had used the interracial marriage topic in club, and the mood had changed somewhat at AC since then. Things were a little more sensitive.

This time around it was my own club. I had only really desired one position of leadership with any enthusiasm since I arrived at AC, and that was to be a club president. I was afraid that with the image of a "free thinker" which I had developed the previous school year, I might not be given the influence and responsibility of an Ambassador club, but I heard through the ever-active grapevine that a somewhat influential friend of mine had convinced some skeptical and hesitant faculty members that I should be a club president. I was grateful. I had the opportunity to select my own officers, so Wayne Janes, Bob McBride, Gary Smith, and John Griffin made up my "administration" ... It was a lively, outspoken, and even sometimes thoughtful bunch. Mr. Mark Kaplan was our director, and since it was his first time in such a post, he contributed an enthusiasm which often gave the club a shot of inspiration.

On the evening of Nov. 18th we experienced one of the most stimulating topics sessions I'd participated in during 3-1/2 years of club at AC. I was topics master and I presented the same topic on interracial marriage as I had on April 30th of the last semester.

Immediately junior John Griffin, a former black roommate of mine, who had thoroughly researched the subject from every conceivable aspect, rose and gave about a three minute defense of the point that interracial marriage was not a sin in God's sight. A freshman then brought up a scripture he felt was to the contrary and Griffin again rose for another few minutes to counter his argument. Another rose to challenge him and John dispatched him as well. He spoke for another few minutes, quoting the Bible and other secular sources. He hit it from all angles, Biblical, biological, social, historical. The club members and Kaplan were surprized and slightly overwhelmed. The discussion went on for 15 or 20 minutes with Griffin the master of it all.

In his evaluation of the session Kaplan, who had apparently never heard anything quite like it in a club before, suggested that perhaps we could take the discussion to Mr. Dart. He apparently wasn't aware that it had been an "underground" issue for about a year. The administration was well aware of it.

Interracial Marriage

Here is still another echo of John Griffin. A fellow Big Sandy student wrote me in 1988:

> I remember John Griffin well. I sat at the same dining hall table with him once and was struck by a profound comment he made: "All things are relative." Wonder what became of him. Also, there is an anecdote about John Griffin and ____ that goes far to point out where the WCG was really coming from on interracial dating. This was before I knew ____. Seems she and John Griffin got into a heated discussion about some academic point and, while pressing a point, ____ touched him momentarily on the arm.
>
> A few days later she was called into [Dean of Students] Mr. Kelly's presence, who informed her that there were rumors going around concerning her and John Griffin, and he wanted to know if she knew of those rumors and if there was any basis to them. He apparently was satisfied by her explanation that the arm touch was all, and that was that.

That was the way things were. I myself heard a story—secondhand but I believe it to be reliable—concerning a senior white male student and a sophomore female black student during my freshman year. He had driven her into nearby Tyler for some innocuous errand as a courtesy since she had no car and they were friends. According to the white senior student, Mr. Kelly had called him in to his office and asked him if he had taken the young black woman in to get an abortion. (The answer was no, nor was there any basis for the question.) But back to John Griffin.

~ ~ ~

At the student level, I don't know of anyone who didn't like John Griffin, including those with whom he engaged in spirited debate. He was just that kind of person—engaging, lively, and upbeat, such that even if one didn't agree with him, one still liked him. The administration's view of Griffin, however, may have been a different matter. Here they had magnanimously let him in even though he was black, and he was ungratefully taking advantage of their beneficence by pointing out absurd contradictions in their policies with razor-sharp logic, making them look like idiots—and worse still, talking about it right and left indiscriminately to other students, all of whom liked him and a good number of whom thought he made excellent sense. My mention of Griffin to the deputy chancellor as in the background of my paper was only one of a number of points at which Griffin came to their unwelcome attention.

I don't know the circumstances, but at some point Griffin disappeared without graduating. In retrospect, how could it have been otherwise. He shone too brightly. He was too much for the institution to handle. I wonder where he is now. He was missed.

A graduating student at Big Sandy is disqualified from employment in the "Work" because of the interracial marriage doctrine ...

Another African-American fellow student at Big Sandy when I was there was Murdock Gibbs. Gibbs was one of the most decent persons there was: thoughtful, considerate, and he had a conscience.

It was Gibbs who passed on to me this behind-the-scenes glimpse into American politics. Shortly before he came to Ambassador College in Big Sandy, Gibbs had occasion to talk with the first African-American mayor in Alabama, the mayor of Tuskegee, Gibbs' hometown. This mayor told Gibbs about George Wallace, the governor of Alabama. Wallace had gained national prominence for being a hard-liner on segregation and always got the white racist vote, both in Alabama and throughout the United States in 1968 and 1972 when he ran for President. (I remember how white racists in Akron, Ohio at the gas station where I worked just *loved* George Wallace.) But this black mayor told Gibbs that Wallace was no racist. Wallace only *talked* like he was, *pretended* to be racist, to get the votes he needed to get elected! Privately he treated the black leaders fine, gave them what they needed, worked along well with them. When Gibbs

Interracial Marriage

told me this I marveled that while a lot of people are racist and pretend not to be, this was the first I ever heard of the reverse (if it was true). But this is a digression.

Gibbs entered Ambassador College at Big Sandy the year after I did, but Gibbs was about four years older than me as I recall. The reason he was older as a freshman had to do with his having been refused admission to Ambassador College Big Sandy in earlier years because of the color of his skin, since Ambassador College was not accepting single blacks until 1971. (Of course they did not say that in his rejection letters, which never gave a reason.) When he was refused admission to Ambassador College the first time he applied in 1968, he went to one of his second choices, prestigious Brandeis University in Massachusetts which had offered him a scholarship. Every year after that he would apply to transfer to Ambassador College and get turned down again, never being told why. The first three years he was turned down Gibbs did not even realize that Ambassador College had a policy not to admit blacks. After about three years of his applications being turned down a local white WCG minister clued him in to what was going on, and then later black WCG ministers in New York City confirmed it to him. Still Gibbs kept applying.

After four years Gibbs graduated from Brandeis in 1972 with a B.A. Following his graduation from Brandeis Gibbs then received an acceptance letter from Ambassador College (in response to his annual application #5). But Gibbs was on summer vacation in Cleveland, Ohio at the time and there was a slight delay in him receiving the letter due to the forwarding. By the time Gibbs got the letter and promptly made contact with the Admissions Office at Big Sandy to accept the happy news, he was told it was *too late!*—in the delay they had accepted another black guy in his spot! They were filling a quota of four black men and four black women that year so that there would be the right number for blacks to date among "their own kind." Under no circumstances could there be a fifth black male admitted when there were only four black females for them to date. Since the quota for black male students was unfortunately now filled, Gibbs was just out of luck again, no matter how well qualified he was and despite his having been sent a letter of admission.

Gibbs then moved to New York City in the fall of 1972, landed a job as a publicity writer for McGraw-Hill, and applied yet another time to Ambassador. He received an acceptance letter in the summer of 1973, and at last was able to come to Ambassador College, his dream. He started in the fall of 1973. He was selected as freshman class president.

If anyone would have made a good pastor of a church congregation one would think of Gibbs. He had it all: sincerity, empathy, dedication, people skills, teaching skills, outstanding reputation, the works. He completed the full ministerial training program at Big Sandy and was interviewed for the job for which he had trained and was, to all outward appearances, fully qualified. This would be spring 1976. But there was a slight problem: Gibbs was an honest man. They had ways of screening for that. One stock question the ministerial hiring committee asked the aspiring seniors being interviewed was this: "Do you disagree with any church doctrines?" The correct answer to this question was "No." (Whether or not it was true.) Any answer other than an unqualified "no" was a practically certain kiss of death.

Gibbs appeared before the three-man hiring committee, which consisted of Dean Blackwell in charge, and two other ministers, David Robinson and Norvel Pyle. The first question these men of God asked Gibbs was how he felt about interracial marriage. (That was not the first question asked of white ministerial candidates.) Gibbs disclosed truthfully that he did not see where in the Bible interracial marriage was a sin, and that he personally could not kick someone out of the church over this issue. Gibbs was therefore disqualified from being hired as a minister. All three agreed with the thumbs-down. Though I remember Gibbs well and remember being puzzled that he had not been hired, it was only years later when I came across the following newspaper account by accident that I learned why. This is from the 1996

Interracial Marriage

Worldwide News (the in-house WCG newspaper) reporting on a church symposium on racial healing:

> Murdock Gibbs, a local church elder from the Dallas, Texas, North church, related how Ambassador College at one time did not accept blacks. Mr. Gibbs asked: How would you feel if your children could not attend the school you were donating so much money to?
>
> Mr. Gibbs eventually attended Ambassador and was interviewed for the ministry shortly before graduation. "I told them I didn't feel that interracial marriage was a sin. I didn't think it was something that would determine someone's salvation. That it wasn't something I would kick someone out of the church over."
>
> The presiding minister replied: "Well, until we prove to you that it is a sin, you will never be used in this work."
>
> Mr. Gibbs said: "From that point forward I said, 'God, if you want me to be used, it's up to you. I'm not going to try to work through men and please men.' And about a year ago I was ordained an elder in what I consider is a new Worldwide Church of God."[30]

... while, amazingly, headquarters simultaneously denies to the PUBLIC that a doctrine against interracial marriage even exists!

In an article in the American mass-circulation monthly *Christianity Today*, a journalist reported to that magazine's readership that he had been told by officials of the Worldwide Church of God in Pasadena in the spring of 1976 that there *was no doctrine* against interracial marriage. The journalist, Joseph Hopkins, reported that unnamed officials at Pasadena had told him: "we cannot and do not forbid people of different racial or ethnic backgrounds to marry even though such marriages may not be wise."[31]

I do not remember hearing anything about this at the time. And based on the experience of Murdock Gibbs at Big Sandy

---

[30] Thomas Hanson, "Pasadena Church Conducts Racial Healing Weekend," *Worldwide News*, July 23, 1996.
[31] Joseph Hopkins, "Armstrong's Church of God: Mellowed Aberrations?," in the April 15, 1977 issue of *Christianity Today*.

cited above, it seems long-time ministers at Big Sandy doing ministerial hiring interviews also were unaware that the doctrine they were punishing Gibbs for not believing was not believed at headquarters either, and in fact, according to the report, was not a doctrine of the church.

The *Christianity Today* report, it should be noted, was not a misquote or a mistake. (The particular journalist, Hopkins, was otherwise scrupulously accurate.) In fact, what headquarters told *Christianity Today* seems to have been a sound bite for public consumption which never was implemented. Surprisingly, it appears headquarters at Pasadena indeed was poised to make a change in the doctrine on interracial marriage in 1976 (though it seems virtually no one at Big Sandy, including at the senior ministerial level, knew this at the time they torpedoed Murdock Gibbs' employment prospects). According to Church of God historian Richard Nickels, papers for the headquarters Systematic Theology Project issued at Pasadena in late 1976 included a written statement on "Race and Ethnic Relations in the Church" which stated that the church would no longer teach against interracial marriage.[32] But few church members in the Worldwide Church of God seemed aware of this. I do not think it was announced by most ministers to their congregations. If it was, it was cancelled in 1978 when Herbert Armstrong condemned the entire Systematic Theology Project as a plot done behind his back and fired the ones who had prepared it.

The doctrine against interracial marriage as it was carried out in God's Church

Wesley Webster was a later Ambassador College (Pasadena)-trained African-American who did become a Worldwide Church

---

[32] Richard Nickels, "Biblical Doctrine. Fundamentals of Belief and Analysis of the Doctrines of Various Sabbath-Keeping Groups" (4th edition, 2003) (http://giveshare.org/doctrine/doctrine11.html).

of God minister. He has written of his experiences with race issues in the 1980s. Webster writes:

> I can remember a very unfortunate experience that I once had when I was being trained in the Ministry [of the Worldwide Church of God] in 1987. The Assistant Pastor had me assist him in visiting a new contact and prospective member. The young lady was of mixed parentage. Her mother was white, and her father was black. She was very light in complexion, but her brother was very dark. Before inviting her to Church, the Assistant Pastor had to inform her that we did not allow interracial dating and marriage in the Church. We had no clear scriptures to support our point. However, the minister went on to explain that since she was not clearly in either racial group, she would have to decide before attending services which race (skin color) she would date. Her decision once approved would be final and lifelong. For approval she was required to write an essay explaining her decision which was to be sent to Pasadena along with a photograph, before a final decision could be made.[33]

This is what the doctrine meant in practice: a young woman forced by these ministers to choose what skin color of man in the future she would be forever forbidden to love and marry, no matter how honorable and good that man might be and even though she herself shared the same skin color. Webster also recounted the day he learned he was accepted to Ambassador College.

> I'll always remember the day that I found out that I was accepted to go to Ambassador College. I'll always remember because the Pastor was instructed to inform me and make sure that I understood interracial dating at Ambassador was strictly forbidden. White males were not subjected to this questioning. This was definitely a form of racial discrimination and reflected the racist view that black men are desperately desirous of white women. These views are a carry over from the slavery and Jim Crow periods of the United States' history.

---

[33] Wesley Webster, "Does God's Word Forbid Interracial Marriage?" (http://www.biblestudy.org/basicart/interace.html).

Interracial Marriage

Impact in individual lives

Around 1990 a man identifying himself as a Worldwide Church of God member wrote to William F. Dankenbring, a former writer for the *Plain Truth* magazine now running an independent publishing ministry. The distraught letter writer was dumbfounded to hear Worldwide Church of God headquarters claim the church had never broken up interracial marriages (as distinguished from forbidding new ones to happen). The letter writer said they were *lying*; he claimed *his* interracial marriage had been broken up by church officials because of the doctrine against interracial marriage. The author of this letter wrote:

> In the Worldwide News of July 30, 1990 ... Joseph Tkach said: "Herbert W. Armstrong did not require interracially married converts to separate." This is a lie, Mr. Dankenbring. How do I know it is a lie? I know it is a lie because I was forced to separate from my beautiful, loving, wonderful wife—only because of her skin color!!!
>
> I have suffered untold misery over the years, repenting of my longing for this woman, never fully being able to get her out of my memory. Now the Church is telling me that no one was ever forced to leave their mate because of interracial marriage.
>
> I am going crazy, Mr. Dankenbring. I can't stand this. My beautiful wife is now married to someone of her own race, and every time I think of her living with another man I have to repent of my anger and sorrow in the loss of the best thing that ever happened to me ... I just can't believe this!
>
> I can't sign this. I'm still a member and couldn't take being disfellowshipped ... This is too much. Help me ... I don't know how I can live with this.[34]

The writer of this heart-wrenching letter did not identify himself because of fear that his loving fellow Christians would ostracize him if he did. Was this man's story true? Another letter Dankenbring received said:

---

[34] Quoted in Wm. F. Dankenbring, "What Does the Bible Teach About the Race Question?" (http://www.triumphpro.com/race_question.htm).

Interracial Marriage

> I was forbidden to marry the person I intended to marry because that person had mixed blood of two races ... that decision hurt me and my family a lot and now that the doctrine is changing it makes me feel sick inside at how I separated from my mixed-race friend, only because of her race.[35]

Ronald Dart on interracial marriage

In 1979 Ronald Dart, for many years in high position in the Worldwide Church of God, and who appeared to have done nothing with my paper on interracial marriage or the arguments in it in those years despite his letter to me saying he would, left the Worldwide Church and joined with Garner Ted Armstrong's new church, the Church of God, International, headquartered in Tyler, Texas. Mr. Dart soon became Number Two man in Garner Ted's church. In 1987 I sent Dart a draft of an earlier version of the present chapter. Dart responded:

> The segments in your paper on race relations are an interesting illustration of the problem of change in any organization. There were many of us who were uncomfortable with the college's policy, but not even Herbert W. Armstrong could change that policy by fiat—amazing as that sounds. Racial feelings were too deeply rooted in everyone concerned, and there are some changes that have to be made over time as people grow and learn. They cannot be forced. I believe this is one of those questions.

I hate to say this, but this reminded me of the time I saw the American evangelist Jerry Falwell on television commenting on the subject of apartheid in South Africa. This was back when South Africa was still white-minority ruled and practicing apartheid. (Conservative Christian leaders such as Falwell were among the strongest supporters of the racist regime.) Falwell said that the problem in South Africa was that apartheid existed, but no one liked apartheid. According to Falwell, the blacks didn't

---

[35] Quoted, Dankenbring, "What Does the Bible Teach About the Race Question?"

like apartheid, and the whites didn't either. It was something that was inherited that no one today supported or wanted, but it still existed. (Therefore, the white government of South Africa should not be condemned, since they were against apartheid too.) There was this unjust system in place, enforced brutally by laws and police, but no one was responsible since everyone was against it. So Falwell's logic. Unfortunately Ronald Dart's statement sounded too much like Falwell's unconvincing apology for the South Africa regime. It brought back memories of the 1960s in which I heard, as a child, whites telling blacks they needed to be more "patient" in seeking equality before the law—after all, it was only 100 years after blacks had been promised equality, and these things take *time* and *cannot be forced*.

Certainly changes of attitudes take time. But what did Dart, who was in a position to do something, do to encourage the process? Dart had the no-interracial dating policy, which was certainly racist since it was so singularly and emotionally focused on African-Americans, enforced by those under him at Big Sandy. I do not remember Dart ever giving a sermon or Bible Study showing that the doctrine against interracial marriage was unbiblical. As the most influential and respected administrator and teacher at Big Sandy, he could have changed attitudes significantly by as little as a single effective Bible study on the topic. But so far as I am aware, it never happened.

Meanwhile, senior student Murdock Gibbs was being told at Big Sandy, on Mr. Dart's watch, that he, Gibbs, was banned from employment in his field of training unless he would believe and enforce the doctrine against interracial marriage—a doctrine without any valid basis.

~ ~ ~

How was interracial marriage handled in the new church led by Garner Ted Armstrong and Ronald Dart? How did Dart's "changes that have to be made over time" work out in practice in the Church of God, International? In September 1990 *Ambassador Report* reported:

> The significance (or lack thereof) of race and the way in which the world's races should interact is another doctrinal area undergoing sweeping changes in the WCG. Whereas HWA saw the Anglo-Saxon "race" as having a special past and future historical role, Tkach increasingly emphasizes the complete equality of all races. Whereas HWA was known to have refused to marry interracial couples, Tkach has stated that while his church is not trying to encourage interracial marriage, he now strictly prohibits ministers from refusing to marry a man and a woman because they are of different races (WN, July 30, p. 1).
>
> As Tkach himself acknowledged (p. 5), the topic of interracial marriage is an emotionally charged one in WCG circles. Even in the Church of God International, once thought to be more "liberal" than the WCG, interracial couples have had difficulties being accepted by fellow church members and have even been denied marriage by some ministers. For instance in 1986 when CGI ministers refused to marry one CGI couple because he was white and she was black, the couple was forced to go to a Baptist minister to have their wedding performed.
>
> The couple, now Mr. and Mrs. (C. A. and Doreen) Foland, left CGI to help found the Sabbath-keeping Church of Our Lord Jesus Christ, which is pastored by former WCG minister Ross May. The Folands have appeared on a number of talk shows and their personal trials have been documented in newspapers ...

A glimpse of the Worldwide Church of God African-American experience

The following is from a recent email exchange I had with an African-American who was a student at Big Sandy when I was there:

> Me: When I looked at the *Envoy* [Ambassador College yearbook] for 1974 a few months back I was surprised to notice 100% white faces in all four classes of Bricket Wood shown (unlike Pasadena and Big Sandy). How come I didn't remember that? Or did I know it and forget it? Did you know that?

Interracial Marriage

Reply: Because you're white. And it really wasn't an issue that affected you. If you saw a Bricket Wood photo of only women, you probably would have questioned what was going on—you being a male, this would directly affect you and your perceptions.

I guarantee you, every time a black WCG family or person looks at a photo of AC—paging through the *Envoy* or some other idyllic portrayal of life at AC, we're thinking, "Where are the black people?"

Me: When you came to Big Sandy, was there a formal mechanism in which you were instructed not to date non-blacks?

Reply: No, but other church literature—*Plain Truth* and booklets—implied or clearly stated that "God" placed the races in their boundaries and never intended racial mixing. The Big Guns from Headquarters adamantly preached racial separation, especially folk like Gerald Waterhouse who had the whole racial plan of God figured out.

Of course, this doctrine made no sense when they tried to explain Noah and his sons starting the human race and other races ... we were told that God allowed Noah's sons to marry outside of their races, that is, Ham (white) married a black lady; Japheth (white) married an Oriental/yellow lady; and Shem (white), of course, was like Noah—"perfect in his [bloodline] generations," and married a white lady.

Yeah, black folks and other minorities heard this kind of preaching for years ... but this was "God's Church." He would set things straight, some felt. Others recognized it as racist and either fumed quietly or left the church.

What can one say. It was so wrong. In earlier days in America white slave-owners heard sermons preaching that blacks had no souls and were not human, were under the "curse of Ham," and so on. Biblical exegesis legitimizing hurtful attitudes and actions toward other groups of human beings in the name of God is an old, old story.

The doctrine of Anglo-Israelism formerly held by the Worldwide Church of God and continued in many of the splinter groups—even though the self-understanding of many of the groups holding the Anglo-Israel doctrine is that they are not racist—nevertheless underlies institutional racism, with its

Interracial Marriage

language of "Israelite" (whites) versus "stranger" (blacks). More on Anglo-Israelism later.

The long night ends in the Worldwide Church of God on this issue

In mid-1989 the first edition of the present book, *Showdown at Big Sandy*, appeared with an earlier version of the present chapter featuring my 1974 student paper on interracial marriage written when I was at Big Sandy. In September 1989 *Ambassador Report* reported my book's availability and favorably reviewed and recommended it. The book, and my interracial marriage paper and chapter within it, became known within Worldwide Church of God circles at that time. It was also at about this time that William Dankenbring, whose publishing ministry critical of the Worldwide Church of God had a substantial readership, published a partly derivative version of my interracial marriage paper under his own name, giving its arguments wider currency.[36] He blasted the WCG over this issue.

Whether either of these things played a role in what happened a few months later I do not know, but in July 1990 the Worldwide Church of God formally ended its doctrine that the Bible forbids interracial marriage. By decision of Pastor General Joseph Tkach, Sr., the doctrine and policy of the Worldwide Church of God came to be in agreement in almost every particular with what students such as John Griffin, and my 1974 sophomore paper, had argued on this subject so long ago at Big Sandy.

~ ~ ~

In 1994-95 the Worldwide Church of God, led by Joseph Tkach, Sr., and then Joseph Tkach, Jr. following the death of Tkach Sr. in September 1995, astonished observers in the religious world

---

[36] See Chapter 9 for details.

by repudiating the distinctive doctrines of Herbert Armstrong, expressing sorrow for the hurt and abuses of the past, and becoming a Sunday-keeping evangelical church. The transformed, humbler WCG—a church which had for so long attacked and condemned other Christian ministries—was embraced and welcomed by evangelicals like a prodigal son coming home. It was either breathtakingly courageous, a Damascus-road experience of a church repenting as a body, or else it was wholesale apostasy and a cruel abandonment of historic roots, depending on how one viewed it. Feelings ran very deep. The changes caused massive defections of ministers and members many of whom switched over to several major and a large number of minor "splinter groups" (as all sides refer to the phenomenon without opprobrium).

By far the largest and most important of the splinter groups is the Cincinnati, Ohio-based United Church of God, started in 1995 by a number of former high-level WCG ministers. Hundreds of WCG ministers and 12,000 members went over to the new UCG. The UCG announced their default doctrines were the ones of the WCG *before* the Tkach sweeping reforms, although they set up procedures to study and correct doctrines by top ministerial consensus as needed.

And so it was that from 1995 until 2005 the United Church of God *resumed* the *old* doctrine against interracial marriage, although their stated reasoning was different than Herbert Armstrong's in arriving at the same conclusion. No longer were the traditional alleged biblical reasons forbidding interracial marriage of the old WCG cited; they explicitly acknowledged that those reasons were bad exegesis and baseless. They acknowledged that the Bible nowhere directly forbids interracial marriage. Instead, the UCG's stated reasoning until 2005 was that the Bible (a) gives many examples of recommending marriage within one's own extended family and community (rather than with different cultures or parts of the world), and (b) gives the ministry the task of counseling members with wise advice on social issues, such as the problems that face interracial marriages for social reasons.

These two stated reasons became the new Bible foundation for the (all-white) UCG governing ministers' formal position that as a denomination they officially opposed interracial marriage—sight unseen in advance, in all cases, no matter who the people or what the circumstances. There were too many social problems, they explained, too much racism in the world for the UCG to approve an interracial marriage, due to the problems that would beset such a couple. (The UCG headquarters prohibition of interracial marriage was for the parties' own good, arising from the ministers' biblical mandate of care for the brethren, you see.) Same conclusion as the old WCG, different way of getting there from the pages of the Bible.

But in August 2005 the Council of Elders of the United Church of God approved a study paper announcing for the first time that that church body has no doctrine against interracial marriage. Unlike the Worldwide Church of God when it changed on this issue, the UCG's statement appears unaccompanied with any formal statement of sorrow for the effects their former teachings and attitudes meant for their black brethren. But they did, in 2005, come to consensus on ditching the biblically indefensible doctrine itself, for reasons virtually identical to those of John Griffin and my student paper at Big Sandy of 1974, and of the WCG of 1990.

Closing comments from today

The whole notion of "three races" which was so basic and widespread in these discussions is bogus. There is *no such thing* as "three races" in any scientific sense. There are only multiple ethnicities in history which are largely socially constructed and self-defined. The "three races" idea was a 19th century notion, deeply racist in its origins, that is discredited today in anthropological circles.

Of interest for those wishing to do further research is a field called "whiteness studies" and a subset of that focused around a journal called *Race Traitor*. From one of the editors of this publication:

> *Race Traitor*, whose first issue appeared in the fall of 1992 [had] the slogan "Treason to whiteness is loyalty to humanity" on its cover. The aim was to chronicle and analyze the making, remaking, and unmaking of whiteness. My book on the Irish was the story of how people for whom whiteness had no meaning learned its rules and adapted their behavior to take advantage of them; *Race Traitor* was an attempt to run the film backwards, to explore how people who had been brought up as white might become unwhite ... The goal of abolishing the white race is on its face so desirable that some may find it hard to believe that it could incur any opposition other than from committed white supremacists. Of course we expected bewilderment from people who still think of race as biology. We frequently get letters accusing us of being "racists," just like the KKK, and have even been called a "hate group" ... Our standard response is to draw an analogy with anti-royalism: to oppose monarchy does not mean killing the king; it means getting rid of crowns, thrones, royal titles, etc. ...[37]

And from an online description:

> One group of people involved in these discussions advocate a strategy they call race treason, and are grouped around articles appearing in the journal *Race Traitor*. The adherents' main argument is that whiteness (as a marker of a social status within the United States) is conferred upon people in exchange for an expectation of loyalty to what they consider an oppressive social order. This loyalty has taken a variety of forms over time: suppression of slave rebellions, participation in patrols for runaways, maintenance of race exclusionary unions, participation in riots, support for racist violence, and participation in acts of violence during the conquest of western North America. Like currency, the value of this privilege (for the powerful) depends on the reliability of "white skin" (or as physical

---

[37] Noel Ignatiev, author of a book entitled *How the Irish Became White*, quoted in the Sept.-Oct. 2002 issue of *Harvard* magazine (http://www.harvard-magazine.com/on-line/0902135.html).

Interracial Marriage

anthropologists would deem this construct, the phenotype of historical North Atlantic Europeans) as a marker for social consent. With sufficient "counterfeit whites" resisting racism and capitalism, the writers in this tradition argue, the privilege will be withdrawn or will splinter, prompting an era of conflict and social redefinition. Without such a period, they argue, progress towards social justice is impossible, and thus "treason to whiteness is loyalty to humanity."

In *Race Traitor*, the editors cite as basis for their proposed actions a call by African American writers and activists—notably W.E.B. DuBois and James Baldwin—for whites to break solidarity with American racism. Since that racism involves the awarding of various forms of white privilege, some have even argued that every white identity is drawn into that system of privilege. Only identities which seek to transcend or defy that privilege, they argue are effectively antiracist. This essential argument echoes Baldwin's declaration that, "As long as you think you are white, there's no hope for you," in an essay in which he acknowledges a variety of European cultures, a multiracial American culture, but no white culture per se which can be distinguished from the maintenance of racism.

Race Traitor advocates have sought examples of race treason by whites in American history. One historical figure consistently valorized by *Race Traitor* (a publication favorable to the tenets of whiteness studies) is John Brown, a Northern abolitionist of European descent who battled slavery in western territories of the United States and led a failed but dramatic raid to free slaves and create an armed anti-slavery force at Harpers Ferry, West Virginia.[38]

Now before (fellow white) readers of Christian-biblical grounding get their hackles up over this (and I do purposely quote the above to be provocative), consider three questions. Think:

(1) Is there any biblical basis to such a notion of classification as a "white race" in history?

Are Italians part of the "white race"? Why? Are Russians? What about Assyrian Christian Iraqis and other Iraqis who descend from the Assyrians of old? What about Jordanians? Are Arab tribes who claim descent from Ishmael? Are Spaniards part

---

[38] From the Wikipedia article "Whiteness Studies."

of the white race? Are Portuguese? Are Greeks? Are Poles? How about Muslim Shi'ite Azerbaijanis from the Caucasus? How about *Armenians* and *Georgians* and *Chechens* from the Caucasus area, otherwise known as *Caucasians*, or in Russia known negatively as *blacks* (because their skin is typically darker and more "ethnic" looking than that of Russians)? Are these Caucasians, who are Russia's *blacks*, members of the "white race"? (Remember, historically Armenians and Georgians from the Caucasus started out *defining* the so-called Caucasian/white race.) Are Hungarians part of "the white race"? Rumanians? Czechs? Gypsies (Roma)? Albanians? Serbs? How about the Persians of Iran, Iran's largest ethnic group, who descend from the ancient Aryan Persians?

> (2) What *is* the actual basis for such a notion of a "white race" in history?

Same questions as above, repeated. How did some of these groups get to be members of "the white race," while others did not? Who decided, and why? And finally,

> (3) Has this notion done more good or harm?

I leave these questions open, to encourage reflection.

CHAPTER 5

BIG SANDY SCHOOL DAYS: 1974

The dissident rebellion of 1974 during my sophomore year referred to in the previous chapter started when the pastor of the Worldwide Church of God congregation in Shreveport, Louisiana (only eighty miles away from Big Sandy to the east) told his congregation one Sabbath that headquarters was doing a cover-up. He said that when Garner Ted Armstrong had been secretly put out of the church by Herbert Armstrong two years earlier, it wasn't just because handsome, blue-eyed Garner Ted needed rest. The reason for Garner Ted's disappearance, he said, was Garner Ted's affair with a stewardess on his jet. The Shreveport pastor added that Garner Ted had a penchant for gambling, headquarters was in a big mess and was wasting a lot of money, and the church doctrine forbidding remarriage after divorce was wrong. Finally, the pastor said the whole business of taking money from people to preach the gospel to the world was a big scam. The scripture clearly said an angel will do this job, not human beings (Rev 14:6). This was not a normal Sabbath sermon.

When this startling event happened (i.e. a pastor saying these things), an irate Garner Ted and half the firepower in Pasadena converged on the bewildered Shreveport congregation. Garner Ted was not in a good mood. He didn't appreciate the stories about stewardesses and gambling. He said there were no more female crew members on his jet and whatever happened in the past was none of their business. As for gambling, so what if he had blown a few thousand dollars in Las Vegas in one night? It was his own money. Garner Ted likened the action of their pastor to someone who reached his hand down into a pile of wet manure and smeared it all over their sweet, innocent faces. He called for a curse from God on the next person who spread a rumor. Needless to say, the Shreveport pastor found himself suddenly unemployed. He and a number of Shreveport members began meeting independently, greatly reducing the Worldwide Church of God congregation. All of this happened around late November/December 1973.

The fires of rebellion spread to Big Sandy

Several student friends of mine went to Shreveport one Sabbath soon after to find out for themselves what was going on. (Understandably, this was contrary to the wishes of the Big Sandy administration.) These students attended both services— the approved Worldwide Church of God services in the morning and the dissident services in the afternoon. They brought news back to campus of what was happening in Shreveport. What I heard shocked my tender ears. But I tried to talk my friends out of going further in this direction. I couldn't defend the church's past mistakes, but all that was over. Anything relating to Garner Ted was, after all, in the past. The way I saw it, just because a scandal or two surfaces is no reason to leave a church where truth is being taught. It was important to keep sight of the *big* picture. The dissidents, sadly, had let themselves fall into a bad attitude.

At first it seemed as if the Shreveport blowup might blow over. Formidable Ronald Dart, the resident Big Sandy administrator, returned from meetings in Pasadena and assured us that the Work was now "stronger than ever." But it turned out that what had happened in Shreveport was only the proverbial tip of the iceberg. In fact, the unexpected uprising in Shreveport actually served to trigger a chain reaction which wrecked more far-reaching plans. For there had been larger plans afoot among high-ranking ministers across the country. Many of the top ministers believed that, for the good of the church, Garner Ted

Big Sandy School Days: 1974

Armstrong would have to go. One of the biblical qualifications for ministers is to be "of good reputation." Garner Ted hardly qualified. Herbert Armstrong himself would have to change from being so autocratic and authoritarian. These ministers believed the church should be governed with more accountability. An improved church government would involve the ministers in making key decisions, no longer having to wait on Herbert Armstrong's personal whim to make desperately needed changes. The divorce and remarriage doctrine which had so cruelly ripped apart so many homes would be changed. And tithing as it was applied was far too onerous and would be made voluntary.

Feeling blocked at every turn in bringing about needed reforms, these high-ranking ministers planned to apply pressure on the board of directors to shove young Garner Ted Armstrong out and tell old Herbert Armstrong it was time for him to be eased into some kind of honorary retirement. The ministers' plan for Herbert was for him to do public relations work as a figurehead. Then these ministers would go to work to try to straighten out the mess the church was in.

Back at Ambassador College at Pasadena, Ernest Martin, head of the Theology Department, resigned in January. He wrote a pointed letter to Herbert Armstrong telling Herbert he must quit being so bullheaded about rejecting clear Bible truths from his researchers. (Of course he didn't put it in quite those words.) Concerned church officials decided the letter would upset Herbert if he read it, so they wisely never let him see it. Instead, they put Herbert Armstrong on the phone to Ernest Martin. Armstrong asked Martin to please reconsider and come back. Martin declined, saying he couldn't return without more changes than Herbert Armstrong would be willing to consider.

In late February, Garner Ted Armstrong called a huge meeting at Big Sandy for all ministers in the region. It took place in the "Gold Rooms" adjoining the student dining hall, and it lasted seven hours. As I ate lunch that day, I wondered why this unexpected meeting just a few yards away was taking so long.

Big Sandy School Days: 1974

Inside, Garner Ted was angrily confronting some of the region's ministers with what he had learned about their ungrateful collusion against him and his father. At one point one pastor asked Garner Ted point-blank if there was any truth to the stories that he had had affairs with Ambassador College coeds. Garner Ted, lying through his teeth, denied that *anything* of that kind had *ever* happened. That puzzled the pastor, since one coed's father was in his congregation and had told him a slightly different account of Garner Ted.[39] At the conclusion of the

---

[39] According to David Robinson (minister and department head at Big Sandy): "Rod Meredith [headquarters evangelist] told me in his office, with Raymond McNair present, that as early as 1965, he had proof that GTA had been seducing college girls, and from that time, this occurred regularly until it became much more generally known, culminating in the rather widely publicized events of 1971 and 1972. I asked him if he had gone to Mr. [Herbert] Armstrong about it, and he said that he had. 'What,' I asked, 'did his father say?' Rod said that his father would always forgive Ted when he demonstrated repentance by shedding tears and begging for forgiveness. Raymond explained that Ted was a professional repenter. He said that nobody could repent like Ted" (David Robinson, *Herbert Armstrong's Tangled Web*, 1980, p. 138).

Another account: "Around 10:30 p.m. [on Jan. 30, 1972] Garner Ted came home from a Los Angeles Lakers basketball game and was stunned to find his father, most of the headquarters leadership, and Stan Rader waiting in his living room. Upon learning the purpose of their visit, he flew into a reactionary rage during which he openly admitted he had had illicit sexual relations with some 200 women—and that was his 'conservative estimate'—during his two decades of association with his father's church. Among his consorts were literally dozens of youthful, wide-eyed coeds, plus several who became executive or ministerial wives. On this occasion Ted was given an official letter of disfellowship" (reported in *Ambassador Report*, 1977). Apparently Garner Ted, angry, asked if they wanted to hear names, which he warned might embarrass some present. There was also a story circulating at Big Sandy that Garner Ted had threatened suicide that night, and apparently had a gun in the house with which to accomplish it.

Garner Ted Armstrong's own self-assessment: "Al, let's get one thing straight! I'm a no good, fornicating, adulterating son of a bitch! ... Put me behind bars, slip my food to me, keep me in solitary confinement, but just don't take my microphone away because I must preach the message God has

Big Sandy School Days: 1974

tumultuous meeting Garner Ted suspended three pastors and the pastors' regional director before closing with prayer.

Having preempted the collusion before it came to fruition in the Big Sandy region, Garner Ted found himself in charge of fire control from now on. Events moved quickly. Dissident ministers across the country now planned to stand before their congregations simultaneously and tell the full story about headquarters' scandals. Garner Ted doused this flash fire by canceling Sabbath services across the whole country on March 2. He rushed members a letter saying, "Stay home, pray, and fast." He had already sent an urgent message to his father who was on his way to the Philippines (where he was scheduled to preach at his first international campaign). Herbert Armstrong and Stanley Rader (Herbert's ever-present lawyer) quickly turned the nose of the jet around and rushed back to Pasadena to destroy the rebellion.

When Herbert Armstrong learned of the plans to turn him into a sort of Colonel Sanders Kentucky Fried Chicken figurehead, he took a dim view of such plans and their authors. Herbert didn't intend to be put out to pasture on a modest pension just yet.

Nor was Herbert Armstrong inclined to consider any talk of loosening up on the tithes members were commanded to mail in the first thing out of their paychecks. Herbert Armstrong was not about to start compromising with the Law of God. And Herbert Armstrong sure did not see this as any reform movement. Herbert, enraged, called it what it was: it was the *work of Satan!!!*

A new church is formed

Many of the dissident ministers and segments of their congregations, having gotten nowhere with headquarters, broke off from the Worldwide Church of God, particularly on the east coast around the area of Washington, D.C. and a regional

---

given me" (said to Al Carozzo, May 16, 1973, according to Carozzo quoted in *Ambassador Report* in 1977).

director there named Kenneth Westby. A new church was organized called the Associated Churches of God. It was an association of congregations without a central authority. The new church would not break up marriages of remarried persons as did the Worldwide Church of God. In the new church tithing was no longer required. The seventh-day Sabbath was continued but the holy days were regarded as optional. When the dust settled, the immediate Worldwide Church of God losses were about 40 ministers out of 600, and 2000-plus members out of 50,000. Gone were three out of eight regional directors in the United States and two vice-presidents at headquarters. The two vice-presidents, who resigned the same day, were David Antion, director of United States church administration, and Albert Portune, treasurer.

Tall, dark-haired, Lebanese-American Antion was the pastor of the Akron, Ohio church in 1968 who baptized my father. Then in 1971-74 he was a reform-minded director of the United States ministry. Now his term had come to an abrupt end because of his sympathies for the dissident ministers' plight. (After being exiled to Hawaii for two months to think things over, Antion did however heed Herbert Armstrong's appeal to return to Pasadena to teach classes.) Antion was well-loved by the Akron, Ohio church, and as director of church administration in Pasadena he had made a serious, intelligent attempt to bring about reforms that, if they had been successful, could have made the Worldwide Church of God story very different and better. Antion was one of the elite (he was intelligent, savvy, and he was family, namely Garner Ted's brother-in-law), and yet he stood out in actually caring about, and risking himself to stand on behalf of, the church members who had been (not to mince words) horribly abused by an uncaring headquarters. Though Antion was criticized by some for returning to teach at Ambassador College after his high-profile showdown with Herbert Armstrong failed, there is a broad consensus on the part of observers that Antion was two or three cuts above many of the rest. He was one of the better apples in the barrel, so to speak.

Big Sandy School Days: 1974

~ ~ ~

Garner Ted Armstrong gave sermons at Big Sandy during this time. He announced the beginning of the new breakaway church the Sabbath after it happened. For the first time, Garner Ted talked about the months he had been out of the church back in 1972. He told of the tears he had shed, the sleepless nights, and his repentance. He quoted Paul who said, "I am not worthy to be called an apostle." He drew an analogy from that to the forgiveness he had received and his restoration to Number Two position by his father. Then Garner Ted told of the harshness in the church which must, must go. I was certainly moved by this sermon. I, with others in the congregation, was almost in tears. It was as if there was a cleansing and a catharsis.

Subsequent sermons of Garner Ted Armstrong dropped from these noble tones of grace and mercy. As it became clear that initial damage reports showed 95 percent of the church was still intact, Garner Ted regained his confidence. He likened the dissidents to cattle rustlers going after cattle rounded up by others who did the hard work (and you know what they did with cattle rustlers in the Old West). He said the Worldwide Church of God paid its ministers better than any other denomination in America. Garner Ted could not understand how, after being paid so well, these dastardly ministers could still turn disloyal against the hand that fed them. Finally, Garner Ted didn't like all the gossiping going on, particularly about him. As Garner Ted put it in one inspiring metaphor: "People just love to dive into the slop-trough of rumors and wallow around in it and love the smell." Defiant Garner Ted said that he was right at his father's side, now that he was restored, because his father wanted him there. Only God or his father could remove him now. He thundered, "If I ever leave, *don't follow me!!*"

Mr. Dart vigorously defended the Armstrong father-and-son team in his sermons. Mr. Dart was one of the inner circle of headquarters who responded to the crisis. He came down very hard on the dissidents. But at the same time he also recognized some of the problems which had led to the revolt. In one class he told us, "We have had our own Protestant Reformation in a sense." (This was a disarmingly accurate analogy.)

Mr. Dart's basic position was: there are responsible ways and irresponsible ways to go about changing an organization. The dissidents, of course, had chosen the irresponsible ways. The responsible way was to go up the line through channels. As for Garner Ted's sins, Mr. Dart stressed, "Sometimes it's best not to work for someone who's perfect. A man who has never sinned can be a harsh taskmaster." On the other hand, he pointed out, "In all of the issues raised by the detractors, one thing that has not been challenged is the personal integrity of Herbert W. Armstrong. His character is as pure as the driven snow."[40] In sermons and student forums Mr. Dart countered the dissidents' arguments as follows (from my notes):

> There have been problems, and mistakes have been made, but we're working on resolving them ... Apostasy is nothing new. The New Testament is filled with it ... The dissidents don't believe tithing is a law. One of them suggested eight percent as a good percentage for freewill giving. Perhaps they should be called the Discount Church of God ... The dissidents want democratic processes. Are we to become like the Baptists who vote on everything and have floor fights at conventions? ... They say they want to get rid of human authority and be governed by Christ alone. But whenever you have a group of people, someone must be in charge. The only religious body which practices no human authority consistently is the Religious Society of Friends ... Not all dissidents were operating from wrong motives. But they are in with some who are. Not all dissidents were in it for the same reasons. At first, some wanted to see things changed from within. The dissidents left when they realized the changes they were asking were impossible within the framework of this organization ... If these defecting ministers are sincere, let them do as Mr. Armstrong did in the 1930s and resign their salaries and go preach the gospel to the world. That is the honorable thing to do and the biblical way. They should not be trying to get members away

---

[40]   Direct quote.

Big Sandy School Days: 1974

from us ... There are some things which you cannot change and continue to be what you are. Can you imagine the Church of God without the holy days? Can you imagine it? ...

Students question their instructors

Some of my close friends became dissidents. I talked and argued from the Bible with them, trying to turn them from the error of their ways. I was dismayed at the spreading cynicism, criticism, and departure from a focus on the commission to preach the gospel (which was being done through the Work). One day, about twenty students who had attended an unapproved meeting off campus held by an ex-minister were fired from their student jobs by Dean of Students Ronald Kelly. It was explained that the college would not use tithes sent in by poor members and widows to subsidize ungrateful students who were giving support and money to greedy dissidents bent on destroying the church. (This was the interpretation placed upon attending a single meeting to hear both sides of the story.)

Somehow, Howard Clark (Big Sandy's resident faculty gadfly) survived. He was on sabbatical this year. This meant he was not teaching classes. He was ill the day of Garner Ted's showdown in the Gold Rooms and hence missed the action there. But his home out in the woods seemed like a magnet for student ferment. I noticed friend after friend innocently believing in the church go out to meetings at Clark's house. They they would return as different persons. With distressing frequency, they often packed their bags soon after and left college. I never went to Clark's place myself. If I had, maybe I, too, would have left, and the story of this book would be different. It did not take an overabundance of perceptive ability to see that Howard Clark's house was a roaring hotbed of student dissidence. But Clark denied he was stirring up trouble. He was, he said, just encouraging students to think for themselves. (Surely no one would object to that.)

Big Sandy School Days: 1974

But what about the suspicions that controversial Howard had *something* to do with all these students leaving the church (which in some coincidental way seemed to happen right after their going out to his house)? Why no, Clark said, he was in the church and believed in the church. He denied that he ever suggested that anyone should leave the church. Of course, when Howard Clark said "church" he meant the invisible, spiritual church, not in the worldly organizational sense like the Worldwide Church of God. Clark's answers would frustrate those who were suspicious of him, but colorful Howard Clark had enough chutzpah that he managed to keep on being Howard Clark—until he got canned.

A year earlier, when I had my talk with Clark during my freshman year, he had cautioned me: "Don't put your faith in an organization." But still, he said, even with all the organization's faults, the truth was still here. But later, I was shocked to hear Clark, at lunch in the student dining hall, say in his characteristic ringing voice: "When you send money out to Pasadena ... it's *gone!*" This robust, hearty commentary on headquarters' use of widows' mites brought peals of laughter from surrounding students at Clark's sheer audacity.

There had been a belated attempt on the part of headquarters higher-ups to find a better use for Clark's misdirected abilities. Herbert Armstrong announced to the church that about a half dozen of the top church evangelists and speakers (in addition to Garner Ted Armstrong) would give public appearance campaigns in various cities. One of the prospective names announced by Herbert Armstrong, surprisingly, was Howard Clark. At the fall Feast of Tabernacles in Penticton, British Columbia, in 1973, Herbert Armstrong introduced Howard Clark to the assembled multitude as the next evangelist in the church. But the campaigns, or at least Howard Clark's role in them, never came to pass. There was no explanation. What happened is simply nothing happened.

Maybe it was just as well. Clark explained to me in later years that by this time he had come to realize he couldn't in good

Big Sandy School Days: 1974

conscience promote the outfit any more. Several other faculty members besides Clark quietly served out the academic year resolving not to return.[41]

Naturally, headquarters forbade members from attending the dissident meetings on threat of disfellowshipment. This was, of course, for the members' own good. Church officials pointed out that at dissident meetings there were criticisms. When members learned, for example, the extent of the luxurious living of headquarters brass paid for by their hard-earned offerings, this tended to produce in members what church leaders called "bad attitudes." (This was, of course, bad.) Furthermore, this kind of talk resulted in a lack of unity among God's people. (This was also bad.) Therefore, the church applied the obvious solution. No members were to attend dissident meetings. In this way, members would not hear the troubling information, and unity would be preserved. (That was good.)

I write a paper proving Herbert Armstrong's authority

I know this will sound unbelievable, but some of the dissident students were even going so far as to say there was no need for a headquarters or central earthly authority for Christians. I wrote a paper (now lost) for the benefit of a couple of my deluded, unfortunate friends. My paper said that in the early church James (the brother of Jesus) was clearly the leader at headquarters, running the show whenever key decisions were made. I had not heard a lot said about James before, so for me this was original research.

My paper's conclusion was that James was in charge of the church in New Testament times. Therefore Herbert Armstrong was in charge today. For some reason my dissident friends found

---

[41] As later told to me by Clark, the end for him happened this way. Dart had a paycheck made out to Howard Clark in front of him and asked Clark, "Well, are you with us?" When Clark did not give the right answer, Dart tossed Clark's check into a wastebasket, indicating Clark was fired.

my paper unconvincing, as clear as this logic was to me. I was told a few days later that my paper had been a featured topic at Howard Clark's house at one of his Bible studies with dissident students. They had gone over it and the various scriptures I had quoted, and Clark had refuted it. I took it as sort of a backhanded compliment when I was told that Clark said of me on that occasion, "He may be misguided, but at least he's studying the Bible for himself. That's more than most of them are doing."

I stayed with the church. I was learning too much of substance about the Bible from the classes and sermons even to consider leaving. I felt such a bond of loyalty to Herbert Armstrong. His monthly letters radiated love and sincerity from the heart. He had a vision to carry Christ's gospel to the suffering, lost world just as he had had the vision to build the Ambassador Colleges. If it had not been for Herbert Armstrong, where would we all be? I shuddered to think about it. Ambassador College would not even exist. The Work would not be getting done. And I would not have been called to a knowledge of the truth. I would be out in the world not knowing the purpose or meaning of life, without direction. I owed so much to Herbert Armstrong. How could anyone turn on one who had done so much for us?

First visit to headquarters: seeing where God lived; washing feet; and yo-yos

During the spring break of 1974 I was one of five students who combined to take a trip to Pasadena. My four fellow students were Guy Swenson, Tom Adams, Dennis Houglum, and Tim O'Connor. All were valued friends and remained so throughout my college years. All were pure-hearted, examples of the church's best. Since I was pure-hearted myself, that made all five of us pure-hearted. The trip, my first through the southwestern states, was like a dream. I loved the miles and miles of cactus, the bright reds and purples of desert colors, and the occasional roadrunner we would see scampering away into the distance. It took us twenty-four hours to drive straight through.

Big Sandy School Days: 1974

We arrived late at night in Pasadena. The campus was quiet and peaceful. It was my first sight of headquarters in person. As I gazed in awe at everything, I saw the impressive new Auditorium looming seven stories tall. The Auditorium, one of the most beautiful buildings in southern California, had been Herbert Armstrong's dream for years. The Auditorium had high columns rising out of an artificial pool and bridged walkways. It seated 1250 and was acoustically perfect. The finest materials and furnishings for it came from all over the world.

Herbert Armstrong refrained from calling his dream building a Temple (that would be sacrilegious), but the analogy was clear in the minds of church members. Herbert Armstrong called it, instead, a "House for God" or "God's House." (These terms soon dropped out of active use, but they were the standard vocabulary at the time.) Members (including me) contributed millions over and above regular tithes and offerings to a Building Fund to make God's House possible. Now I saw what I had helped build. It was almost complete. It was supposed to have been finished by Passover, but the final touches were still being done. The Vienna Symphony Orchestra, conducted by Carlo Maria Giulini, had been flown in at a bargain cost of $250,000 to formally open the Auditorium. This was going to happen while we were right here in Pasadena.

I saw the solemn words engraved on the inside wall of the Auditorium foyer: "Dedicated to the honor and glory of the Great God." I felt both proud and humbled to be part of this church as I read these simple words. Just a year earlier I had come close to losing my faith altogether. But through the grace of God my eyes had been opened to see glimpses of heavenly glory, and I had been spared the awful alternative of not knowing my purpose in life.

There were to be three consecutive opening nights for the Auditorium—April 7, 8, and 9. No tickets were sold. Admission was by invitation and all seats had long since been reserved. Nevertheless, I resolved to try to find a seat for one of the opening nights. Each night there was a waiting list of people who would be admitted at the last minute to take the seats of no-shows. I didn't make it the first night, but on the second night I was admitted. I couldn't believe the luxury—the huge chandelier in the foyer, the thick carpeting, the plush seats, the tuxedoed dignitaries. I was ushered to an excellent seat in the middle near the front and heard a spectacular orchestra.

The opening of God's House coincided with a new American fad called "streaking." When people "streaked," they would run stark naked through public places just for the shock value. Rumors flew that there would be streakers on the Auditorium's opening night. There were. I didn't see them, but the news spread fast. A man and a woman had come running through the campus with no clothes on. Security personnel and volunteering students gave chase. The man was caught in a dramatic flying tackle in a flower bed. The woman was also apprehended, I hope more gently. As they gave her something with which to cover up, however, the woman had a complaint. She complained that the Ambassador College males kept looking at her.

None of this, of course, affected what went on inside the Auditorium. The beautiful concert wasn't disrupted. I felt very proud to be part of the Worldwide Church of God. I felt grateful for the immediate friends I had in every city. It was like a worldwide, close-knit family. At Big Sandy I had developed the best friends in my life. Together we shared the excitement of learning truths of the Bible every day. I felt like I was under grace.

Just before the concerts there was the Passover service—my first time as a participant (only baptized members could participate)—with bread, wine, and footwashing. We heard Herbert Armstrong preach twice during our week there. Herbert Armstrong's message on the plan of God inspired me with its beauty and the prospects of the glory of the ages to come. He made reference to the dissidents, of course. He quoted 1 John 2:19: "They went out from us, but they were not of us; for if they had been of us, they would have continued with us." Herbert Armstrong was as proud as a peacock over the Auditorium. As

Big Sandy School Days: 1974

was to be expected, some, naturally, had criticized the lavishness and cost of the Auditorium. The church said the bill for the Auditorium was $12 million. Dissidents said the true tab, when everything was added up, came out closer to $24 million. Herbert Armstrong said he would tell us who was the true author of this criticism. To no one's surprise, the culprit was: "Satan!—because Satan hates beauty!" But beauty was, after all, the mind of God. Naturally, Satan would only stir up criticism when our pastor general Herbert Armstrong imitated God's love of beauty and luxury. Misuse of funds? Those funds had been donated and earmarked for the Auditorium. If those funds had *not* been spent on the Auditorium, *that* would be misuse of funds.

We stayed in bunks in an unused attic of one of the men's residences. I made new friends, talked back to the parakeet in the student center which greeted everyone with, "Hello! Hello!," ate the tasty food served to students, visited the library, and compared notes with Pasadena students on some of their interesting courses.

I also met a friendly, slightly-built oriental man named Eddie Koo. Eddie Koo told me that he personally had brought the yo-yo to the United States from the Philippines after World War II and that he used to be a famous yo-yo champion. Now Eddie Koo was Herbert Armstrong's personal barber. (So far as I could determine, his expertise in yo-yos and his barbering for Herbert Armstrong was simply coincidental.) Likeable Eddie Koo told me what it was like to be in the church in the late 1940s and early 1950s and see the campus grow. His first Feast of Tabernacles was a memorable experience for him. "I kept asking myself," he said, "how can it be that God's True Church would have only eighty-seven people in it in the whole world?" That was an interesting question.

Finally it was time to return to Big Sandy. Again we drove straight through in twenty-four hours. I had been to headquarters—on the occasion of the opening of the dream Auditorium, no less. I had heard the world famous Vienna

Symphony Orchestra. I had seen the glory of the Work for myself.

I felt unbelievably sad for those students who had turned dissident and had left college. Most likely, they would never experience the wonder of the Work or know the almost incommunicable feelings I had.

Big Sandy summer days

After the eventful spring term of 1974, things quieted down over the summer. I stayed on campus during the summer working the eight-hour night shift at the switchboard. In the mornings I took some classes during which I often had trouble staying awake. I also took flying lessons. Fortunately, I did not have trouble staying awake during my flying lessons.

I didn't have much money, but I spent what I didn't have on flying. I flew a Cessna 150 two-seater, one of the aircraft owned by the church. My flight instructor was tall Martin Regtien, a Dutch student who had transferred from the Bricket Wood campus of Ambassador College in England to Big Sandy. Regtien was a thoroughly competent flight instructor. But he also had a flair for unexpectedly showing off stunt tricks that would put your stomach in your throat, while he had a wicked grin and enjoyed the adrenalin rush. Fortunately he was a trained acrobatic pilot and was never unsafe. It only seemed that way while I was trying to keep my lunch down. I ran out of funds before getting my license (I didn't become a pilot until much later in Oregon), but I soloed many times. I loved it. Flying alone, high above the Texas landscape, the aircraft doing what I wanted it to do, I felt exhilarated. Somehow, God seemed closer. Sometimes I wished I could stay high in the air, free as a bird, forever, and never come back down to earth.

~ ~ ~

Big Sandy School Days: 1974

One summer class I particularly remember was American history. It was taught by one of my favorite instructors: dedicated, always-interesting Mark Kaplan. Kaplan invited a fellow student, Perry Hoag, to give several guest lectures. Muscular Perry Hoag was a combination of many gifts. He was a former "Mr. Alaska" (as in weight lifting and body building). He was also a walking refutation of the idea that weight lifters have no brains. Hoag had a vocabulary no one could match, neither students nor faculty. He always used his flair for polysyllabic tongue-twisters humorously and would have people rolling in the aisles, so to speak, with his creative use of big words. Everyone liked talented, good-natured Hoag.

Hoag had driven all the way from Alaska to Big Sandy the previous fall on a huge, dream motorcycle. (I don't remember what kind it was.) Unfortunately, Hoag's machine was stolen his first night on campus. (The theft was never solved.) Hoag lived in the same dorm as I, and I got to know him well. Once we visited a hellfire and brimstone revival meeting in nearby Tyler. Afterward, Hoag told me that he barely restrained himself from getting up during the open "testimony" portion of the service. In past times, he said, he was capable of putting on quite a show. I believed him.

Hoag filled me in on his background. He came to Big Sandy from the University of Alaska. He had been active in the campaign of Minnesota senator Eugene McCarthy, the peace candidate who had challenged the standing president, Lyndon Johnson, for the Democratic nomination for President in 1968. Filled with idealism, Hoag had campaigned heavily for McCarthy, only to be soundly disillusioned when McCarthy lost. At that point he decided the system was rigged and gave up on trying to change it. Hoag came to Big Sandy with the dream of a better world to come. In his lectures on American history, Hoag traced the flow of the ideas of John Locke on the American Revolution.

Much later, I would look back on those lectures and see the incongruity between the ideas which went into the American

Revolution and the model of "benevolent dictatorship" which the church practiced today on its own membership and could hardly bear to wait to administer to the whole world tomorrow. (As Herbert Armstrong always put it, it would be necessary to "force people to be happy.")

It is true that, on rare occasions, certain Benevolent Dictators-to-be among the church hierarchy fell a trifle short of the ideal of Total Benevolence. But the hapless members were placated with the promise: "If you learn obedience now, in *this* life, and break that 'independent' spirit, *you too* will get to be a Benevolent Dictator over whole cities of people *in the millennium!*"

(For the benefit of the unenlightened, I will explain a trivial point. The benevolent dictatorship of God's government, as the imitation was attempted on earth, is easily distinguishable from police state human dictatorships. The difference is that the *benevolent* dictatorship rules in the people's best interests, for their own best good—never for self-enrichment or private gain. This was the obvious difference between God's headquarters government at Pasadena and, say, corrupt Third World dictatorships.)

~ ~ ~

I also got to know crusty Dr. Lynn Torrance (1918-2004). He was the college registrar. Torrance was an ex-prisoner of war of the Japanese in World War II—a survivor of the famous Bataan Death March of 1942. (He told me the key to survival under enemy occupation: "Never draw attention to yourself.")

Thankfully, those days were behind him. Now, Dr. Torrance taught freshman English Composition classes, ran the Registrar's and Admissions offices, and helped students plant gardens. Torrance had a wry sense of humor. He was known for favorite sayings, always said in a spirit of affection, such as, "Let's use our heads for something more than hat racks." And, "Students will go as high as you kick them."

Big Sandy School Days: 1974

~ ~ ~

One final person of note taking courses at Big Sandy with whom I became acquainted that summer was athletic trainer Harry Sneider from Pasadena. Sneider was one of the most courteous, decent persons I met in the church. He was on the physical education faculty at Pasadena and trained Olympic athletes. He told me about the job he'd been assigned of taking care of Bobby Fischer, the world chess champion. After winning the world championship at Reykjavik, Iceland, in 1972, the brilliant, eccentric Fischer had gone to church headquarters at Pasadena to learn more about the truths of eternal life. (He gave a good portion of his $156,000 Reykjavik winnings to Herbert Armstrong.) Herbert Armstrong had asked Harry Sneider and his wife to host Fischer, see that he was accommodated and be someone Fischer could talk to. A chess aficionado myself, I was highly intrigued by Fischer's interest in the church. Some chess authorities considered Fischer in his prime the most brilliant chess player that had ever existed, alive or dead. In one of the mysteries of the chess world, Fischer lost interest in chess and gave it up. Later, he lost interest in Herbert Armstrong's path to eternal life and gave that up too.

"Double or nothing?": showdown at Big Sandy
with student equivalent of Stanley Rader

Late that summer at Big Sandy I had my one and only experience with gambling. But first I have to introduce the key personality: Tim Sobitz, Jr., fellow Akron, Ohio cohort, sharp dresser extraordinaire, and frequent short-term Corvette owner.

Tim Sobitz, Jr. was the remaining half, besides me, of the Akron, Ohio contingent of our entering freshman class. (A third Akron member of our freshman class, Sharon Catron, fell in love and married a graduating senior at the end of her first year.) I knew Sobitz well during our last years in high school.

Big Sandy School Days: 1974

Sobitz had gotten into Ambassador College through characteristic chutzpah. He had applied the same time as I, but unlike me, he had been turned down. Not letting this minor detail deter him, he simply flew to Big Sandy (using luggage borrowed from me), talked to Dr. Torrance, and persuaded Torrance to let him in.

Sobitz loved fast cars, sharp dressing, and golf. (A picture of him playing golf with Garner Ted Armstrong graced his desk at Big Sandy.) Sobitz's student job his freshman year was painting cars in the Transportation Department where I also worked. (Sobitz's father, Tim, Sr., a church member, ran a successful auto body refinishing business in Akron. The Sobitz family lived in the former home of their friend Art Arfons, a world-famous racer who at various times in the 1960s and 1970s held the world's land speed record.) But Sobitz didn't stick around long at the Transportation Department. With a gift for finding the plush jobs, he soon moved to Purchasing, and then to the Festival Department.

Somehow Sobitz and I started playing poker one evening late in the summer of 1974. It wasn't long before Sobitz innocently suggested we play for a dollar. Sure, I said, why not. Sobitz won. I started to reach for a dollar to pay up. Sobitz said, "Let's go double or nothing." I thought, well, I'll win the dollar back, what have I got to lose? Sobitz won. "Double or nothing?" he asked. He won again. Another double or nothing and now I owed him $8. I decided to quit at that point and pay out $8 but Sobitz just smiled and persisted with, "Double or nothing? Come on, Doudna, double or nothing?" I succumbed, hoping to return to zero. Another showdown of the cards—and I lost again.

Now I owed him $16. Each time I was vowing that if I won I'd quit when I broke even. At $16, this was more than I really cared to lose. (That point had been passed at about the $2 point.) Again, Sobitz persisted in double or nothing, and I lost again! Now I owed him $32!

Being true to my word, this was a debt I would pay, though it was now distinctly more than I had in my pocket. Smiling Sobitz

Big Sandy School Days: 1974

was relaxed and happy, while I was beginning to turn various shades of green.

Sobitz, meanwhile, was as cool and calm as ever. Gently he pressed to go double or nothing again. I knew Sobitz had already won over $150 playing golf from another classmate—who paid. Sobitz was also known to win money at pool. In appearance and style, he resembled a much younger version of church attorney Stanley R. Rader, now that I think about it.

There was no way I was going to risk a $64 debt in poker. I was not enamored with helping to finance Sobitz's Corvettes in this manner. I proposed we switch to chess. Unfortunately, he knew better than to do that and refused, even when I offered a substantial handicap. It was an impasse.

Then I said, "Well, let's compromise. You won't play chess and I won't play poker. Let's go double or nothing on Monopoly." He persisted in pressing for another poker hand, but (my senses at last having returned) I refused to give in. If he didn't agree to Monopoly, the game was over (and I'd pay him the $32). He finally agreed. Meanwhile, I vowed inside that if I won this one I'd never gamble again in a thousand years. If I lost, I'd pay the $64 and also never gamble again. I didn't tell Sobitz, but I knew what I was doing at Monopoly. He bit, and we got out the Monopoly game. With exceedingly heightened concentration and $64 at stake, I wasted no time in quickly winning without any problem. I didn't owe Sobitz a thing. I didn't gamble anymore, either.

There are several lessons that might be gleaned from this little episode. But to readers with ears to hear, I commend two morals in particular from this harrowing experience.

First, be careful of gambling with smiling, well-dressed Stanley Rader look-alikes, particularly if you hear the words: "Double or nothing?"

And second, the best winning strategy in some games is to not start playing in the first place.

Big Sandy School Days: 1974

Facing the future with Big Sandy in my eyes

Throughout the second semester of my sophomore year I had planned not to return to college the next fall. This was not because of any lessening of my heart in the church. A significant factor was a shortage of money. However, even more fundamentally I didn't see what a third and fourth year in college at Big Sandy would do for me or what purpose there was in staying. It was *comfortable* being on campus at Big Sandy. But I asked myself what purpose there was beyond being comfortable. The college was not accredited and its degree was of little value in the outside world. I had devoted a lot of energy learning as much Bible knowledge from the available classes and faculty instructors as possible during my sophomore year—and so I felt I had gotten what I came for.

During the summer, some of the Worldwide Church of God pastors had come to the campus for some kind of refresher training. One was young, dedicated George Kackos, a pastor from Wisconsin Dells, Wisconsin. He was staying in my dorm. One night he stayed up late into the night talking with several of us, particularly me. He was intrigued by my studies on various topics of the Bible. When I told him I was leaving Big Sandy, he invited me to locate in his church area. He wanted to "build a church area," as he put it, and he felt that my energy and studies would be an asset. I decided I would do so.

Leaving Big Sandy after two years

As the summer closed I left for Akron where I visited my folks and bought a car. I went to the Feast at Lake of the Ozarks, Missouri, and returned briefly to Big Sandy for more flight instruction. Then I traveled to Pasadena. I went to Pasadena with the idea of contributing my Bible research ability to headquarters. (This is just what headquarters was holding their breath waiting for.)

Big Sandy School Days: 1974

I took the direct approach. I asked two leading figures at Pasadena—Herman Hoeh and Dr. Charles Dorothy—if I could be employed doing research. As previously noted, Dr. Hoeh, whom I had gotten to know from his visits to Big Sandy, for many years had been the leading doctrinal authority in the church next to Herbert Armstrong. Dr. Hoeh was sympathetic to me. But he explained with a hint of embarrassment that he had no job and no office of his own, let alone a budget. He was not, therefore, in a position to offer me a job. However, he took me around with him for a day visiting various friends of his.

Dr. Hoeh seemed to like me enough that I got the impression it might have been different if he had had funds in his control. It mystified me how someone this important in the church would have no job or office. I was too polite to ask for details on how this odd circumstance had come to pass.

Dr. Dorothy, one of the most well-loved and intelligent teachers and researchers in the church, headed the Theological Research Project and didn't know me from Adam. But Dr. Dorothy was courteous and polite to this ex-Big Sandy sophomore (me) who showed up from out of nowhere. I earnestly tried to tell him about the great research breakthroughs I and my friend Russ Gmirkin were making in our studies, and that Dr. Torrance and Dr. Hoeh liked my work. I asked if there was any minimum-wage employment doing research in Pasadena. Dr. Dorothy was kind and considerate. But he compassionately explained that he had all the employees he needed and nothing in his budget for what I had in mind. He said there might be a possibility of a small payment from his budget for individual research articles from time to time, but no job was available.

It was frustrating. What I wanted more than anything else on earth was somehow to have room and board so I could study and research eighty hours a week. I cared not at all about money, status, or position. It was the sheer love of discovery, the thrill of seeing hidden patterns for the first time, of hunting up hidden treasures in the pages of scripture and on library shelves, of contemplation of timeless mysteries, of finding further dazzling, glorious truths of God!—which motivated me for its own sake. For room and board—for $100 a week—and an occasional pat on the head, Russ Gmirkin and I would have cranked out more research than any students had ever done since Dr. Hoeh himself had arrived on campus in 1947. Never would the headquarters dollar have bought more theological bang for the buck. However, there wasn't $100 a week available in anyone's budget. The $24 million Auditorium had taken all the spare change. Headquarters was just too strapped for cash.

At Big Sandy, Dr. Torrance had been sympathetic to me when he learned of my heart's desire. Of course he had no place in his registrar's budget for hiring creative biblical research on the side. Besides, he wasn't even a minister. Biblical research was supposed to be the task of the ministers who were more qualified to study into such things. Dr. Torrance offered to be a referral to help bring about this kind of situation for me. But there were no funds at Big Sandy for this kind of research. I had asked deputy chancellor Mr. Dart at Big Sandy. He had replied that there was "nothing in the budget." When I didn't get anywhere at Pasadena either, I thought, "Well, I tried. I guess it's the will of God that I not be at Pasadena." I said good-by to my Pasadena friend Russ Gmirkin and took off for Wisconsin.

Return to Big Sandy by way of Madison, Cedar Rapids, and Memphis

From Pasadena, I drove across the country to Wisconsin Dells, Wisconsin. A high point along the way was stopping in Salt Lake City to visit the centerpiece of another unusual American religious phenomenon: the Mormon Temple. I remember thinking, "What a combination of fine people and strange ideas."

In Wisconsin, George Kackos, Worldwide Church of God pastor, and his wife Merry welcomed me to their area and were very hospitable. I set about seeking employment in nearby Madison. Kackos was a hard-working pastor filled with ideas

Big Sandy School Days: 1974

and energy. He talked to me about my assisting him in his duties of visiting members and holding outlying Bible studies for isolated brethren. The first Sabbath I accompanied Kackos to church since I was his guest. I was startled when members hurried to hold doors for me and carry my briefcase—just because I was with the minister! Fortunately, I got to know some of the normal people right away and escaped that kind of unfamiliar limelight.

Unfortunately I didn't find work in Madison, Wisconsin. Not finding work was an eye-opener. I was astonished to learn that my two years at Big Sandy taking unaccredited Bible courses for some strange reason just hadn't qualified me for much in the job market.

I then went to Cedar Rapids, Iowa. For four days I learned the art of cleaning windows from the legendary Russ Rigdon, a church member there. Rigdon, who started from nothing himself, helped hundreds of church members find high-paying, honest employment, self-esteem, and work that did not conflict with the Sabbath or holy days. I first learned of Russ Rigdon through my friend and fellow student Tim O'Connor. O'Connor, also from Iowa, had built a profitable sideline window washing route around Big Sandy. He spoke highly of Rigdon and had urged me to contact him.

I called Rigdon from Madison. I was hungry and motivated. He and his wife Mary took me in and opened up their home in hospitality to me. Rigdon taught me his streamlined, unbeatable "system." He showed me how to clean a window spotlessly with one smooth, swirling motion of the squeegee in seconds. Then he taught me how to use an extension pole to clean the higher windows. My first day he had me clean the same sliding glass door and other windows at his home over and over for several hours. After I passed this crash course, he took me with him to do real customers. He showed me how to obtain new customers, how to keep existing ones happy, and how to set up a schedule. He told me every tip of the trade that would help me. I sent him an unsolicited $500 out of the blue a couple of years later as a

Big Sandy School Days: 1974

token of gratitude, but it cannot repay what it meant to me to learn how to make money instantly anywhere on earth.

From Cedar Rapids I drove to Memphis, Tennessee, intent on starting a business and making my fortune. I didn't know a soul in Memphis. I just looked at a map, picked it out, and drove into town. (A return to Madison was not an option. Besides my not being enthused about working outdoors in the winters there, more importantly there was already a Rigdon-trained self-employed church member cleaning windows there. Rigdon had asked me to go to a city where I wouldn't be competing with anyone in the church already in business.) In four days in Memphis I established and started twenty-one window cleaning customers among retail stores. In retrospect that was a respectable start. But having nothing against which to compare it, I decided it wasn't happening fast enough, so I drove out of town.

I returned to the Big Sandy area in November 1974 and found employment in nearby Longview, Texas, about twenty miles east of Big Sandy, delivering two rural newspaper routes. I lived in a rented room in Longview. In January 1975 I enrolled again as a student at Big Sandy for one class—a men's third year speech class under Dean Blackwell. I commuted to the campus for this class two days a week and attended Friday night Bible studies and Sabbath services on campus. I was back at Big Sandy again.

PART TWO

CREATIVITY

CHAPTER 6

HOW I TRIED TO PROVE THE UNITED STATES IS EPHRAIM, NOT MANASSEH

One of the basic doctrines of Worldwide Church of God founder Herbert Armstrong was "British-Israelism," also known as "Anglo-Israelism." This theory says the Anglo-Saxon peoples of the United States and British Commonwealth are descendants of the Lost Ten Tribes of Israel, which were carried into captivity by the Assyrians in 732 and 721 BC.

According to this remarkable theory, the northern tribes of Israel lost their language, adopted different customs, and migrated into Europe where they settled in northwest Europe, Scandinavia, and the British Isles. The United States and the British Commonwealth are identified as the descendants of Joseph's two sons, Ephraim and Manasseh, who were to become a "nation and a company of nations" (Gen 48:19). The tribe of Dan, in accord with prophecy and scriptural precedent (Josh 19:47; Judges 18:11-12; 18:29), is believed to have left its name's "mark" in various areas of its tribal peregrinations, i.e. the Danube River, the Don River, Denmark, and so on. Early settlers of Ireland called the "Tuatha de Danaan" are also identified as of the seafaring tribe of Dan (Judges 5:17). A sheet used internally in Ambassador College classes gave suggested, less certain identities for the ancestries of other European nations as follows: Belgium is the tribe of Asher; Finland is Issachar; France is Reuben; Iceland and Norway are Benjamin; the

Netherlands is Zebulon; Sweden is Naphtali; and Switzerland is Gad.

Jeremiah, the prophet, is believed to have transported a Tea-Tephi, daughter of king Zedekiah, the last king of Judah, to Ireland to marry into the line of a Prince Herremon, thus continuing Israel's royal lineage. This royal line then continued unbroken through transfers to Scotland and finally England, where it continues down to the present day with Queen Elizabeth and Prince Charles. In this way biblical promises to David that his kingly line would never cease to reign on earth are believed fulfilled.

~ ~ ~

Herbert Armstrong wrote a book explaining the Anglo-Israel theory, which came to be titled *The United States and Britain in Prophecy*. It is probably the most persuasive presentation of Anglo-Israelism in existence. It certainly spread the idea more widely than any other means. The 1986 edition contained the impressive statistic that over 5,025,000 copies of this book had been distributed in the English language since 1942, not counting editions in Dutch, French, German, Norwegian, and Spanish. I would say the Anglo-Israel belief and Herbert Armstrong's book on the topic was instrumental in more conversions to the Worldwide Church of God than any other single doctrine or piece of literature.

In the earliest versions of the book Armstrong claimed the knowledge of modern Israel's prophetic identity was specially and divinely revealed to him as the key to understanding end-time prophecy, not learned from any man. Even the 1986 edition retained statements such as "The Lost Master Key Has Been Found" (title of the first chapter), and "The prophecies come alive once their doors are opened by this now discovered master key!" (pp. 3-4). In fact, the majority of Herbert Armstrong's book was copied, without footnote or acknowledgement, in many passages word for word, from an earlier book entitled *Judah's*

United States/ Ephraim

Sceptre and Joseph's Birthright, written by Joseph H. Allen (first edition 1902).

Surprisingly, this earlier literary source for Herbert Armstrong's book was sold openly at the Ambassador College student bookstore at Big Sandy when I was there, and was purchased and read by many students. Successive revisions of Herbert Armstrong's book published by the Worldwide Church of God never included this bibliographic reference, nor, incidentally, any information on how readers could check or even find another set of sources relied upon for the theory, the annals of ancient Ireland.

A brief word of explanation for the uninitiated

The appeal of Anglo-Israelism is fundamentally this: the prophetic portions of the Bible (which is the inerrant Word of God) are believed to be written for the end-time, which, as is plain to see, is now. Given the impeccable logic of this starting point, it is considered inconceivable that the United States—so dominant in the world today—would not play some central role in biblical prophetic texts dealing with the end-time.

Now an external observer might suggest that seeing one's own country as "Israel" is not the only conceivable option here. It is at least theoretically conceivable (the external observer might suggest) that one could go a different logical direction, and look at parallels between the United States of today and biblical imagery associated with one or another of the mighty gentile powers of old. Say for example Babylon, which turns up in the book of Revelation as a mighty end-time power who rules the world and its seas, and the reaction to whose downfall at the end sounds like that video of Osama Bin Laden laughing about the fall of the Trade Towers in New York City.

Critical scholars will tell you that the overheated images of Revelation and the allusion at Rev 18:20 to the saints laughing uproariously at the mighty city Babylon and its civilians within it going up in smoke is simply *first century AD Christians* absolutely gleeful about Rome burning to the ground—nothing at all to do with *today*. Therefore, these critical scholars try in vain to tell the fundamentalists of today, one can't just go around saying that "Babylon" of Revelation is this or that power in the world *today*, far removed in time and space from those texts' original context. (But then, "Babylon" already was being used as a cipher for some contemporary power at the time of the book of Revelation—so updating of ancient prophecies to one's current last days is nothing new. If it was OK to reuse "Babylon" for an end-time then, what's wrong with a few more reuses of "Babylon" in later end-times?—the fundamentalist might respond to the critical scholars.)

Of course not all ancient gentile superpowers were bad. There was an occasional good one, like Cyrus's Persia. One could have America be a good gentile superpower, if that is more to taste.

But Herbert Armstrong did not go in any of these directions, of seeing the world's superpower at the end time as reflected in biblical prophecies of end-time superpowers. Herbert Armstrong saw America not as ancient Assyria or Babylon or Persia allegorically replicated on the world stage today, but instead as ... Israel, and not as a metaphor but by genetic descent.

The argument that the United States is Israel basically consists of the following four points. First, some of the florid prophecies of physical blessings and greatness to Abraham's descendants, if the wording is taken completely literally, it is argued, were not completely fulfilled by Israel anciently. Second, the house of Israel and the house of Judah were separate and never reunited. Third, prophecies concerning the house of Israel in the end-time show them to be in captivity, which means they must exist in our time as an identifiable people (and distinct from the Jews). And fourth (you already heard this once, but it won't hurt you to hear it again), the greatest nation on earth in our time would not be ignored in Bible prophecy.

Within this ideological template, the rest is more or less filling in the blanks. For good measure one will want to rig up a bit of

United States/Ephraim

ancient history to undergird it, stir thirty minutes, and cook until done.

Those were the days

> "For over thirty-five years, on the WORLD TOMORROW program, and in the PLAIN TRUTH magazine, I have been shouting God's prophecies to our people—that we are going to have such total DROUGHT and disease epidemics that it will take one third of our people! And, unless our people as a nation wake up and REPENT of these SINS, we shall be INVADED, and once more TAKEN CAPTIVE AS SLAVES. You may scoff. You may ignore. But NOT FOR LONG! In the near future it will STRIKE! *You won't scoff then!*"
> --Herbert Armstrong, 1971 (*Which Day is the Christian Sabbath?*)

Herbert Armstrong began his ministry in the early 1930s in the years leading up to American involvement in World War II. Herbert Armstrong broadcast a prophetic picture that saw a Mussolini-led revived Holy Roman Empire conquering Britain and America, the modern house of Israel. Israel (Britain and America) would be reduced to national captivity as punishment for its sins. In this, Herbert Armstrong departed from traditional Anglo-Israel or British-Israel teaching. Most Anglo-Israelites modestly saw the British Empire as the Kingdom of God on earth and destined for increased prosperity.

According to articles in early issues of *The Plain Truth*, Mussolini, not Hitler, was to be the world-ruling Beast. This was because Mussolini was Italian or Roman. The Axis powers were portrayed as the final revival of the Holy Roman Empire which was to be the end-time Beast Power. Hitler would become subordinated to Mussolini, who would take over Axis leadership. The Catholic Church would become allied with the Axis powers. The forces of Mussolini and the Pope would converge on Jerusalem, there meeting eastern armies in battle, which would be interrupted by the return of Christ. Detailed predictions were made for the outcome of specific battles and military strategies, which, however, all failed to materialize. A date for the return of Christ was set for 1936, 2520 years after 585 BC. (Armstrong believed the "times of the Gentiles" had begun with the fall of Jerusalem in 585 BC.)

Christ didn't show up at the appointed time. When Mussolini was killed by Italian partisans, Herbert Armstrong said Hitler would be the prophesied Beast instead. Hitler would be victorious in his Russian invasion. Then he would turn on Britain and America and reduce our nations to captivity.

Again, things didn't turn out as Herbert Armstrong predicted. World War II ended in victory for the Allies, instead of the predicted defeat and captivity. Hitler and Germany were in ashes, not dominating the world. But Herbert Armstrong did not give up. He did not believe his prophetic understanding had been wrong. Instead, after the Nazi defeat, Armstrong became convinced Hitler was really alive and in hiding in South America. The final beast, who "was and is not" (Rev 17:11), lived. World War II had merely set the stage for the true scenario which would be World War III.

A revived Germany would lead a reunited Europe, which would be a Catholic-endorsed final resurrection of the Holy Roman Empire. This German-led European power would carry Britain and America into national captivity. One-third of Britons and Americans would be killed in war. One-third would die of pestilence and disease. The remaining one-third of the people would be taken into captivity, deported over to Europe as slaves, and undergo a repeat of the Nazi concentration camps (Ezek 5:12). Germany might be devastated from war damage at the moment, but Germany would rise again and return to ascendancy. Hitler would return to lead the revived Nazis.

Fueling Armstrong's theory of a secretly alive Hitler (besides the absence of his body—he had been cremated) was Revelation 13:3, which says the whole world would "wonder" at his (believed) resurrection from a deadly wound to the head. (The world was under the impression Hitler died of a self-inflicted gunshot wound to the head.) The German people were identified as descendants of the ancient Assyrians. The coming captivity of the United States and Britain at the hands of the Germans would be a repeat of the ancient Assyrian conquest of the house of Israel.

This is the background to why Herbert Armstrong focused upon Germany, rather than the more common fundamentalist Christian target of that time, the Soviet Union, as the coming evil empire and mortal enemy of America.

By the time I came to Ambassador College as a student in the early 1970s, the belief that a surviving Hitler would return to become world dictator had been dropped for obvious reasons of age. But the Beast's nationality as German, heading a German-led United Europe and destined to be America's and Britain's captors, remained just as strong. West and East Germany would be reunited. The Beast would be a new German strongman. Particular attention was focused on West Germany's right-wing Franz Josef Strauss (1915-1988) of varying political fortunes as a potential candidate for world Beast.

West Germany's surprising post-war economic recovery and ascendancy were eagerly monitored. *Plain Truth* articles reported on the development of the Common Market and moves toward European unity. Herbert Armstrong frequently reminded his listening audience that he had predicted Germany's recovery to economic and political might even in the face of general post-war despair over the bombed-out nation's prospects. Now, finally, one of Herbert Armstrong's predictions was coming true.

It is true that Germany of the postwar era is a friendly ally, not an enemy, of the United States and Britain. But this was no real objection to *Plain Truth* staff writers and news analysts. They believed West Germany could "change overnight." The new, industrialized Germany was viewed as a Frankenstein monster built by the West which would bring about the West's ultimate downfall. (Franz Josef Strauss, incidentally, was invited and came to Ambassador College in Pasadena as an honored guest in 1969, with Worldwide Church of God leaders carefully attempting to conceal from Strauss the real reason for their interest, which was having him pegged as possible future world-ruling Beast!)

Lightning strikes

With this background I come to the story of my own attempt to improve the Anglo-Israel theory. According to the theory, the United States is identified as Manasseh, oldest son of Joseph. (Joseph, the favored one of Jacob's twelve sons, inherited the birthright promise which originally had been made to Abraham and passed down through his son and grandson Isaac and Jacob.) The British Commonwealth is identified as from Joseph's younger son Ephraim. Ephraim was prophesied to exceed his older brother Manasseh in greatness and to become a "company of nations" (Gen 35:11; 48:8-22).

The terminology of "Manasseh" meaning the United States, and "Ephraim" meaning the British Commonwealth, though it may sound strange to non-biblically attuned ears, was commonly used in the Worldwide Church of God. One night in the winter of '73-'74, while I was at my midnight to 3:00 a.m. student job at the night switchboard, the blinding realization suddenly struck me that the prevailing identification of the United States as Manasseh was wrong! We were not Manasseh but Ephraim! It was Britain who was Manasseh! I saw as clear as day that the church had these identifications precisely the reverse of what they ought to be.

It happened that Mr. Dart was not only the resident administrator at Big Sandy but also personally taught men's second-year speech class. (Women took a first year of speech class but then home economics after that, not public speaking.) At the time that I was struck with my brilliant idea about Ephraim, Mr. Dart had just given our class one of the most memorable speech assignments of the year. This was the "hostile audience" speech, also known as the "heckle speech."

Each of us were to choose a controversial topic for our subject. We would then attempt to persuade our audience to a different point of view than our listeners would normally hold on whatever was the topic. Two students in the class (unknown to the speaker) would be selected by drawing lots to be allowed two heckles apiece during the course of each six-minute speech. The heckles could be any questions or comments one wished to say to interrupt or contradict the speaker. (Plus, Mr. Dart reserved unlimited heckling rights for himself.)

Mr. Dart explained that a clear question from an audience normally ought to be addressed by a speaker. But if the question couldn't be heard or understood, we should simply assume the audience couldn't hear or understand it either and ignore it. Talk about live drama! Some of the funniest moments of the whole year came during these heckle speeches. I decided my topic would be to prove the United States was Ephraim instead of Manasseh.

Just to make sure I was not stepping out of bounds and being a bit *too* controversial in challenging a church doctrine in a classroom situation like this, I took the precaution of calling Mr. Dart at home the evening before my speech was scheduled. I asked if he would have any objection to my proposed topic. Mr. Dart responded with a chuckle. He said, "I think you'll have a hard time proving it, but go ahead."

Six minutes is not a long time to develop any topic. I knew in that time period I would have to cover ground quickly. The big moment arrived and I launched into my subject. I set up the issue, made one or two points quickly, and was picking up steam when a question came from the audience: "But what about Ezekiel thirty-two verse forty?" (Or whatever the verse was.) I couldn't mentally place that scriptural reference. I answered, "What about it? What does it say?," hoping to quickly find out what the point was so I could refute it or use it to further my own purposes and move on. My heckler, Guy Swenson, normally a friend outside the classroom, persisted: "Look it up for yourself!" A second heckler chimed in and demanded an answer to the same verse, too.

With valuable time and momentum slipping away, I quickly tried to find the chapter and verse ... and discovered it didn't exist! I had been thrown a chapter and verse number which didn't exist! I looked up and there was Swenson with a big grin on his face and the rest of the class enjoying the drama as I acidly pointed out I couldn't answer objections based on verses that don't exist. I returned to my sequence of argument, but my hecklers had done better than I, and before I knew it my six minutes were over.

In his evaluation, Mr. Dart pointed out I had made a double mistake. The first was asking my heckler what the verse said. This gives the floor to the heckler. A smart heckler will simply seize the opportunity to start making his own speech and the original speaker will be without an audience. Second, when I didn't get an answer when I asked what the verse said, I should have treated it like any other unintelligible question or comment, ignored it, and proceeded as before. Of course my subject was too broad for six minutes. As for my argument itself, Mr. Dart commented that Britain as Ephraim, as the leading tribe, would also lead the rest of Israel in its decline.

In spite of the above comic relief I forged ahead with my research over the following months. I wrote a lengthy, formal paper on the subject at my parents' home in Akron, Ohio, at the end of that summer in 1974.

~ ~ ~

My paper was entitled "The United States in Prophecy: The Case for Identifying the United States with Ephraim (not Manasseh)" (September 30, 1974). Lest there be any misunderstanding, I do not hold to these beliefs today. In fact in the next two chapters I intend to thoroughly dismantle the Anglo-Israel argument.

Friends have told me, however, that that particular paper was one of the most compelling papers I ever wrote, if one overlooks the slight problem that it is not true. It has produced remarks such as, "You've got *me* convinced the United States is Ephraim, and I don't even believe in this stuff!" and so on.

The argument that the United States is Ephraim, not Manasseh: how I did it

It starts with the blessing on the biblical patriarch Jacob. In Genesis 35:11, Jacob was promised his progeny would become "a nation and a company (*qahal*) of nations." In Genesis 48:19-20 Jacob blesses his two grandsons, Manasseh the older and Ephraim the younger, but Jacob pointedly gives the greater blessing to the younger Ephraim. Jacob said that although the older Manasseh would become "a great nation," he would be surpassed by his younger brother Ephraim who would become "a fullness (*melo*) of nations."

The expression "company of nations," as the King James Version rendered Gen 35:11, was interpreted by Anglo-Israelites as fulfilled in the British Commonwealth. This is the "trunk of the tree" as to why Britain is identified as Ephraim by Anglo-Israelites.

But, I pointed out, this was based on a misunderstanding. Analysis of the word *qahal*, "company," in its uses in the Hebrew Bible shows it is used of armies or assemblies and refers to a single political unit. The plural *goiim*, "nations," on the other hand, does not mean multiple *political states* (as in "British Commonwealth of nations"). Rather *goiim* means peoples or tribes or ethnic groups. I read the blessing on Ephraim as that Ephraim would become one political entity ("a company") consisting of multiple ethnic groups.

Therefore "company of nations" is a misleading rendering if "nations" is understood in the modern sense of nation-states. The expression *qehal goiim* is better rendered "company of peoples" and means a single political entity, a single state, composed of multiple *goiim*, multiple "tribes." This is what was promised to the younger Ephraim, who was to be greater than his older brother Manasseh.

United States/Ephraim

The whole key to this, as I saw it then, was in the earlier typical fulfillment of "company of nations" as the ancient house of Israel. Here I have to explain "typical fulfillment" for the benefit of any unfamiliar with this term. The notion of duality of prophecy is central to all who see biblical prophecy as written for the end-time. In this view, the biblical record has earlier, partial fulfillments of prophetic themes. Very commonly there will be a prophecy directed toward a particular ancient empire which is the target of God's wrath at the moment (according to the prophet). Depictions of disaster to befall the ancient evil ruler or power will be given in florid detail, usually accompanied by or embedded within an oracle foretelling the end of the present order of the world in a cataclysm ushering in a new age. Often these ancient empires did suffer downfalls in agreement with the biblical oracles.

(Biblical scholars and historians will tell you that many of these prophecies were written after the fact, *ex eventu*, and then attributed to earlier times, so that it only looks like fulfilled details of ancient true prophecy.)

But even when there were downfalls of ancient empires that fulfill biblical prophecies, if there is an eschatological overlay to the prophecy, that part of the oracle did not come to pass. (After all, the mere collapses of world-ruling Assyrian or Babylonian empires anciently were not actually associated with the dawning of a new everlasting age of peace, and so on.) The end of the present age continues to be still future, after all of these thousands of years.

And so the ancient fulfillments of these prophecies are understood to have been only forerunners, "types," prototypes, trial runs, or whatever word you want to give to it. They illustrate some of the themes of the prophecy (and are useful to study for this reason). But they are not the *real* fulfillment of those prophecies, which is for our time. This schematic understanding of prophecy is basic within this way of looking at the world. The earlier partial fulfillments long ago in history are "types" or

United States/Ephraim

echoes of what is to come. The true fulfillment which will happen in the latter days (that's our time) is the "antitype."

I noted that the ancient ten-tribed house of Israel, which was distinct from the southern house of Judah, was the *type* of the "company of nations" promised to Jacob. The "house of Israel" consisted of multiple distinct ethnic components, the ten tribes. And yet the whole house of Israel was often called (for example throughout much of Hosea) "Ephraim," by the name of the leading tribe. So "Ephraim" was both the leading tribe of the house of Israel and also the name which came to be used for the whole house of Israel. This was *the type*, the typical or partial fulfillment, of the "company of nations."

This was my point: the ancient house of Israel was a single political entity. It had multiple tribes or ethnic components, but it was a single political entity. It was not a "commonwealth" of multiple nation-states. It was a single state, analogous to the United States.

In my paper I noted that "United States" means in English, literally, a "company of political states," and "state" is, of course, used synonymously in English for "nation." Therefore "United States" is, by a pun, "company of nations" in its very name. Of course the fifty states in the United States are not independent, but then neither were the *goiim* or "nations" in the earlier fulfillment of "company of nations," the ancient house of Israel. This I saw as the point missed by Anglo-Israelites.

The problem was caused by semantic confusion over the meaning of *goiim* which is sometimes rendered into English as "nations" and then confused with the modern English use of "nation" as a state, which is not the sense of the Hebrew *goiim*. I tried to cut through the semantic confusion. The biblical "company of *goiim* (peoples)" was to be a single nation or political entity, not multiple nations or political entities. This was fulfilled in type by the house of Israel anciently, and, I argued, by the United States today.

The other part of Jacob's blessing of Genesis 35 was that another part of his descendants would become a single "nation" or people, *goi* (as in "*a nation* and a company of nations"). The ancient typical fulfillment of this, I argued, was the house of Judah anciently, which was considered—at least according to one biblical tradition—a single tribe (1 Kgs 11:36; 12:20-21).

So *qehal goiim* is actually misleadingly translated "company of nations." It does not mean a commonwealth of multiple states. That confuses the biblical meaning of *goiim* with the modern meaning of "nation" as "political state." The "company" is the political state foreseen for Ephraim, and it is singular—a single political state. Again, the proof of this, I argued, was in the nature of the ancient typical fulfillment, the house of Israel of old. I wrote:

> As the house of Israel was composed of equal members under one sovereign authority, so are other biblical "companies," and so is modern Ephraim—the United States of America ... Manasseh was to become a great nation, and only one modern nation is known as being "great" in *its* very name—Great Britain ... The United King*dom* and the United State*s*. A nation and a company of nations. To those of us who have strongly believed that the United States is Manasseh this requires some adjustment in thinking. The important thing to grasp is that the United States fits both the *type* and the *biblical interpretation* of "company of nations."

Arguing logically

After making this positive argument based on the meaning of the expression *qehal goiim*, I then argued that there were contradictions in the existing view as commonly held. Believers in Anglo-Israelism kept insisting Ephraim was the British Commonwealth, then often in the next breath would speak of Ephraim as if it was just one of those multiple nations, namely the United Kingdom, or even just England.

> Let us now, on the other hand, follow through to its logical conclusion the traditional line of reasoning which contends that Ephraim is the British Commonwealth. All of the nations comprising the

United States/ Ephraim

company or fullness of nations *are* Ephraim, not colonies under Ephraim's direction.

If Ephraim really has become many separate and sovereign peoples, then Ephraim = Great Britain, Ephraim = Canada, Ephraim = Australia, Ephraim = New Zealand, and Ephraim = other English settlers in British colonies worldwide.

If Ephraim really has become all of these nations, then Australia, for example, is as much Ephraim as is Great Britain. Then when Hosea and other prophets speak of "Ephraim" doing this or doing that, just who is meant—will Britain, Canada, Australia, and New Zealand simultaneously "call to Egypt" and "go to Assyria" (Hos 7:11), to cite but one of many similar scriptures?

Perhaps it seems like belaboring the subject, but it is essential to understand this matter first, as it is the trunk of the tree, and virtually 100 percent of the objections to the identification of the United States with Ephraim are sure to arise from this single point of the "company of nations" Ephraim was to become. Those who support the traditional view must deal with the inconsistency of holding that Ephraim is the British Commonwealth and then applying prophecies concerning Ephraim toward only one of that "company of nations" instead of all of them ...

The other settlements of Britain are Manassite just as French settlements are French (of Reuben) and Dutch settlements are Dutch (of Zebulon). The fact that Britain has colonies in no way proves she is a company of nations. Britain is a single nation in the same way that other Israelite nations with colonies are still single nations.

After arguing this foundation, I then argued that other features of the promise to Ephraim pointed to the United States rather than England.

Ephraim was *younger* than Manasseh. Isn't the United States younger than Britain?

Younger Ephraim was to surpass older Manasseh in *greatness.* "His younger brother [Ephraim] shall be *greater* than he [Manasseh]," said Jacob. Hasn't the younger United States now surpassed older England in greatness, in that order?

Manasseh was to be great *first*, in relative sequence. Then Ephraim was to be *greater, second.* (This is Jacob's blessing sequence, in Genesis.) Wasn't Britain great first, then the younger United States surpassed Britain in greatness?

United States/ Ephraim

Ephraim was to have greater *population* than Manasseh. Hosea 13:15 alludes to Ephraim being "fruitful among his brethren." The very name "Ephraim" itself means "doubly fruitful." Wasn't Britain's population (1970s numbers) about 60 million, against the younger United States' much larger 200 million?

When Isaiah 49:2 says, "These [Jacob] shall come from *afar*, and, lo, these come from the *north* and from the *west*, and from the land of Sinim," isn't North America an equally good, if not better, fulfillment of this "northwest" direction from the Middle East, as the British Isles?

And what about the prophecies in which Israel is pictured as returning from the "isles" (Isa 49:1; Jer 31:9-10)? Anglo-Israelites said this was the British Isles. But critics of Anglo-Israelism kept pointing out that the Hebrew for "isles" is better rendered "coasts." I argued that this perceived criticism of Anglo-Israelism actually became an argument in support of Anglo-Israelism if the United States is Ephraim.

> Which land is a land of "coasts"—a desirable "habitable spot"? It is the United States which has one of the longest usable coastlines of any nation in the world ... The same Hebrew word *yam* is translated "sea" and "west." The "isles of the sea" or "coasts of the sea" of which the prophets sometimes speak can just as easily be translated *"coasts of the west."* The United States! The critics' objection to the translation of "isles" is no objection at all—it only confirms the case for Israel's true identity.

Then I focused on Canada, the "lesser" Israelite country in North America, like a brother to the north of the United States, although (unlike the United States) it is attached to England. I noted that of all the ancient tribes of Israel, Manasseh was the only one divided geographically. I suggested it was no coincidence that of all modern Israelite nations it is Britain whose settlements are so widely separated.

Anciently the Israelites after leaving Egypt are said to have come into Transjordan with the Jordan River to their west, and

United States/ Ephraim

then crossed the Jordan to enter the Promised Land to the west. But part of Manasseh (along with the whole tribes of Gad and Reuben) chose not to cross the Jordan. The rest of Manasseh crossed to the west with the other tribes of Israel (Numbers 32). I saw a parallel. In our time part of Manasseh chose to cross westward and became Canada, while the rest of Manasseh remained behind as Britain. All of Ephraim crossed over westward, then as now.

I listed what I saw as parallels between Canada as the lesser Manasseh to the north, compared to the greater, more powerful Ephraim of the United States on its southern border. (This gets *really* creative here, so hang on.)

> In one sense, modern Manasseh can be considered Britain and Canada both, corresponding to the two parts into which Manasseh anciently was divided. At West Manasseh's southern border was Ephraim, the longest border between any two tribes of Israel. Canada and the United States share the longest unprotected border in the world, and the longest border between Israelite nations. West Manasseh was also bordered on the west by "the great sea to the west," the same great sea that all Israelites pushed toward when they first settled the Promised Land.
>
> As Joshua 17:10 puts it, "the land to the south being Ephraim's and that to the north being Manasseh's, with the sea forming its boundary." Very similar to the United States and Canada. West Manasseh had "ten portions" of Canaan (Josh 17:5). Canada has ten provinces. West Manasseh's land area was larger than that of Ephraim's. Canada occupies a larger land area than the United States ... "Such are the *ten thousands* of Ephraim, and such are the *thousands* of Manasseh" (Deut 33:17). The populations of the United States and Canada are about 200 million and 20 million respectively, the exact proportion of Moses's statement. East Manasseh was probably greater in numbers than West Manasseh (1 Chron 12:31, 37). Britain's population is greater than Canada's. East Manasseh settled before West Manasseh and Ephraim. Britain was a nation before Canada and the United States ... The North American continent, from Jerusalem's latitude northward, has been given to the descendants of Joseph—the better portion going to Ephraim, the lesser to Manasseh.

United States/Ephraim

I even had Alaska and Australia worked into this scheme in terms of "polar opposites" or "ends of the earth," with Israel in the latter days extending to the northwest and southeast extremities of the world, from the perspective of the Middle East. To the extreme northwest is Ephraim—Alaska. To the extreme southeast is Manasseh—Australia. (I *told* you I was creative.)

And it is basic in Anglo-Israel theory that there was a "seven times" postponement of blessings on Israel, interpreted as 2520 (360 x 7) years from 722-718 BC when the Assyrians took the northern house of Israel into captivity. Church literature always said this time period ended with the Louisiana Purchase of 1803. Wasn't it the United States (rather than Britain) which fulfilled this to the exact year?

In every way, I argued, the younger, greater United States is the correspondence with younger, greater Ephraim. England is *Manasseh*.

> To say that Britain at one time was greater than the United States—that she *used to* be greater in the 1800s—is entirely unsatisfactory. *What about now?* Prophecy was written for the twentieth century, not the eighteenth or nineteenth. One of the strongest and most persistent objections to the "Anglo-Israel" theory is Britain's ignoble decline and current second-rate status. Yet it confirms modern Israel's true identity and the truth of Jacob's words if we but realize that our nation, the United States, is Ephraim.

As clear as I thought my argument was up to this point, I realized that right about now an alert British-Israel theorist, even if unable to immediately answer the foregoing, might come back with a trump card objection, which goes like this. It is basic to the theory that the throne of England is the throne of David. (According to the theory, when the house of Judah went into captivity the throne of David was transplanted to the house of Israel [Ezek 17:22-23].) Would not the throne of David be in Israel's leading tribe? Does this not weigh in favor of England being Ephraim?

United States/ Ephraim

To which I answered in my paper, no, just the opposite, it weighs in favor of the *United States* being Ephraim. Look at the American Revolution, I argued. The American Revolution parallels the revolt of Ephraim against the throne of David. Anciently, a company of tribes led by an Ephraimite (Jeroboam) revolted from the throne of David over the issue of taxation (1 Kings 12). Thousands of years later, American colonists revolted from the throne of David in England over the same issue—taxation. In both cases the rebels rejected monarchies. In both cases the king was arrogant and unwise, would not listen to sound advice from counselors, and ordered collection of taxes which made revolution inevitable. Just as in times of old, modern Ephraim would not have David's throne rule over them: "So Israel has been in rebellion against the house of David to this day" (1 Kings 12:19). Ephraim anciently separated from the mother nation ruled by the throne of David. The United States separated from Mother England ruled by the throne of David. Just as the ten tribes led by Ephraim and the name of Israel were rent away from David's throne (1 Kgs 11:11), in modern times the name of Israel, prophetically speaking, was taken from David's throne in England and given to Ephraim, the United States.

> Ephraim was to separate from *Manasseh* (Genesis 48). Past history suggests that Ephraim would rebel against *David's throne* ... We thus see two independent prophetic lines converging in the American Revolution. It was a rebellion against *both* David's throne *and* Manasseh—because David's throne was *in* Manasseh! ... Can we see the connection between the throne of David and *Manasseh*?

I noted additional biblical clues suggesting a throne of David/ Manasseh connection. 1 Chronicles 12:19 says, "Some of the men of Manasseh deserted to David when he came with the Philistines for the battle against Saul." See? Manassites in affinity with David.

At the time of the entrance into Canaan, five prominent Manassite women are said to have come to Moses and asked for a land inheritance (Num 27:1-11). They got the inheritance. I counted a total of five women, all of David's line, who solely ruled Britain. They are: Mary I (1553-1558), Elizabeth I (1558-1603), Anne (1702-1714), Victoria (1837-1901), and Elizabeth II (1952-   ). *Five* Manassite women received inheritances. *Five* women on David's throne exercised sole reign of Britain. Now are you seriously going to tell me that is *coincidence?*

(Those versed in English history might object that Mary II, who reigned 1689-1694, is missing in this list, which would make the number six instead of five. But I had that covered. I quoted a reference work which said that her reign was jointly with her husband William III and "the administration was exclusively in the hands of William." So she doesn't count.)

I noted that in 1 Chronicles 2:21 the granddaughter of *Manasseh* married into the family of Judah from which King David was descended. Centuries later the throne of David was transplanted when the daughter of the king of Judah married into the royal family which now rules in Britain, modern *Manasseh*. Almost the same circumstances, but in reverse. I was just amazed.

Then I gave the *coup de grace*, a point which I titled in my paper "The Sting," because I thought it so elegant. Of all of the kings of Israel and Judah, there was only one whose name was the same as one of Israel's tribes. That was king Manasseh of Judah, descendant of David, the longest-ruling king of either house. And it was because of king Manasseh that the house of Judah went into captivity (according to the authors of the Bible). "Surely this came upon Judah at the command of the Lord, to remove them out of his sight, for the sins of Manasseh, according to all that he had done" (2 Kgs 24:3; 2 Kgs 21:11, 23:26, and Jer 15:4). I wrote:

> The captivity of Judah was brought about because of king Manasseh's wickedness. It was *because of Manasseh* that David's throne was transplanted! Transplanted to where? To England—*modern-day Manasseh!* How ironic! Truth is stranger than fiction!

United States/ Ephraim

> King Manasseh sat on the throne of David. Now David's throne sits in Manasseh. *Because of* king Manasseh!

(Now aren't you amazed too?)

I noted that Hosea and other prophets are filled with allusions to an end-time witness coming out of Ephraim. Wasn't the headquarters of God's Work in the United States? I cited John 11:54 as symbolism of the true church at the end situated in Ephraim: "Jesus therefore no longer continued to walk publicly among the Jews, but went away from there to the country near the wilderness, into a city called Ephraim, and there he stayed with his disciples."

Finally, in any argument challenging a paradigm it is necessary not only to make a positive case for the new view but also to offer an explanation for why the mistaken idea formerly seemed convincing. I had that covered too. I closed on this note:

> Why, then, is the belief so prevalent that the United States is Manasseh, and Britain Ephraim, when every indication is to the exact opposite? The answer is very simple. Everyone who teaches the truth of Israel's identity has been strongly influenced by the original British-Israelites. The British-Israel people teach that Britain is Ephraim. The reason they teach this is because British-Israelism began, and was popular the past century or two, in Britain. At that time Britain was greater than the United States. Seeing the prophecies of Ephraim being the greatest of Israelite nations, they logically applied the designation of Ephraim to themselves. They did not foresee the United States surpassing and eclipsing Britain in terms of power. In fact, this very turn of events has caused embarrassment to British-Israelites as well as delighting skeptics of the theory. Britain's decline is difficult to explain when Gen 49:22 plainly states that Ephraim would be *greater* than Manasseh and the greatest nation on earth.
>
> This is why the belief was begun that Britain is Ephraim. The theory was propounded *in Britain* at a time when Britain was the greatest nation on earth up to that time. The British-Israelites were right about Britain being Israel, but they had the identities of the United States and Britain backward. Perhaps the time has now come to unravel the confusion ... Herbert W. Armstrong very early realized the truth of Israel's identity and its significance, this truth

> being the key which unlocks Bible prophecy. Today the Worldwide Church of God is the most prominent group in the United States advocating Israel's true identity ... Of those other groups in America who do understand Israel's identity, none understand the true gospel, they are often anti-Semitic, and usually they foresee continued blessings for our people, not coming calamity ... Until now it seems no one has realized that the United States is Ephraim. But this is indeed the case ... Would not this realization give us added motivation to warn America of what is coming?

Well, dear reader, there you have it. I had a few other things thrown in, but that was the core of the argument. I thought at the time that the argument was practically open and shut, a dunk shot. I had little doubt that when people had time to think it over and consider it, it would be seen as just obvious.

I put my heart into preparing this paper explaining this. I did little else for about five weeks but write this paper at my parents' home in Akron, Ohio, setting my accumulated thinking and notes of the past months into this single organized presentation. I saw my paper as changing the Worldwide Church of God, and the Worldwide Church of God as changing the world. In this way I saw the potential of my paper to impact history.

How would headquarters react? What would happen after that? How would it all turn out? These were my questions as, tingling with excitement, I left my parents' home to return to Big Sandy.

Unexpected reaction at Big Sandy

Back again at Big Sandy I gave this paper to a good friend on the faculty, the resident instructor in Hebrew. I sought his critique and comment preparatory to submitting my paper to headquarters. I was *completely* taken by surprise by his reaction. Unfortunately, my faculty friend, quite knowledgeable on historical matters due to having had Orthodox rabbinical training, and now zealous for the church interpretations of scripture, took strong, emotional exception to my research.

In the first place, he felt my conclusion was wrong because I didn't realize, he said, that the British Empire in its prime had been greater than the United States is currently.

But even more importantly and seriously, he went on, I was questioning Mr. Armstrong. This was *very serious*. As a student having completed only two years of Ambassador College, I did not, he said, have the background or training to be qualified to do this. This was the only instance of any of my papers throughout my Ambassador College years receiving a negative response. In retrospect, that has got to be regarded as something close to miraculous, in light of the experiences of so many others. I attribute my good fortune, if not to a sort of perverse divine humor, to my evident and transparent sincerity of attitude as well as my careful exercise of good judgment on where to submit new ideas. Even in this instance, my faculty friend's reaction, however discomfiting in its effect, was conveyed in sincerity as a friend to a friend. He earnestly pleaded with me to *reread* Herbert Armstrong's book, *The United States and British Commonwealth in Prophecy*, with a *prayerful* attitude, in order, he hoped, that I would see where I was wrong. He said he regretted having to say such harsh things and hoped I would understand he meant his words in the sense of Proverbs 27:6, "Faithful are the wounds of a friend." For my part, I felt a sick feeling in the pit of my stomach.

I had viewed my research not as *questioning* Mr. Armstrong, but as *improving* upon Mr. Armstrong's work. It was not a challenge but a contribution! It grieved me that I had been so misunderstood. I decided to put the paper aside until a later time when I could feel emotionally clearer about it.

Meanwhile, still reeling from the unpleasantness of having a respected friend question my attitude toward the church (I being a sensitive soul), I was stopped on a sidewalk by one of the ministers and speech instructors, Richard Ames. Mr. Ames wanted to speak to me about my talking to other students about the United States being Ephraim. A coed student had overhead me discussing this idea and had come to him quite upset about it.

How could she know what was true anymore if everything was being questioned like this? I felt dismayed to hear this. I said I had not meant to upset anyone, felt very badly that I had, and that I had always tried to exercise discretion in talking about ideas but apparently had misjudged this time. I asked Mr. Ames who it was so I could go to her and try to make things right. He declined to say who it was. I asked him to convey my regret and apology for upsetting her. (I never knew whom I had upset.) The conclusion, Mr. Ames said, was I was not to discuss any further ideas of the United States being Ephraim with other students. Mr. Ames didn't object to my believing what I liked on the matter. No judgment was expressed on the idea or me, nor was any curiosity expressed on the topic. It was simply communicated to me that I was not to talk about it any more.

Later that day at supper in the student dining hall I experienced my first test in obedience to this edict. The word had spread to a few more student friends of my interesting idea. One was a senior who was later hired and sent out as a ministerial trainee after graduation. He was as faithful and believing in the church as he could be. He frequently came to me to discuss biblical things or get my opinion on certain scriptures. He sat down and with much eagerness said, "So and so said you believe Ephraim is Manasseh. Tell me why you think this."

I felt on the spot, mindful of the instruction I had received not to discuss it. I carefully answered, "No, that's not correct. I believe Ephraim is Ephraim." I hoped somehow the subject would be changed.

My poor friend looked completely nonplussed and persisted. "But so and so *said* you believe Ephraim is Manasseh. I want to know why you think this. Tell me—I'm really interested!"

I replied, "No, I've never thought Ephraim is Manasseh. I think Ephraim is Ephraim." By now other students at the table who saw the semantic confusion could barely restrain their mirth. I began to feel ashamed of myself for taking advantage of my friend's unwitting misstatement of words. I explained as simply

United States/ Ephraim

as I could that I was not allowed to discuss it, and the subject was dropped.

I complied with the instruction I had received. I did not discuss the idea further. I never submitted my paper to anyone else. It wasn't long before I began to suspect flaws here and there in the historical evidence for Anglo-Israelism. I even began to suspect the theory might have been fabricated to justify English hegemony. This removed my incentive to do anything further with the paper.

And so it was that what could have been a striking improvement in the Worldwide Church of God "identity of Israel" teaching was effectively buried ... all because an unknown coed had become upset at hearing the idea and had gone for counseling to a minister, who solved the problem by imposing a gag order.

CHAPTER 7

AFTERWARD ON ANGLO-ISRAELISM, PART I

Having applied prodigious creative energy to improving the Anglo-Israel theory in the previous chapter, it's my sad duty now to report it was a complete hallucination.

My Ephraim paper looked so good at the time. Let there be a lesson in this. As we live in the world, there will be many plausible sounding ideas presented to us. They will seem logical. They will sound persuasive. Others will believe them. Their only problem is they often just don't happen to be *true*. But the very appeal of the idea or the packaging with which it is presented may deflect attention from asking underlying questions which every person ought to ask every time a salesman or a speaker or a writer makes a claim, namely: what are the sources, how primary are they, how reliable are they, and do the primary sources say what it is said they say?

As an exercise in applying this kind of examination to a belief that, at least in certain circles when starting from certain presuppositions, *sounded* plausible, I will focus upon one feature of Anglo-Israel belief in particular: the idea that the throne of England today descends from king David of Israel. I will show that this idea is as loony as the moon being made of green cheese.

But to set the stage first, before examining stories of ancient kings, migrating prophets, and rescued damsels marrying foreign princes, here is a thumbnail history of Anglo-Israelism—and how it took root in the church of Herbert Armstrong.

Afterward on Anglo-Israelism, I

A short history of Anglo-Israelism

Although isolated individuals had proposed the idea as far back as the late 1500s, the Anglo-Israel idea first came to wider public attention with ex-sailor Richard Brothers (1757-1824), in London.[42] In 1794 he published a treatise entitled *A Revealed Knowledge of the Prophecies and Times*, which contained "Great and Remarkable Things Not Revealed to Any Person on Earth." It foretold the end of King George III's reign and a reestablishment of an Israelite kingdom composed of the Lost Ten Tribes who were in England. Brothers also saw visions in which he learned that he himself was a descendant of David, which led logically to his demanding that the crown of England be given to him. He declared that he was "Apostle" of a new religion, and that he was "the Nephew of the Almighty."[43]

The English authorities just had no sense of humor. When Brothers predicted death to King George III, the stuffy English authorities rudely charged God's Nephew/Apostle with treason. Upon closer examination, they decided he was nuts instead and committed him to a lunatic asylum. The story might have ended there but for a fortuitous event. A member of Parliament and a famous Oriental scholar, Nathanael Halhed, became Richard Brothers' disciple. Halhed was able to get Brothers released to a private asylum. From this improved condition of confinement Brothers published further prophetic pamphlets and gathered a

---

[42] I am indebted for much of the information in this section on the history of British-Israelism to Cecil Roth, *The Nephew of the Almighty* (London: Edward Golston Ltd., 1933), and the entry on British-Israelism in J. Gordon Melton, *Encyclopedia of American Religion*, 2 vols. (Wilmington, N.C.: McGrath Publishing Co., 1978), I, 446-451.

[43] Just as Herbert Armstrong thought he was the Lord's *strong arm* by which the Bible says the Lord will rule earth, so Richard Brothers realized he was descended from David through a *brother* of Jesus. Hence his nephew-uncle relationship to the Almighty.

growing number of followers on the outside, although he was derided and satirized by the popular press of his day.

Brothers made some predictions which failed to come to pass, but his following of supporters received a definite shot in the arm with the English defeat of Napoleon in 1815. This seemed to confirm in the popular mind that England was on the receiving end of divine favor. Several more influential persons came to believe Brothers' amazing idea that the Britons were Israelites. Brothers died in 1824. A biographer of Brothers, Cecil Roth, concluded:

> The candle which Richard Brothers lit in the world ... is not yet extinguished. Even now, a hundred years and more after his death, there are millions of persons on both sides of the Atlantic who implicitly believe in the theory which he first launched, that the Lost Ten Tribes are to-day represented by the Anglo-Saxon race ... Other theories may perhaps show a greater plausibility. There is none other, however, which can boast in its support the authority of an ex-officer of the British Navy, who was at the same time Prince of the Hebrews and Nephew of the Almighty.

Regrettably, Herbert Armstrong never gave any credit to his earlier prototype. But let us continue.

In 1840 a Scotsman named John Wilson published *Our Israelitish Origins*. Wilson's appearance of scholarship and oratorical abilities generated further public interest in the idea. In 1850 Wilson's book was published in America. It found isolated disciples but did not take off until after World War I.

In 1880, Joseph Wild, pastor of the Union Congregational Church in New York, published *The Future of Israel and Judah*. This Anglo-Israel expositor was no right-winger. Wild was a social visionary. Chapter 10 of his book was entitled "Manasseh and Communism." Subheadings in this chapter include: "Communism of the Gospel," "Future System of Government,"

"America a Type of the Millennial Government," "Growth of Socialism," and "True Relations of Employer and Worker."[44]

In 1887, M.M. Eshelman in Illinois published *Two Sticks*, after being converted to the British-Israel idea by an eighty-year old immigrant. But the real statement of American Anglo-Israelism was Joseph H. Allen's previously-mentioned book of 1902 entitled *Judah's Sceptre and Joseph's Birthright*.[45] This was the source for Herbert Armstrong's book.

Anglo-Israel fervor increased after 1917 when Britain took charge of Palestine and sponsored Jewish settlement. In that context, the accession in 1936 of Edward VIII, known to those close to him as "David," looked like an imminent fulfillment of the prophecy in Ezekiel 37:21-24, "I will ... bring them to their own land ... they shall be no longer two nations ... My servant David shall be king over them." Unfortunately, this idea bit the dust when the new king fell in love and abdicated his throne the same year in order to marry an American woman.

The movement in America reached its height in the 1930s and 1940s with congregations, radio broadcasts, and even two seminaries (such as Dayton Theological Seminary, from 1947 to the early 1950s, whose graduates and teachers were influential for decades after). The anti-Semitic publisher of Henry Ford's Dearborn, Michigan newspaper, W.J. Cameron, became a convert and promoted the theory.[46]

---

[44] "America has a grand commission, a glorious work to perform, and victory will perch upon the banner of Manasseh at last ... It is the special providence of this country that all men, of every country, race, and colour, may dwell together in peace and harmony, and on this grand, small scale, give to the world a type of the millennium day" (Joseph Wild, *The Future of Israel and Judah, Being the Discourses on the Lost Tribes, from How and When the World will End* [London, 1880], 104-110).

[45] J.H. Allen, *Judah's Sceptre and Joseph's Birthright* (1st ed. 1902; Merrimac, Mass.: Destiny Publishers, 17th ed., n.d.).

[46] As brought out in the study of Albert Lee, *Henry Ford and the Jews* (New York: Stein and Day, 1980), Ford bankrolled a number of anti-Jewish books and people.

Afterward on Anglo-Israelism, I

Herbert Armstrong discovered Anglo-Israelism in some of his earliest studies. In fact as early as 1929—five years before he started his radio broadcast ministry, when he was in poverty in Oregon with barely enough for his family to eat—Herbert Armstrong wrote letters expressing his realization that his destiny was to take the gospel of Anglo-Israelism to *the whole world*.[47] In that year, 1929, he wrote a nearly 300-page manuscript—the message he was to take to the world—and mailed it to a leading figure in the Church of God (Seventh Day), headquartered in Stanberry, Missouri, Andrew Dugger. Six months later Armstrong received back a reply from Dugger, typed on a train late at night. In this letter, Dugger said Armstrong was surely right in what he had written. (Early editions of Armstrong's *Autobiography* included a photograph of this letter.)

But the Church of God (Seventh Day) did not adopt this new truth Herbert Armstrong had presented. This proved quite disillusioning to Herbert, who described his submission of this manuscript to headquarters and the response it would receive as a crucial "test to help settle the question of whether this was, in actual fact, the true Church of God." They flunked the test. Herbert Armstrong told the sad story of what happened:

---

[47] Herbert Armstrong wrote in a letter in 1929: "I was made to see clearly that I have been given a commission to get this warning message out with the loud shout to the world. The true, full message never has been carried at all, much less with the shout. I don't see how I am to do it. The Lord will open the way, and I must simply trust him and look to him for guidance. The means will be provided and the way opened, I am sure" (letter, HWA to Brother Hobbs, Feb 6, 1929). In another letter the same year he wrote: "I feel that a great message based on this Israel truth has been revealed to me which must be powerfully broadcasted to the whole world without delay" (letter, HWA to Lt. Col. MacKendrick, March 4, 1929). These letters are cited in Ralph Orr, "How Anglo-Israelism Entered Seventh-day Churches of God: a history of the doctrine from John Wilson to Joseph W. Tkach," at http://www.wcg.org/lit/prophecy/anglo/howanglo.htm.

> Did this Church accept and proclaim this vital new truth—the KEY that unlocks the doors to all PROPHECY? ... This Church refused then to accept it or preach it or publish it ...[48]

Herbert Armstrong decided not to wait on headquarters. He started his own ministry and went on to become Anglo-Israelism's most successful expositor of all time. As he had envisioned so long ago in 1929 when hardly anyone believed him, Herbert Armstrong did, indeed, take this message to the whole world.

Rather than the anti-Semitism which by now had come to characterize other American exponents, Herbert Armstrong used Anglo-Israelism to identify *with* Jews. In his *Autobiography*, Armstrong claimed personal descent from Edward I of England, and from there back to King David. Unlike his unfortunate earlier predecessor Richard Brothers, Herbert Armstrong never demanded that the throne of England be turned over to him—at least in this age in advance of Christ's return. (Near the end of his life Armstrong did, however, apply certain prophecies of millennial rule by a Davidic descendant, normally regarded as referring to Christ, to himself, citing his alleged Davidic descent in this regard.)

Critique of Anglo-Israelism on historical grounds

Crucial to the theory is the belief that an unbroken line of Davidic descent continued to rule over Israelites after being transferred to the British Isles via the prophet Jeremiah. Jeremiah is supposed to have brought the daughter of the last Jewish king, Zedekiah, to Ireland to marry into the reigning Irish Milesian royal family. As explained in Herbert Armstrong's book, *The United States and Britain in Prophecy* (hereafter abbreviated *USBP*):

---

[48] Herbert Armstrong, *Autobiography of Herbert W. Armstrong* (rev. ed., 2 vols; Pasadena: Worldwide Church of God, 1986-87), I, 359-362.

Afterward on Anglo-Israelism, I

An elderly, white-haired patriarch, sometimes referred to as a "saint," came to Ireland. With him was the princess daughter of an eastern king and a companion called "Simon Brach," spelled in different histories as Breck, Berech, Brach, or Berach. The princess was named Tephi or Tea-Tephi.

Modern literature of those who recognize the national identity of the Anglo-Saxons has confused this daughter of Zedekiah, with an earlier Tea, a daughter of Ith, who lived in the days of David.

This royal party included the son of the king of Ireland who had been in Jerusalem at the time of the siege. There he had become acquainted with Tea-Tephi. He married her shortly after the city fell. Their young son, now in his late teens, accompanied them to Ireland.

A descendant of the ancient King Herremon, this young man has usually been confused with his much earlier ancestor Gede the Herremon—who married his uncle Ith's daughter Tea. The son of this later young king and the Hebrew princess continued on the throne of Ireland and *this same dynasty continued unbroken* through all the kings of Ireland; was *overturned* and transplanted again in Scotland; again *overturned* and moved to London, England, where *this same dynasty continues today* in the reign of Queen Elizabeth II ...

In view of the linking together of biblical history, prophecy, and Irish history, can anyone deny that this Hebrew princess was the daughter of king Zedekiah of Judah and therefore heir to the throne of David? That the aged patriarch was in fact Jeremiah, and his companion was Jeremiah's scribe, or secretary, Baruch?[49] [Emphasis in original.]

But what is the evidence that this happened?

Neither Herbert Armstrong nor the Worldwide Church of God's *USBP* ever said. Throughout all of its editions, *USBP* gave no footnotes, cited no title or page number of source documents, had no bibliography. It simply asserted. In one of the most creative leaps of *USBP*, the statement was made:

With the facts of biblical history and prophecy in mind, one can sift out the legend from the true history in studying ancient Irish annals.

---

[49] Herbert Armstrong, *The United States and Britain in Prophecy*, 9th ed. (Pasadena, Calif.: Worldwide Church of God, 1986), 98-102.

> Throwing out what is obviously legendary, we glean from various histories of Ireland the following ...[50]

Then follows the Jeremiah/Zedekiah's-daughter story, simply stated as fact.

That was the sum total of evidence offered by *USBP* for this crucial point. If you missed it, read it again.

The Tea-Tephi/Jeremiah legend

In preparation for the writing of this section, I searched out and examined a number of old Anglo-Israel books, as well as primary and secondary sources on the Irish annals, in an attempt to more accurately understand the basis for the Jeremiah/Zedekiah's-daughter legend.

I found that Anglo-Israel books invariably repeat the same Tea-Tephi story, each in slightly different words, each claiming that the story is in the annals. Yet I found it difficult in the Anglo-Israel sources to actually find a reference to *where* in the annals their story finds support. Herbert Armstrong's *United States and Britain in Prophecy* gave no reference. Joseph Allen's earlier book did not. They all seem to draw from previous Anglo-Israel writings. They speak so confidently it sounds like there must be something in the annals to which they refer. The *names* mentioned in the Tea-Tephi legend appear in the annals, true enough, but I discovered they are totally different persons in the annals than the Anglo-Israel legend makes them out to be. The annals simply don't say what the Anglo-Israel literature, or the Worldwide Church of God's publications on the subject, *said* they say. It is a legend that someone somewhere within Anglo-Israel circles began, stated it as fact, and it has been repeated as fact within Anglo-Israel circles ever since. It comes down to the present day with Worldwide Church of God-derived spin-off

---

[50]   Armstrong, *USBP*, 98.

groups continuing to repeat it to millions. It may make an interesting story, but it is completely *fabricated*.

It would be as if I were to take any random writing of primeval origins from anywhere in the world which had a few names in it, and in total disregard for what that document said *about* those names, I arbitrarily said, "This one was Abraham. That one was Isaac. That one was Rebekah. They sailed halfway around the world and showed up in this legend." The Jeremiah/Tea-Tephi legend of the Irish annals has no more basis to it than this.

Perhaps this is why so few of the numerous Anglo-Israel books and writings I was able to examine give quotations from the annals themselves, or cite chapter and verse in the annals. They simply assert. I was not aware of *how* baseless these assertions were until I researched the Irish annals for myself.

Examining the Irish annals

What the originators of the Tea-Tephi legend did was simply combine famous, known figures in the annals, many centuries apart, and splice them together in a totally imaginary reconstruction.

For example, who is Ollam Fodla? In Anglo-Israel theory, and as stated in the *USBP*, he is Jeremiah, the aged prophet.[51] In fact, Ollam Fodla appears in the Irish legends as one of the greatest native Milesian kings. I will now quote from the annals. A poem in one of the annals called the Book of Leinster, and identified by one of Ireland's early authorities on the annals, Eugene O'Curry, as written around the time of the birth of Christ and of a very high degree of authenticity, has this to say of Ollam Fodla. Does this read like a description of the biblical Jeremiah?

> Ollamh Fodhla, of furious valour,
> Who founded the Court of Ollamh,

---

[51] Armstrong, *USBP*, 102.

> Was the first heroic king
> That instituted the Feast of Teamair [Tara].
> Forty sweet musical years
> He held the high sovereignty of Errin [Ireland];
> And it was from him, with noble pride,
> the Ultonians took their name.
> Six kings of valiant career
> Of Ollamh's race reigned over Errin;
> For two hundred and ten full years,
> No other person came between them ...[52]

The ancient poem continues with an account of Ollam's six reigning descendants. The annals say Ollam founded a college and was an enlightened ruler, known as "Doctor of Wisdom." This is said of the famous *king* Ollam Fodla. The name "Ollam" thereafter meant a wise man. The Anglo-Israelites *arbitrarily* said Ollam Fodla was Jeremiah, even though the *annals* say he was a *native Milesian king*. The Jeremiah identification is a complete fabrication.

Herman Hoeh, the leading historian of Anglo-Israelism in the Worldwide Church of God, was aware of the king named Ollam Fodla. In his Irish kings list in his *Compendium of World History*, he had an Ollam Fodla dated 714-674 BC, with the appended comment, "Not the later prophet Ollamh Fodhla."[53]

Dr. Hoeh's *Compendium*, completed in 1963, was published in-house and was used as a textbook at Ambassador College during my years at Big Sandy. It was Hoeh's work more than any other that was the basis for the way history was understood in the Worldwide Church of God. At some stage in the late 1960s Dr. Hoeh withdrew his *Compendium* from circulation to the public and to the church membership (students in Ancient History classes at Ambassador College could still get it), stating that some of its material was not accurate. Unfortunately Hoeh never

---

[52] Eugene O'Curry (ed.), *On the Manners and Customs of the Ancient Irish* (1st ed., 1873), 2 vols. rev. ed. (New York: Lemma, 1971), I, 8-9.
[53] Herman Hoeh, *Compendium of World History* (2 vols.; Pasadena, Calif.: Ambassador College, 1970), I, 430.

Afterward on Anglo-Israelism, I

specified exactly which material ought to be rejected and which he still stood behind as valid, and the *Compendium* continued to be the basis for understanding of history within the church.

(I asked Dr. Hoeh once in 1974 if he would publish another edition of the *Compendium* and offer it to the public. Hoeh told me no, because he didn't want the paper it would use to contribute to a paper shortage in the world! This seemed to me something less than an adequate reason for refraining from publishing one's work, but out of respect I didn't press the matter.)

But to return to Ollam Fodla, who appears in the *Compendium* as an Irish king and who is supposed to be different from the "later prophet Ollamh Fodhla": in fact there is no second, later Ollam Fodla in the Irish annals who may be identified with Jeremiah. There is only the *one* famous King Ollam Fodla.

Likewise, there is no second Tea-Tephi. Tea appears in the annals as the wife of one of the original Milesian brothers, Heremon. Anglo-Israel theory says this Tea was Zedekiah's daughter. But this doesn't fit chronologically, since this Tea would be dated at either 1000 BC or 1700 BC, depending on which chronology in the annals is preferred. The 1700 BC date is from the traditional *Annals of the Four Masters*.[54] But Hoeh followed a different dating system of O'Flaherty's *Ogygia* which gives the 1000 BC date. Hoeh wrote: "The original and correct history of the Milesians in Ireland has, however, been preserved unaltered only in the Domestic Annals, the official history of ancient Ireland. They may be found in O'Flaherty's *Ogygia*." In this system Tea is about 1000 BC.[55]

Zedekiah's daughter and Jeremiah, however, lived in the mid-500s BC. The *USBP* therefore said there was a "second" Tea in the mid-500s BC who was Zedekiah's daughter. As Hoeh said:

---

[54] "Ireland," *Britannica* (11th ed.); O'Curry, *Manners and Customs*, II, 3. According to the chronology of the *Annals of the Four Masters*, the Milesians (led by Miled and sons) came to Ireland in 1694 BC.
[55] Hoeh, *Compendium*, I, 417.

> The *Annals of the Four Masters* reads: "Tea, the daughter of Lughaidh, son of Itha, whom Eremhon married in Spain." This Tea is an altogether different person from the Tea who came more than four centuries later to the Irish Isles. The British Israel World Federation ... is unwilling to believe the history of Ireland as it is plainly recorded. The Tea who married Ghede the Heremon was a daughter of Lughaidh, the son of Ith, uncle of Miledh (Milesius) ... These events occurred in David's reign, not Zedekiah's.[56]

But this "second" Tea proposed by Hoeh and in *USBP* was a sheer fabrication, since there is no "second" Tea in the Irish annals which, after all, are supposed to be the sources.

Admittedly, a problem occurs either way Tea-Tephi is interpreted. The problem with the Anglo-Israel Tea-Tephi being the daughter of Jewish king Zedekiah is:

> (a) she ("Tea") is the cousin of Milesian founding King Heremon;[57]
>
> (b) her father is said to have been Lughaidh, a Milesian, not Zedekiah, a Judean;
>
> (c) she comes from Spain, not Palestine; and, finally,
>
> (d) she is about five hundred years too early, according to the *Ogygia*

The problem with the Worldwide Church of God's "second" Tea-Tephi in the time of Jeremiah is:

> (a) primarily, that she doesn't exist

The "second" Tea-Tephi, like a "second" Ollam Fodla, was completely invented.

---

[56] Hoeh, *Compendium*, I, 425.
[57] Heremon's father Miled (founder of the Milesians) was a nephew of Ith, grandfather of Tea. Tea married her cousin (Seusmas MacManus, *The Story of the Irish Race*, 4th rev ed. [1944], 8).

Afterward on Anglo-Israelism, I

What about Tea's marriage to "Heremon"? Heremon was the founder of one line of the Milesian kings. But Heremon lived 1000 BC or 1700 BC, which is centuries too early for Zedekiah's daughter to have married him. British-Israel theory said Zedekiah's daughter was Heremon's wife Tea-Tephi. But since the *Compendium* had already ruled out this Tea in favor of an imaginary "later" Tea-Tephi, Dr. Hoeh and *USBP* simply went down the list of kings until one was found five hundred years later at approximately the right time, and arbitrarily said, "Here! This one must have been the 'Heremon' we're looking for that Zedekiah's daughter married!" It happens that his name wasn't Heremon, but that trifling detail was solved by suggesting that Heremon became a title that could be applied to any king descended from Heremon. (But this does not appear in the annals.) Thus a "second" Heremon was added to the "second Tea-Tephi" and "second Ollam Fodla" to make the British-Israel legend work. Strangely, none of these figures, who just happen to have duplicate names to known leading figures in the annals, appear themselves in the annals.

What about Baruch, Jeremiah's scribe back in Palestine? (Baruch is a figure who accompanies Jeremiah throughout the book of Jeremiah.) The *USBP* stated,

> With [Ollam Fodla/Jeremiah] was ... a companion called "Simon Brach," spelled in different histories as Breck, Berech, Brach, or Berach ... can anyone deny ... that his companion was Jeremiah's scribe, or secretary, Baruch?[58]

In the first place, nothing in the annals links Ollam Fodla with Simon Brach. Second, Simeon Breac (Brach) is identified in the annals, according to *Britannica* (11th ed.), as a famous ancient warrior before the Milesians ever arrived in Ireland. Other records in the annals spell his name "Breas" and say he was a leader of sea-robbers.[59] This name was lifted out of its context in

---

[58] Armstrong, *USBP*, 100-102.
[59] MacManus, *Story of the Irish Race*, 3-4.

the annals nearly 1000 years earlier and arbitrarily said to be "Baruch, the scribe" who accompanied Jeremiah to Ireland in the 500s BC.

Actually, there is a second tradition of Simeon Breac in the annals. O'Flannery's *Ogygia* has "Siomon Breac" as a Milesian king in the 400s BC. It is surprising that both Dr. Hoeh's *Compendium* and Joseph Allen's *Judah's Sceptre* had "Siomon Breac"—which they had already identified with *Baruch*—listed in their line of Irish kings several generations after Tea-Tephi, without comment or a hint of embarrassment.[60] The *Compendium* lists Siomon Breac's reign as 483-477 BC.

It is evident that if Siomon Breac was an Irish king generations after the alleged arrival of Jeremiah and Tea-Tephi, and if he was descended from earlier Irish kings, then he cannot be the biblical Baruch with Jeremiah.

Need it be asked if there is a "second Breac" (actually a "third" Breac, in light of the two traditions in the annals), answering to the biblical companion of Jeremiah named Baruch, in the annals? There is not. The story of Jeremiah bringing Zedekiah's daughter over to Ireland is an obvious cut-and-paste job, taking prominent names in the Irish annals separated by many centuries and making the most superficial, gullible identifications. If anyone checks the story of the annals themselves and stumbles across these things, the explanation was that there were "second" Ollam Fodlas, Heremons, Tea-Tephis, and Breacs—these "second" personalities all just happening to have such famous names and of whom, strangely, the Irish legends know nothing—and all conveniently at the right time, unlike their inconveniently dated famous namesakes.

Actually, there was not even a *first* Tea-Tephi. The original Milesian queen in question was named simply "Tea," not "Tea-Tephi." A mention of a much earlier "Tephi" appears in the annals—but she was the daughter of a leader of a Celtic settlement in Spain, married to a British king named Canthon,

---

[60] Hoeh, *Compendium*, I, 431; Allen, *Judah's Sceptre*, 374.

and had nothing to do with Irish royalty. In 1861, a British-Israel expositor named F.R.A. Glover combined "Tea" and "Tephi" into one person, in the first book to promote the "Tea-Tephi" theory. Glover was the inventor of the story of "Tea-Tephi" and Jeremiah.

With some difficulty I obtained Glover's book.[61] I found that Glover made numerous flying leaps philologically, claiming key Irish names were really Hebrew words simply because consonants matched.[62] (In fact, not a single Irish name/Hebrew word match claimed by Glover is convincing.) Starting with the premise that Jeremiah brought over a daughter of Zedekiah to Ireland, Glover scoured the Irish annals for possible points of contact and rigged up the Jeremiah/Tea-Tephi story that has been perpetuated ever since.[63] (Interestingly, Glover did not propose that the Milesian King Siomon Breac was Jeremiah's scribe Baruch. That was a post-Glover embellishment from someone else.)

Glover's questionable conjectures were adopted as gospel truth by other Anglo-Israelites, including Joseph H. Allen and Herbert Armstrong.

Again, not the slightest attempt at documentation appeared in Herbert Armstrong's glossy, public presentation of *The United States and Britain in Prophecy* which circulated by the millions.

---

[61] F.R.A. Glover, *England the Remnant of Judah and the Israel of Ephraim. The Two Families under One Head. A Hebrew Episode in British History* (2nd ed. [1st ed. 1861]; London, Rivingtons, 1881).

[62] For example: "The name of Tara [famous site in Ireland], adopted at that time, is, in itself, an evidence that the Law of the Two Tables, called by the Hebrews Torah (pronounced taw-rah), was there set up at that time" (Glover, *England the Remnant of Judah and the Israel of Ephraim*, 77).

[63] Glover uncritically assumed all sorts of things, including a belief that the Irish people were descended from Canaanites driven out of the Promised Land by Joshua! ("The people, who had constantly led Israel astray with idolatrous practices, were there [in Ireland] in great force. Those who had escaped or fled from 'Joshua the Robber,' had transferred to Ireland, all that, for which they were driven out of the land of Canaan" [Glover, *England the Remnant of Judah and the Israel of Ephraim*, 84].)

In spite of the book's tone of authority in citing the legend as fact, it is evident the tale did not come from headquarters researchers reading the annals directly and summarizing them for public consumption. It was simply lifted from Joseph H. Allen, even down to details. For example, Allen wrote that Jeremiah was "a patriarch, a saint."[64] The *USBP* said Jeremiah was an "elderly, white-haired patriarch, sometimes referred to as a 'saint.'"[65] The adjectives "elderly" and "white-haired" evidently were added by Herbert Armstrong, a minor touch of artistic license.

Although *USBP* never cited from the annals directly, I did find a rare statement in an Anglo-Israel book identifying where in the Irish annals one common Anglo-Israel claim is supposed to be found: that Tea-Tephi came from *the east*. The reference is cited as from the *Chronicles of Eri* at Trinity College, Dublin. The relevant passage comes in a narrative of the legendary wanderings, thefts, and counter-thefts of the Irish Lia Fail stone. The passage reads:

> For being but few to journey on the land, they would move on the face of the waters in search of their brethren, led by two of the race, to the extremity of the world of land to the sun's going, as they had heard. And they were driven from their course. The vessel was borne to this land [Ullad] and here was broken, but all the men came save with Lia Fail.[66]

Anglo-Israelites arbitrarily said, without any evidence beyond their say-so, that the "two of the race" mentioned are Jeremiah and Baruch. Since "to the sun's going" meant they were headed west, this meant they were coming from the east. Do you now see how logical it is that they could have come from the Middle East? Then from another passage from the same ancient source:

---

[64] Allen, *Judah's Sceptre*, 228.
[65] Armstrong, *USBP*, 100.
[66] Quoted in John Fox, *The World's Greatest Throne* (1949), 27-28, reproduced in an appendix of Keith Hunt, *In Defence of David's Throne* (Kelowna, B.C.: The Biblical Church of God, 1987).

Afterward on Anglo-Israelism, I

> Chiefs of Iber, Gaal of Sciot, look on this stone ... Be thus: guard well this blessed gift; and in what land this messenger shall stay, a Chief of Iber shall bear sway.

There you have it, plain as can be: "A Chief of *Iber*," meaning a *Hebrew* Prince. "Iber" equals "Hebrew," get it? (The ancients thought "Iber" was a totally unrelated word meaning Spain, and philologists say "Iber" comes from a Basque word *ibar*, "valley," but what do they know?) The daughter of Zedekiah brought to Ireland by Jeremiah and Baruch with her Irish Milesian husband therefore made the line of Irish royalty *Hebrew* thereafter!

Are there ancient records or legends of any people on earth—in many of which references may be found somewhere to two people traveling, and names with syllables in them—from which the same kind or genre of conclusions could not be generated?

Perhaps the forgers of the Jeremiah legend would have been better off if they had invented totally fictitious names rather than taking famous characters in the annals (one from here, one from there ...) and so obviously revealing where they got the names. If Jeremiah brought Zedekiah's daughter to Ireland, it went wholly unnoticed in the ancient Irish annals, assertions in Anglo-Israel literature notwithstanding.[67]

A question and an answer

On November 24, 1987, I wrote the Worldwide Church of God and asked where in the Irish annals the story of Tea-Tephi and Jeremiah was found. To that, I received this response: "You also asked for information regarding Princess Tea-Tephi. This information is available in booklet form from: The Covenant Publishing Co., Ltd., 6 Buckingham Gate, London SW1E6JP, United Kingdom."

---

[67] The *Annals of the Four Masters* and background discussion concerning the Irish annals can be found at Hugh McGough, "Irish Kings," http://www.magoo.com/hugh/irishkings.html.

I wrote the Covenant Publishing Co., and to my astonishment received back a letter dated March 11, 1988, from Secretary Richard Hall, with an enclosure giving a policy statement from six years earlier refuting beyond any doubt that there even was a Tea-Tephi. The statement explained that there is a Tea in the annals, and an earlier Tephi, which had been wrongly combined into one person in 1861 by Rev. F.R.A. Glover, but there is no "Tea-Tephi" in the annals.[68]

In other words, not only was the Worldwide Church of God unable all along to quote from the annals themselves to support assertions in the *USBP*, but the source to which a questioner was referred mailed back evidence completely blowing the theory out of the water.

The Lia Fail stone

Many kings and queens of England and Scotland have been crowned over an ancient block of sandstone which used to rest under the old Coronation Chair at Westminster Abbey, the "Stone of Scone." (It was returned to Scotland in 1996.) Much legend surrounds this stone. Anglo-Israel theory sees in this a crucial supporting link. The theory says this stone was Jacob's pillar stone which was brought to Ireland by Jeremiah and became the famous Irish "Lia Fail" coronation stone. The Lia Fail stone is then supposed to have been transferred to Scotland in the 6th century AD where it became the "Stone of Scone." Then in 1296 AD it was transferred (Scots say "stolen") from Scotland to England by Edward I.

---

[68] W.E. Filmer, F.M. Nithsdale, T.A. Price, and H.E. Stough, "Tea-Tephi or Scota," *The Message*, Issue 5 (London: Covenant Publishing Co., c. 1982). The Covenant Publishing Co. believes the connection of the Irish royalty to David happened instead through a "Scota," wife of Miled. This idea is not an improvement to the theory, however. "Scota" appears in the annals as a daughter of an Egyptian Pharaoh, not as a daughter of Zedekiah. Also, she is at least 500 or 1200 years too early, according to Irish chronology.

Afterward on Anglo-Israelism, I

Indeed the Irish Lia Fail stone has an ancient and legendary history. But what the *Irish* legends say about the Lia Fail stone, as distinguished from Anglo-Israel theories, is that the stone was brought to Ireland by an Israelite in the time of *Moses* (not the time of the later Jeremiah). According to *Britannica* (11th ed.), another version of the legend was that the Lia Fail stone was brought to Ireland even earlier—even before Israel left Egypt—by the Tuatha de Danaan.[69] Scripture also says nothing about Jeremiah lugging around a huge, special stone from place to place. Many scholars believe Jacob's pillar stone was the shrine at Bethel which Josiah stamped to powder (2 Kgs 23:15).

Even more to the point, however, the Scottish Stone of Scone is not the Lia Fail stone of the Irish legends. The true Lia Fail never left Ireland. Two ancient Irish texts unambiguously testify to the contemporary presence of the Lia Fail stone at Tara in Ireland in the 10th and 11th centuries AD—five and six centuries, respectively, *after* Anglo-Israelites, and Herbert Armstrong, said that the Lia-Fail stone was moved to Scotland in the 6th century.[70] In fact the Lia Fail stone was found in modern times by excavators at Tara, the most famous site in Ireland. It is an upright granite stone, and it is still there to the present day. (The archaeological identification of the Lia Fail stone at Tara is

---

[69] According to the annals, the Tuatha de Danaan brought the Lia Fail to Ireland 200 years before the Milesians arrived ("Ireland," *Britannica*, 11th ed.).

[70] The British-Israelite claim that the Lia Fail was transferred from Ireland to Scotland in the 6th century AD is refuted by a "poem of Cuan O'Lochain in the *Dinnseanchus* that the Lia Fail was at Tara in the time of the writer (10th century)" and by "the Irish translation of Nennius, made in the eleventh century, [which] has appended to it a list of the *Mirabilia* or wonders of Erin, among which are the three wonders of *Teamar* or Tara; and the third is 'the *Lia Fail*, or stone which sounded under every king whom it recognized in the sovereignty of *Teamar*.'" The references are from John O'Donovan, 1836, and William Skene, *The Coronation Stone*, 1869, respectively, which were provided by a medieval historian, Alfred P. Smyth, to Ambassador College, Bricket Wood, graduate Bill Moore. Moore reported this in a letter to *Ambassador Report*, March 1988.

standard and is brought out in a number of current authorities.) The Irish Lia-fail stone did not come from Jeremiah—and it never left Ireland to go to Scotland or England. It never was other than Irish, and it never went anywhere.

As for the Scottish Stone of Scone which used to be in Westminster Abbey—the sole artifact claimed for the Jeremiah/Zedekiah's-daughter legend—it is known to have been quarried in Scotland, not the Middle East.[71]

It's not so hard to claim ancestry from David

According to the *Compendium*, the original Milesian brothers Eber and Gede the Heremon, after landing in Ireland, founded a town and made it their new capital. They named it Tea-mur, the town of Tea. It became known as Tara.

One old name found attached to the site of Tara was preserved as "Dowd's Town," which Hoeh said meant, literally, David's Town.[72] At the time of the founding of Tara, Hoeh went on, the legends refer to an event involving a beautiful woman who was "sorrowful to a harlot" (from a poem of Cuan O'Lochain). Hoeh suggested this was an allusion to David's daughter Tamar (2 Sam 13). Hoeh suggested David brought her up to Ireland near the end of his reign, taking time out from his palace turmoils recorded in the scripture to cruise up to Ireland to found "Dowd's Town" and give his daughter Tamar in marriage to an Irish prince of an earlier Hebrew line. (After this David sailed back to Judea again where he died and was buried, according to this story.)

The reader may wonder what point this narration of detail serves. Here is where I will—(tongue in cheek!)—make my *own* historical claim to be personally descended from David!

---

[71] Skene, *The Coronation Stone* (1869); Melton, *Encyclopedia of American Religion*, I, 447.

[72] Hoeh, *Compendium*, I, 425-26. The *Compendium* says the name "Dowd's Town" is attached to an area three miles north of Tara Hill, according to B.M. Ordnance Survey maps, Ireland, 91, 101.

Afterward on Anglo-Israelism, I

My last name is Doudna, and all Doudnas in existence—with this spelling—descend from John Doudna (1744-1811), a sailor who landed on shore in North Carolina in 1770, illiterate and penniless, after barely surviving a shipwreck. Of English origin, John had been kidnapped as a child from a wharf, and never saw his parents again. He had been raised by a ship's captain on the sea, had fought in the Battle of Quebec under General Wolfe (1759), and remembered that his last name was pronounced "Doudna." Arriving safely on land after the shipwreck, John Doudna renounced the sea, found work as a farmhand, and married the farmer's daughter. They were Quakers, migrated to Barnesville, Ohio, and (this being before birth control) had fourteen kids. That is the origin of all the Doudnas. No Doudnas up to now have been able to trace John Doudna's origins any further back. I have undertaken considerable personal effort, including a trip to London in early 1985, to see if I could solve this mystery.

That all known Doudnas, no matter where you may find them in the world, trace their descent from the same John Doudna confirms that John Doudna's last name was spelled the way he remembered it sounded, as distinguished from how his parents' name was written.

In England, I found the names "Doudney" and "Dowdney" are common, most strongly in Somerset and Devon. I concluded that this probably was the true English name of John Doudna. But where did the Doudneys come from? (I reject as apocryphal a tale that the name originated when John Doudna was asked his name upon arrival in America. According to that story he answered "don't know" and that became misunderstood and written down as an answer of "Doudna.") Although Doudneys are well-established in England, I suspected they had migrated from somewhere else. One theory among Doudneys with whom I have talked is that they came from French Huguenots from the River Aude region in France (D'Aude).

However, I found names similar to Dowdney seemingly more common in Ireland than elsewhere—names such as Dowd,

Dowdal, Dowde, and Dowden. Even in my study of the Milesian king lists in the annals I noticed the frequent appearance of "na" endings on the names (i.e. Eadna, Seadna, Muimne, Luighne, Feorgna, Cearmna, Fiachna). Because of this, I came to suspect that Doudna origins may go back to Ireland, not France. But where *in* Ireland might the Doudnas have originated?

No solution suggested itself until I reread, in preparation of this chapter for the first edition of this book, the mention of "Dowd's Town" in the *Compendium*. Seeing this led me to wonder if the Doudna name might literally be connected with that place-name. Lacking other leads, I consider it, at the least, an intriguing possibility. Since the *Compendium* says this town was founded by King David of Israel, this would mean the Doudnas, or originally, Dowdneys, carry the name of King David, originating from the town which he founded. "Doudna" or "Dowdney" would mean "born of David." With a little further imagination it could be suggested that Doudnas descend directly from David's daughter Tamar, brought to Ireland at the founding of Dowd's Town. A dim memory of our true origins might be hypothesized from the coincidence that my father's name is "David Ephraim Doudna." (My great-grandfather's name was Ephraim Doudna, and his father was Hosea Doudna, who was a son of the original John Doudna.) This would make me a son of David by surname going directly back to King David, after whom, by this interpretation, all Doudnas are named.

If Herbert Armstrong could lay claim to direct descent from David, I thought I might add my own claim, which probably has at least equal historical merit. I will refrain, however, from laying claim to the throne of England.

(As I said, this is tongue in cheek—I do not believe Dowd's Town or my ancestry has any connection with King David.)

The lesson from this excursion into creative etymology is that finding coincidences of similar-sounding syllables in unrelated languages (i.e. "Dowd's Town" from "David's Town") is, on a scale of strength of evidence from 0 to 10, 10 being highest, about, say 1/10,000 or less. There are only a small number of sounds from which all human vocalizations must be composed. Some consonants, like "d" and "s" and "b" and "n," appear even more frequently. Of the hundreds of thousands of words and names in hundreds of languages, to find words with two, three, or four consecutive syllables in one language to be similar to words in another language is only to be expected by the laws of probability. There is no basis for drawing causal or derivative conclusions from this kind of reasoning. Yet this is exactly the level of reasoning that finds, for example, "Isaac's sons" in "Saxons"; the Hebrew "Covenant Man (Berit-Ish)" in "British"; or the name "Baruch," the scribe of Jeremiah of Jerusalem, in the Milesian king "Simeon Breac," a hemisphere away in Ireland.

CHAPTER 8

AFTERWARD ON ANGLO-ISRAELISM, PART II

The outside reader may wonder with amazement: "How can people actually believe that ancient Israelites were white folks who migrated to Europe and became switched into Anglo-Saxons?"

Much of what passes for history in groups such as the old Worldwide Church of God and its successor organizations is indeed, to put it kindly, baseless. (It would never get to first base at any gathering of professional historians.) The outside observer may be appalled at the distortions and misstatements, undocumented assertions and leaping to conclusions that are believed as gospel truth by avid readers of church literature.

Speaking as one who was there in youthful days, I hasten to shed light on why these ideas seem credible. What the outside observer often overlooks is that, to the believer, the issue is not framed in terms of: "What does a fair survey of the relevant historical records tell us?" Rather, the belief comes out of a perception that the Bible requires such a system of belief. That, combined with a lack of familiarity with what is currently published in the relevant fields, can lead to outlandish beliefs.

At Big Sandy I believed, along with everyone else, that Americans and Britons were Israelites. I was aware that, as one thoughtful, older Worldwide Church of God member diplomatically put it in conversation with me once, "It would be nice if the historical evidence was a bit stronger." Nevertheless, the biblical arguments in the theory's favor seemed intriguing and persuasive.

But in the months following my writing of my paper on Ephraim, I began to have troubling second thoughts. Did the ancient Israelites really migrate to Europe and become switched into Anglo-Saxons? That sure wasn't what the encyclopedias said. According to the encyclopedias, the Anglo-Saxons originated in lands far to the north of the Middle East. They were not Hebrews native to the Middle East. To say that Anglo-Saxons came from Hebrews is like saying that Alaskan Inuit are really African Zulus.

I decided I would try to get some answers.

Learning history at Big Sandy

> "The idle genealogies Paul talked about refer to pagan cosmogonies and cosmologies, not to what we are learning in this course."
> --lecturer, Ancient World History class, Feb. 4, 1974, from my class notes

Quiet, bespectacled, red-haired Allen Manteufel (1935-1978) was the instructor in my sophomore Ancient World History class. He taught out of Dr. Hoeh's *Compendium of World History*. He supplemented this with his notes from assorted other rare and arcane books, the only copies of which were often in Pasadena. (We could not even see a copy of most source materials for what we were learning.) I found Mr. Manteufel's classes fascinating. It was the feeling of learning rare, exciting knowledge hidden from an outside world that goes about its daily tasks oblivious to understanding its true origins and history. For example, the following is verbatim from my Ancient World History class notes of February 8, 1974.

> Noah took his sons on a world tour to show them the world around the Mediterranean in 10 years. He began by the Black Sea, circled the Mediterranean, and left a colony on the Tiber River in Italy. Noah then retired to Armenia. Noah sent out regular contingents of

Afterward on Anglo-Israelism, II

colonies as the population grew. He took another world tour in 2210 BC and spent 9 years in Spain. Then Noah arrived in Italy, found Gomer had died and the Italians were being corrupted by Ham. Noah kicked out Ham and ruled Italy himself. Noah died and gave the land to Saturn and one of Joktan's kids.

(It was definitely, as the Ambassador College student handbook accurately said, knowledge unattainable at other universities.)

I stopped by Manteufel's office one day. I asked: "Mr. Manteufel, are we really the literal, physical descendants of Israel? If it wasn't for the biblical reasons for believing this, how strong would the historical evidence in itself be for this?"

Pleased at my interest in this area he had made his specialty, he answered, "The evidence is very good." He said the work of an historian named Sharon Turner had proven the origins of the Anglo-Saxons from the Black Sea. This was the same location, he said, as the Israelites were last known to have disappeared.

Manteufel is dead now. But who was Sharon Turner and what was in Sharon Turner's work which had convinced Manteufel?

Were the Scythians Israelites?

Mr. Manteufel was referring to one of the most common ways in which British-Israelites traced the Anglo-Saxons from the Israelites. It goes basically like this:

(1) The Israelites taken into captivity became the Scythians by the Black Sea.

(2) Anglo-Saxon origins are traced from the Scythians.

The second step of this two-part linkage—the claim that the Anglo-Saxons came from the Scythians—was the thesis of English historian Sharon Turner. He published his work, *The History of the Anglo-Saxons*, in 1799-1805. Turner (who was not a British-Israelite) was an able historian for his time. He was an early pioneer in recovering Anglo-Saxon history and writings. It was Turner who, in 1805, brought the epic poem "Beowulf" to the world's attention.

Turner's theory on Anglo-Saxon origins from Scythians is not, however, accepted by historians today. Turner traced the Saxons from the Scythian tribe of the "Sacae." But archaeology in the twentieth century by Soviet scholars established that the Scythians came to the Black Sea from Western Siberian origins. Historians do not believe Europeans came from Siberian or Mongolian peoples. Hence, Turner was mistaken.

Furthermore, there is no basis for saying the Israelites in Assyrian captivity became a people of central Asians which existed centuries earlier and migrated to the north of the captive Israelites decades before the Israelites were there. In other words, the Anglo-Saxons weren't Scythians, and the Scythians weren't Israelites. Both steps of the two-step linkage are wrong.

Those ubiquitous "Lost Israelites"

The "Lost Israelites" were identified in Worldwide Church of God literature not only as Scythians but with many other significant peoples of the time (perhaps for good measure). The *Cimmerians* (the Scythians' mortal enemies) were also identified as the Israelites.[73] An ancient Greek people called the "Tuatha de Danaan" was identified as the Israelite tribe of Dan. The *Celts* were identified as Israelites by evangelists Dibar Apartian and Raymond McNair.[74] Herbert Armstrong identified the Celts' conquerors, the *Anglo-Saxons*, as Israelites, in *The United States and Britain in Prophecy*. In an article entitled "Where did the Twelve Apostles Go?," and in his *Compendium of World History*, Dr. Hoeh said the *Parthians*, the rival empire on the

---

[73] Dibar Apartian, *Les Pays de Langue Francaise Selon La Prophetie* (rev. ed.; Pasadena, Calif.: Worldwide Church of God, 1982).

[74] Apartian, *Les Pays de Langue Francaise Selon La Prophetie*; Raymond F. McNair, "Key to Northwest European Political Origins" (thesis, Ambassador College, Pasadena, 1963), 13.

Afterward on Anglo-Israelism, II

Roman empire's eastern frontier, were Israelites.[75] Hoeh said the ancient *Pelasgian Sea People* in Greek annals were Israelites.[76] Hoeh also thought maybe the "White Indians" or "*Nephtalite Huns*" of India were Israelites from the tribe of Naphtali.[77] Undoubtedly there are more that I have missed.

Hoeh even had Hebrews in the Greek world and in Ireland before Abraham was born! "In 2068 [BC] Parthalon and a band of Hebrew warriors arrived from the Greek world [to Ireland]," Hoeh wrote in the *Compendium*.[78] (Those Hebrews got around!)

The problem with these identifications is they just aren't true. The Tuatha de Danaan existed in the Mediterranean before there was an Israelite tribe of Dan. The Celts existed before Israel went into captivity.[79] The first century Parthians are distinguished by Josephus from the tribes of Israel.[80] The Pelasgians were early inhabitants of Greece. And the White Huns or "Ephthalites" were a tribe who came from central Asia into India in the fifth century AD.[81] The Cimmerians are a special case and require comment.

---

[75] Herman L. Hoeh, *Compendium of World History*, 2 vols (Pasadena, Calif.: Ambassador College, 1967-69 reprint [1st ed. 1962-63]), II, 303-305.
[76] Hoeh, *Compendium*, I, 409.
[77] Hoeh, *Compendium*, II, 305-306.
[78] Hoeh, *Compendium*, I, 417-418.
[79] The Celts were in southwest Germany and eastern France in 1500-1200 BC according to reference sources. Meanwhile, 2 Kings 17:23 says the Israelites were in captivity in the land of the Assyrians (present-day Iran) "until this day," i.e. 500s BC or later.
[80] The Parthians frequently challenged the eastern borders of the Roman empire. Josephus refers to the Israelites as Israelites (*Ant* 11.5.2), not Parthians. (Josephus calls the Parthians "Parthians.") The "kings from the east" of Rev 16:12 likely allude to Parthians. The Parthians were descended from earlier Asiatic Scythian roots according to reference sources.
[81] Hoeh's total evidence for the Ephthalite Hun identity was the similarity of the name to one of the tribes of Israel, and that they were called "white."

Cimmerians and Anne Kristensen[82]

The Cimmerians are widely and correctly identified as "Gomer" of Japheth in the Genesis table of nations.[83] However a Danish scholar, Anne Kristensen, argued in a study published in 1988 that the Cimmerians or *Gimirru* who appear in Assyrian sources were Israelites working in the Assyrian army, posted in Assyrian fortresses.[84] Anglo-Israelites have leapt on this. Other scholars are then cited who say the Scythians and Cimmerians were interchangeable, and then this is put together with legends of Celts and others anciently claiming to come from Cimmerian origins. Presto!—the Anglo-Israel theory is true after all! Not so fast.

First of all, although Kristensen makes an argument that the Cimmerians were working for the Assyrians, it does not

---

[82] I thank Selim F. Adali, a graduate student at the University of Sydney who is doing a dissertation on the Cimmerians and the Medes, for kindly reading this section after I wrote it and suggesting several corrections and rewordings. Any remaining errors are of course my responsibility.

[83] Allen Godbey summarizes: "Gen 10:2 says the Ashkenazim are 'sons' of Gomer (that is, political sons) ... The classic Kimmerians are universally recognized in the Hebrew Gomer ... The Kimmerians were expelled from their ancient home on the northwest of the Black Sea about 660 BC. The Scythians drove them into Asia Minor where they shattered the kingdom of Lydia; but their brief triumph in the west was followed by the Scythian wave from the east, about 637, which shattered the Kimmerian power, leaving them a fragment of the country held later by the Iranic Katapatuka (Cappadocia). The Armenians called this Gimirr. So Genesis 10:2f. reflects the moment of Kimmerian dominance in western Asia Minor, and any Ashkenazim Jews in that region are political 'sons' of the conquering Gomer. The overthrow of this Gomer power is shown in Ezekiel 38:6 where Lydia (Gog, Guggu, Gyges) is master in Asia Minor, and Gomer is but one of many petty vassals of Lydia" (Allen Godbey, *The Lost Tribes a Myth* [Durham, N.C,.: Duke U. Press, 1930], 228-69).

[84] Anne Katrina Gade Kristensen, *Who Were the Cimmerians, and Where Did They Come From?: Sargon II, the Cimmerians, and Rusa I* (trans. from Danish by Joergen Laessoe; The Royal Danish Academy of Sciences and Letters No. 57; Copenhagen, 1988).

Afterward on Anglo-Israelism, II

follow from this (if this is the case) that these Cimmerians were Israelites.

And second, many Anglo-Israelites cite Kristensen with a very poor or non-existent understanding of her case or argument. It is common in Anglo-Israel literature to see Kristensen cited, and then her thesis homogenized with views which Kristensen's thesis opposes, namely that the Cimmerians were a northern nomadic people who came down from the north, with the idea being that some deported Israelites "joined" these northern nomads. In this way Anglo-Israelites get the Israelites into Cimmerian history and (claimed) connections to Europe, without having to take the risky step and hard work of addressing the quite different traditions of Cimmerians of Herodotus, explaining Cimmerian place-names to the north, archaeological issues, and so on. But that is exactly what Kristensen does, and the correctness of her case *requires* that she be correct on this. That is, Kristensen argues that there *are* no distinct Cimmerians other than the Israelites, and that the Cimmerians *are* deported Israelites, and nothing else. If one is not going to go the whole route with Kristensen, one cannot cite her conclusion as somehow adding support to a modified interpretation of the traditional view which is in conflict with Kristensen's argument. But this is what some Anglo-Israelites do.

Kristensen argues for locating the Cimmerians of the Assyrians texts south of an ancient kingdom called Urartu. According to Kristensen, the Cimmerians of 714 BC are in the employ of the Assyrians manning Assyrian fortresses. These issues are under debate among scholars. A key point of dispute is where *Gamir* is, a location of the Cimmerians to which allusion is made in Assyrian texts. If Gamir is to the north of Urartu (as traditionally), then Kristensen's thesis cannot be correct that the Cimmerians are working for the Assyrians (since Urartu was to the north of the Assyrian empire). But Kristensen and a few other scholars argue for locating Gamir to the south of Urartu. Specialists in Cimmerian studies continue to debate this, though the stronger scholarly weight seems to favor the northern location.[85] (Personally, having studied Kristensen's monograph, I think Kristensen's argument concerning the Cimmerians as part of the Assyrian army of Sargon II is brilliantly argued but almost certainly wrong.[86])

---

[85] In 1990 G.B. Lanfranchi, an expert on neo-Assyrian texts, argued that the Cimmerians in Mannae and Media were part of the Assyrian army, and for a "southern" location for Gamir, both points in agreement with Kristensen. However Askold Ivantchik, a leading authority on Cimmerians (see note 92), reports that in 1994 Lanfranchi told him he is instead "now inclining" to view Gamir as located to the north of Urartu, in agreement with Ivantchik and against the thesis of Kristensen (Ivantchik citing an oral comment of Lanfranchi in 1994, in A.I. Ivantchik, "The Current State of the Cimmerian Problem," *Ancient Civilizations from Scythia to Siberia* 7/3-4 [September 2001]: 307-339). The late I.M. Diakonoff (Russian linguist and Assyrian authority) is also cited by Ivantchik as agreeing with the northern location of Gamir (Ivantchik, "Current State," 313). On the other hand a 1997 dissertation by Hermann Sauter of Saarland University (Germany), published in 2000, supports Kristensen's argument of a southern location of Gamir and that the Cimmerians were part of the Assyrian army (H. Sauter, *Studien zum Kimmerierproblem* [Bonn: Habelt, 2000], available online at http://www.kimmerier.de/start.htm).

[86] My reasons for thinking Kristensen's argument that the Cimmerians are part of the Assyrian army is likely wrong include the following considerations: (a) Assyrian policy was to incorporate deported peoples into Assyrian citizenship, which would include army service, in a national identity as "Assyrian" (see S. Parpola, "Assyrian Identity in Ancient Times and Today", at www.nineveh.com/parpola_eng.pdf). Would an Assyrian army unit be known in Assyrian reports by an ethnic name in the manner proposed? (b) If the Cimmerians were Assyrian citizens/soldiers in 714 BC (per Kristensen), would they have become independent and warred against Sargon II (721-705 BC) only 9 years later, as Assyrian records indicate? Is this a plausible outcome of deportees in the Assyrian army, when other deportee populations typically assimilated and were loyal to Assyria? Are there other parallels of Assyrian military units going independent and attacking Assyria in this period? (c) If the Cimmerians were deportees, and if the Cimmerians were easily confused with Scythians, this almost requires the Scythians to be closely related to the same source of origin as the Cimmerians, which escalates further the amount of historical revisionism required. And after 705 BC the Scythians and Cimmerians not only are both independent of Assyria but war with each other. Where did the Scythians, this distinct people so similar to the Cimmerians, come from? Is it not simpler and less complicated

Afterward on Anglo-Israelism, II

But what if Kristensen's argument concerning the Cimmerians being in the Assyrian army *is* correct? Here is where Kristensen's further argument from this point dramatically weakens.

Kristensen says: if the Cimmerians are in the Assyrian fortresses near Urartu, this fits the pattern of the Assyrians making use of deportees in their army. In this case the Cimmerians may be far from their homeland (in keeping with general population movement policies of the Assyrians). On this hypothesis, the Cimmerians would be from somewhere else. Who would they be? Kristensen answers: they are deportees from the house of Israel. Kristensen supports this proposal with two arguments: a name identification argument and a geographical juxtaposition argument.

On geographical juxtaposition, Kristensen argues that the "cities of the Medes" to which the Israelites are biblically said to have been deported are associated with the area of the Cimmerians. This involves argument concerning toponyms and placements of toponyms, which Kristensen provides. But the actual proof of the Israel/Cimmerian identity, Kristensen says, comes from an identification made in Anglo-Israel circles of the Assyrian name for the house of Israel, *bit-Omri*, with the Assyrian name for the Cimmerians, *Gimiri*.[87] Kristensen writes:

---

to suppose the Cimmerians and Scythians are related peoples in an area outside of Assyrian control, in keeping with the traditional view? (d) In the Assyrian spy report cited by Kristensen which tells of a defeat at Gamir of a king of Urartu in the time of Sargon II (which Kristensen says is the same as an Assyrian victory credited to Sargon II over Rusa, king of Urartu, of a different account), why is there no verbal allusion internal to the spy report text that Gamir *is Assyrian* (if Kristensen is correct)? (Kristensen does on p. 83 cite a line rendered "The Urartian, since he […] went [to] Gamir [now(?)] is very afraid of the king my lord," but given the lacunas and brokenness of the text I do not see that this proves, as Kristensen claims, that "Sargon and the Assyrians were engaged in the battle with Rusa in Gamir.")

[87] Kristensen here cites an article in the July/Aug. 1984 Norwegian edition of the *Plain Truth* magazine, published by the Worldwide Church of God, by Robert Boraker entitled "The Origin of the Scandinavians."

Afterward on Anglo-Israelism, II

In reality, the answer as to who the Cimmerians were has been given long ago and has been known since the last century, perhaps even earlier. Not, however, by established scholarly research but by a long series of people who showed up with different backgrounds: people who asked themselves the question, What did in fact become of the Israelites who were deported, already at the time of Tiglath-Pilesar III and later on, after the conquest of Samaria in 722, to Assyria, and in the latter case also to the cities of Media. For them there is no doubt: the Cimmerians were Israelites who came from the northern kingdom of Israel and wherever and whenever Assyrian and later sources refer to Cimmerians, we are in fact dealing with deported Israelites ...

The proof which has been provided for the identity of the Israelites with the Cimmerians is of a philological nature. The northern kingdom of Israel was known by several names at the time, among them, *Beth-'Omri*, the House of 'Omri, named after the founder of Samaria, Omri, the king of northern Israel who lived in the 9th century. When the Assyrians referred to North Israel, they always used the name Beth-'Omri which was rendered as *Bit-Humri*. When Omri could be rendered as "*Humri*," then according to Pinches it shows that at the time the name was pronounced "Ghomri, in accordance with the older system before ghain became ayin" [citing Pinches 1903]. Inasmuch as the Assyrians "had no *gh* in their language, they had to represent it by a character which may be transliterated *Kh*, *Gh*, or *H*, according to choice. In Assyrian, therefore, Beth-Omri is renderable by *Bit-Khumri*, *Bit-Ghumri* or *Bit Humri*, as may be preferred," so Hannay writes, and he goes on to saying, "The Assyrian word which may be transliterated *Khumri*, *Ghumri*, or *Humri*, expressed the same idea, and stood in the same degree of relation to its Hebraic etymon 'Omri as did the Babylonian word *Gimiri*, or *Gimirra*." When historians have failed to find the exiled Israelites in the sources of the time, Boraker maintains, it is due to the circumstance that the Assyrians did not call them "Israel," but designated them as "Bit-*Humri*" or the like. "At the time of Esarhaddon [680-669 BC] ghomri was written Gimirrai (Cimmerians)."

These are the arguments of those scholars. But it is not only at the time of Esarhaddon that the term *Gimirraja* occurs. Yet, in the letters

---

Kristensen writes: "I thank [Robert C.] Boraker for having placed his vast knowledge of this wide subject at my disposal through our correspondence" (Kristensen, *Who Were the Cimmerians?*, 119 n. 407).

Afterward on Anglo-Israelism, II

dating to the reign of Sargon [721-705 BC], this term, KUR GI-MIR-AJA, occurs in one single letter only (ND 1107). Otherwise, at the time of this king, we find terms like KUR GA-MIR (ABL 197, ob. 9), KUR GA-MIR-RA (ABL 146, obv. 6 and 9) or LU$_2$GA-MI$_3$-RA-AJA (ABL 112, obv. 4). It may be taken for granted there is a linguistic relationship between *'Omri* and the terms used for the Cimmerians, but one may wonder why the Assyrians would have applied these terms for deportees from the house of Omri when so far, in their inscriptions, they had used the term *Humri*? The arguments adduced by the students of the Ten Tribes amounts to the possibility that there may have been two different ways in which the Assyrians attempted to render the Hebrew *'Omri*. Incidentally, the Hebrew word for Cimmerians, *Gomer*, appears to be rather close to the older form *'Omri*.[88]

I have given this extended quotation of Kristensen not only to give the argument for the word connection but to show the fundamental weakness of the argument.

Kristensen cites the similarity between the Assyrian term for Israelites, *bit-Omri*, and the Assyrian term for the Cimmerians,

---

[88] Kristensen, *Who Were the Cimmerians?*, 118-120. Kristensen continues: "I am in no way blind to the fact that the idea of connecting the Cimmerians with deported Israelites will rouse an immediate wave of contradiction, if for no other reasons, then psychologically. We have for so long become accustomed to the idea of the Cimmerians as a nomadic horseborne people from the North Pontian steppes that, quite naturally, we would find it difficult to accept the idea that we are in fact dealing with a people which is already well known in history, such as Israelites. An untrustworthy tradition as that of the classical conception of the Cimmerians can be repeated for so long, indeed for millennia, that truth, once it appears, is unlikely to appear for our benefit. I myself was utterly skeptical, not to say extremely reserved, when I first encountered this hypothesis in print. But it forced me to take up the question of the earliest history of the Cimmerians, and as the premises of the commonly accepted opinions of this people began to crumble, and an entirely new picture began to take shape, I had to admit that the students of the Ten Tribes must have seen the truth. The result of the analyses which have been undertaken in the present contribution concerning the Cimmerians and their first appearance in 714 [BC], as well as probings into their history in the next century provide us with a geographical, chronological and an historically solid basis of the theses of these scholars which so far has not been available" (pp. 120-21).

Gimiri. Kristensen endorses the argument that the two names are variants of the same name and refer to the same people, through a plausible spelling variant. But the fact that the names as used by the Assyrians are *not* spelled the same is a major problem for the theory. The Assyrians knew how to refer to Israelites when they were speaking of Israelites. They had a term for Israelites. If they were referring to *Israelites*, they would use the same term instead of the different (though similar sounding) name. The names Omri and Gimiri are similar but not the same. Why (if they are the same people) did the Assyrians not use *exactly* the same name? Kristensen offers no explanation for this. The more likely interpretation is that the two names sound similar simply by coincidence, and that the reason the Assyrians use two different names (even if sounding similar) is because these are the names of two distinct peoples. If the names *were* naming the same people there would be only a *single* name used for the one people, and this question of why the two names would not even have come up.[89]

With the failure of the only alleged proof cited by Kristensen for the identity, namely the argument that the similar names means identity, there simply is nothing substantial that remains calling for a Cimmerian/Israelite identity.

The geographical proximity argument is not substantial. First of all the Bible does not know of any of the resettled, deported Israelites becoming army units in the areas to which they were deported. (More likely, resettled peoples became citizens and subject to taxes and military service like other citizens, and those who were drafted became part of the regular army which could

---

[89] Mere similarity in names is usually far from enough to prove identity. Here is an unfortunately typical example of reasoning from an Anglo-Israel website: "Why some of those folks have been traced to Japan!! One of the most common Japanese names is Sakai. And their warriors have a name, Samurai, that is so close to the name of the Israelite capital, Samaria, that the connection between Israel and Japan is virtually cemented ..." ("The Assyrian Tablets: Hard Evidence," no author or date, http://asis.com/~stag/tablets.html).

go anywhere.) The Cimmerians, if they *were* the Assyrian army in that location, could be posted to that area from any conquered people (or alternatively, mercenaries from non-conquered allies), and not necessarily from the peoples settled there in other capacities. If the Cimmerians *were* deportees in the Assyrian army, there were many populations, not just Israelites, which could be candidates for being the Cimmerians. (But the notion that the Cimmerians were deportees in the Assyrian army is not secure.)

No ancient historian thought that the Cimmerians were the Tribes of Israel. The Greek historian Herodotus (484-425 BC) did not think that. He thought the Cimmerians came from the north, from Central Asian origins. Josephus did not think so. Josephus thought the deported Israelites were thriving on the eastern side of the Euphrates in his day (*Ant.* 11.5.2), not to the west and far to the north where the Cimmerians were located. If the Cimmerians were openly named and known as Israelites by the Assyrians how was this knowledge so completely lost to ancient historians?

Even the authors of the Bible, with all of their interest in the house of Israel, do not know of a Cimmerian/Israelite identity. In the Bible the Cimmerians are "Gomer," which is from Japheth, and distinct from the Israelites from Shem (Gen 10:2). Kristensen does not address this. For Kristensen's thesis to work it must be assumed that not only Herodotus and other ancient historians did not know the Cimmerians were Israelites, but the writers of the Bible *also* had no idea Cimmerians were actually Israelites. Is this really plausible?

At the end Kristensen attempts to wrap up loose ends. She wants to account for Cimmerian toponyms found north of the Black Sea and also for why Herodotus thought the Cimmerians came from north of the Black Sea. Kristensen solves this by arguing that the Cimmerian/Israelites, after breaking free of their Assyrian overlords and going into Asia Minor where they attacked the kingdom of Lud, then spread to different places including north of the Black Sea. The alternative is that

Herodotus had it basically right that the Cimmerians, as well as the Scythians, came from the north to begin with. The best current discussions of archaeological finds appear to favor the northern origin of the Cimmerians and Scythians.[90]

To put it succinctly, there is no positive evidence for Kristensen's suggestion that the Cimmerians are Israelites, and seemingly overwhelming arguments against it. And again, the necessary prerequisite, namely that the Cimmerians were located to the south (as opposed to the north) of Urartu, and were working for the Assyrians (as opposed to being a distinct people north of the Assyrian empire), is not established in terms of winning over most scholars.

The Russian scholar Askold Ivantchik has argued well that the Cimmerians are to be identified archaeologically specifically with what scholars have called "Early Scythian" sites.[91] The Cimmerians are culturally similar to the Scythians who also are found with "Early Scythian" assemblages, although the Scythians are a different people than the Cimmerians according to contemporary written descriptions. The sites of the Cimmerians in Anatolia, which archaeologically are called "Early Scythian" sites, show a nomadic people with a material culture relationship to Central Asian precursors. These are not the material remains of exiles from Samaria or the Middle East. Ivantchik cites texts in which the Assyrians know the contemporary Cimmerians and Scythians as distinct peoples (refuting the idea of some scholars that Cimmerians and Scythians are interchangeable). Yet their similar archaeological remains show cultural similarity, and the later Babylonians mixed up the two peoples. Therefore although the Scythians and Cimmerians were different (the Assyrians know them as different, and they war with each other), they weren't *very* different. They were confused anciently as being the same

---

[90] See note 92.

[91] A.I. Ivantchik, "The Current State of the Cimmerian Problem," 324-339.

Afterward on Anglo-Israelism, II

people.[92] If the Scythians and Cimmerians are *both* Israelite, is it not odd that no ancient historian knows this about the Scythians either?

Kristensen apparently saw this implication concerning the Cimmerians and the Scythians as related peoples, and at the end of her monograph seems to hint at a revised understanding of the Scythians as Israelites or Jews as well. These are the final words of Kristensen's study:

> [W]ho are the Ashkenazim [Jews]? The name is identical with the Hebrew term for Scythians, Ashkenaz, which corresponds to the Ishguza of the Assyrians. How could it ever have happened that one main group of European Jews should have become known as "Scythians"? Is it merely a case of "misunderstanding" or "a curious development"? Isn't the truth, rather, that the last word remains to be

---

[92] For information on the cutting edge of Cimmerian studies, see the review of A.I. Ivantchik, *Kimmerier und Skythen* (2001) by B. Baebler in the *Bryn Mawr Classical Review* 10 (2004) (http://ccat.sas.upenn.edu/bmcr/2004/2004-10-29.html). The reviewer writes: "To avoid the problems caused by the cultural similarity of Cimmerian and Scythian archaeological remains, I[vantchik] narrows his focus to those areas of Anatolia for which the written sources bear witness to the presence of Cimmerians but not Scythians. Instead of concentrating on material from the Cimmerians' homeland in the steppes, which cannot be linked to contemporary written sources, he analyzes the archaeological remains of those regions which were the goal of the Cimmerian military campaigns and therefore mentioned in the cuneiform accounts. Four burial complexes are analyzed (two on the acropolis of Norsuntepe on the upper Euphrates; two in the vicinity of Imirler and Amasya); it can be shown that the architecture of the tombs' stone vaults and the bimetallic battle pickaxes ("Streitpickel") with the picture of a bird of prey on them were very probably distinctly Cimmerian. These features appear also in graves of Southern Central Caucasia; there lay the "country of Gamir" where the king of Urartu was beaten by the Cimmerians in 714 BC. Apart from these peculiarities, however, the Cimmerians belonged to the same archaeological culture as the early Scythians ... The archaeological cultures of the Cimmerians and Scythians are almost identical, but the cuneiform texts distinguish them clearly and they occupied different territories; most probably they were related Iranian peoples. This volume is certainly the best and most solid book on Cimmerians and early Scythians available today."

said about the descendants of Abraham, Isaac and Jacob, the children of Israel?[93]

In short, Kristensen's 1988 monograph consists of a main argument—that the Cimmerians were part of the Assyrian army as opposed to independent of the Assyrians—and an unproven conjecture at the end of her main argument which does not follow from her main argument: that the Cimmerians are identical with the deported Israelites. The key point to realize is that the main argument, which is the bulk of Kristensen's thesis and itself disputed, provides no evidence for the conjecture of interest to Anglo-Israelites at the end of the book, which is not demonstrated with evidence.

The Anglo-Israelites' use of Kristensen is a case of Anglo-Israelites looking across the smorgasbord of legitimate scholarship and finding a scholar who argues a point which serves a purpose. In much of this literature the method seems to be: simply that a scholar's argument "works" is all that is needed; quote the scholar, declare point proven, extrapolate the conclusion way beyond what the point is capable of proving even if it is correct, case closed. But this is no way to do history.

The Cimmerians, after being driven west by Scythians, flourished briefly in Asia Minor but their power seems to have been broken in 637 BC by Scythians. Although the Cimmerians are first mentioned in written records in 714 BC, the continuity between Cimmerian material culture ("Early Scythian") and Central Asian antecedents argues that the Cimmerians existed before the house of Israel went into captivity.[94]

---

[93] Kristensen, *Who Were the Cimmerians?*, 132.

[94] Dr. Hoeh had the Cimmerians long predating the Israelites. According to Hoeh's *Compendium of World History,* in 1489-1429 BC some Germans and Amazons "proceeded down the Danube valley to the Black Sea and on through the Crimea and the Palus Maeotia to Armenia and Cappadocia and the Taurus mountains. Here they were known as the Cimmerians" (*Compendium*, II, 21-22, citing the *Bavarian Chronicle*).

Afterward on Anglo-Israelism, II

In conclusion, there is every evidence, including biblical, that Cimmerians were biblical "Japheth" peoples, related to Scythians, and had nothing to do with Israelites. No ancient historian, nor the Bible, knows of a Cimmerian/Israel identity or a Scythian/Israel identity. There is nothing indicating this in Assyrian records. There is nothing known of Cimmerians in terms of language or archaeology that links them with Israelites. There are extensive grounds to associate Cimmerians with Scythians, and neither the Cimmerians nor the Scythians originated from deported Israelites.

Every claim under the sun

Every claim under the sun has been made for the "Lost Ten Tribes." A distinguished seventeenth-century Hebrew scholar, Manasseh ben Israel (1604-1657) of Amsterdam, considered emigrating to Brazil after publishing his findings that he had discovered the Lost Ten Tribes in South America (in Ecuador, to be specific). (Some natives had recited the "Shema" in Hebrew to him, and told him through an interpreter that they were Israelites descended from the tribe of Reuben, and he believed them.) The Red Karene tribes of Burma, discovered by Baptist missionaries, were supposed to be the Lost Tribes (they worshiped a god named "Ywwah" and "looked like Jews"). In 1819 it was reported that some Afghan clans called themselves "Usofzais" or "Josephites" and claimed Israelite ancestry, at least for their chieftains. They claimed ancestry from Kish, the father of Saul. This was popularized in a book in 1841 by Asahel Grant which claimed the Nestorians and the Yezidi tribe of devil-worshippers of Afghanistan were the Lost Ten Tribes. Before long some Europeans decided the whole Afghan people represented the "lost ten tribes."

The Abyssinians were claimed to be the Lost Tribes because of temples of Yeha (= Yahu) found at Axum. (Actually, the temples derive from pre-Christian Jewish trading posts.) The Masai tribe of today's Kenya was claimed to be Israelites. The

Israelitish origin of the Japanese people was infallibly demonstrated by a book in 1879. (The last king of Israel was Hosea, died 722 BC. The first king of Japan was Osee, 730 BC. Need one say more?) The aboriginals of Australia were claimed to be Israelites (because they practiced circumcision). The Malays of Malaysia were claimed. The American Indians were claimed. Via Joseph Smith, this last idea survives as Mormon doctrine today, but it was widely believed earlier.[95]

The Ahmidiyya Movement in Islam (whose mosque in Washington, D.C. I have visited) believes that, after surviving the crucifixion, Jesus went to the descendants of the Tribes of Israel in Afghanistan and Kashmir. There he married a local peasant woman named Mary, settled down and had a family, lived to the ripe old age of 120, and is buried in the city of Srinegar today at a tomb of "Yuz-Asaph." The tomb is owned and cared for today by Jesus's descendants, who will tell you more of the story for a modest donation.

At least two pre-World War II British-Israel books that I have seen claimed that the Japanese were another branch of Manasseh that split from the branch that became the United States.[96] That one was short-lived, however. After Pearl Harbor, the ancestors

---

[95] Information in this paragraph is summarized from Godbey, *The Lost Tribes a Myth*, 1-6, *The Jewish Encyclopedia*, and Shalom L. Goldman, *God's Sacred Tongue: Hebrew and the American Imagination* (U. of North Carolina Press, 2004).

[96] Japan as Manasseh was argued in W.G. MacKendrick, *The Destiny of Britain and America*, rev. ed. (Toronto: McClelland, 1922), 259-69; and M.H. Gager, *The Heritage of the Anglo-Saxon Race*, 3rd rev. ed. (Haverhill, Mass.: Destiny Publishers, 1941), 112-15. The argument was that as ancient Manasseh was divided into two parts, modern Manasseh is in two parts, the United States and Japan. Allegedly startling parallels between the Shinto religion and the law of Moses were also claimed, such as that they both had priests, and so on. The idea that the Japanese were Manassites apparently first surfaced in British-Israel circles in 1905. After the Anglo-Japanese Alliance of that year a pamphlet appeared, rudely taking away the United States people's Manassite ancestry and "claiming that Japan, not America, was the true Manasseh" (John Wilson, "British Israelism," in Bryan Wilson, ed., *Patterns of Sectarianism* [London: Heinemann, 1967], 349).

of the Japanese from thousands of years ago understandably were quickly changed back into Gentiles again.

The Mormons believe Christ appeared and taught in the Americas several hundred years after his time in Palestine in order to minister to descendants of the Lost Ten Tribes in the western hemisphere. The Ten Tribes had migrated eastward through Asia and over the Bering Strait to become the Indian tribes of North and South America. In New Zealand, in 1986, I came to know an intelligent, professional Maori woman who was also a believing Mormon. She explained to me the belief of Maori Mormons that her people, the Maoris, and all Polynesian peoples came from the Americas and were branches of the lost Israelites. She personally had received a vision and a blessing, she told me, in which she received certain, confirming knowledge that she was of the tribe of Ephraim. (Actually Polynesians and Maoris came from Asia, according to most authorities.)

One article cites literature in Finnish going back to the 1700s in which the Finns, Lapps, and Estonians are identified as from the Lost Tribes of Israel.[97] (A 1769 book is cited which argued that "many villages in Finland bear an exact resemblance to the names of various places in Persia, where peradventure the carried-away Israelites lived for a certain length of time" and besides that, "there are many ancient customs among the Lapps and the Finns that appear to have a great deal in common with the Israelitish ones," such as a veneration by the Lapps of Saturday as more holy than Sunday.[98])

My favorite statement identifying what became of the ancient tribes of Israel, however, is from a Scottish lawyer named John

---

[97] R. Salomaa and A. Reipas, "The Identity of Finland," undated (http://www.giveshare.org/israel/finland.html).

[98] According to sources I checked, the Lapps had an annual holiday called *muistinsuovatta* (Memorial Saturday) which took place in the autumn, on the Saturday before October 26. If there were other Saturdays of importance to Lapps I could not find them. Lacking further evidence, this seems an insufficient basis upon which to propose the Lapps came from Samaria in the Middle East.

Finlayson. Finlayson was a disciple of the illustrious Richard Brothers. In 1849, Finlayson wrote:

> So that nearly all the Germans, English, Lowlanders of Scotland, Easterlings of Ireland, are the descendants of the Hebrews—. But two-thirds of France are also so; as well as the Persians and those of the Barbary States—one half of the Russians, Poles, Swiss, Italians, Spaniards and Greeks are so, and they abound in the Turkish Empire and adjoining states, and even in China, Japan, and Ethiopia—nearly all the North Americans are so ...[99]

Germany

In the universe of the old Worldwide Church of God and its successor groups, the Anglo-Saxons and most other major peoples in Europe are Israelites—with one *gigantic* exception. One people right in the heart of Europe which were *not* claimed to be Israel were the Germanic tribes of Germany which produced the Anglo-Saxon tribes. In this mental universe Germany today is *Assyria*, not symbolically or metaphorically but through genetic descent, in the same way that the Germanic tribes who settled elsewhere than Germany are *Israelites* through genetic descent. (Is that clear?)

Dr. Hoeh explained this theory of German origins in his *Compendium* and in a two-part *Plain Truth* article "Germany in Prophecy" in December 1962 and January 1963. Both of these sources were soon made unavailable to church members. (The Germany/Assyria belief remained firm and basic to the church's prophetic picture, but the only written explanations for the Germany/ Assyria belief were unavailable to church members.) Hoeh explained in these articles that the ancient Assyrians were the Hittites, and the Hittites migrated to Germany and became Germans. Both of these claims are far-fetched according to

---

[99] John Finlayson, *The Last Trumpet and the Flying Scroll* (London, 1849), 32, quoted in Wilson, "British Israelism," 351.

Afterward on Anglo-Israelism, II

current historians. (That, of course, is no objection to one inside an hallucination.[100])

Putting aside the inconvenient historical issues underlying the Assyria/ Germany identification, there is a logical problem internal to the hallucination: Anglo-Saxons and Germans are of the same origins. They are the *same peoples*. The Saxons *came from* Germany. In the Finnish and Estonian languages the very word for "Germany" is *Saksa*, "Saxon."

Therefore if Germans came from Assyrians, it follows that the predominant ethnic components of Britain and the United States also are Assyrian. By this reasoning the United States would be Assyrians, not Israel. But the ancient superpower Assyria gets a bad rap in the Bible (even though their own self-image was that they were moving peoples to new promised lands for those peoples' greatest good and blessings—in language like the land-inheritance promise to Abraham in Genesis).

Germany's ancestors are severed in most versions of Anglo-Israelism from the ancestors of Britain and the United States. Germany's role as enemy to Britain in two world wars proved to most British-Israelites that Germany's ancestors did not qualify to be Israelites. The Germans' ancestors were instead Israel's ancient mortal enemy, the Assyrians. In my own survey

---

[100] Another alleged evidence cited by Hoeh for a German/Assyria identity was that the ancient city of Trier, Germany's oldest city, claims a tradition that it was founded by a Trebeta, son of Ninus, king of Assyria. The problem here is that this legend is of medieval origin and of no historical value. "The legend arose in the eleventh century during and as a part of the Investiture Controversy, presumably in order to make Trier worthy to be another Rome, as indeed it once had been" (Frank L. Borchardt, "Forgery, False Attribution, and Fiction: Early Modern German History and Literature," *Res Publica Litterarum* 9 [1986]: 27-35 [http://www.duke.edu/~frankbo/pdf/Forgeryhtml.htm]). Another comment on the Trebeta/Ninus legend: "'I wouldn't place too much credence in that,' says Hans-Albert Becker, director of Trier's Tourist Information Office. 'It's probably a legend concocted by one of my predecessors in the Middle Ages'" (John Dornbert, "Trier—Germany's Oldest and 'Most Splendid City'," *German Life*, April/May 1997 (http://www.germanlife.com/Archives/1997/9704_01.html).

of old British-Israel books, I noticed the Assyria-Germany identification began appearing frequently in British-Israel literature after World War I. (Before World War I many British-Israelites considered the Germans fellow-Israelites in good standing.[101])

In all of this, it can be seen that once you determine how ancient history "ought" to be, based on who is currently one's enemy at the moment, the controls of mere analysis of facts simply fly away. Past "reality" becomes anything it is desired to be.

The views of Herbert Armstrong (the world's leading Anglo-Israel exponent) on race: "no defiance will be tolerated"

From wrong ideas, attitudes, and beliefs, holocausts can emerge. In his 1985 book, *Mystery of the Ages*, Herbert Armstrong hallucinated ideas of how it was *going to be* in the World Tomorrow, when he would be helping Christ rule and reeducate the world:

> It seems evident that the resurrected Noah will head a vast project of the relocation of the races and nations, within the boundaries God has set, for their own best good, happiness, and richest blessings. This will be a tremendous operation. It will require great and vast organization, reinforced with power to move whole nations and races. This time, peoples and nations will move where God has planned for them, and no defiance will be tolerated ...[102]

One wonders why Herbert Armstrong assigned this job of forced removals, relocations, and ethnic cleansings to Noah. The ancient

---

[101] For a detailed history of 19th century British-Israelism and internal debates concerning whether Germany was Israelite or not, see the study of Richard Simpson, "The Political Influence of the British-Israel Movement in the Nineteenth Century" (Sept. 2002; http://www.originofnations.org/books,%20papers/MA_dissertation_BI.pdf).
[102] Herbert Armstrong, *Mystery of the Ages* (New York: Dodd, Mead, and Co., 1985), 342.

Afterward on Anglo-Israelism, II

Assyrians were so much more experienced and efficient at this type of thing. (Similar views on defiance, too.) The Nazis might also merit consideration for the task. Even the United States experience in the brutal "Trail of Tears" relocation of Cherokees to Oklahoma in 1830-1840 might suggest another set of candidates with the requisite abilities to carry out the divine will according to Herbert Armstrong.

Herbert Armstrong thought Adam was white and Eve was white. Without citing the slightest scriptural evidence, he thought it was just obvious. "It is evident that Adam and Eve were created white. God's chosen nation Israel was white. Jesus was white."[103] (According to the theory, God created the genes for races of color in white Eve. Then, amazingly, some of white Eve's children turned out yellow, while others turned out black.)

At the time of the Flood, Herbert explained, "Noah, only, was unblemished and perfect in his generations—his ancestry. He was of the original white strain."[104] The Flood came upon earth because of integration of the races, said Herbert Armstrong.[105]

That is, God hated interracial marriage so much that he exterminated nearly the whole world for it, except for the family of righteous Noah, half of whom were interracially married. Noah had three sons: Shem, Ham, and Japheth. (All the world descends from these three.) Shem was white and married to a white woman.[106] Ham, also white, had a black wife who had black children, while Japheth had a yellow wife who had yellow children.[107] (At least, this is how Herbert Armstrong explained it.) The Israelites, of course, were white. Herbert Armstrong explained: "WHY did God raise up this special Hebrew nation as 'the chosen people'? ... The probability is that these people were

---

[103] Herbert Armstrong, *Mystery of the Ages*, 148.
[104] Herbert Armstrong, *Mystery of the Ages*, 148.
[105] Herbert Armstrong, *Mystery of the Ages*, 341-42.
[106] Herbert Armstrong, *Mystery of the Ages*, 154.
[107] Herbert Armstrong, *Mystery of the Ages*, 154.

all—or nearly all—of the white racial strain, unchanged since creation."[108]

The Israelites, who were of "the original physical racial strain," which was white, were "of a superior heredity."[109]

No one native to the Middle East has white skin today. The idea is fabricated out of whole cloth. But Herbert Armstrong wrote it as if it was true, and many believed it was true, because Herbert Armstrong wrote it.

At the time I was at Big Sandy (1972-75) the Worldwide Church of God was claiming that racial bias was eliminated from its literature and public statements. But it is evident that, formal policy of the church notwithstanding, Herbert Armstrong had not updated his blatantly racist personal views.

Were the ancient Israelites white folks?

You might ask how Herbert Armstrong or his acolytes could claim to get the half-baked idea that ancient Israelites were white folks *out of the Bible*. Well, they did. True, you would practically never hear an actual verse cited to support the point, but the way they talked made it sound as if the Bible said something like that *somewhere*—even if it was not quite clear exactly where. (As Herbert Armstrong explained, it was just "evident.") It was not easy for me to find a written biblical explanation for this belief within Worldwide Church of God literature. But I finally did. I found it in an Ambassador College thesis written in 1963 by an early and loyal student of Herbert Armstrong, Raymond McNair, entitled "Key to Northwest European Origins." This M.A. thesis was never published or made available to church members, and the majority of Worldwide Church of God members probably were unaware of its existence.[110]

---

[108] Herbert Armstrong, *Mystery of the Ages*, 166.
[109] Herbert Armstrong, *Mystery of the Ages*, 168, 170.
[110] Raymond McNair's 1963 Ambassador College thesis "Key to Northwest European Origins" is available at http://www.originofnations.org/key.htm. That this link is found on Raymond McNair's "Church of God—

Afterward on Anglo-Israelism, II

Here is how McNair explained this idea is found in *the Bible*. Did not Isaac tell his son Jacob to marry one of the daughters of *Laban* (Gen 28:1-2)? "Laban" in Hebrew means "*white*"! Laban, being named "white," therefore was a white person. Sarah is said to have been "very fair" (Gen 12:11, 14), proof that Sarah too was white. David was of a "fair countenance" (1 Sam 17:42). The woman of Song of Solomon 5:10-11 says, "My beloved is white and ruddy." She also is called "fair." Lamentations 4:7 says the Nazarites were "whiter than milk." All of these were therefore white people. Esther, "fair and beautiful" (Esther 2:7), was another white woman. There you have it, plain as can be. The Northwestern Nordic Europeans are the descendants of the dispersed white ("fair") Israelites.

The problem with all this is that Hebrew *yfh*, "fair," means shining, not white. It is like saying someone today looks "radiant." It is not a statement of skin color. It has nothing to do with Sarah or Esther being white.

On the other hand, I have seen literature from African-American sources quote equally irrefutable biblical evidence direct from the inspired King James Version proving that the patriarchs and Israelites were *black* people. For example, Job says, "My skin is black" (Job 30:30). Jeremiah said, "I am black" (Jer 8:21). The Jews of Jerusalem said their skin was black (Lam 5:10). The "fair" woman in the Song of Solomon herself says she too is "black" (Song 1:5-6). How much plainer can these be?

These uses of "fair" and "black" as clues to racial physiognomy remind me of a humor piece written by my fellow student and now long-time friend Earl Smith. (Always one with a down-to-earth commentary on the human condition, Earl was editor of the *Portfolio*, the student newspaper at Big Sandy, during his

---

21st Century" home page (http://www.cog21.org/), combined with the absence of any known retraction from McNair over the years, suggests that the thesis's author still stands by the arguments quoted here. This thesis is in any case the only written statement I could find from a Worldwide Church of God source of actual argument (as distinguished from simple assertion) that the Bible says the Israelites were white people.

junior year, 1974-75.) Earl's topic for this memorable article was biblical principles in dating and marriage. He entitled it "Never Marry a Stranger." Turning to Genesis, we read that "Adam knew his wife." That's right, he talked with her, spent time with her, learned her interests, her likes and dislikes—he really got to know her. The problem in modern dating is people are marrying who don't yet know one another. But the patriarchs are an example for us; they knew their wives. This biblical principle to know one's wife is confirmed in the injunctions not to "marry a stranger." Again and again the Bible tells of the problems that befell those who married strangers before they became sufficiently well-acquainted.

Too bad that article was never published. Earl wrote another one on "the International Baby Conspiracy." He waxed eloquent with creative exegesis of biblical prophecies about wisdom in the mouths of babes and babes ruling the world. Skeptics may doubt, but Earl backed up his solemn warnings with empirical examples drawn from real life showing the ancient prophecies coming to pass. The tiny conspirators try to fool us by acting innocent, Earl went on, but they know more than they let on. (How else can their disruptions which always happen at the most *inopportune times* be accounted for?) Then he finished with his coup de grace: the end-time ruling power called "Baby-lon."

That one was never published either. I always thought Earl's talents were underutilized at Ambassador College. There is no telling what could have happened if he'd been hired to write booklets.

McNair quoting Sayce

Raymond McNair also had an historical argument (as distinguished from the biblical one just given, above) purporting to prove that the ancient Israelites were white. McNair quoted the famous Assyriologist Archibald Henry Sayce (1846-1933) as follows. This is the quote from Sayce:

Afterward on Anglo-Israelism, II

> The names of the Jewish towns captured by the Egyptian King Shoshenk [c. 900s BC] ... recorded on the walls of the temple of Karnak are each surmounted with the head and shoulders of a prisoner. Casts have been made of the heads by Sir Flinders Petrie, and the racial type represented by them turns out to be Amorite and not Jewish ... It is plain that the Amorite belonged to the blond race. His blue eyes and light hair prove this incontestably. So also does the colour of his skin, when compared with that of other races depicted by the Egyptian artists. At Madianet Habu, for example, where the skin of the Amorite is pale pink, that of the Lebu or Libyan and the Mashuash or Masyes is red like that of the Egyptians, though we know that the Libyans belonged to a distinctively fair-complexioned race. In a tomb (No. 34) of the Eighteenth Dynasty, at Thebes, the Amorite chief of Kadesh has a white skin, and a light red-brown eyes and hair...[111]

McNair then says the Egyptian heads identified as Amorites were really Jews, not Amorites. McNair corrected the learned Sayce on this point (who said the opposite). McNair insisted that, no matter what the Egyptians who drew the reliefs, and Sayce, thought, the Amorites were "descendants of Ham (through his son, Canaan), and were dark-complexioned like all of Ham's descendants."[112] Therefore, it follows that the Amorites could *not* be white as the Egyptians portrayed them. No, according to McNair the Amorites were actually *black*.

In other words McNair did a bait-and-switch with Sayce's argument. According to McNair, the Amorites portrayed by the Egyptians were not, as the Egyptians and Sayce said, *Amorites*. Rather, McNair said, they were *Jews* or Israelites. (The evidence for this being: they were found in cities of Judah and because of the biblical evidence that Israelites were white [cited above].) McNair is therefore saying something that no ancient testimony says. Sayce argued that much of the population of southern Judah c. 1000 BC was Amorite of foreign origin (rather than native Jewish or Israelite). But McNair said that the Egyptians were

---

[111] A.H. Sayce, *Races of the Old Testament* (1891), 115-16 and 167-68 cited at McNair, *Key to Northwest European Origins*, 49.
[112] McNair, *Key to Northwest European Origins*, 49.

actually portraying white Jews and Israelites and calling them Amorites, rather than portraying actual Amorites. McNair explained:

> But, as already mentioned, undoubtedly this name "Amorite" was used by the Babylonians, Egyptians and others to denote generally the blond races which were living in the Palestinian area—races which had supplanted the original Amorites.[113]

McNair does not bother to explain how the Hamite Libyans, also fair-complexioned like the Amorites according to Sayce, should be interpreted. Reality becomes what McNair says it is. The irony is McNair presents this analysis as if he is citing ancient evidence that Israelites were white. But neither the ancient Egyptians nor Sayce said that.

Here are two other perspectives on the Egyptian Amorite head portrayals. The first is from Allen Godbey, *The Lost Tribes a Myth*:

> Some other Egyptian reliefs show as men of Amor (the Amorites) a tall, yellow-haired, blue-eyed, heavy-jawed folk, widely different from the conventional Asiatic of Egyptian art. They strongly suggest some of the Indo-European folk shown by the records to have settled in Asia Minor and the Lebanon mountains ...[114]

And second, from the *Encyclopedia Britannica*:

> Egyptian illustrations of the New Kingdom show the Palestinian Amorites to have been a race much more like the northern Europeans than the Semites; long headed, with blue eyes, straight nose, and thin lips.[115]

The key point here is that these are *Amorites* being described, not Israelites. This is the elementary point upon which McNair's

---

[113] McNair, *Key to Northwest European Origins*, 51.
[114] Godbey, *The Lost Tribes a Myth*, 83.
[115] *Encyclopedia Britannica* (14th edition, 1939), I, 829.

thesis is mistaken. The Egyptians frequently depicted Asiatics and *shasu* in quite different manner than the seemingly Caucasian characteristics portrayed for people the Egyptians label *Amorites*. It is curious in passing to note that Num 13:32-33, Deut 3:11, and Amos 2:9 suggest the Israelites remembered the Amorites of legend as being tall in comparison to the shorter Israelites.

There is, in short, no basis for supposing the ancient house of Israel and house of Judah consisted of white folks.

How is history to be evaluated? (Some reflections)

What is one to say to all this? To begin with, historians deny the ten tribes were "lost." Anglo-Israelites say that "after leaving Assyrian captivity, [the 'Lost Israelites'] first inhabited the land just west of the Black Sea before migrating northwest."[116] That's to the *northwest* they are supposed to have migrated.

But Josephus, writing late in the first century AD, says the exiled ten tribes were *east* of him at the time he was writing (*Ant.* 11.5.2). Josephus did not consider them lost. At the outbreak of the Jewish Revolt in 66 AD, Josephus says, there were communications from Judea to the ten tribes to the east, beyond Rome's eastern frontier, seeking their assistance in the War against Rome. That is in the opposite direction from where Anglo-Israelites have them headed.

The exiled descendants of the ten tribes probably for the most part assimilated into their new Assyrian identity as other deported populations did,[117] while others may have maintained some memory of their ancient home in the places at which they had been resettled. The Jewish Diaspora was regarded as including members of all the tribes (Acts 26:7). James 1:1 in the

---

[116] Herbert Armstrong, *The United States and Britain in Prophecy*, 9th ed. (Pasadena, Calif.: Worldwide Church of God, 1986), 98.

[117] See the Parpola article, "Assyrian Identity in Ancient Times and Today," in note 86 on the relatively rapid assimilation of deported ethnic groups into their new identity as Assyrians as part of the Assyrian nation.

New Testament has the letter of James addressed to the "twelve tribes scattered abroad." There is no secret meaning in this. The Jewish dispersion understood itself as consisting of all twelve tribes. The Semitic Middle Eastern people of the ancient kingdom of Samaria (Israel) certainly did not become switched into tall, blond Anglo-Saxons.

The reconstructions of Herman Hoeh's *Compendium of World History* drew heavily on medieval legends and European king-lists. Most of these annals and king lists trace back to Noah and other biblical figures. Many claim Jewish ancestry. These claims are not surprising in light of coming out of the Middle Ages with Christian-biblical interpretations forming the basis for what was believed to be true in science and history.

Historians regard these literary sources as legendary. It may be analogized to how historians view the stories in Genesis, with patriarchs living 900-plus years with names of later famous cities and civilizations and the traits of the later peoples revealed in events in the patriarchs' lives. Historians regard Genesis and stories like it occurring in the literatures of other peoples as something like archetypical propaganda (not to be taken as literally factual). But to the scripture-believing world in which the *Compendium*, like the earlier medieval European histories, was produced, all history is properly to be plugged into the biblical account as basic. Historians who do not do this are believed to be making a methodological mistake: they reject on principle the idea that God supernaturally intervenes in history.

The world of the *Compendium* is a world in which most European monarchies descend from Israelites, in which numerous famous ancient peoples were really Israelite colonists by other names, in which ancient Israel was a major world seafaring power, in which biblical personages like Joshua and David sailed to the British Isles and back again. This projects outward to the whole world the view of the Hebrew Bible, which is written with Israel giving history its meaning and focus.

It was perfectly clear in the world of the medieval historians, grounded as they were in the belief that scripture was the foundation of all knowledge sacred and profane, that Israel was the focus of history. This was as clear and as obvious to them as it was that the earth was the center of the universe. But historians today are biased toward archaeology, combined with critical techniques toward literary-legendary sources. The Hebrew writings are given no special status; there is no double standard. They are to be judged by the same standards applied to any ancient literature. But in the world of the *Compendium*, the Bible must *not* be considered like other ancient literature. It is unique. It is in a class by itself. It is the standard by which all else—including even the results of archaeology—must be interpreted. It is rejection of divinely revealed knowledge to reduce the Bible to the same standards applied to all ancient literature.

As noted previously, to the believer the issue is not framed in terms of what a fair survey of the relevant historical records say. Rather, the belief comes out of a perception that the Bible requires such a system of belief. If external corroboration can be found, fine. But if not, it does not matter. In the end, within the world of the hallucination, the hallucination is its own evidence for itself.

For further appreciation of true cases of unfounded beliefs taking root in popular imagination told in entertaining style, see the classic Charles Mackay, *Extraordinary Popular Delusions and the Madness of Crowds*.[118] (Highly recommended.)

Postscript

In any consideration of American self-conception as Israel, whether by descent or allegory, any thoughtful person must ponder the devastating effects this idea has had in practice. As Mark Noll, George Marsden, and Nathan O. Hatch, in *The Search for Christian America*, summarize:

---

[118] Charles Mackay, *Extraordinary Popular Delusions and the Madness of Crowds* (2nd ed., London, 1852).

> Since the Puritans considered themselves God's chosen people, they concluded that they had the right to take the land from the heathen Indians ... They had explicitly biblical rationale for their policies. They regarded themselves as the new political Israel ... The result was worse than if they had made no attempt to find a Christian basis for politics ...[119]

Randall Balmer writes in a bibliographic essay at the end of that book:

> As Henry Warner Bowden establishes in *American Indians and Christian Missions*, successive waves of European colonizers approached the Indians differently, but generally agreed that the "savages" needed to be Christianized ... conversion to Christianity more often than not entailed a conversion to European manners. Yet, converted or not, the Indian rarely was assimilated into the white man's culture. When the Indians could no longer tolerate encroachments on their territory and rose up in armed resistance, the white man used these uprisings to justify an unrestrained violence against the "savages" which amounted nearly to genocide ... Dee Brown's brilliant study *Bury My Heart at Wounded Knee* traces Manifest Destiny's relentless and fatal pursuit of the American Indian in the nineteenth century ...

A language of superiority was engendered in the Worldwide Church of God by the Anglo-Israel belief, even though the self-conception of many church leaders was that this belief was not racist. In this view of the world, the "non-Israelite" nations and peoples were spoken of as "heathens" and "like animals." The "animal" metaphor applied to "gentile" nations within Worldwide Church of God culture and language was common and routine, almost unconscious. The so-called "Israelite" nations were not, however, given the "animal-like" metaphor. I remember the Worldwide Church of God pastor in Akron, Ohio, Bryce Clark, speaking in repeated sermons of American Indians as "heathen savages" who had no right to the land in America

---

[119] Mark Noll, George Marsden, and Nathan O. Hatch, *The Search for Christian America* (Westchester, Ill.: Good News Publishers, 1983), 36.

Afterward on Anglo-Israelism, II

(God had given North America to Israelites, i.e. European colonizers). It was a rhetoric of justification for ethnic cleansing of native Americans.

Garner Ted Armstrong would refer to Inuit peoples, as he did in May 1974 in Pasadena on the occasion of the dedication of the new Auditorium, as "grunting savages ... people up at Point Barrow, Alaska, who knew nothing but hair seals and whale blubber." Garner Ted would go hunting in Alaska. "Grunting" was Garner Ted's interpretation of hearing Inuit talk in their native tongue, the Inuit language. Since he could not understand it, it was "grunting."

At my first Feast of Tabernacles, at Mount Pocono, Pennsylvania, in 1969, I heard Roderick Meredith, at that time superintendent of U.S. ministers for the Worldwide Church of God, say to the assembled thousands that if he were President he could end the war in Vietnam in one hour—maybe even thirty minutes. He sort of paused and smiled when he said it, and repeated "maybe thirty minutes," to let the words sink in and make sure no one missed his point. It sounded like he was talking about nuclear annihilation of North Vietnam. The statement was never rebuked, retracted, clarified, nor, to my knowledge, did anyone walk out. The Vietnamese people, of course, were gentiles, not Israel. Their lives didn't count as much as American (Israelites') lives.

Going back earlier, there was the Cuban missile crisis of 1962. I was eight years old at the time. I sat in wide-eyed alarm with my brother, mother, and father around a radio as President John F. Kennedy spoke to the nation of the discovery of Soviet nuclear missiles in Cuba pointed at us, the unacceptability of this situation, and of his ordering a blockade of Cuba to force the Soviet Union to back down. When Kennedy's address was over, my father looked at us and said, "We just don't know what will happen." I went to bed that night with my stomach in my throat. Would I get the chance to grow up? Or was it all to end horribly while I was still a child? Americans, and the world, held their breath to see how the Russians would respond. As the clock ticked, second by second, minute by minute, hour by hour, the Russians, under Khrushchev, finally blinked, and pulled their missiles out of Cuba. The Soviet ambassador told his American counterpart with emotion in the midst of his humiliation (paraphrased), "We have backed down this time. But you will *never do this to us again.*"

One of the participants in the decision-making circles of that crisis was Robert Kennedy, the President's brother. Robert Kennedy wrote a book about it, entitled *Thirteen Days*. In this book, Robert Kennedy said that the United States decision makers estimated that there was a one-third chance of nuclear war when they ordered the blockade. Historians have not disputed the accuracy of that risk assessment.

The December 1962 issue of the *Plain Truth* magazine, however, carried an article bewailing the fact that the United States had not bombed the daylights out of Cuba during the Cuban missile crisis. The reason President Kennedy had not ordered air strikes, it was explained, was because he feared escalation into a nuclear war with Russia. The *Plain Truth* regretted that Kennedy did not understand Bible prophecy, for if he did, he would have known that "God says plainly Russia will not ever attack the United States with an all-out nuclear bomb war!" (No such war was prophesied; therefore there was no risk of it happening.) If Kennedy had only known the prophecies of the Bible, the article went on, Kennedy would have been able to have "DEALT with the animal-like minds of gentile leaders in no uncertain terms!"

And in the next month's *Plain Truth* (Jan 1963) Herbert Armstrong wrote:

> God commanded the Israelites to drive out all the inhabitants of Canaan—and to destroy their idols and places of false worship. That is a pretty close parallel to the U.S. driving Castro and anti-God Communism out of Cuba.

Afterward on Anglo-Israelism, II

This is the dark side of Anglo-Israelism in its old Worldwide Church of God form. Targets of conquest, if not literally claimed to be descended from Canaanites, became figurative Canaanites (communists in Cuba). They became non-human. They were to be attacked, dispossessed, and exterminated in the name of God by the superior Israelites (Americans). It was an ideology of American exceptionalism, a legitimization of earthly dominion and conquest in the name of God.

~ ~ ~

In July 1995, the Worldwide Church of God repudiated Anglo-Israelism, announcing in its *Pastor General's Report* that Anglo-Israelism lacked any credible evidence and would no longer be taught.

Herbert Armstrong's vision to take the message of Anglo-Israelism to the whole wide world, however, lives on. The largest splinter or successor group of the old Worldwide Church of God, the United Church of God headquartered in Cincinnati, Ohio, continues to teach and spread the Anglo-Israel theory, via the internet, printed literature, and media networks. Dozens of smaller groups representing the legacy of Herbert Armstrong do so as well.

Surprisingly, the first edition of *Showdown at Big Sandy* of 1989 unwittingly and against my intentions turned out to have fueled the Anglo-Israel theory among certain of these groups. That bizarre story is told in the next chapter.

CHAPTER 9

THE FURTHER ADVENTURES OF THE EPHRAIM/ U.S. THEORY: CHAOS THEORY IN ACTION

In 1987-88 as I was preparing the original manuscript of *Showdown at Big Sandy* and looking for a publisher, someone gave me the name of William F. Dankenbring, a former writer for the *Plain Truth* magazine. He had his own publishing business marketing books to Worldwide Church of God members.

Dankenbring had been laid off from his job as a writer for the *Plain Truth* in the summer of 1974 (in the same layoff that had rendered his boss, Dr. Hoeh, without an office which I found so odd when I visited Dr. Hoeh in Pasadena later in 1974). To support himself and his family, Dankenbring started a publishing business while remaining a Worldwide Church of God member in good standing. Dankenbring published books that were compatible with and supported church teachings. Then Dankenbring would offer these books for sale to church members at Feast of Tabernacles sites. Dankenbring published titles of hardbound books such as *A New Case for Creation, The Keys to Radiant Health, Beyond Star Wars, Ascent To Greatness, The Last Days of Planet Earth, Overcoming Satan, The Ultimate Source of all Supernatural Phenomena,* and *Escape from Armageddon.* Most of these titles were authored by Dankenbring himself, but several were written by others (e.g. two books, *Health Secrets from the Bible* and *The Ultimate Source of all*

Supernatural Phenomena, by Ronald Wlodyga, and *Ascent to Greatness* by Raymond McNair).

Headquarters, apparently including in his last years Herbert Armstrong himself, took an increasingly dim view of Dankenbring's entrepreneurial activity in the realm of teaching spiritual truths and publishing activities associated therewith. (God gave a monopoly on that to headquarters, remember.) And despite Dankenbring's prolific writing for the *Plain Truth* in earlier years, he had never been ordained a minister. (Non-ordained members *definitely* were not supposed to teach other members spiritual truths.) In January 1987 Dankenbring fell under the bloody axe of headquarters.

Supposedly Dankenbring's capital crime meriting execution was he had published some obscure prophetic argument related to the 2300 days of Daniel having come to an end in 1967 with the Arab-Israeli Six-Day War. Though it is hard to see how this could be offensive to anyone, Herbert Armstrong's successor Joseph Tkach, Sr. nevertheless arbitrarily decreed *ex post facto* that Dankenbring's publication, by his own publishing company, of his own argument for how to count 2300 days prophetically, had crossed some kind of line. Tkach, exercising his new absolute powers that a year earlier Christ had inspired Herbert to sign over to him a few days before Herbert departed this life, said "off with his head." And so Tkach's minions had Dankenbring summarily executed, i.e. disfellowshipped and marked without a hearing after three decades of loyal service to the church. This did not endear headquarters to Dankenbring, to put it mildly.[120]

---

[120] Dankenbring: "I was cast out of the Church of God in a vicious pogrom, in January, 1987, without a trial or hearing ... in a venal, visceral miscarriage of justice ... When I was told of the decision ... I immediately phoned to set up an appointment with Dr. Hoeh, or Mr. Salyer. Neither one returned my phone calls. I asked Mr. Reier, the local pastor of the Imperial A.M. Church to set up an appointment for me to see Mr. Salyer. He later phoned and said he was unable to do so ..." (W.F. Dankenbring, "Crisis in the Worldwide Church of God—the Good, the Bad, the Ugly") [http://www.triumphpro.com/crisis_in_the_worldwide_church_of_god.htm]).

Further Adventures of the Ephraim/U.S. Theory

Dankenbring's company was called at that time "Triumph Publishing." Unaware of the details of this history and not knowing much about Dankenbring (but told that he was in business), I sent my unpublished *Showdown at Big Sandy* manuscript to Triumph Publishing in late 1987, thinking he was a small publishing house, asking if he would be interested in publishing my book. Dankenbring declined to publish *Showdown at Big Sandy* on the grounds that my secular message was not in keeping with his publishing mission. Fair enough, I thought, I would look elsewhere for my publishing needs. But then the story took an unexpected turn, from my point of view.

After declining to publish my book, Dankenbring adopted the ideas of several of my chapters and papers in the *Showdown at Big Sandy* manuscript, which he rewrote into articles and tapes marketed to his mailing list. Dankenbring mined my manuscript freely for material. A number of his tapes and articles had lengthy sections of paraphrases of my material, interspersed with his own elaborations and research. These included material from my chapters on the 7000-year plan, the God-family discussion, interracial marriage, and so on. But above all, Dankenbring liked my paper from my Big Sandy days arguing that Ephraim was the United States. Dankenbring found the Ephraim/U.S. idea so compelling that he made it a centerpiece of his prophetic ministry thereafter. But he ignored my *rebuttal* of Anglo-Israelism which was the point of it all.

The rebuttal of Anglo-Israelism may have been *my* intention in telling the story of my paper on Ephraim/U.S. in the manuscript that I had sent Triumph Publishing Company in hope that my book might be published. But as any good literary critic will tell you, authors don't control meanings of texts, readers do. And Dankenbring was no ordinary reader. To my astonishment it became clear that Dankenbring saw it as his personal divine calling to broadcast this *truth* as he saw it (that the U.S. is Ephraim) to the world which the Worldwide Church of God had suppressed (from me) over fifteen years earlier. It did not matter to Dankenbring that I no longer believed it. In his view God had used me, a young, innocent student at the time, no matter what became of me later. If God could speak through Balaam's ass (Num 23: 28-31), he could speak through a sophomore at Big Sandy who later drifted back into the world. (This last wasn't Dankenbring's exact words, but conveys the approximate sense.)

Dankenbring's adoption of the Ephraim/U.S. idea and advocacy of it took me by surprise on three counts. First, I never imagined that when I sent my manuscript to a publishing house, that after turning down the manuscript for publication, pieces of the manuscript I had submitted would be paraphrased and expanded into booklets and tapes sold by the publishing house. Second, I did not anticipate that the "Ephraim/ U.S." argument would be more compelling than my debunking which had accompanied it (which was the point of the whole thing). And third, I did not anticipate that my Ephraim/U.S. argument would be published *without* my debunking attached to it (showing readers not only the hallucination but how to get back out again).

I am satisfied that Dankenbring did not intend or think he was doing anything wrong. Since (as he saw it) Ephraim as the United States was the key to opening up prophecy for the end-time, in his view he was carrying out a vitally important mission—and even saw his own ministry prophesied—in speaking this truth to the world that had come to him (however it did). He credited me by name as his source. He energetically argued the Ephraim/U.S. idea in many articles and publications, and continues to do so to the present day. In so doing Dankenbring made the Ephraim/U.S. idea an issue in the splinter groups of the Worldwide Church of God which continue to believe in Anglo-Israelism. I was only sporadically aware of this over the years, but from the sidelines I watched with amazement.

The earliest that I can find from Dankenbring on this subject on the internet is an undated article entitled, "Who is the United States in Bible Prophecy?"[121] Here is Dankenbring in that article

---

[121] William F. Dankenbring, "Who is the United States in Bible Prophecy?" (www.triumphpro.com/united_states_in_prophecy2.htm). There

Further Adventures of the Ephraim/U.S. Theory

telling essentially the same story I have just told, but from his perspective:

> The real identity of the United States has never been truly understood—until this time of the End! The first to discover this amazing new truth did so in 1974—but was put under a "gag order" not to speak about it to others! Nevertheless, the truth will not be suppressed for long! The time has come to reveal the SHOCKING IDENTITY of the United States of America in BIBLE PROPHECY! No truth would be more incredible—more dumbfounding—more sensational! ... Here is the incredible truth! ...
>
> For years, after studying the booklet, *The United States and British Commonwealth in Prophecy*, which I first read in 1956-7, I was convinced that the Anglo-Saxon peoples indeed were descended from the patriarch Jacob, whose name was changed to Israel. I was persuaded, as Herbert Armstrong taught, that the British peoples were the descendants of Ephraim, the younger son of Joseph, and that the United States was descended from Manasseh, Joseph's elder son. However, even then certain things in prophecy did not add up—did not make sense—to me, the way Herbert Armstrong explained it!
>
> I first heard this identification challenged by a friend several years ago, it may have been in 1974 or thereabouts, who asked me if I really thought the United States was Manasseh, and the British Commonwealth Ephraim, in prophecy. He pointed out some factors which I agreed seemed to cast some doubt on the standard interpretation, as handed down by Herbert Armstrong. But, with other things on my mind, including the many problems the Church was going through in those days, I again put the matter from my mind ... I did not get back to thinking about the "U.S. Identity problem" until a graduate [*sic*] of Ambassador College, Big Sandy, Texas, sent me a copy of a sensational manuscript he had written over the years, detailing his experiences at Big Sandy, and his run-ins with administrators there. He was an active scholar, creative, highly intelligent, and made many valuable contributions in the writing field—but somehow his brilliance and expertise became "lost" and ignored in the ongoing controversies that embroiled the Church, and his research and scholarship were ignored and suppressed.
>
> It was this man, Greg Doudna, who put me back on track of seeking out the true identity of the United States in prophecy. In his

---

is a present-tense allusion in this article to Richard Ames doing the "World Tomorrow" telecast in Pasadena, which Ames did between 1986 and 1994.

> unpublished papers, entitled "Showdown at Big Sandy," which he inquired about me publishing at the time, were some articles or chapters of Biblical research which were literary and scholarly gems. Although I did not agree with everything he wrote in his monumental tome, much of it was extremely valuable. Unfortunately, from my viewpoint, Mr. Doudna later seemed to throw out all his research and beliefs, due in no small part to the spiritual crises which seemed to rock and dog the Church in those not-so-halcyon years.
>
> Chapter Four of his book, entitled "the United States in Prophecy," was possibly the biggest "bombshell" in the entire book. In this chapter Doudna presents a paper he wrote September 30, 1974, entitled: "The United States in Prophecy: The Case for Identifying the United States with Ephraim (not Manasseh)."
>
> Although Greg Doudna does not hold to these beliefs today, when he presented his paper one person remarked to him, "You've got me convinced the United States is Ephraim—and I don't even believe in this stuff!" Friends told him it was one of the most compelling papers he ever wrote. But how did Doudna's research come about? It makes for a tantalizing tale of intrigue and humor, suspense, and irony ...

Dankenbring then goes on to tell the story I recount in the present book in Chapter 6, of my presentation for the second-year "heckle speech" assignment at Big Sandy, and so on, down to the reaction of Mr. Ames who stopped me on the sidewalk and forbade me to speak further of the idea. Dankenbring was outraged at Mr. Ames' action.

> Can you imagine the effrontery, the blustering egotism and spiritual tyranny, being exercised by Richard Ames, at this point? He was being totally cavalier and unfair, totally unbecoming a true minister of Christ—and intimidated a poor Church scholar, much like the Catholic hierarchy intimidated Galileo concerning his telescopic discoveries in the Middle Ages, threatening him with excommunication and calling his work "heresy." Richard Ames, modern inquisitor, is now one of the chief television personalities on the "World Tomorrow" broadcast put forth by the Worldwide Church of God ... Doudna complied with the instruction he had received. He did not discuss the idea further. He never submitted his paper to anyone else. So that which was intended to be an improvement in the Worldwide Church of God teaching on the British-Israel connection was effectively "buried ... all because an unknown co-ed had

Further Adventures of the Ephraim/U.S. Theory

> become upset at hearing the idea and had gone for counseling to a minister, who solved the problem by imposing a gag order." What was this incredible new truth—new revelation—which the Worldwide Church of God ministry succeeded at least temporarily in banning, gagging, and suppressing? It is time you saw the incredible evidence ... [paraphrase of my paper follows along with Dankenbring's elaborations and comments] ...

From Dankenbring's point of view, he was divinely called with a mission to publish the truth of the Bible to the world. So it was only logical, from his point of view, that he write and speak what in his view was true, from whatever source it came. There was no sign of malice on Dankenbring's part. But I give this background to tell how unexpected, and at times disconcerting, the outcome was to me.

With a lot of work I did get my story out the way I intended it to be told—except practically no one ever saw it. In 1989 I published *Showdown at Big Sandy* through University Microfilms International (UMI), of Ann Arbor, Michigan (even though it was not a dissertation).[122] University Microfilms International was an "on-demand" publisher—they produced softbound or hardbound copies on order from microfiches of manuscripts on file.

Showdown at Big Sandy was favorably reviewed in *Ambassador Report* in September 1989 and became known and publicly available at that time. Now, I thought, my debunking of Anglo-Israelism, into which I had poured so much time and research, would get out to the WCG world where it was needed. But few copies actually were produced or circulated, and I did not promote or advertise the book further myself, which in any case had cost me dearly. (The cost of the copies I sent out for free paid out of my own pocket far exceeded the ten percent royalties that I received from UMI for book orders that came in to them. I

---

[122] G. Doudna, *Showdown at Big Sandy: Youthful Creativity Confronts Bureaucratic Inertia at an Unconventional Bible College in East Texas* (Ann Arbor, Mich.: University Microfilms International, 1989).

shipped dozens of copies to people at my reduced author's cost in order to make it more affordable to those who wanted the book. And there certainly was no compensation to me for the time and work that went into writing and editing the manuscript.) So far as I can tell, my book made little impact. Of course I don't know how far the copies that did go out might have reached, but I got the impression that it was not read by many. In all of the bibliographies in print, or which can be downloaded off the internet, about the Worldwide Church of God or Anglo-Israelism (up to the present as I write this in August 2006), my 1989 book has never been seen on any of these lists—even though it was published in both hardbound and softbound, contained detailed research, and, according to the review in *Ambassador Report*, was well-written and substantive. It is as if Worldwide Church of God and Anglo-Israelism bibliographers never knew my 1989 book existed.

William F. Dankenbring's publishing ministry, however, was a different matter. Dankenbring's articles and tapes were widely known and publicized in Worldwide Church of God circles. Dankenbring's scathing attack articles on corruption in the WCG and doctrinal differences were a major thorn in their side. Through Dankenbring's activity my Ephraim/U.S. theory from my Big Sandy student days entered the world of Anglo-Israel and Church of God splinter groups discourse. Within Church of God splinter groups which continue to hold to Anglo-Israelism, nearly everyone now has heard of the Ephraim/U.S. theory and has an opinion about it. Now you know how it started. It is an example of chaos theory at work, in which random, accidental things lead to chains of events that take on lives of their own.

About a decade later there was a further development. A former associate of Dankenbring named John Keyser decided to go into business for himself. He started his own website (or stole it from Dankenbring, depending on whose version is to be believed) called "Hope of Israel Ministries." In 2001 Keyser published an online article under his own name entitled "Jeremiah in Ireland: Fact or Fabrication?," most of which was

Further Adventures of the Ephraim/U.S. Theory

plagiarized practically word for word from my discussion of the Tea-Tephi story in the Irish annals published in my 1989 book.[123]

I never heard of Keyser until coming across my name in his article on the internet, which has spread widely. Keyser opens his article with paragraphs of my writing represented as his. After a few paragraphs of this he then shifts to quoting a few lines from me (attributed to me by name), and then returns to paragraphs of my writing claimed to be his, and so on, for most of the remainder of the article. That is, close paraphrases from my writing in the first edition of *Showdown at Big Sandy* written as if in the voice of Keyser are punctuated by attributed quotes, then back to close paraphrases represented as the voice of Keyser. However although Keyser cites my name, he gives no bibliographic information for my book in his article, not even the book's title, or information on how a reader could find it.

In the lines quoted from me Keyser altered many of my words to all-capital letters inside the quote marks, whenever he wanted to emphasize something I was saying. This made it look like I was shouting. Then he put this on the internet, and this article was picked up by others on the internet interested in Anglo-Israelism, and proliferated. In this way my criticism of the Tea-Tephi story came to the attention of Anglo-Israel researchers in a form wholly unplanned by me and not of my doing, in a way that my own book from 1989 failed to accomplish.

And so in this way, not through my intent, pieces of my Anglo-Israel discussion in my 1989 *Showdown at Big Sandy* entered the world of Church of God Anglo-Israel discourse and took on a life of its own.

I tell the story of my paper on the Ephraim/U.S. theory as part of my story at Big Sandy, but I hope the chapters on Anglo-

---

[123] John Keyser, "Jeremiah in Ireland: Fact or *Fabrication*?," Sept.-Oct. 2001 *The Berean Voice* 2/5 (Sept-Oct 2001): 71-87 (http://www.hopeofisrael.org/bvdown.htm). The same article is linked within and appears to chronologically precede a piece of writing dated 1996 at this site: http://www.biblemysteries.com/library/coronation.htm. The actual date of origin of the Keyser article is obscure.

Further Adventures of the Ephraim/U.S. Theory

Israelism will be more than simply part of this story. I intend these chapters to be a public service for persons within Church of God splinter groups whose leaderships still teach the Anglo-Israel idea. Take it from me: the idea *is nuts*. I intend these chapters to be read as a unit and to be a case study in critical thinking: to show how I worked my way through hallucinatory ideas and out of them, and how if you are there, you can too.

A synopsis of the further adventures of the Ephraim/U.S. theory

As noted, William Dankenbring adopted the Ephraim-United States idea from my unpublished manuscript of *Showdown at Big Sandy* which he received from me about the end of 1987 and turned down for publication. Appalled at learning that the Ephraim/U.S. idea had been suppressed in 1974, Dankenbring saw himself as divinely commissioned to broadcast the Ephraim/U.S. truth to the world in the latter days. The Ephraim/U.S. idea has never ceased to be central to Dankenbring's ministry and remains prominently featured on his "Triumph Prophetic Ministries" website.

Due to the tenacity and energy with which Dankenbring has promoted the Ephraim/ U.S. idea, controversy was inevitable. I summarize briefly what I have found from the internet (undoubtedly there are discourses not known to the internet which are missed here).

The first non-Dankenbring reference to the Ephraim/U.S. idea I see on the internet is a 1996 online book by Raymond McNair, *America and Britain in Prophecy*, published by the now-defunct Global Church of God. McNair was one of the early students of Herbert Armstrong and for many years was a Worldwide Church of God evangelist and executive. In this book McNair has a section "Ephraim and Manasseh—Which is Which?" in which McNair gives a refutation of what he has heard are three main arguments set forth in favor of an Ephraim/U.S. identification. McNair appears to be responding to the impact of Dankenbring,

Further Adventures of the Ephraim/U.S. Theory

although Dankenbring is not mentioned by name. Here is McNair:

> In recent years, however, some have concluded that the United States is modern Ephraim and that Britain, Canada, Australia and New Zealand are Manasseh. This view is based, primarily, on three arguments. 1) America is the "multitude of nations" because it is composed of 50 states; 2) the U.S. at its height, was "greater" in wealth and power than Britain at *its* height; and 3) the U.S. is "younger" than Britain—just as Ephraim was younger than Manasseh ... Let's look at them one at a time.
>
> First, could the 50 states of the Union be considered 50 "nations"? ... Emphatically, no! America is "ONE nation under God, indivisible" (as stated in the U.S. Pledge of Allegiance) ... Second, was the American zenith of greatness really higher than Britain's? Absolutely not! The British directly ruled a quarter of the earth's land and nearly a third of its population ... The tremendous military supremacy *Britain* enjoyed during *its* heyday lasted far longer than America's ... Third ... because Scripture makes it very clear that God, through Jacob, "set Ephraim *before* Manasseh" (Gen 48:20), their two positions should be reversed—Ephraim being made 12th and Manasseh becoming 13th ... Thus Ephraim would inherit the birthright first and Manasseh would follow. And that is exactly what happened—the 1800s were the "British Century" and the 1900s have been the "American Century."
>
> It should be crystal clear. Modern Ephraim is definitely the U.K., Canada, Australia and New Zealand, while Manasseh, without question, is the U.S.A.[124]

Next appeared a series of pro-Ephraim/ U.S. articles in the November 1996 issue of *Servants' News*, an independent Sabbatarian publication edited by Norman Edwards. (Norman's brother Russ Edwards was a fellow student in my class at Big Sandy.) In this issue of *Servants' News* there was an article by Harry Curley entitled, "Will the Real Ephraim Please Stand Up?",[125] and another one by Lyle Timmins entitled "Ephraim,

---

[124] Raymond McNair, *America and Britain in Prophecy*, 1996 (http://www.abcog.org/abp4.htm).

[125] Harry Curley, "Will the Real Ephraim Please Stand Up?" *Servants' News*, November 1996 (www.servantsnews.com/sn9611/s961114.htm).

Manasseh, Texas and the Bill of Rights."[126] These articles argued that Ephraim is the United States. Norman Edwards himself endorsed Ephraim as the U.S. and published rejoinders to Raymond McNair's arguments of 1996 quoted above.[127]

The next issue of *Servants' News*, December 1996, contained a letter in which a reader asked Norman Edwards where the Ephraim/U.S. idea came from. In his answer Edwards showed no awareness of Dankenbring's role or my 1989 book.

December 15, 1996
Dear Mr. Edwards,
  Very recently, I was shown a copy of your November *Servants' News* which contained several articles on Ephraim being the USA and Manasseh being Britain. I am curious and wish to know what reference source material(s) was/were used to inspire the writing of these articles—if this can be divulged? Several years ago, I learned about this and became convicted on it (it's a reversal from what I had learned in WCG, which I no longer attend), and the person I learned it from received information about it from someone who attended Ambassador College in the early 1970(s). I think it is encouraging to see people print the Truth when it is adequately proven ...
    John Gordon
    Nashua, NH

Response: The first person from which I first heard about the Ephraim and Manasseh reversal was Harry Curley, the writer of one of the related *Servants' News* articles. Harry worked at the WCG headquarters during the 1970s through the 1990s, but I think he came to the conclusion on his own. I have heard the idea from a number of others since then. I did not use any one else's material for my article.—N[orman] S[cott] E[dwards]

---

[126] Lyle Timmins, "Ephraim, Manasseh, Texas and the Bill of Rights," *Servants' News*, November 1996 (www.servantsnews.com/sn9611/s961115.htm).

[127] N. Edwards, Ephraim and Manasseh—Which is Which?" (Response to McNair 1996), *Servants' News*, November 1996 (http://www.servantsnews.com/sn9611/s961117.htm).

Further Adventures of the Ephraim/U.S. Theory

The next item on the internet in chronological sequence is dated February 1997, from Rick Sherrod, a former chair of the history department at Ambassador College. Sherrod, who has a PhD in modern British history from Michigan State University, advocates Anglo-Israelism and has devoted his research abilities to building on the arguments of Herbert Armstrong in favor of Anglo-Israelism. After leaving the Worldwide Church of God in the 1990s Sherrod has been active with the United Church of God.

This online document from 1997 is identified as a "booklet draft." In it, Sherrod notes that a United Church of God minister in Elkhart, Indiana named Steve Sheppherd had given a series of Bible studies arguing that the United States is Ephraim. Sherrod describes and, in his view, refutes Sheppherd's case. "Sheppherd inverts our traditional identifications of Ephraim and Manasseh, and raises several interesting, if not valid points, arguing each of them well," writes Sherrod. Sherrod responds that in light of (a) biblical hints that opposition to monarchy is associated with Manasseh's character as illustrated by Gideon the Manassite who opposed setting up a king, and (b) Britain's relatively greater power in its time than the United States's relative power today, the traditional understanding that Ephraim is the British Commonwealth is "quite satisfactory."[128]

A few months later, in the May 1997 *Servants' News*, Norman Edwards reported a change of heart. He had previously embraced Ephraim as the U.S. in his November 1996 issue, as noted above. But Edwards now reported having received some correspondence defending the traditional view, causing him to back off from the Ephraim/U.S. idea. Edwards wrote:

> We received a lot of comments on these articles, and a lot more information supporting the "traditional view" ... After reading much of this information, and realizing that there was much more available,

---

[128] Rick Sherrod, *Israel in Prophecy. Where are the Lost Ten Tribes. Booklet Draft*, February 1997 (http://www.geocities.com/simplyberean/sherrod.pdf), paragraphs 109-128.

this writer had to change his opinion and realize that he needs more study before reaching a conclusion ... [129]

In this issue Edwards cited excerpts from an Anglo-Israel writer named Yair Davidy who argues, among other things, that the name of the biblical Manasseh's son "Machir" (1 Chron 7:14) may be reflected in the name "America."[130] (And I bet you always thought the name came from Amerigo Vespucci!)

The next item on the internet I see in chronological sequence is a doctrinal study paper on Anglo-Israelism, dated January 1999, published by the United Church of God.[131] In this study paper the ministers of the United Church of God (who apparently all, or most anyway, still believe in Anglo-Israelism) address the U.S.-Ephraim idea and reject it. The study paper recommends retaining the traditional U.S.-Manasseh view, in language echoing Sherrod's second reason ("b") noted above: "England's greatness in relative terms has outstripped anything which the world has ever seen."

In 2002 the Ephraim/U.S. idea picked up a surprising convert: none other than Kenneth Westby, the leading figure in the 1974 Worldwide Church of God dissident ministers' revolt.

On August 17, 2002 Kenneth Westby hosted a radio program on the subject "America ... Ephraim or Manasseh?" Westby's radio program featured guests Clyde Brown and Gary Arvidson, as well as Westby himself, all three arguing in favor of the U.S./Ephraim identity.[132] On this program Westby and Clyde Brown said they learned the idea from Arvidson. Arvidson said he

---

[129] Norman Edwards, "Ephraim and Manasseh Revisited," *Servants' News*, May 1997 (www.servantsnews.com/sn9705/s70509.htm).
[130] Quoting from pages 369-70 of a book by Davidy entitled *The Tribes*.
[131] The "Lost Tribes" of Israel. Doctrinal Study Paper, "Chapter 6. The Incredible Story of Ephraim and Manassseh," no author named, United Church of God, January 1999 (http://www.giveshare.org/israel/losttribes israelucg/chapter6.html).
[132] A transcript of this radio program is available at http://www.godward. org/archives/Special%20Articles/EphraimTranscript-1.htm.

Further Adventures of the Ephraim/U.S. Theory

learned the idea from the 1996 article in *Servants' News* by Harry Curley.

This radio program was reported in the August 30, 2002 issue of *The Journal. News of the Churches of God*, published in Big Sandy, Texas. Editor Dixon Cartwright ran an article, written by himself, entitled: "Trading Places: Could America be Ephraim in Prophecy?" Ken Westby was quoted from the radio program as saying the United States is so powerful that he sees no choice but that the United States is Ephraim. Westby:

> For example, I see the United States as the leader of NATO. Basically all the tribes of Israel follow our lead. In that sense we represent a company of nations. There has never been such a grand leader in the history of the world.

Dixon Cartwright's article in *The Journal* got a reaction. Outraged letters appeared in the November 2002 issue of *The Journal* from overseas, expressing shock at the nerve of upstart Americans claiming to be Ephraim, with no respect for what the mighty British Empire once was.[133]

> We were staggered by Dixon Cartwright's article ... Do we understand correctly that the American brethren and many others around the world agree with Ken Westby, Gary Arvidson and Clyde Brown? Who said America is "vastly greater" than Britain? Where was the United States of America between about A.D. 900 and 1900? How do we measure greatness? By gross national product or the size of the military arsenal? Historically Britain's power was greater than America's has ever been. We have all heard the saying that "the sun never set on the British Empire." In 1900 Britain owned 20 percent of the land area of the earth, and 23 percent of the world's population was ruled by the British monarch. What land of any consequence has America ever ruled outside of North America?
> Lewis and Kathleen McCann
> Milton Keynes, England

---

[133] *The Journal. News of the Churches of God*, issue 70 (Nov 30, 2002) (http://www.thejournal.org/issues/issue70/letters.html).

Further Adventures of the Ephraim/U.S. Theory

As a Benjaminite, I'd like to remind my brother Joseph's forgetful descendants Manasseh that their younger brother Ephraim was given the double-portion blessing of the firstborn by grandfather Jacob. No amount of snatching and waving Ephraim's flag can give America the birthright promise ... There never has been a multitude of American nations, just one nation with a multitude of ethnic communities, with some overseas properties. Further, the royal throne of King David's lineage has remained in the British Isles ever since Jeremiah brought King Zedekiah's daughters to Ireland around 569 B.C. ... If America was the leading tribe of the house of Israel, then the royal line of Davidic kings would be in the U.S.A. .... Today Queen Elizabeth II sits on the lineal throne of King David! Her Majesty sure don't rule from the U.S.A., and Christ sure ain't coming back to Washington, D.C. ... Where was Manasseh at the height of the British Empire, the greatest empire the world has ever seen, which took place between the golden jubilee (1887) and diamond jubilee (1897) of Queen Victoria? "The British Empire: 500 Years That Shaped the World (1497-1997)," published by *The Daily Telegraph*, contains a short history of the following British imperial territories, consisting of 375 million people who came under the sway of British rule at a time when earth's population was considerably smaller than it is now ... America has been the dominant power in the world starting only from the latter part of World War II, in the 1940s. The English are clearly Ephraim. As usual, Herbert W. Armstrong makes more doctrinal sense than the revisionists in the church who claim superior insight.
    Geoff Neilson
    Fish Hoek, South Africa

These letters were followed by one from Dankenbring.

I read with interest your article "Trading Places: Could America be Ephraim in Prophecy?" [*The Journal*, Aug. 30, 2002], based on new views entertained by Kenneth Westby, Gary Arvidson and Clyde Brown. I knew all these men when I was at Ambassador College. Your article, however, failed to mention that this subject is not really new; I have been teaching and writing about this matter since 1992. We ran another article on it in *Prophecy Flash* last year and again in the May-June 2002 issue of *Prophecy Flash*. To my mind, the real credit for bringing this truth to light originally belongs to Greg Doudna, a student at Ambassador College, Big Sandy. The thought came to him, as I recall, as he was working the switchboard late at

Further Adventures of the Ephraim/U.S. Theory

night, and he began to explore the subject in great detail and eventually wrote a fascinating paper on it—much to the chagrin of Ronald Dart and administrators at the college. The Worldwide Church of God wanted nothing to do with anything that remotely contradicted the writings and teachings of Herbert W. Armstrong, no matter how reasonable, well researched and scholarly in presentation. Their minds just were not open. However, the evidence for the United States being modern Ephraim is formidable. My original article gives much credit to Greg Doudna for beginning the research into this subject and his conclusions.
William Dankenbring
Pasadena, Calif.

New Zealander Gavin Rumney in his online journal *Ambassador Watch* of December 15, 2002, described the whole debate as a lot of nonsense:

> The classic Armstrong rehash of British Israelism taught that Britain was identified in prophecy as the tribe of Ephraim, while the United States was Manasseh. In recent times some on the dippier fringe of Armstrongism have adopted a "new truth." Herb, it seems got it back to front. America is Ephraim and Britain is Manasseh. Confused? Ken Westby attempts to ride to the rescue with the transcript of a discussion on the subject. Joining Ken are Clyde Brown, a former colleague of Ernie Martin in the Foundation for Biblical Research, and another FBR old timer, Gary Arvidson, both advocates of the flip-flop position. All very fascinating, if you're interested in following a discredited theory past the point of total absurdity.[134]

The next item appeared in 2003 in an online publication named *Perspective*, edited by Michael Germano. Germano was dean of faculty at Ambassador College, Pasadena, in the 1970s and is widely regarded as having been one of the most capable administrators in Ambassador College's history. Germano is not a believer in Anglo-Israelism. But he wrote an article reporting on the Ephraim/ U.S. debate in an April-June 2003 issue of *Perspective*. Germano wrote:

---

[134] *Ambassador Watch*, issue 32, Dec 15, 2002 (no longer accessible online).

Further Adventures of the Ephraim/U.S. Theory

Prophecy buffs who prophetically identify the United States of America and Great Britain as the end-time Israelite tribes of Manasseh and Ephraim face a new challenge. Ephraim and Manasseh, the sons of Jacob's son Joseph, were descendants of Abraham, Isaac, and Jacob. Their grandfather Jacob adopted them. Several advocates of the theory claim that the prophetic identities of the two tribes must be reversed. The switch has raised the hackles of some ...

In "Trading Places: Could America be Ephraim in Prophecy?" [*The Journal*, Aug. 30, 2002], editor and publisher Dixon Cartwright discussed, among other things, the content of a Virtual Church Program hosted by Kenneth Westby on August 17, 2002. It was a phone-panel discussion with Westby as Moderator—and with Dixon Cartwright, Clyde Brown, and Gary Arvidson participating. The question at issue was: Is Ephraim the United States of America? ...

The leading proponent for the America = Ephraim and Britain = Manasseh identification has been William F. Dankenbring the founder-leader of Triumph Prophetic Ministries. His position is set forth in "Heraldic Emblems Prove the Modern Identity of Ephraim!" (2002) and "A New Look at End-Time Ephraim!" (2002). Dankenbring credits Greg Doudna, a former student at Armstrong's Ambassador College as the originator of the idea. The present day "reformed" Worldwide Church of God no longer makes such a claim and has rejected the concept on a number of grounds. The belief does, however, remain as a common thread among many of its derivatives including the United Church of God, the Living Church of God, and the Philadelphia Church of God. Each of these entities have published material espousing the doctrine.

An international conference on prophecy, being organized by Kenneth Westby, is to include a section on "Trading Places for Ephraim & Manasseh." Arvidson, a principal advocate of the USA is Ephraim in prophecy dogma has challenged writer Steven M. Collins to an oral dual over the issue: Which entity is Ephraim: The United States or Britain? Collins authored *The "Lost" Ten Tribes of Israel ... Found!* (Collins 1995).[135]

---

[135] Michael Germano, "The United States and Great Britain in Prophecy," April-June 2003 issue of *Perspective* (vol. 6, no. 2) (http://www.bibarch.com/Perspectives/6.2A.htm).

Further Adventures of the Ephraim/U.S. Theory

And so the world turns. That is the most recent item I see on the internet about this.

Closing reflections

In my dreams I would rather see myself credited with helping to put the Anglo-Israel idea in the grave where it belongs. The idea is factually untrue as an historical claim and has borne bad fruit in its application (referring to the national-chauvinistic views associated with it).

For any readers who are concerned that a motive to warn America of its errant ways would be gone without Anglo-Israelism, I suggest reading Noam Chomsky, *Understanding Power*.[136] This book has the power of Orwell's *1984*, except that whereas Orwell tells timeless truths through fiction, Chomsky's *Understanding Power* is nonfiction.

---

[136] Noam Chomsky, *Understanding Power* (New Press, 2002). Footnotes to this book, which are encyclopedic and an education in their own right, are available online at http://www.understandingpower.com.

CHAPTER 10

IS GOD REPRODUCING?

If you asked me when I was at Big Sandy why I was in the Worldwide Church of God, I would have told you that the reason was the God-family doctrine. That, to me, was the heart of everything.

Now you might ask: just what is this "God family" business, and what about it was so compelling?

A simple idea

> "All living things reproduce themselves. Is God alive? Is God reproducing?"
> —from my Big Sandy notebook

The doctrine that humans on earth are destined to become Godkind—to be made into the same nature and substance as God though remaining individual beings as distinct sons, and thus to become literal God-beings—was the vision of human destiny that converted me. In his writings and sermons, Herbert Armstrong emphasized that God is reproducing, that Jesus was the "first-born among many brethren" (Rom 8:29), that human purpose and destiny is to become begotten and born as sons of God in the same way as Jesus Christ—that our destiny is to become born as gods.

It was a soaring, electrifying thought and message. I marveled that almost nowhere else on earth, it seemed, were the basic biblical expressions "sons of God," being created "in God's image," and the promise to Christians to inherit everything that

Christ inherited, interpreted in the sense of a growing family of God consisting of a Father and many born sons.

In this view, those who receive the Holy Spirit in this age are conceived of the Father but as yet unborn, like an embryo god impregnated and growing within its mother's womb. Christians in this age are inside the church, unable to see the Father face-to-face. After this conception or spark of new life from God the Father in this life, there is growth in this unborn state. The birth, being born a god, occurs at the resurrection at the time of Christ's coming. That will be when transformation occurs, like a caterpillar being born or changed into a butterfly.

God reproducing ... it was a sweeping theology, neither Jewish nor conventionally Christian, often condemned as blasphemous. I prayed, believed, and looked at the stars at night at Big Sandy, humbled by the scope and magnitude of this plan of the ages to which only a select few human beings in this present age seemed privileged to know. Somehow, by the unsearchable grace of God, I had been called to a knowledge of this truth, while most of the rest of humanity lived in ignorance.

This vision of God reproducing through human beings was the heart of everything to me at Big Sandy. It exceeded the wildest science fiction fantasy, yet it was true, and it was going to happen. Within this sacred canopy my prayers were answered, miracles happened in my walk with God, and my spirit flourished and reached to the stars.

Some historical perspective

The doctrine of the God-family (a two-plus, open Godhead) conflicts with the traditional Christian doctrine of the Trinity (a three-person, closed Godhead). The Trinity was enforced by Roman emperors as doctrine throughout the Empire after it won out over "Arian" views at the Councils of Nicea (325 AD), Constantinople (381 AD), and Chalcedon (451 AD).

The basic difference between Trinitarianism and Arianism was this: Trinitarians said Jesus Christ was equal with and of the

Is God Reproducing?

same substance as God the Father, in a sense that humans could *not* attain. Arians said that Jesus Christ, even though having attained the full glory of divine sonship through obedience, was nonetheless subordinate to God the Father. Arians said that because of Christ, humans now *could* attain to the same divine status as had Christ.

In the Trinitarian view, God personally, in the form of the Son which was part of Himself, temporarily descended to take on human limitations in order to redeem fallen mankind. The possibility that Christ could have failed was unthinkable. Arians said that Christ, the first of God's primeval creations, acted as a perfect example for the rest of God's creation. Arians said that Christ indeed could, conceivably, have failed. But Christ prevailed, paving the way and making it possible for the rest of humanity to attain to divine status as well.[137]

Both sides slaughtered each other in wars over hundreds of years, until at last the Trinitarians won, thereby establishing the Trinity as orthodoxy. Ever since, the Trinity, a word which is never found or defined in the Bible, has been used as the principal litmus test, the most fundamental defining point above all others of orthodoxy and heresy in Christianity down to the present day.

---

[137] "The Arian hermeneutic cannot be misconstrued: what is predicated of the redeemer must be predicated of the redeemed ... the central point in the Arian system is that Christ gains and holds his sonship in the same way as other creatures ... As these passages in scripture describe Christ's election as Son of God, so do they proclaim the sonship of believers in the same mode—through obedience, through willing God's will. That is the soteriological basis of the religion of Arian Christians, daring enough to appeal and to scandalize" (Robert C. Gregg and Dennis E. Groh, *Early Arianism—A View of Salvation* [Philadelphia: Fortress Press, 1981], 50, 69). See also Joseph T. Lienhard, "The 'Arian' Controversy: Some Categories Reconsidered" (*Theological Studies* 48 [1987]: 415-437).

Is God Reproducing?

How the doctrine entered Herbert Armstrong's theology

The doctrine of the God-family did not come into Herbert Armstrong's theology until 1953. Here is a firsthand account of how this happened from one who was there, Roderick Meredith. Writing in 1979 Meredith recounted:

> Back in the early 1950's Mr. Armstrong began to say to us, "Fellows, I've begun to realize how ... God says that everything reproduces after his kind. And the physical was created as a type of the spiritual. We all reproduce after our kind, so why would not God reproduce after His kind? And if my sons are human like I'm human, why would not God's sons be God like God is God? But," he said, "I don't know. This concept comes into my mind. It's almost like God put it there. But I'm sort of afraid of it because it sounds blasphemous. We've never believed that before." He brought up some more examples, and he said, "Well, let's keep thinking about it and discussing it from time to time."[138]

Here is a fuller account from Meredith written in 2005:

> I cannot help but remember the late spring of 1953 when I sat in the graduate class under his [Herbert Armstrong's] immediate guidance. For right in front of our eyes, Mr. Armstrong began to postulate and finally to fully understand the awesome purpose for human life ... As I sat there with Mr. Armstrong and with Herman Hoeh, Raymond Cole, Richard David Armstrong, Kenneth Herrmann and my uncle, Dr. C. Paul Meredith, I began to realize that Jesus Christ was indeed inspiring our discussion and revealing to us a transcendent truth of tremendous significance. Over several weeks of discussion, Mr. Armstrong directly asked those of us in this class to challenge him—to *disprove* him if we could—on this exciting "new" truth that seemed almost "too much" to grasp at first glace. We tried.
>
> But, as the class continued through that spring of 1953, Herman Hoeh contributed a number of key scriptures and concepts which simply added to the validity of what Mr. Armstrong was beginning to realize. As I was already in earnest preparation for teaching a class on Paul's epistles, I was able to explain how certain inspiring

---

[138]   Roderick Meredith, Sermon Summary, *The Christian Art of Meditation* (Pasadena: Worldwide Church of God, 1979), p. 3.

Is God Reproducing?

statements of Paul also added to and amplified this vital understanding. It was an exciting time. In the years since those hearty discussions, it has become increasingly obvious to me that God led his servant, Herbert Armstrong, to a full understanding of one of the most inspiring truths ever revealed to mankind. This revelation by God to Mr. Armstrong—through His Word—was certainly a major highlight of Mr. Armstrong's life![139]

I asked Ken Herrmann, who was also there, about this myself. Herrmann told me much the same as above, how he remembered Herbert Armstrong talking about the idea in classes, asking, "Can this be true? Is this blasphemy?" On the question of whether there was Mormon influence in the origin of the doctrine in Herbert Armstrong's thinking, Herrmann told me he saw no sign of Mormon influence in those discussions, although he admitted that Herbert Armstrong had read of different religions earlier in life and that could have influenced him.

How the Worldwide Church of God was more orthodox than most of its critics (though both would be shocked to learn it)

Readers uninvolved with Christianity may not sufficiently appreciate the degree to which other Christians regard the God-reproducing doctrine, as it was held by the Worldwide Church of God, as blasphemous. Few teachings of the Worldwide Church of God, in fact, aroused greater fury from Christian critics than this one.

The critics took offense at the God-reproducing doctrine since it says humans can "become equal with God." The Worldwide Church of God (in common with the rest of Christianity) held that Jesus Christ is divine. Since it is plain that the New Testament teaches that Christians are to inherit everything Christ inherited and become everything Christ is, it was only logical,

---

[139] Roderick Meredith, letter to members of the Living Church of God, Jan 16, 2005; no longer available online.

within this theological world, to speak of "becoming God" and "the God family."

The critics, however, charged that this doctrine of human deification was the original heresy. These critics pointed out that Genesis says the original temptation from the devil was to become "like God" (Gen 3:5). To this, the Worldwide Church of God responded that the devil also can quote truth (Matt 4:1-11); the wily old serpent indeed was referring to true human destiny. The temptation, it was explained, was in the wrong means Mr. Satan offered of attaining Godhood (through the tree of knowledge of good and evil), not in the statement of human deification itself.

A survey of evangelical "anti-cult" literature sold in Christian bookstores confirms the emotions aroused by this point. For example, Bob Larson, host of a nationally syndicated Christian radio talk program, said in his book, *Larson's Book of Cults*:

> Perhaps the most dangerous Armstrong doctrine is the contention that deity is an attainable goal of man ... This view ... robs Christ of his unique position as eternal God. Man, who was created by Christ, is thus elevated from his finite position to a status equal with Infinity.[140]

Josh McDowell and Don Stewart, in their book, *Understanding the Cults*, were quite dogmatic.

> There is no teaching whatever in the Scripture that suggests God is a family ... The idea that man will some day be God can be found nowhere in the Bible. God is God by nature. He was, is and always will be God. Man cannot attain Godhood for he is finite, limited by his nature ... The [Worldwide Church of God's] totally unbiblical doctrines about God being a family, salvation by works, the new birth not taking place until the resurrection, along with their other

---

[140] Bob Larson, *Larson's Book of Cults* (Wheaton, Ill.: Tyndale House, 1982), 184.

Is God Reproducing?

teachings signify them to be a non-Christian cult that should be avoided.[141]

And finally the late Walter Martin, the evangelicals' expert above all on cults, in the 1985 edition of his encyclopedic *The Kingdom of the Cults* called the teachings of the Worldwide Church of God "a gospel of confusion unparalleled in the history of American cultism."[142] Martin wrote:

> Armstrong ... exceeds even the Mormon fantasy, boldly teaching what appears to be a pantheistic unity of God in which all the members of the "family" participate. This is certainly a view which is not shared by any of the inspired writers of the Scripture.[143]

(In this same edition of *Kingdom of the Cults*, Walter Martin also calls the Unitarians, a mainline denomination going back to the Reformation which has produced four American Presidents and too many famous scientists to count, a "cult."[144] How did Unitarians merit definition as a cult in Walter Martin's definition? Because, Martin explained quite logically, Unitarians do not believe in the Trinity, they do not believe in hell, and they replace the authority of the Bible with reason. These things, said Martin, make them a "cult."[145])

I was familiar with anti-cult diatribes like these during my Big Sandy days. These diatribes only confirmed to me how out to lunch these critics were. I read the New Testament with my own two eyes and nothing could be plainer than the God-reproducing doctrine. "It is the Spirit ... bearing witness with our spirit that we are children of God, and if children, then heirs, *heirs of God and fellow heirs with Christ*" (Rom 8:16-17). I used to marvel at

---

[141] Josh McDowell and Don Stewart, *Understanding the Cults* (San Bernardino, Calif.: Here's Life Publishers, 1982), 157-58, 163.
[142] Walter Martin, *Kingdom of the Cults* (rev. ed.; Minneapolis: Bethany House Publishers, 1985), 336.
[143] Walter Martin, *Kingdom of the Cults*, 325.
[144] Walter Martin, *Kingdom of the Cults*, 501.
[145] Walter Martin, *Kingdom of the Cults*, 504-506.

the virulence of the attacks upon the church for its "God-reproducing" doctrine. It was inexplicable to me apart from explanations drawing on God's selective grace and enlightening Holy Spirit. How could Christians or anyone else who read the Bible with their eyes open, I wondered, fail to see that God is reproducing through human beings?

What I did not realize then—and what neither most of the Worldwide Church of God nor most of its evangelical Christian critics realized—is that the God-reproducing doctrine was believed and explicitly taught by almost all of the early church fathers. Rather than being a recent innovation, this belief was ancient and original. The doctrine that humans can become divine, can become gods, was at the very heart of early Christian orthodoxy. Nor was the doctrine lost after an idealized, pure "first generation" in the first century, to go underground for nineteen hundred years until recovered in our time. It was the predominant belief in mainstream Christianity for about the first four centuries. Then it seems to have dropped out of the writings of Western theologians. But it remains basic doctrine in the Eastern Orthodox Church to this day.

The quotations that follow are from major, heavyweight early church fathers. It is ironic that the Worldwide Church of God, which did not care what the church fathers said after the Bible was written, ended up almost uniquely holding a doctrine central to early orthodoxy. Meanwhile, evangelical Christian critics blasted away against the Worldwide Church of God on *this* point, on the grounds that the Worldwide Church of God was *un*orthodox ... oblivious to the fact that in so doing they were also leveling blasts against each of the names below.

> *Irenaeus*: "There is none other called God by the Scriptures except the Father of all, and the Son, and those who possess the adoption."[146] "We are first made men and then gods"[147]

---

[146] Irenaeus, *Against Heresies*, preface, 4. See also 3.6.1-2.
[147] Ireneaus, *Against Heresies*, 4.38.4.

287
Is God Reproducing?

Theophilus: "[that a man] keeping the commandment of God, he should receive as reward from Him immortality, and should become God."[148]

Clement of Alexandria: "To be incorruptible is to share in Divinity."[149]

Hippolytus: "And thou shalt be a companion of the Deity, and a coheir with Christ ... For thou hast become God ... because thou hast been deified, and begotten unto immortality ... For the Deity, (by condescension,) does not diminish aught of the dignity of His divine perfection; having made thee even God unto His glory!"[150]

Athanasius: "The Word was made flesh in order that we might be enabled to be made gods."[151]

Gregory of Nyssa: "For just as He in Himself assimilated His own human nature to the power of the Godhead .... so, also, will He lead each person to union with the Godhead if they do nothing unworthy of union with the Divine."[152]

Eusebius: "The Word of God [Christ] is now God as He had been man, in order to deify mankind together with himself."[153]

Augustine: "If God humiliated Himself to such an extent as to make Himself man ... this was in order to exalt men to such an extent as to make of them gods."[154]

The Eastern Orthodox church has never ceased to believe the doctrine that human beings will be made divine. The *Westminster Dictionary of Theology* summarizes:

---

[148] Theophilus, *ad Autolycus*, II, 27.
[149] Clement of Alexandria, *The Stromata* 5.10.63.
[150] Hippolytus, *Refutations*, 30.
[151] Athanasius, *Against the Arians*, 1.39
[152] Gregory of Nyssa, "On Perfection," in *Saint Gregory of Nyssa: Ascentical Works*, trans. Virginia Woods Callahan (Wash. D.C.: Catholic University of America Press, 1967), 116.
[153] Eusebius, *Demonst.* iv, 14.
[154] Augustine, Sermon 166.

Is God Reproducing?

> Deification (Greek *theosis*) is for [Eastern] Orthodoxy the goal of every Christian ... It is possible for man to become like God, to become deified, to become god by grace. This doctrine is based on many passages of both OT and NT (e.g. Ps 82:6; II Peter 1:4), and it is essentially the teaching both of St. Paul, though he tends to use the language of filial adoption (cf. Rom 8:9-17; Gal 4:5-7), and the Fourth Gospel (cf. 17:21-23).
>
> The language of II Peter is taken up by St. Irenaeus, in his famous phrase, "If the Word has been made man, it is so that men may be made gods" (*Adv. Haer* V, Pref.), and becomes the standard in Greek theology. In the fourth century St Athanasius repeats Irenaeus almost word for word, and in the fifth century St Cyril of Alexandria says that we shall become sons "by participation" (Greek *methexis*). Deification is the central idea in the spirituality of St Maximus the Confessor, for whom the doctrine is the corollary of the Incarnation: "Deification, briefly, is the encompassing and fulfillment of all times and ages, and of all that exists in either" ... St Symeon the New Theologian at the end of the tenth century writes, "He who is God by nature converses with those whom he has made gods by grace, as a friend converses with his friends, face to face" ... It should be noted that deification does not mean absorption into God, since the deified creature remains itself and distinct. It is the whole human being, body and soul, who is transfigured in the Spirit into the likeness of the divine nature, and deification is the goal of every Christian ...[155]

I knew nothing of this when I was at Big Sandy—all these ancient dead church fathers talking like that so long ago. This information was never brought out in classes at Big Sandy. If any faculty members or students were aware of this history and tradition, I never heard of it. I knew only that the God-reproducing doctrine rang true to me from the New Testament. It was as plain as the rising sun to me that the Bible teaches that Christians will inherit every reward and glory now given to Christ (John 14:3; Heb 2:10-11; Rev 3:21). And if Christ is divine, that means we would be too.

---

[155] Symeon Lash, "Deification," in *The Westminster Dictionary of Christian Theology*, eds Alan Richardson and John Bowden (Philadelphia: Westminster Press, 1983), 147-48.

Is God Reproducing?

"Mass apotheosis" and New Testament scholarship

In the late 1960s, James Tabor, then a faculty member at Ambassador College, Pasadena, left Herbert Armstrong and his employ to pursue a PhD at the University of Chicago for the next nine years. Tabor did his dissertation on the concept of mass *apotheosis* in the thought of Paul of the New Testament. (*Apotheosis* means humans becoming gods.) The *Journal of Religion* named Tabor's dissertation one of the ten best scholarly studies on Paul of the 1980s. Tabor argued that human deification was at the very heart of Paul's gospel:

> Paul's understanding of salvation involves a rather astounding (at least to modern ears) scheme of "mass *apotheosis*" ... The equation of Jesus the Son of God, with the many glorified sons of God to follow is God's means of bringing into existence a family (i.e. "many brothers") of cosmic beings, the Sons of God, who share his heavenly *doxa* [glory].[156]

Tabor situated Paul's thought in its contemporary Mediterranean context, and gives a glimpse of the intoxicating appeal of the idea. Tabor:

> I would relate the Pauline concept to what Nilsson calls a "new cosmology" which emerges in the Hellenistic period .... the great gulf is increasingly transcended by a more general idea of *apotheosis* as potential not only for heroes, emperors and rulers, but for anyone and everyone. More specifically I would relate Paul's concept of many sons of God to a host of Jewish texts in and around the Second Temple period which speak of the destiny of both individual and select groups in terms of heavenly transformation, glorification, or even enthronement.[157]

---

[156] James Tabor, *Things Unutterable: Paul's Ascent to Paradise in its Greco-Roman, Judaic, and early Christian Contexts* (Studies in Judaism; Lanham, MD: University Press of America, 1986), 9, 12.

[157] James Tabor, "Firstborn of Many Brothers: A Pauline Notion of Apotheosis," *Society for Biblical Literature 1984 Seminar Papers* (Chico, Calif.: Scholars Press, 1984).

Is God Reproducing?

Paul's notion of Christians becoming gods, in other words, took place in a context of *democratization* of who could become a god. No longer kings and rulers only, but ordinary blokes, servants, slaves, working stiffs, women, *anybody—everybody* could become a god! Think of it—this was potent stuff. It must have been like science fiction to the early gentile Christians as they did their rites and ascension rituals, secure in the knowledge that they were on their way to becoming *gods like Jesus*. It is a vision, a storyline, worthy of a Star Trek movie.

In the rest of this chapter I will sketch several ways I interacted with this doctrine when I was at Big Sandy. Bear in mind this is description, not *apologia*. I am describing what was then.

The Holy Spirit

The Holy Spirit, as in the Jewish conception, was considered to be the power or working of God but not an active person in its own right. In the instances in the New Testament in which the Holy Spirit is spoken of as "he" and as if it performs actions of its own, this was regarded as personification language, similar to "the wind blows" (John 3:8), Abel's blood crying out from the ground (Gen 4:10), or "the mouth speaks" (Matt 12:34). A favorite example every freshman at Big Sandy learned in Ronald Kelly's Church History class was the King James Version translation of Acts 12:10: "They came unto the iron gate that leadeth into the city; which opened to them of *his* own accord." Obviously an iron gate is not a "him." The Greek pronoun translated "he" and "him" for the Holy Spirit likewise, it was explained, should be rendered "it." On the other hand, the Hebrew for "Spirit" of God is most often feminine. Few Christians today seem inclined, however, to speak of the Holy Spirit as "She." (In fact some early in Christianity's history did think of the Holy Spirit as feminine, but that's another story.) The simplicity of the God-family idea was that just as human

Is God Reproducing?

marriage pictures the marriage of Christ to the church, human reproduction pictures God the Father reproducing sons. The objection to the Trinity was it has no human analogy, no family analogy, no earthly way of being understood. It came from the realm of Greek philosophy rather than biblical analogies of family and agriculture. The conclusion was: the "Spirit of God" seemed to be an idiomatic way either of speaking about the power or working of God, or simply another way of speaking of God. There was another analogy: when we as humans speak of our spirit, we do not mean a separate entity. Similarly, the "Spirit of God" was read as another way of saying "God."

How the doctrine entered the Worldwide Church of God that Christ was not the first Son of God

One question raised during the time I was at Big Sandy was over a teaching in Herbert Armstrong's booklet, *Just What Do You Mean—Born Again?* In previous editions of this booklet Herbert Armstrong had always said Christ was the first to have been begotten of the Holy Spirit of God the Father. But attention had been called to statements in the Bible in which ancient luminaries before Christ were said to have had the Holy Spirit.

Originally, it was explained that these former luminaries were not actually begotten as were Christ and Christians. The Spirit may have worked with or spoken through them (just like it spoke through Balaam's ass [Num 22:28]), but the Spirit had not *begotten* them. That sounded like a reasonable explanation to me. But in the fall of 1973, during my sophomore year at Big Sandy, a revision was noticed in a new edition of the *Just What Do You Mean—Born Again?* booklet published from Pasadena. The new edition said the aforementioned luminaries of old indeed *had*, in selected instances, been begotten as sons of God.

This headquarters change in the status of the ancient patriarchs and prophets was not announced. The change became noticed at Big Sandy when a student who had read the new booklet brought up the matter in a class one day. This came as a

Is God Reproducing?

surprise to the astonished instructor who had just finished teaching it the old way. Inquiry was promptly made to Pasadena about the matter. (I do not know whether this inquiry included the suggestion that the next time headquarters changed a doctrine maybe they might let Big Sandy know about it.)

A memo came back from headquarters evangelist David Jon Hill giving an explanation for the change. A faculty member kindly showed the memo to me. I read Hill's explanation carefully, and it produced some thinking of my own on the matter. The more I thought about it, the more I concluded that Herbert Armstrong's original version had been right after all. Did not Hebrews 11:39-40 say the past luminaries "did *not* receive what was promised, since God had foreseen something *better* for us"? Did not Christ say the least in the kingdom of heaven (the begotten sons of God) are greater than the greatest of the prophets, namely John the Baptist (Matt 11:11)? Did not Christ say he would have to die first and go to the Father before anyone could receive the promise of the "Counselor"—the Holy Spirit of the Father (John 16:7)? And, if Christ was not the first begotten Son of God the Father—*who was*?

Herbert Armstrong's original version had been correct, I believed, and the change had been a mistake. But my thinking and study on this never made it to the stage of becoming a submitted paper.

Worldwide Church of God teaching thereafter remained that Jesus was not the first begotten son of God.[158] Since a begotten son is a son, this meant Jesus was not the first Son of God in Worldwide Church of God doctrine. I never made an issue of it, but I always thought this was a little screwy.

---

[158] "Before Jesus was conceived by Mary, He was not the SON of God ... Jesus was NOT the *first* begotten *in the sense* that Abraham, David, and Old Testament prophets were begotten" (Herbert Armstrong, *Just What Do You Mean—Born Again?* [Pasadena, Calif.: Worldwide Church of God, 1972], 25).

Is God Reproducing?

Jesus as the God of Israel before his human conception (or, "God is not an amoeba!")

Christianity early on struggled with a basic problem. It was bedrock doctrine that there was only one God. Yet in the New Testament there are two beings whom Christians deem to be "God"—God, and Christ. Finding a satisfactory solution to this troubling incongruity of how two beings add up to no more than one God generated much energy and learned discourse in the first centuries of the development of Christianity. This conundrum in turn led to an adjunct question, "Who was Christ before his human birth?"

Theologians wrestle with these issues to this day—there are tons of arguments one can read. There is the unitarian argument, the binitarian argument, the Trinitarian argument, and various permutations and corollaries thereof. Every formulation seems designed to exclude what are considered errors in opposing positions—yet every formulation seems to enshrine paradoxes of its own. Attempts are made to explain and defend the formulations logically, and when that fails, the tried-and-true fallback is stated: the truth of God is a *mystery, beyond human comprehension.* (Yet this defense is only considered valid for one's favored formulations—the non-favored formulations are subjected to withering criticisms on the grounds of logic.)

Then there is the question of whether the Bible is necessarily consistent on these things. Is it possible that Jesus held no different than prevailing Jewish views? In this case it is likely Jesus would have been unitarian, since Jews were. Or did Jesus innovate from what other Jews thought? Or did Paul innovate from what Jesus and Jews thought? Or did later Christianity innovate from what Jews, Jesus, and Paul thought? If these questions are of interest to you, you will have to work them out for yourself. Here, I am simply setting forth the Worldwide Church of God position on some of these questions at the time I was at Big Sandy.

Is God Reproducing?

It was Worldwide Church of God doctrine that Jesus Christ was the Hebrew God "Yahweh" before his human conception. But during my days at Big Sandy this tenet came under question from some quarters.

A particularly well-documented research paper by an ex-Worldwide Church of God member from New Jersey found its way to me in which were assembled many New Testament scriptures equating Yahweh of the Hebrew Bible with the *Father* of the New Testament, instead of *Christ* as the church taught.[159] (To cite just one example of scriptures this paper cited, Hebrews 1:1-2 says, "God spoke of old to our fathers by the prophets; but in these last days he has spoken to us by a Son.")

Approaching the matter logically (as was my nature), I set up the question and enumerated the options in syllogistic form. To the question, "In New Testament times, who was Israel's Yahweh," the leading possibilities were: (1) he was the Father, (2) he was Christ, (3) he was both.

(This last option was proposed privately by a friend during my Big Sandy days. He said the one God of Israel had become two separate beings by New Testament times, and that Christ was "a function become a person," or a function which became incarnated. I strenuously objected to what I called "this amoeba theory of God," and as perfect friends we debated the matter for several hours once in an all-night diner in nearby Tyler—to the amazement of staff and diners in neighboring booths. But we could not come to agreement in this modern version of a debate on how many angels could dance on the head of a pin.)

The key argument in church literature and in our classes at Big Sandy ran something like this. Israel's Yahweh interacted with humans directly in physical ways. In Genesis 18, for example, Yahweh and two buddies drop by Abraham's and Sarah's tent for dinner. (Unfortunately, the festivities were

---

[159] The photocopied paper was titled, "Was Jesus the God of the Old Testament?" No date and no author was identified on the copy I received, but I was told its author was a Richard C. Condon of New Jersey.

Is God Reproducing?

marred when Abraham and Sarah got into an argument with their distinguished guests.)

The New Testament, however, paints a different picture of God the Father. The New Testament says no one has *ever seen* God (John 1:18). The New Testament says the Father was unknown until revealed by Jesus (John 1:18). How could Yahweh of Israel, who was Abraham's guest for dinner, be reconciled with the New Testament portrait of the never-seen God the Father?

Mainstream theologians have answers to these questions, of course, involving terms like anthropomorphism and agency and whatnot. But there wasn't a whole lot of reading of mainstream theologians at Ambassador College, Big Sandy. Mostly it was just the Bible as interpreted and taught by the class instructors (who had been trained by Herbert Armstrong). There would usually be some use of *Strong's Concordance*, sound-bite quotes from commentaries, and some Josephus thrown in. But the thinking was, the Bible isn't terribly complicated if one truly wanted to know God's will, and the world's wisest aren't called to an understanding of the truth anyway, so why waste a lot of time on worldly scholars' ideas?

It was explained to us in our classes at Big Sandy that the New Testament Father was *not* Yahweh of former times. Instead (so the theory went) Yahweh of old gave up his glory to *become Jesus*. In the scheme of the theology classes at Big Sandy, it was not Jesus who was the new arrival in New Testament times. It was *God the Father*, revealed by Yahweh/Jesus.

Furthermore, just as Yahweh was husband to Israel of old, Christ is husband to the church. But Israel's Yahweh was not known as a personal "Father" to individuals in the Hebrew Bible. (This last fact was not generally recognized, but I noticed it and considered it significant.) Meanwhile, in the New Testament Christ is a husband but not a father, and God the Father is a father but not a husband. This seemed to reinforce the argument that Yahweh the *husband* was Christ the *husband*. I wrote a paper about this, entitled "The Two Plans of the Two Gods (The

Father and the Son—Their Respective Plans Compared)" (December 1974). I wrote, "The plan of the Father is to beget sons. The plan of the Son is to acquire a wife. These plans are distinct. The human family is a synthesis of the two plans."

That was what it seemed like then, anyway. But theology is tricky. Just when you think you have everything nailed down into an elegant synthesis, you see things slipping out under the edges that just won't fit. You modify your definition to account for those, and you forget about something else over there, and behind you, which now has slipped out. Eventually the temptation becomes almost overpowering to either become arbitrary and dogmatic ("I'm weary of ambiguity and uncertainty. I have decided what I am going to believe, and that's that") or else become agnostic about finding the ultimate definition which accounts for everything biblical. This second path is often defended in terms of it being good to focus on basics that one knows, and OK to leave more complicated questions unanswered. There is a story that Karl Barth, the German theologian, once was asked if he could summarize the theology of the Bible in one sentence. He answered: "Jesus loves me, this I know, for the Bible tells me so." That, of course, is a children's song. But in a world that is often loveless and broken, what power there has been in that.

Eventually the sense grew in me that there may be no single, consistent biblical thought on the nature of God. It is as if the Bible is descriptions of God written by a committee. Every time opposing views would be submitted from members of the committee, some inspired chairperson would declare both opposing positions simultaneously true (and if you can't understand that, that's because you need to pray for more of God's Spirit), bang a gavel, and go to the next question. Or maybe that better serves as an analogy to later church councils. The Bible may be more like the Jewish story about when you get three rabbis together you will get four opinions. And maybe there is something to be said for having sacred literature with multiple voices, multiple perspectives, rough edges, uneven and with surprises around the corner. Isn't that a richer, more interesting ancient text than if it were a single polished treatise by a single author?

New worlds, new universes

In sermons at Big Sandy it would be speculated that we would create new worlds, and that our new creations of peoples might go on to create new universes of their own. And so on, new creation going on for infinity, with no limits on time and space. It was a vision of the entirety of the universe, the cosmic scheme of things, based upon the principle of eternal, continuing creating. Our capacity for creating is what makes us "in the image of God," I believed. In all of these matters I was conscious that we "see through a glass darkly" (1 Cor 13:12) with comprehension comparable to that of an unborn child in its mother's womb imagining the outside world. Still, I thought I was seeing glimpses of wonderful things which could hardly be put into words for their glory.

Does God grow and learn?

In contrast to conventional Christian conceptions of a perpetually static, forever unchanging, omniscient God who can't be surprised, never learns because He already knows all, and never grows, the thinking in classes and sermons at Big Sandy was that God was omnipotent but not omniscient; God does not know future human choices. It was emphasized that God, no less than humans, learns from the growth of His children. The biblical statements that God "changes not" were not regarded as inconsistent with this. These were understood to mean God never changes in His unfailing love and mercy (Mal 3:6). They were not regarded as denying that God learns and grows, as shall we also, for all eternity.

Such a concept of a learning and growing God—I came to even use the world "evolving" toward the end of my time at Big

Sandy—seemed more living and biblical to me than the static, unchanging, non-growing conceptions of God drawn from classical Greek thought inherited by Christian orthodoxy.

I had no knowledge then of terms such as "process theology" or "open theism." But that is essentially where these ideas were headed for me, without knowing the language for it.

Was Israel betrothed or married?

I also came to believe that Israel had never been married to Yahweh as was taught in our classes at Big Sandy and in church literature. Rather, Israel was betrothed to Yahweh—the same as the New Testament church is pictured as betrothed but not yet married to Christ.

In ancient Israel, the covenant of marriage was made at the time of betrothal (Ezek 16:8). Following this, there was a betrothal period. Then came the wedding feast which celebrated the woman leaving her father's house to live in her husband's house. It dawned on me that the covenant between Yahweh and Israel at Sinai was a *betrothal covenant*, not a *wedding* as was taught by Herbert Armstrong.

In the Bible, unfaithfulness during the betrothal period is termed adultery. This is because a betrothed woman was considered a wife even thought the wedding was still future (Deut 22:23-24). The terms "husband" and "wife" are used of betrothed men and women (Matt 1:18-20; Rev 21:9). The prophets likened Israel's sins to adultery, and the northern house of Israel was given a written "decree of divorce" from Yahweh (Jer 3:8). Israel became called "Not my people" (Hosea 1:9). This "decree of divorce," I came to see, occurred during the betrothal period—not after the wedding. The wedding feast for Israel remained future at the appearance of the future Messiah in power (Isa 62:4-5; Hosea 1:36).

John the Baptist likened himself to the "friend of the bridegroom" sent before the Messiah (John 3:28-30). It was not that Israel and Yahweh/Jesus *already* were married in the sense of being past the wedding. Instead, Israel never made it to the wedding. The marriage feast was to begin the millennium (Jer 3:14; Hos 2:16). But Israel never attained the age envisioned by the prophets in which Yahweh would dwell with his people himself. Therefore it was a misunderstanding when Herbert Armstrong always said that Israel *was married* as the church *will* be at Christ's coming. In fact Israel never made it to the wedding feast (in the metaphor).

I came up with this idea on Israel's betrothal on my own. I proposed the idea once at Big Sandy in an open lecture classroom in the fall of 1975. I got about two-thirds of the idea expressed before the instructor caught on to the fact that I was proposing a change from what Mr. Armstrong taught. When the instructor noticed this he quickly took over and moved the subject elsewhere, and the idea was never taken up again. That's as far as this one got.

The issue of the "Sacred Name"

An issue that drew continuing small numbers of members away from the Worldwide Church of God was what was known as the "Sacred Name." This was a belief or doctrine that the name of God was not "God," which derives etymologically, like most words in the English language, from non-Hebrew origins. Rather, the true name was "Yahweh," the Hebrew name revealed in the Bible. It was important to identify and address the Almighty by this true name and not substitute titles. Small groups of this conviction often kept the sabbath and holy days. They usually believed it was wrong even to use the term "God."

The outside world may wonder, "Who cares?" But you have to understand that in the soil of Worldwide Church of God origins—the Church of God (Seventh Day) and associated groups—the "Sacred Names" issue was one of the most controversial and divisive issues of all. Forget Christmas or Easter or steeples being pagan. That's small potatoes. The name "*God*" is pagan! That is *really* separation from the world's false churches. All of the language of the sacredness of and praise toward the name of Israel's Yahweh, "hallowed be thy name," the persecutions "for my name's sake," the prophets facing the prophets of Baal ("Lord") in the name of Yahweh, and so on, were interpreted to mean the *name Yahweh*. Just as the world had substituted Sunday for the true Sabbath on the seventh day, it was argued, so the world has substituted "God" for Yahweh.

The major "Sacred Names" figure was Jacob O. Meyer of Bethel, Pennsylvania. He was the leader of a group called the Assemblies of Yahweh. Losses of some Worldwide Church of God members to this group and its doctrines prompted publication of a Nov.-Dec. 1972 special issue of *The Good News*, the magazine for the Worldwide Church of God membership. This issue was specifically devoted to the "Sacred Names" subject. It contained a series of articles from headquarters researchers exploring various points and refuting key "Sacred Names" contentions.

I met Jacob Meyer once by accident at a roadside stop in Missouri. I was driving to the 1974 Worldwide Church of God Feast of Tabernacles site at Lake of the Ozarks. At a highway rest stop I spotted a station wagon with a bumper sticker saying something about the name "Yahweh." Curious, I introduced myself to the bearded patriarch of the family. (He looked like my childhood conception of an Old Testament prophet.) To my surprise, he introduced himself as Jacob Meyer. He was on his way with his family to *their* Feast of Tabernacles site which was being held somewhere else in Missouri.

During a short, interesting conversation, I asked Meyer if he had seen the recent issue of the *Good News* devoted to refuting the "Sacred Names" doctrine. (It is fair to say he was the direct cause of it.) He said, "Yes, and I can refute every point in it."

Meyer claimed the name "God" was the name of a pagan deity. He flipped open a Bible and showed me two verses, right while we were standing, in which appeared the name "Gad" in reference to Baal or pagan deities (Joshua 12:7 and 13:5). People who worshiped "God" today, Meyer said, were worshipping

Is God Reproducing?

these same pagan deities just like ancient Israelite idolaters. This was new to me and gave me a start. "God" was Baal? Later research however showed there is no etymological relationship between the Germanic "God" and the Semitic "Gad"—the similarity in sound is simply coincidence. I noted that Jews, who understand and respect the Hebrew name of God and refrain from idolatry, do not object to the use of the substitute term "God." Nor, for that matter, does the Bible itself. The Bible frequently uses "God" ("Elohim") instead of "Yahweh." It was as plain as day to me that the Bible itself frequently used substitutions. The bottom line of the "Sacred Names" contention is that it is objectionable to use *substitutions* for the correctly-pronounced name of Yahweh. But every time Genesis uses "Elohim," for example, this is a substitution, for "Elohim" was the Hebrew equivalent to our "God" or "gods." Although "Sacred Names" literature could almost snow one with other points and details, this fundamental fact stood out to me. To me, this rendered the "Sacred Names" argument baseless.

~ ~ ~

It was also common in "Sacred Names" circles to postulate the New Testament was originally written in Hebrew or Aramaic. Even if it was conceded that Paul may have written his letters in Greek, the claim was that Paul would have originally used the name Yahweh in Hebrew in his Greek epistles (analogous to certain Septuagint manuscripts in which the Hebrew YHWH appears in the Greek text). Then this was lost and/or corrupted in later copying of Paul's epistles, such that all surviving texts translated into today's Bibles are from the corrupted editions, without YHWH surviving. This doesn't seem too plausible in light of 1 Cor 8:5-6, where multiple *theoia* worshiped by pagans are contrasted to the one *theos* worshiped by Christians. And at Acts 17:23-24 Paul pointed to "the altar of the unknown *theos*"—which was *theos* (that has been verified archaeologically). Paul said *that* deity, *that theos*, was the *theos* that he, Paul, worshiped.

"Sacred Names" groups also often replaced the name "Jesus," *Iesous*, with "Yahshua." All of the instances in which Greek *Iesous* appears in Greek texts were believed to be the work of later editors corrupting the original text. In this view all surviving New Testament manuscripts stem from corrupted versions. A wide-ranging conspiracy is postulated, so successful that no known testimony exists reporting this substitution happening or objecting to such systematic editing. I realized that unusual scholarly claims combined with a wide-ranging conspiracy theory were essential to the Sacred Names theory. The "Sacred Names" case against "God" therefore was not analogous to the case against Christmas. With Christmas, the basic facts are not in much dispute (the issue is rather the significance or interpretation one attaches to matters of general knowledge). But in the case of the "Sacred Names" claims, the most important facts upon which the case rests cannot be found verified in any encyclopedia. That was the key difference.

Conclusion

And so the "God-reproducing" vision was what I regarded as the gem of the theological system of those days. Who else had this truth of the God family? That proved this church was the true church of God.

Of course the fallacy in this is that an idea or insight, no matter how good it may seem, is no basis for joining or staying with a group which otherwise has more than a few screws loose upstairs. But I didn't realize that at the time.

As for the idea itself, today I regard the idea of mass *apotheosis* as an unproven hallucination, even if it was at the heart of Paul's theology in the ancient Mediterranean world in which Christianity emerged. But it certainly seemed convincing when I was in classes at Ambassador College at Big Sandy so long ago.

CHAPTER 11

DESERT ROMANCE

In Genesis, the twenty-fourth chapter, Abraham sends his servant on a journey to procure a bride for his son Isaac. The bride, Rebekah, agrees to go with the servant on the long return journey to marry this man, Isaac, whom she has never seen. The resolute, dashing servant takes the young Rebekah across shifting sands, burning sun, blazing heat and starry nights, protecting her from attack of bandits and abductors. She is safe in his strong, bronzed arms. One arm is on the reigns of the stallion upon which they ride, ready at a moment's notice to unsheathe his shining sword with which he is capable of felling ten or a hundred in her defense. The other is around her as he carries her at a gallop across the desert into the sunset ...

This servant uses his intelligence to navigate their journey around harm's way. He is fierce in her defense, but utterly and completely gentle toward *her*, for he would never think of being harsh toward *her*. He transports the damsel through unknown, uncharted lands. He delivers her sound and whole (untouched in any way other than in purest chivalry) to her gallant, waiting, handsome husband at the other end, who has been thinking only of her all this time. The woman is the church. Her waiting husband is Christ. The servant is the minister who leads her to Christ.

Even if this may be just slightly embellished (the actual story involved travel on much less romantic camels, for instance), the story is there in Genesis. I wrote a paper built around this story during my Big Sandy student days and submitted it to one or more sources at headquarters but do not recall to whom. Here is a condensed version of that paper.

"The Servant and the Woman"
Greg Doudna
November 15, 1974

The church is presently Christ's betrothed wife, to be married to Christ at His coming (Gen 3:15-16; Eph 5:25-27; Rev 12:1-16). The marriage of Isaac and Rebekah, told in Genesis 24, is recognized as a type of Christ's marriage to the church. Abraham is a type of God the Father, Isaac a type of Christ, and Rebekah a type of the church. Abraham sent his servant to find a wife for Isaac. The servant represents the human instrument God sends to call His own.

The story is a perfect picture. Abraham was out of Rebekah's sight during the entire narrative, just as God the Father has never been seen by the church (John 1:18). The servant asked Abraham what happens if the woman won't go with him (Gen 24:5). Abraham answers, "But if the woman is not willing to follow you, then you will be free from this oath of mine" (24:8).

The servant did find the right woman: Rebekah. She said "Yes" to the servant's offer of marriage to Isaac, left her entire family, all her acquaintances, and everything she knew, and followed this servant to a land she never had seen before. The church is in the same state as Rebekah was on her journey with that servant. The church is on a journey to meet Christ, but she will not see Him until His second coming and the marriage supper of the Lamb (Rev 19). Like Rebekah, the church is on a long journey in a strange land, not having received the promises yet—a journey which will end in her marriage to a Husband she has never seen.

The servant was promised that God's angel would help in the accomplishment of his mission (24:7). When he arrived at Nahor he went to the place where a wife for Isaac would most likely be found. Of all the young women coming to draw water from the well near Nahor, the servant had faith that one had been "appointed" by God for Isaac (24:14). He prayed to God for help. When Rebekah drew water for his camels, the servant knew Rebekah was the one.

The servant wondered "whether the Lord had prospered his journey or not" (24:21). The first thing the servant did after he had been shown the right woman was he "bowed his head and worshiped the Lord" (24:26). The servant was invited to Rebekah's father's house. "Then food was set before him to eat, but he said, 'I will not

Desert Romance

eat until I have told my errand'" (24:33). The servant stated the purpose of his mission to Rebekah's family, which can be likened to proclaiming the gospel, and after finishing said, "And now if you will deal kindly and truly with my master, tell me: and if not, tell me; that I may turn to the right hand, or to the left" (24:49).

Rebekah was asked directly, "'Will you go with this man?' She said, 'I will go'" (24:58). So Rebekah, who was "very fair to look upon, a virgin" (24:16), "followed the man" and "the servant took Rebekah, and went his way" (24:61).

At the end of the journey Isaac and Rebekah met "in the field in the evening" (24:63). "The field is the world", says Matthew 13:38. Isaac had gone there "to meditate". The servant pointed out Isaac to Rebekah, just as modern servants point the church to Christ. Isaac "took Rebekah, and she became his wife, and he loved her" (24:67).

CHAPTER 12

MEAT OFFERED TO IDOLS

This chapter deals with a paper I wrote in my Big Sandy days which argued that a common reading of a particular argument in the writings of Paul was in error. The subject was "meat offered to idols," which sounds a little obscure. To explain this involves leaving today and going back into the world of the New Testament. If you are interested in the letters of Paul, you may find this chapter of interest. (I promise a couple of surprises and curve balls.) But if not, you will not lose anything in terms of the story by skipping forward to the next chapter.

Boundary issues

There is ancient testimony concerning some Jews disliking all the gentile imposters pretending to be Jews who seemed to be running around. Sometimes they would grab some gentile who was setting himself up in public as an authority or a teacher on Jewish law. They would take him into a back alley and make him an offer he couldn't refuse: either become circumcised right then and there, that very moment, or die. Given the choice of alternatives, often there was one new fully-converted Jew that came staggering out of the back alley, probably not too interested in walking for the next few days. At the same time, when word of this got around, for some odd reason there were a few less gentiles in the neighborhood interested in teaching the Jewish law or adopting Jewish ways without undergoing conversion.

The early Christian historian Hippolytus of the third century AD tells of this.[160]

~ ~ ~

Ancient sources tell of widespread interest in things Jewish in the Roman and Greek world—a large-scale phenomenon of Judaizing gentiles. Perhaps they were soldiers posted on the eastern frontier who had "gone native." Perhaps they were disaffected intellectuals fascinated with various and eclectic forms of Jewish speculative thought. Perhaps they were upper-class women drawn to traveling wonder-workers who came to town with flashing eyes and charming accents talking about Jewish mystical rites and salvation schemes. However it worked, these gentiles would desert their traditional and ancestral gods and culture, and act out their fascination with this eastern religion, the religion of the Jews. They might visit synagogues, hear Jewish texts read and studied, adopt Jewish ways and customs. In some cases they might convert to becoming Jews. But many, it is clear, went part way but not all the way toward Jewish conversion. There were lots of "part"-Jews, would-be Jews and "imposter" Jews, depending on who was doing the describing.

In this context the New Testament is filled with echoes of some fundamental dispute over the issue of gentiles who had turned from their gods to the Jewish god, in this case (as told in the New Testament) associated with a Jewish mediator-figure named Jesus. The dispute was over whether such gentiles should be required to be circumcised, i.e. become Jews (convert). The New Testament tells of conflicts between the apostle Paul and a "circumcision party" of the Jews. This conflict is a major theme throughout Paul's letters and the book of Acts.

The "circumcision party" of the New Testament appears to reflect the ideological position which Hippolytus's vigilantes

---

[160] Hippolytus, *Refutation of all Heresies*, 9.21.

Meat Offered to Idols

carried out forcibly. Here is a key point: contrary to popular conception, the motivation of this "circumcision party" appears *not* to have been to increase the numbers of converted Jews. Rather, the motivation of the "circumcision party" appears to have been to *reduce* the number of claimants to Jewish identity on the part of those who were not willing to become full Jews in fact. It was a turf and boundary issue.

~ ~ ~

According to Acts 15, James the brother of Jesus chairs a meeting in Jerusalem on this issue and sums up a decision after discussion and debate. The decision was that gentiles who believed in Jesus should not be required to convert to being Jews. A letter was sent to the gentiles who had turned to the Jewish God telling them to keep what would later be called the "laws of Noah" applicable to all tribes of mankind apart from the Jews.

> "The apostles and elders and brethren send greetings to the brethren which are of the Gentiles in Antioch and Syria and Cilicia. Forasmuch as we have heard, that certain which went out from us have troubled you with words, subverting your souls, to whom we gave no such commandment ... it seemed good to the Holy Spirit, and to us, to lay upon you no greater burden than these necessary things; that you abstain from meats offered to idols, and from blood, {and from things strangled,} and from sexual wrongdoing, from which if you keep yourselves, you shall do well. Fare you well" (Acts 15:1-29).

The three or four rules cited by James and the other Jewish leaders of Acts 15 were prohibited categories of behavior. The term "laws of Noah" is a later rabbinic term not in the Bible, but it explains the background of the Acts 15 decree. The "laws of Noah," as the later rabbis defined them, were the standards that God required of gentiles to be saved. The later rabbis listed seven Noachian rules. Acts 15 has only three or four such rules (depending on a manuscript dispute—the item "things strangled" is not in some manuscripts), but it is obviously some earlier version of these rabbinic laws of Noah.

The first prohibited category, "meat offered to idols," is the subject of interest here. No one disputes that the letter of Acts 15, said to be issued at the direction of James, the brother of Jesus, prohibits eating meat offered to idols. But now there is a curious phenomenon, which is the point of this chapter. In the world of traditional and evangelical Christian biblical exegesis (including, on this point, the Worldwide Church of God during my Big Sandy days), it was and is a practically universal interpretation that Paul held a *different* view. Paul is believed to have said in his first letter to the Corinthians not to eat such meat if it offended someone—otherwise (if no one was offended), it is acceptable to eat it.

For anyone reading this who is unfamiliar with this issue, just ask some Christian nearby who is well-versed in the New Testament. Ask your New Testament-literate friend what Paul's position was on eating meat offered to idols. If you do, you can verify for yourself the accuracy of what I am saying concerning the common interpretation of Paul's view on this point.[161]

You might think that Christians' exegesis, particularly those inclined toward biblical inerrancy or fundamentalism, would *not* have Paul teaching something different than James in Acts 15.

---

[161] For example David Treybig, United Church of God pastor: "Paul explained that 'an idol is nothing' (1 Corinthians 8:4) in clarifying that it was permissible to eat meats that had been sacrificed to an idol" (D. Treybig, "Does the New Testament Abolish Meat Distinctions?," *The Good News*, July-Aug 1997 [http://www.gnmagazine.org/issues/gn11/uncleanmeats.htm]). Herbert Armstrong: "In New Testament times, clean meat offered to idols was prohibited if it had been polluted by strangulation or if the blood were remaining in it. Otherwise the meat was permitted to be eaten if it did not offend anyone" (H.W. Armstrong, "Is All Animal Flesh Good Food?" (3rd edition [1st edition 1958]; Pasadena: Worldwide Church of God, 1978). Worldwide Church of God web site in 2006: "Paul later seemed to rescind, under special circumstances, the regulation against eating meat that had been offered to idols (1 Corinthians 8:4-13)" ("The Covenants and the Sabbath. Part 2: The New Testament" [http://www.wcg.org/lit/law/sabbath/cov-sab2.htm]).

Meat Offered to Idols

But in this particular case, and oddly, that expectation is *not correct*: the prevailing view among Christians is that Paul *did* have a different view on this point than James in Acts 15. Most Christian exegetes, even those who believe in inerrancy or near-inerrancy, seem quite comfortable with this. At Big Sandy the teachers in our classes were comfortable with this.

~ ~ ~

Not me. I *did* see a problem with James and Paul disagreeing on this issue in the New Testament, in my Big Sandy days, even if no one else did. I carefully studied Paul's discussion of the issue of meat offered to idols in 1 Corinthians chapters 8 to 10. The more I read Paul's words closely, the more I became convinced that Paul was being misread on this issue—that Paul was actually saying the opposite of what everyone around assumed. The way *I* read Paul, he was arguing *against* eating meat offered to idols, in *agreement* with James, and what people assumed was Paul's position was actually Paul's quotation of Corinthians' objections which Paul was refuting!

I wrote a paper to show that the usual reading of Paul in 1 Corinthians 8-10 was *not* correct, that Paul did *not* say it was permissible to eat meat offered to idols. My paper was entitled "Meat Offered to Idols: Did Paul Permit What James Forbade?" (November 2, 1974). I sent my paper to headquarters, to the Theological Research Project at Pasadena, thinking I would straighten out headquarters on this minor point. (My paper failed to have this effect.) Here is how my argument went.

My paper started with the injunction from James which is clear and not in dispute (i.e. that James said not to eat meat offered to idols). I noted that according to Acts, Paul himself supported and preached this injunction (Acts 16:4). And in Rev 2:14 and 2:20 Christ himself condemns meat offered to idols. How then could Paul have said differently elsewhere? I asked. In fact he did not, I argued. In the passage at issue, 1 Cor 8-10, I argued that confusion had resulted from misunderstanding Paul's quotation of Corinthian objections. It was not Paul but the Christians at Corinth who were saying, "But we know the idol is nothing," "But we have knowledge," and "All things are clean." The Christians at Corinth were eating meat offered to idols. By reading Paul's answers to their arguments, we can get a glimpse of their arguments in defense of their practice. Paul is answering a letter the Corinthian Christians had sent him (1 Cor 7:1). In his answer to the Corinthians, Paul quotes, then answers, their arguments. My insight—I came to this through my own reading of the structure of Paul's argument—was that what the Corinthians were saying, people had been mistakenly reading as if this was Paul's own view!

It requires careful attention to Paul's rhetoric. The Corinthians said, "But the idol is nothing" (the false gods don't exist). The Corinthians cited this as a reason why it was acceptable to eat meat offered to idols. In Paul's answer (I argued in my paper) he quotes their statement, and begins his answer by partly agreeing with them, establishing common ground. Paul answers that of course we know the idol is nothing. But that is not the issue, Paul says. The issue is that people *think* the idol means something, and that is the issue—that is why it *did* matter. A crucial verse is 1 Cor 8:8. I heard this quoted frequently in classes at Big Sandy and in the wider Christian world to show Paul was saying it did not matter if meat had been offered to idols or not. It reads:

> But meat commends us not to God: for neither, if we eat, are we the better; neither if we eat not, are we the worse (1 Cor 8:8).

But I noticed that when people quoted this, they carelessly interpreted it as if Paul had ended it with "neither if we eat not, are we the *better*." But Paul did not say that. He ends with "neither if we eat not, are we the *worse*." I called attention to this detail. I argued that Paul was not saying here, "It doesn't matter," as so often claimed on the basis of this quotation. Paul was saying, "Are you any worse off *without* that meat? What do you *gain* by *insisting* upon it?" To me, this was not Paul saying either

Meat Offered to Idols

is equally acceptable. It was rhetorical persuasion to the Corinthians not to eat the meat. He was urging them *not* to eat the meat.

Most clearly of all, in 1 Cor 10:20 Paul quotes Deut 32:17 which says pagans sacrifice to demons. Paul says that the gentiles sacrifice to demons, and that eating things sacrificed to demons is fellowshipping with demons, just as when believers eat the Lord's supper it is having fellowship with Christ. Paul concludes, "I do not want you to be partners with demons. You cannot drink the cup of the Lord and the cup of demons" (10:20-22). I argued that these statements could hardly be clearer: *Paul was opposed to eating meat offered to idols*, just like the Acts 15 rule. It mystified me that anyone could read these statements of Paul as anything other than *agreement with Acts 15*.

Then in 1 Cor 10:25-29 Paul deals with a distinct issue: a matter of application of the rule: the issue of meat sold in the marketplace. The problem (as the commentaries explain) is that meat sold in public marketplaces was of various and unknown origins, some of which had been offered to idols. How did the rule apply to meat sold in the marketplace which *may* have been offered to idols, but whose status was not clear? As I argued in my paper, Paul's advice on this issue was this: if the origins of the meat are unknown, it is acceptable to eat. But if someone points out that the meat was offered to idols, then *don't eat it*. If you *learn* that it was offered to idols, *don't eat it*. Paul was not saying it was OK to eat meat known to have been offered to idols if no one was weak in faith. He was not saying it is OK to eat meat offered to idols if no one objects. He was upholding the rule *not* to eat meat known to have been offered to idols.

Of course one possible solution to the question of mixed meat in the marketplace would be to avoid such meat altogether. Paul took a less severe position. He said meat need not be avoided if it is not known to have been offered to idols.

But this is a distinct issue from Paul's position on eating meat *known* to have been offered to idols. On *that* issue, the Corinthian Christians thought it was fine to eat that meat, but

Paul did *not* think that was fine, as Acts 15 *did not*. If it is *known* to have been offered to idols, it *should not be eaten*, said Paul, in agreement with James. This was my argument, which disagreed with the prevailing reading, both scholarly and popular, both within and outside the Worldwide Church of God, of Paul's view on this topic.

I concluded that Paul did not contradict James as commonly thought, i.e. Paul never permitted eating meat that was known to have been offered to idols. I closed my paper with Acts 21:25, showing that several years later Gentiles were still enjoined not to eat meat offered to idols.

I sent this paper to the Theological Research Project at Pasadena, and showed it informally to a few people at Big Sandy. But no response came back from Pasadena, and nothing further came of the paper.

Ahead of its time

It seems my youthful paper was ahead of its time. Nearly a quarter-century later, in 1999, the view I argued in my paper at Big Sandy was argued in a substantial way in the world of New Testament scholarship in a book-length study by Alex Cheung entitled *Idol Food in Corinth: Jewish Background and Pauline Legacy*.[162] A reviewer summarized Cheung's argument:

> This substantial revision of Cheung's Westminster Theological Seminary dissertation is an important work ... it gives exhaustive treatment to the issue of idol food in early Christianity and argues a unique thesis that goes against the grain of almost all scholarly interpretation of this passage. Cheung's thesis is that in 1 Cor 8:1-11:1 Paul consistently and unequivocally opposes the eating of food offered to idols. Paul gives two reasons for his prohibition of this food. It is unloving (ch. 8) and it is idolatry (ch. 10). Paul's only caveat comes at the end of the argument, where he permits Christians to eat without constantly asking questions about the origin of food.

---

[162] Alex T. Cheung, *Idol Food in Corinth: Jewish Background and Pauline Legacy* (JSNTSup 176; Sheffield: Sheffield Academic Press, 1999).

> But once Christians are aware that food has been sacrificed to idols, they must not eat it.[163]

This was followed by another book-length study in 2003 which came to the same conclusion: John Fotopoulos, *Food Offered to Idols in Roman Corinth: A Social-Rhetorical Reconsideration of 1 Corinthians 8:1-11:1*.[164] Alex Cheung commented in a review of Fotopoulos that the former consensus that Paul permitted eating meat offered to idols is "fast becoming a minority position" in New Testament scholarship:

> Fotopoulos maintains that Paul's argumentation is a coherent whole, seeking both to prohibit intentional idol food consumption and to unite the weak and the strong factions, who are divided over the issue. Paul consistently rejected temple dining because it made the Corinthians partners with pagan deities and hence guilty of idolatry. However, food purchased at the market or served at meals in pagan homes could be eaten unless it was known to be sacrificial food, in which case the rhetorical force of Paul's instructions about idolatry would apply, effectively prohibiting its consumption ... the findings of the book are in general agreement with much of my own work (*Idol Food in Corinth*), as Fotopoulos acknowledges ... Along with other recent studies, it successfully challenges the view that Paul sat light to [tolerated] the eating of idol food—a former consensus that is fast becoming a minority position.[165]

How this exegetical issue ultimately will resolve within New Testament scholarship is unclear.

---

[163] Review of Cheung by John Brunt, *Review of Biblical Literature* 05/19/2000 (http://www.bookreviews.org/bookdetail.asp?TitleId=2490).
[164] John Fotopoulos, *Food Offered to Idols in Roman Corinth: A Social-Rhetorical Reconsideration of 1 Corinthians 8:1-11:1* (Tübingen: Mohr Siebeck, 2003).
[165] Alex Cheung, review of John Fotopoulos, *Food Offered to Idols in Roman Corinth*, in *Journal of the Evangelical Theological Society*, 17/3 (2004) (http://www.findarticles.com/p/articles/mi_qa3817/is_200409/ai_n9439104).

Meat Offered to Idols

A non-theologian's reading

Although my paper on meat offered to idols got no reaction from headquarters, I did later receive a reaction to the paper from another source. The author of this reaction is Bobby Clark, a back-to-the-land woman who in her heyday regularly did things like hitchhike to Alaska and work in oil fields in Wyoming before settling down in a rural area to raise chickens. She colorfully disagreed with my paper's thesis. What she lacks in formal biblical studies training (never having had the advantages of an Ambassador College education) she makes up for in bringing a *fresh* viewpoint to timeworn passages of sacred writ. Here is her reaction:

> Paul appears to be a politician. Paul is saying don't pay any attention to James (he's stupid), the issue isn't food, it's loyalty to your friends and practicing only Christian ritual. Now James, whether or not he knew it, was right. Food is an issue ... They didn't have pure food and drug laws back then. James was super practical. If Christians couldn't buy meat from other groups, they'd have to process it themselves. It would be clean and they wouldn't die. Now Paul comes along and says it doesn't matter where you get your food. Hey—you're telling me they agree. No way. According to Paul if all your buddies want to buy black market mutton for a party it's swell just as long as they don't participate in the killing rituals or share the pagans' tables. James and crew were very down to earth working class trash. They had a practical attitude toward survival. Paul on the other hand was an educated Roman city man who undoubtedly never soiled his hands. I doubt he could butcher a sheep if his life depended on it. Nobody with a practical handle on life could say it wasn't important where food came from.
>
> Of course we can take the medieval and illiterate stance that the apostles were demigods-saints. But, if the apostles were human then they had the same group dynamics as all human groups have. By your quotes I can see James making some practical suggestions and Paul playing politician. James says Christ said to do this so we do it. James bases his belief on what Christ said because Christ came up with good ideas. James doesn't try to explain the rules. He just says, "This is the rule." Then Paul comes along and says it's not important, it is important, it's important some times. This way he doesn't offend

Meat Offered to Idols

any Christian faction. Nowadays, he'd agree with the blacks, agree with the KKK, agree with the unions, agree with the business men, and he'd get reelected as a Congressman. If I had lived in 40 AD, I'd not eat blood sacrificial meat because I don't believe in blood sacrifice. I think it's messy and stupid, plus I'd be concerned about how clean it was. It's the same concern I feel about commercial slaughterhouses today. It's why I was a lacto-vegetarian for ten years and will probably do it again ...

I must say this is not an analysis I have seen argued in any New Testament commentary. Yet somehow I see insight concerning the ancient issue in this reaction that has escaped the treatments of trained theologians. If my paper could produce an interesting reaction like this one, perhaps it served a purpose even if it got nowhere at Big Sandy so long ago.

CHAPTER 13

LETTER OF THE LAW AND SPIRIT OF THE LAW

There was no class in Greek offered at Ambassador College, Big Sandy during the years I was there. No class in Greek was offered for the simple reason that, during the time I was there, Big Sandy had no one on the faculty capable of teaching Greek. The Greek alphabet and the basics of how to look up words in lexicons were taught to upper-class theology students, but that was it. This lack of availability of a class in Greek was frustrating to me at the time.

The attempt was made in our classes at Big Sandy to correct the more obvious errors in translation of the King James Version. For example, there are two Greek words in the New Testament which the King James Version translates as "hell." It was explained in our Bible classes that these two words have been a cause of confusion. One of the Greek words, *gehenna*, indeed refers to a fiery destruction at the judgment day. But the other word, *hades*, has a totally different meaning and should never have been translated "hell." It simply means "the grave"—no more and no less. It means being buried and unconscious, awaiting a future resurrection back to life. So when the King James Version of Acts 2:27 speaks of David being "in hell" and then 2:34 says, "For David is not ascended into the heavens," these do not mean poor David has been sizzling like a roasted marshmallow all these hundreds of years. It simply means he is in the grave (*hades*), dead and unconscious, awaiting the resurrection (fortunately for David).

But though some errors such as this one were corrected, the use of the King James Version resulted in other unnoticed or more subtle errors. For example, I discovered to my surprise, toward the end of my Big Sandy years, that the expression "word of God" in the Bible never means written scripture (as commonly assumed, as in the expression "the Word of God" for "the Bible"). Rather, it means spoken truth. I discovered this one day by doing a word study, looking up every use of the expression "word of God." I was amazed at the difference between assumed meaning and biblical meaning of this expression. I never wrote up that finding.

Another discovery I made in those days, equally surprising, was that the terms "spirit of the law" and "letter of the law" never appear in the Bible. A common theme in classes and sermons was that there was an Old Testament "letter of the law" which was amplified or expanded by a New Testament "spirit of the law." The idea was that "letter of the law" and "spirit of the law" stand for two kinds of exegesis or interpretations of the one true law—one way being more literal or nitpicking, the other the principle of the matter. But I came to see that the notion of a biblical contrast between "letter of the law" and "spirit of the law" actually was fictitious and non-existent. I wrote up these findings in a paper entitled, "Does the New Covenant Mean Keeping the 'Spirit of the Law' As Opposed to the Old Testament 'Letter of the Law'?" (March 12, 1975). I wrote:

> Paul does not draw the contrast between a strict "letter of the law" in the Old Testament and an amplified "spirit of the law" in the New Testament ... There are three passages in which "letter" is contrasted with "spirit" [2 Cor 3:3-6; Rom 2:20; Rom 7:5-6]. In each case the meaning has nothing to do with a contrast between a strict, rigid, literal interpretation of the mere words of the law as opposed to the amplified meaning, the intent of the law (the supposed "spirit of the law") ... "Spirit of the law," although so much a part of our vocabulary, and so much a part of our thinking, is not a Biblical term ...

Letter of the Law and Spirit of the Law

In the three relevant passages referring to a letter versus spirit contrast (2 Cor 3:3-6; Rom 2:20; Rom 7:5-6), I argued that Paul was contrasting the law (= "the letter") with the *Holy Spirit* (= "the *Spirit*"). The "Spirit" in these comparisons is the Holy Spirit. What people mean by "the spirit of the law" is what Paul meant when he said "the letter." Paul contrasted the "(spirit of) the law" (= "the *letter*") to the Holy Spirit (= "the *Spirit*").

In this paper I also examined Isa 42:21 which says the Lord will "magnify his law" (King James Version). This was quoted in sermons at Big Sandy as foretelling that Christ would amplify the meaning of the law. I showed in my paper that the Hebrew *yigdil*, rendered "magnify" by the King James translators, means to "make mighty" or elevate the law to a higher status or position of respect, not change or expand its exegetical meaning.

And it was a common notion in classes and sermons at Big Sandy that in the Sermon on the Mount, Jesus contrasted the strict letter of the law of Israel against a fuller "spirit of the law" in which he expanded the law's sense. (Or something like that—nuances varied according to expositor.) Here I argued in my paper in agreement with a stream of scholarly thinking that says Jesus was *not* contrasting his teachings to the law of Israel. Rather Jesus was contrasting his teachings to contemporary misinterpretations of the law of Israel.

(If these things seem obscure, just remember these are the kind of things about which biblical exegetes write dissertations and earn their living arguing.)

In any case, just after I finished writing this paper, by coincidence an article appeared in the *Good News*, the magazine for Worldwide Church of God members, by Raymond McNair. McNair was one of Herbert Armstrong's early students and for many years was deputy chancellor of Ambassador College at Bricket Wood, England. McNair's article was on the very subject of the "spirit" versus the "letter" of the law. McNair's article had all the misconceptions and terminology that my paper showed were unfounded. I sent my paper, with a courteous cover letter, to McNair for his possible edification. I thought he might appreciate learning that most of the premises of his recently published article were without any basis. Sadly, there was no acknowledgement or answer.

I also sent this paper to the director of the Theological Research Project, Dr. Charles Dorothy. I think it was after this paper that a staff member of the Theological Research Project sent me $80 as remuneration for my efforts. In light of my chronic student poverty the check was welcome, but it was unaccompanied by any comment or reaction to the paper itself.

The saga of the late Dr. Charles V. Dorothy (1933-1996)

Charles Dorothy came to Ambassador College at Pasadena as a student in the 1950s. He went on to obtain a graduate degree from the University of Mexico and rose to being head of the Spanish Department of the church. The Spanish Department oversaw church activities in Latin America. Dr. Dorothy and the Spanish Department were headquartered at Big Sandy for a number of years. But a few weeks before I arrived in the fall of 1972, Dr. Dorothy and the Spanish Department with him were transferred to Pasadena. So I just missed him. The transfer of Dr. Dorothy was a real loss to Big Sandy's faculty. Among other things, Dr. Dorothy had been Big Sandy's instructor in Greek.

Dr. Dorothy combined intelligence, learning, and humility in a church where intelligence was, at best, not always valued. At worst it was looked upon with outright suspicion and hostility. Herbert Armstrong, founder and chancellor of Ambassador College, had struggled to where he was by hard work without the benefit of any ivory tower academic instruction or degrees, and was definitely suspicious of intelligence. He would periodically and publicly castigate "some of our own faculty members and ministers going for *outside degrees* at *worldly universities!*" Finally, in his last years, Herbert Armstrong declared war directly on "intellectualism" at Ambassador College. But by that time the war had already been mostly won, even without the help of Herbert Armstrong's personal declaration of war on the kind of independent thinking that he saw contaminating the proper college atmosphere.

At Pasadena, late in 1973 Dr. Dorothy had been reassigned to undertake a new endeavor called the Theological Research Project. This task was intended to be the first formal, published compilation and statement of beliefs in the church's history. In 1977 the Project was taken out of Dr. Dorothy's control and renamed the Systematic Theology Project. When the Project was finally completed a year later, Herbert Armstrong claimed the whole thing had been done all those years behind his back without his knowledge and condemned all the work it had done. The Theological Research Project, which had office space and staff and whose workings were common knowledge and reported in the church newspaper, was no more done in secret than the operation of Ambassador College at Big Sandy. I certainly had not the remotest hint during all the time I was at Big Sandy that the Theological Research Project, or Dr. Dorothy personally, was doing anything other than what Herbert Armstrong wanted done. Nor do I believe Dr. Dorothy had any hint of this either—until it was too late.

All of this is background to show that for many years Dr. Dorothy walked what must have been a continual tightrope. He balanced personal loyalty to Herbert Armstrong against his own scholarly integrity. In October 1974 Dr. Dorothy went to Herbert Armstrong and showed his pastor general that the Bible allows women to wear makeup. (From the mid-1950s until 1974, women in the Worldwide Church of God were forbidden to wear makeup.) Herbert Armstrong had always said he would change if he was shown wrong. 82-year old Armstrong heard Dr. Dorothy out, then issued a decree that all the women in the church throughout the world were now permitted to wear makeup. But, as the saying goes, a man convinced against his will is of the same opinion still. Several years later, after kicking Dr. Dorothy out of the ministry, Herbert Armstrong decided Dr. Dorothy had pulled a fast one on him earlier on this makeup business. As part of his getting the church back on track again, the now 89-year old Armstrong decreed suddenly that all the women in the church in the whole world would henceforth stop wearing makeup again, and no defiance would be tolerated. As Herbert Armstrong put it in his gentle pastoral manner:

> Our women have COPIED THE PROSTITUTES! ... Satan used human reason and makeup and WOMEN to start the ball of liberalism away from God and toward sin to rolling in the Church beginning October, 1974.[166]

~ ~ ~

I realized later that as one of the few real scholars in the church, Dr. Dorothy was under severe pressures. It seemed he was perpetually almost getting fired by jealous rivals or having his offices moved without warning. For some strange reason, these disconcerting catastrophes usually seemed to happen on the days I had appointments to see him. It was what an outside observer might mistake for a circus. Many people would later wonder how Dr. Dorothy put up with it for so many years. If Dr. Dorothy didn't answer all of his mail, the continual uncertainty of his day-to-day work situation or minor things like not knowing where his office would be tomorrow may have been a contributing factor.

At the time, though, in my innocence and naiveté, I was not aware of all of this turmoil behind the scenes. From my distance at Big Sandy, Dr. Dorothy's office and dedicated staff were part of Mr. Armstrong's headquarters team. They were hard at work upon the ambitious task of systematizing the church's various doctrines for posterity. I have no idea what Dr. Dorothy or his staff thought of the steady stream of papers I mailed out to his office. My thoughts were on pounding the keys on my typewriter. I typed away in the excitement of being convinced that my researches would make a difference to headquarters. This was the part *I* could do to help in this great Work.

---

[166] *Worldwide News*, Nov 16, 1981.

CHAPTER 14

QUEST FOR IMMORTALITY

In any religious quest for Truth, sooner or later one comes face to face with the timeless issue of our own temporariness—the inevitable end to all earthly quests and loves, and the question of why this must be so.

In one way of looking at our fleeting mortality, it is but part of the ebb and flow of all things. This perspective is eloquently expressed in Ecclesiastes.

> For everything there is a season,
> and a time for every matter under heaven:
> a time to be born, and a time to die;
> a time to kill, and a time to heal;
> a time to break down, and a time to build up;
> a time to weep, and a time to laugh;
> a time to mourn, and a time to dance;
> a time to cast away stones, and a time to gather stones together;
> a time to embrace, and a time to refrain from embracing;
> a time to seek, and a time to lose;
> a time to keep, and a time to cast away;
> a time to rend, and a time to sew;
> a time to keep silence, and a time to speak;
> a time to love, and a time to hate;
> a time for war, and a time for peace.

The poem seems to be an acceptance of the tides and givens in earthly affairs. It is almost a quiet fatalism, a "letting it be." But another way of looking at these same events—the question I asked while at Big Sandy—was: "Why? Why must these things be?" Did we not envision a time when there will be no death or tears? Why then must death and tears be considered acceptable *now*?

One day I happened to read a non-Worldwide Church of God exposition of a passage in Romans 5. It was explained that Adam's sin had been imputed to us on heavenly books. Then, these sins marked to our account had been wiped clean by imputation of Christ's righteousness to us on the same heavenly books. While this is more or less standard Catholic-Protestant doctrine, it came across to me as metaphysical mumbo-jumbo. As I read Paul's words, a more earthly explanation leaped out to me—that Paul was saying *physical dying of old age* came from Adam's sin. I later learned that this idea was not a new one. But at that time, I was not aware of the existence of this view elsewhere. And I had not heard it in the Worldwide Church of God.

Following is a condensed version of a paper I wrote about this, after which I will tell of its reception. I wrote a first version of this paper in February 1975 which is now lost.

Why Must We Die?
Greg Doudna
May 4, 1975

Adam was created physical, in the image of God. The first mention of death is in the warning: "But of the tree of knowledge of good and evil you shall not eat, for *in the day that you eat of it you shall die*" (Gen 2:17).

Adam did sin, he did eat of that fruit, and he surely died. He *died physically*. He died at 930 years old (Gen 5:5). Should it seem shocking to suggest that if Adam had not sinned there is no reason why he should have died? "Sin came into the world through one man and death *through sin*" (Rom 5:12). Paul says plainly in Romans 5:12-21 that it was because of Adam's sin that physical death passed on to all mankind, just as it was through Christ's obedience that spiritual life is given to Christ's. "The *last enemy* to be destroyed is *death*" (1 Cor 15:26). "Therefore as sin came into the world through one man and *death through sin*" (Rom 5:12)

Adam was given a choice. That choice was between physical life and physical death. Christ's choice was between spiritual life and spiritual death. The results of both of these choices were passed on to their respective descendants. Adam failed. Christ succeeded. We inherited physical death from Adam, and we are the heirs of eternal spiritual life through Christ. Neither comes through our own actions.

We can die from causes other than old age. It is natural death, the aging process, which we inherited from Adam. Unnatural deaths and accidents are of course not inherited from Adam. By "aging" is meant the decaying and wearing out of our human bodies—whatever it is that causes us to grow *old* and *die*. God intended Adam to *grow*, but not to grow old and *die* ... Death, destruction, suffering and tragedy entered by *sin*. Death is not logical, it is not good, it is not our friend (Heb 2:14-15; 1 Cor 15:42-44)!

After God created, "God saw that it was good." God did not create what Paul says is corruption, dishonor, and mortality, and say, "This is good"! If Adam had obeyed God he would have remained in paradise, the ground would not have been cursed, and Adam would not have died of old age.

Death is man's worst enemy. For 6000 years man has searched in vain for some way to circumvent this relentless adversary. There has never been a family, a friendship, a marriage that has not eventually been cruelly torn apart by death. "For this perishable nature must put on the imperishable, and this mortal nature must put on immortality" (1 Cor 15:53-57).

~ ~ ~

My first version of this paper in February 1975 caused a small flurry of interest as it circulated informally among friends at Big Sandy. With growing excitement, I submitted a copy of the paper to the Theological Research Project at Pasadena. I received no response from there. But the deputy chancellor and resident administrator at Big Sandy, Ronald Dart, gave a response to my idea at a Bible study.

Bible studies were held every Friday evening at Big Sandy. Members of the audience could submit written questions for the minister to answer. One Friday in February 1975 someone from the audience asked about my thesis that physical mortality came upon Adam and his descendants through sin. Mr. Dart disagreed with the idea. Cyclic life-and-death mortality of animals existed from the beginning, Mr. Dart said, and animals don't sin. So

Adam's sin brought about something different than physical mortality which was already in existence.

Russ Gmirkin's paper on "newness"

Mr. Dart's reasonable answer stumped me (though I knew my thesis was still right). Not one to let empirical principles of ecology stand in the way of biblically revealed truth, I still had no answer. Fortunately, my creative Pasadena friend Russ Gmirkin came to the rescue and wrote what was probably his most sophisticated theological enquiry of his Ambassador College years. It was a paper entitled "The Concept of Newness."

In this paper, written sometime in 1975, Russ analyzed the biblical concepts of "new" and "old." He argued that these words do not mean (as in English) "recent" compared to "ancient." Instead, he argued, the biblical "new" meant a state or condition, of being refreshed, renewed, incorruptible, never-wearing-out. Similarly, Russ argued, the biblical "old" also meant a state or condition—a condition of wearing out, deteriorating, "aging." A meaning of how recent or long ago in time had nothing to do with it. Both words refer to the nature of present conditions. This word study had enormous theological implications. They ranged from "old man" versus "new man," to "new heavens and new earth," "old" and "new" covenants, eschatological sequence, and so on. Russ explored the topic and its implications in thirty-six single-spaced, closely-argued pages. His first words on the cover were: "Not to be read without explicit permission."

This paper was not written for any class. I think Russ made only two copies of this paper other than his original. Russ sent one copy to the Theological Research Project in Pasadena, where it was never heard from again. He gave the other copy to me. In a key section, Russ quoted from my paper "Why Must Men Die?" (as my paper was originally titled). Russ expanded my concept of Adam's sin bringing physical mortality on *humans* (as in my paper) to Adam's sin bringing physical corruptibility on *all* of creation. The new heavens and new earth prophesied to replace this existing corrupting age (Rom 8:22; 2 Peter 3:13), Russ argued, will end the cyclic, mortality-based, aging-dying-predatorial ways of nature. All will be transformed to a state of perpetual refreshing of all creation in which mortality and dying no longer will be necessary for any living thing. This would be the fulfillment of Paul's words: "The creation itself will be set free from its bondage to decay and obtain the glorious liberty of the children of God" (Rom 8:21).

Russ's explanation was the fuller, visionary answer to Mr. Dart's objection. I had not been able to discover this creative response by myself, but imaginative Russ developed it after reading and being inspired by my paper. Russ's paper on "Newness," incidentally, in another time and place would have been recognized as a significant contribution to theology. (I am absolutely not kidding. There was seriously brilliant stuff in that paper.)

But alas, Ambassador College had no mechanism for recognizing brilliant work being done right under its nose. Russ wrote this paper shortly after flunking out of Ambassador College at Pasadena a second and final time. He had gotten bored with his classes again and had stopped attending. Earlier reservations of Ambassador College officials who wondered whether Russ was indeed "college material" were proven justified. Russ just didn't have what it took to meet Ambassador's academic standards.

A Tale of Two Trees

Russ's paper on "Newness" built on an earlier paper which was like an overture to the later one. This earlier one was entitled "The Fruit of the Fig Tree" (December 1974) and is also worth a moment's attention here.

As everyone knows, in the garden of Eden of Genesis there were two special trees. One was the tree of life. The other was the tree of knowledge of good and evil. As the story goes, God told Adam and Eve not to eat of his prize tree in the middle of the garden, the tree of knowledge of good and evil. If they eat of it, he warned, they would die.

As soon as God was out of sight, the serpent (the wisest animal) seduced Eve into eating the fruit. It's been downhill for the human race ever since. This story in Genesis tells how it all started—the timeless human predicaments, things like having to work for a living, pain in childbirth, women cursed with being dominated by idiotic men, mortality, and so on. This single story with an economy of words explained to the ancient reader how these recurring sources of human grief came to be and why.

Herbert Armstrong interpreted the "tree of knowledge" as representing humans choosing for themselves what was right and wrong. That was the wrong path for humans to go. The tree of life, the right path, Herbert Armstrong explained, was *God's revelation* of what is right and wrong.

Russ's paper argued a different interpretation. Russ correlated the two trees in the garden to what Paul says about the law and the Holy Spirit. Everything Paul says concerning the law was true of the tree of knowledge. It was good, it was holy, it was in the garden. But when it is eaten, it slays. Why? What is the paradox here? Drawing upon insights from Gestalt psychology, Russ said the tree of knowledge represents the way of learning from external authorities. Even if what is taught is 100 percent true (as Paul said of the law), it still kills. The tree of life, on the other hand, represents learning from personal experience. What happened that made Adam and Eve ashamed after they ate of the tree of knowledge, such that they sought to cover themselves? For the first time they had eaten that which they couldn't assimilate. This resulted in that bodily phenomenon which Jesus said (in King James Version language) "defileth a man," namely, that which "goeth out into the draught" (Mark 7:19). Adam and Eve regarded their appearance after this as shameful. This being before the invention of toilet paper or outhouses, Adam and Eve sought to cover their shameful appearance with fig leaves from the tree from which they had just eaten.

Quest for Immortality

The allegory, Russ explained, is that if we swallow knowledge that is not fully chewed, we will produce the spiritual equivalent of that which calls for toilet paper. Swallowing what outside authorities give us without personal chewing and assimilation is what is symbolized, said Russ, by the tree of knowledge. The serpent's offer of the fruit of the tree of knowledge represents the teacher who comes along with something to be believed without being understood. The story is a parable on how what is perfect, good, and holy (knowledge) can turn out to have disastrous consequences. Russ concluded that systems of belief based upon doctrines, no matter how true, if swallowed without personal chewing or if rammed down people's throats will result in bellyaches and diarrhea. Russ developed these allegorical themes in detail. Russ submitted that paper to headquarters too. Not surprisingly, nothing came of it and it was never heard from again. Maybe it gave them acid indigestion.[167]

~ ~ ~

But to return to aging and newness. The Genesis account says that all of nature—all of creation—was cursed as a result of the sin of Adam and Eve (Gen 3:17; Rom 8:20). That is to say, the consequences of human sin pervaded the whole world and, for that matter, the whole universe. (Hebrew writers were not modest about humans being central to the scheme of things.) The prophetic visions of the "wolf shall dwell with the lamb ... and the calf and the lion ... and a little child shall lead them ... they shall not hurt or destroy in all my holy mountain" (Isa 11:6-9), "the creation itself will be set free from its bondage to decay" (Rom 8:21), and so on, I came to read, with Russ, as glimpses of

---

[167] Sometime during my time at Big Sandy I came up with an idea of my own about the two trees. In one of my notebooks I worked out an interesting argument that the two trees—the tree of knowledge and the tree of life, both in the middle of the garden—were actually two different ways of speaking of the same tree. But I never wrote that one up.

a view that earthly creation may someday return to a *death-free* state, even in nature.

There is a biblical theme that the Spirit of God gives life and refreshes all things. I surmised that this must be the biblical image for how all of nature—even down to the level of bacteria—might flourish without need to individually decay or live by destroying other life. In this picture, all life-forms would live as fruitarians or by photosynthesis. (Granted, independent evidence from paleontology may seem to be lacking for this original state of nature. And some skeptics who doubt the literal veracity of this interpretation of Genesis might raise questions such as how soil formation might be affected. But with sufficient imagination, I was sure details like these could certainly be worked out.)

Gmirkin's paper on "newness" pointed out that the book of Revelation ends with the "tree of life," whose leaves and fruit give perpetual healing (Rev 22:2). It is a picture of a return to free access to the tree of life in the garden of Eden from which Adam and Eve were cut off, after which they began to *age*. Think about that—after our primeval parents lost access to the tree of life, they began to *age*. The tree of life is a metaphor for the Holy Spirit. Direct contact with the Holy Spirit (the tree of life) is prophesied to be restored not only to all flesh, but to all that is (Acts 2:17-18; Rom 8:21). Revelation says all creation will then be perpetually fresh, or, to use the biblical term, eternally "new."

Thinking along these lines, in my later Big Sandy days, led me to wonder if the worlds of matter and spirit were even much different (even if they seem very different to us now). I wondered: was physical matter simply some form of hypothetical "spiritual matter" which had been alienated from contact with the Spirit of God—something like pulling a plug out of an electric outlet? Once the "plug" was pulled, did aging begin, and matter became visible?

Then I pondered the implications of relativity theory. I learned of strange mathematical-astronomical worlds and phenomena

Quest for Immortality

such as the mysterious speed-of-light barrier. It is impossible for anything slower than the speed of light to ever attain the speed of light—because it requires energy exponentially increasing to infinity to continue accelerating as the speed of light approaches. At the same time, it is impossible for anything moving faster than the speed of light (the mathematically hypothesized "tachyons") to ever slow down to the speed of light—because in this case, energy exponentially increasing to infinity is required to slow down as the speed of light is approached.

We know this fundamental constant as the speed of light. But *other* universes might know it as something entirely different. They could know of the light-speed constant simply as, say, the conversion factor for matter into energy. I wondered if this fundamental constant might have something to do with the matter-spirit barrier which, using material means, cannot ever be crossed.

And I pondered the strange properties of "Schwarzschild radii" which are found around what astronomers call "singularities" or black holes. Something falling inside this radius will observe the outside universe appear to speed up in time to infinity. This means that the falling object will see, as it crosses this threshold, the whole history of the outside universe speed up and be over in a flash. But for those of us on the outside watching something fall into this radius surrounding a black hole, we will see it hang forever at that threshold of entry, frozen in time for eternity, not moving, ever.

Yes, I thought, things mysterious and wonderful are going on, on macro scales. I failed utterly to identity with a Sartrian, existential despair over meaning. What child, curious and seeing infinite delights and wonders in its new world, feels "existential despair"? If we but open our eyes as the child that sees all things new, and remember there is always Gödel's Theorem (a mathematical proof, developed in the 1930s, which states that no matter what the system, there is always interaction with something outside and beyond it; in other words, there are *no* closed or ultimate systems, no ultimate determinisms) ... can we feel anything other than a sense of adventure, challenge, and discovery?

CHAPTER 15

KEY EVENTS IN THE 1973-74 SACRED CALENDAR (AND OTHER TIMELY TOPICS)

While my other papers from my Big Sandy student days made little headway at headquarters, respect for accuracy constrains me to report the one paper that was an outstanding exception. *This* one almost made it to the attention of Herbert Armstrong *personally*. Here is the story on that.

~ ~ ~

The spring of 1974 was a tumultuous time at Big Sandy. The church was in the throes of upheavals. But as I lived through and pondered the meaning of the times, I noticed something else. I noticed that the spring of 1974 was exactly 3-1/2 years before the end of 6000 years from the creation of Adam, according to the chronology of Dr. Hoeh in Pasadena. These 6000 years were scheduled to finish in the fall of 1977. Since it was believed that there would be a 3-1/2 year period called the Great Tribulation to precede the return of Christ, I looked around for possible fulfillments of the prophetic timetable.

(This interest was simultaneous with my Jubilee year research described earlier focusing on a date a decade later. It became a case of "competing hypotheses.")

Key Events in the 1973-74 Sacred Calendar

It was commonly believed in the church that Christ would return on a Day of Trumpets, since it was believed that the Day of Trumpets pictures Christ's return. (The Day of Trumpets, one of the seven annual holy days, is the Jewish Rosh Hashana in the fall.) In the book of Daniel, there are certain time periods which are said to precede the end of the age. Specifically, these time periods are numbered at 1260, 1290, and 1335 days (Dan 12:7-12).

Therefore, I did a very logical thing. Poring over calendars in an almanac while at my night switchboard job, I began counting back from the Day of Trumpets, 1977. When I counted 1260 days back, I came to nothing significant. When I counted 1335 days back I came to a date in January 1974, again nothing significant. But when I counted 1290 days back, I came, unexpectedly, to a *hit!!*

Prophetically, this day, 1290 days before Christ's return, was supposed to be the day when the "Beast" would cut off the sacrifices of God's people in the temple (Dan 12:11). Counting 1290 days back from Trumpets of 1977 came to the day after Garner Ted Armstrong took the unprecedented step of canceling Sabbath services for the entire Worldwide Church of God. (Garner Ted did this to preempt dissident pastors across the country from turning their congregations away from headquarters on that day.) That was eery. BUT—Garner Ted Armstrong was the *good guy*, not the Beast! I decided that one was a false alarm, only a coincidence. That one didn't make it into any of my papers.

~ ~ ~

Here I was in the spring of 1974, exactly 3-1/2 years before the calculated end of 6000 years. After waiting all through my junior high and high school days, were I and my fellow students now living *in* the end-time, about to see it come to pass before our eyes in Big Sandy?

Key Events in the 1973-74 Sacred Calendar

But where was the Great Tribulation that was supposed to begin 3-1/2 years before the end? As hard as I looked there seemed to be no Great Tribulation engulfing the world, even though it was supposed to be getting underway any day now according to my calendar calculations. It was difficult to escalate even a Worldwide Church of God dissident uprising into that kind of apocalyptic interpretation.

This troubling lack of a Great Tribulation left two possibilities: (a) Christ's return was not going to happen in 1977, or, (b) as ex-registrar at Pasadena and student of astronomical and biblical synchronisms, Ken Herrmann, suggested privately, we might be *in* the Great Tribulation even then—and not know it.

~ ~ ~

How could we be in the Great Tribulation and not know it?

When you're creative, you can interpret what you see in surprising ways. In my innocence and hopes for the return of Christ to come *soon*, I watched with heightened intensity. There was no encouragement of chronological speculations from church leaders. The 1972 disappointment was still too recent. Headquarters was not about to repeat that mistake. But informally, speculation was rife. Mr. Herrmann and I and others actively compared notes as we tried to decipher the hidden meaning of the times.

Mr. Herrmann said he had been thinking about the Yom Kippur War of the previous fall, of 1973. Revelation 12:9 indicates that the Great Tribulation begins with an expulsion of Satan from heaven to earth. When Satan is cast down to earth, he has "great wrath, because he knows that his time is short" (Rev 12:12). The first people Satan might attack, logically, would be the Jews. Had Satan been cast down to earth on the Day of Atonement, 1973?

The Yom Kippur War of 1973 was the occasion of a combined Arab attack on Israel on October 6, the sacred day of

Key Events in the 1973-74 Sacred Calendar

Yom Kippur—the Day of Atonement. Because of Western countries' trade with Israel, the Arab world chose this occasion to implement a catastrophic oil embargo which just about shut down the Western world's economies. Later, it came out that the world was also on the brink of nuclear war, with the United States President, Nixon, putting all U.S. nuclear forces on full alert prepared for a showdown with the Soviet Union. Fortunately, the world survived and hostilities were brought to a halt. The flow of Arab oil to Western countries was resumed, albeit at slightly higher prices.

But though the world had survived, tensions continued. Ever since then, my observant eyes (and those of others) noted, there were, "coincidentally," upheavals in the church. As I looked at the night sky from peaceful, tranquil Big Sandy, I wondered what each next day would bring for the world.

~ ~ ~

If you figure 3-1/2 years *after* Atonement of 1973 you come to a date in the spring of 1977 called Nisan 10 in the Hebrew calendar. Mr. Herrmann pointed out to me that it was on this day, Nisan 10, that Jesus entered Jerusalem triumphantly as Messiah (John 12:12-15). The Nisan 10 entrance of Jesus to Jerusalem, and being hailed as Messiah, was like the Jewish selection of the Passover Lamb on that day, on Nisan 10 (Ex 12:2-3). From this, Mr. Herrmann suggested that maybe Christ might return on a Nisan 10 in the spring—instead of on a Day of Trumpets in the fall—just as he had been proclaimed king when he entered Jerusalem on that day the *first* time. If so, then the predicted period of Satan's wrath, starting 3-1/2 years earlier (Rev 12:6, 14), logically would begin in a fall—Tishri 10, to be exact—the Day of Atonement. Counting back from Nisan 10, 1977, this meant, specifically, the Day of Atonement, 1973—the Yom Kippur War! It worked out to the very day!

But I noticed something more. Just nine days before the Yom Kippur War, Herbert Armstrong gave what he billed as his first "testimonial dinner" to heads of state, and this dinner appeared to have taken place in Japan on the Day of Trumpets, 1973.

Cosmically significant banquets

Lest this last point go over your head, you must understand the significance that was attached to the travel activities and "testimonial dinners" of chancellor Herbert Armstrong. Herbert Armstrong was now spending a large part of his time outside the United States flying around the world in a $3.5 million Gulfstream II personal jet. In the summer of 1973 he turned day-to-day running of the church over to his son Garner Ted. Herbert Armstrong, however, was still in charge. He continued to keep in touch with the membership via monthly letters.

In the course of his travels, Herbert Armstrong, always accompanied by his right-hand man, church attorney Stanley Rader, would speak at banquets in foreign lands attended by dignitaries invited for the occasion. These banquets were called "testimonial dinners."

These testimonial dinners were specifically identified by Herbert Armstrong as the means by which Christ's commission was being fulfilled at the end, in which the gospel would be preached "in the whole world for a witness to all the nations" (Matt 24:14). Herbert Armstrong's reasoning was quite logical. Most Third World countries don't allow access to the media or the public at large. In Gentile kingdoms (as distinguished from the Israelite peoples of the United States and Britain which are democratic countries), Herbert explained, God considers the king to be synonymous with the nation (e.g. Dan 2:21; 2:38-39; 8:22; 11:2). Therefore, when Herbert Armstrong met with heads of state such as King Hussein of Jordan, Anwar Sadat of Egypt, Jomo Kenyatta of Kenya, Haile Selassie of Ethiopia, Indira Gandhi of India, Ferdinand Marcos the dictator of the Philippines (Armstrong particularly liked Marcos), leaders of Japan and mainland China, and others—this was God's witness to these whole *nations* of people. (Just by speaking a few minutes to the ruler of the country.)

After five days and two banquets in China in 1979, for example, Herbert Armstrong announced that he had just carried the witness of Christ's gospel to one-quarter of the world's population. And he explained that he had accomplished this remarkable feat without mentioning Christ.

In actuality, Herbert Armstrong's meetings were glorified photo sessions in which the name of Christ was rarely brought up. Herbert Armstrong would talk in general terms about "the GIVE way of life" and "an age of peace to come on earth." The heads of state would nod politely, be presented with personal gifts of expensive Steuben crystal worth thousands of dollars, and receive glowing puff pieces in the mass-circulation *Plain Truth* in the United States. The members would be told the witness of the gospel was going forth in these foreign lands, and everyone would be happy.

(According to a member of Herbert Armstrong's traveling party in the late 1960s and early 1970s, former evangelist Charles Hunting, these trips involved unrestrained spending and the meetings were almost wholly on a social basis and atmosphere rather than a religious basis. How were the meetings arranged? As a *quid pro quo* for donations to charities sponsored by the dignitaries. For example, $250,000 to King Leopold's Belgian Foundation's work in the Belgian Congo, $250,000 to an Israeli-sponsored International Cultural Center for Youth in Jerusalem, and so on.[168])

The important point here is that what Herbert Armstrong billed as the *first* of these testimonial dinners—the *beginning* of what Herbert Armstrong said was the world's last witness of the gospel before the end—apparently happened on the

---

[168] From a tape of a Charles Hunting radio interview, Clyde Thomas program, WKIS Radio, Orlando, Florida, August 5, 1987 (transcript at http://www.hwarmstrong.com/hunting.htm).

Key Events in the 1973-74 Sacred Calendar

evening of September 26, 1973, the evening portion of the Day of Trumpets.[169]

The timing of the Yom Kippur War and Herbert Armstrong's cosmically significant banquet was startling enough. But then I discovered the "White Horse" of Revelation.

The man on the white horse

The "White Horse" of Revelation 6:2 and its rider are the first of Revelation's seven prophetic "seals." These seven seals constitute the greater part of the book of Revelation. The seer, John, is given a scroll with seven seals. Most of Revelation is John's record of what he sees as this scroll's seven seals are opened, one by one.

When the first of the seven seals is broken, John sees a white horse ride forth. This white horse, then, is the opening of the apocalypse. It is the start of the book of Revelation coming to life in Technicolor vision before John's astonished eyes.

In our classes at Big Sandy it was taught that the White Horse represents religious deception and is a *bad* horse. But in conversations with Big Sandy's long-time registrar Lynn Torrance (the crusty survivor of Bataan of World War II), I

---

[169] Although this testimonial dinner in Japan was prominently reported and a tape of Herbert Armstrong's message that evening was played to the church membership, somewhat surprisingly there never was attention drawn to it having occurred on the Day of Trumpets. But I believed the following confirmed that it did. In a letter dated September 24, 1973, Herbert Armstrong wrote: "I am writing from Tokyo where I look forward on the night of the day after tomorrow, to a very great opportunity. It may be the first time in all history such a thing has happened. I am invited by Prince Mikasa, brother of the Emperor, to explain the Bible—proclaim Christ's gospel of the Kingdom of God—to a most impressive audience. It is the most impressive audience before which I have ever been given opportunity to give Christ's message" (Armstrong, *Autobiography*, II, 529). Based on this, I concluded the dinner occurred the evening of September 26. The Day of Trumpets that year was September 26-27, sunset to sunset.

learned reasons why the White Horse of Revelation 6:2 might be a *good* horse.

Dr. Torrance, who had studied the matter, pointed out to me that the horse didn't simply *appear* white. The horse *was* white. Furthermore, when the White Horse and its rider are said to go forth "conquering," this is the same Greek word *nikao*, "overcoming," which is frequently held out as an ideal for Christians throughout the book of Revelation (e.g. Rev 2:7, 11, 17, 26; 3:5, 12, 21; 21:7).

Herbert Armstrong said his meetings with world leaders were proclaiming the gospel before kings at the end, just as Christ foretold before his second coming (Luke 21:12). Malcontents in the church, however, had an unsettling habit of insisting that a closer look at Jesus's words revealed the gospel coming before kings under circumstances of *persecution*. This was a slightly different picture of meeting world leaders than the style to which Herbert Armstrong had become accustomed. Seeking to resolve this trifling discrepancy, Dr. Torrance suggested that the going forth of the White Horse might be the preaching of the gospel in peace which Herbert Armstrong had now begun. (The witness during persecution would come later.)

Dr. Torrance's comments intrigued me and after studying the matter I became persuaded that Torrance was correct. The White Horse was a *good* horse—the going forth of the gospel. Naturally I improved Torrance's discovery with some embellishments of my own. I pored over the pages of Revelation, like trying to crack a secret code. I was startled to discover never-before-noticed connections between the White Horse and the Philadelphia church of Revelation 3:7-13.

~ ~ ~

The "Philadelphia church" of Revelation was very important to the Worldwide Church of God. The Worldwide Church of God believed it *was* this Philadelphia church.

Key Events in the 1973-74 Sacred Calendar

Chapters 2 and 3 of Revelation describe seven churches to whom John, the seer, is instructed by Jesus in a vision to send letters. These seven churches of the first century were in seven cities of Asia Minor (Turkey). They were, in order: Ephesus, Smyrna, Pergamos, Thyatira, Sardis, Philadelphia, and Laodicea.

It was believed that the descriptions of these seven churches in Revelation represented seven sequential phases or eras of the true church from the first century until Christ's return. The first five eras were believed to be past (though in some cases remnants of former eras remained). The sixth, or Philadelphia era, was the Worldwide Church of God. The Philadelphia church receives high praise from Jesus. The seventh or Laodicean era would arise in the future. It was believed that church would come out of the Worldwide Church of God.

The Laodicean church would still be the true church, but in contrast to the favored Philadelphia church Jesus is not pleased with the Laodiceans. Jesus reprimands them severely for being "neither hot nor cold." He says he is going to spit them out of his mouth if they don't shape up and get their act together. He quotes the Laodiceans as saying, "We are rich and increased with goods." But Jesus says they don't realize how poor they are or are soon about to become. When you get right down to it, Jesus is just pretty disgusted with this bunch (even if they are the true church). Jesus closes with a note of encouragement, though: he beats them only because he loves them—whom he loves he chastens (3:19).

As this was interpreted within the seven church-era scheme, the Laodiceans would consist of spiritually lukewarm brethren in the Worldwide Church of God who, by letting down, would find themselves unworthy to be taken to the earthly place of safety reserved for the faithful, favored Philadelphians. The Laodiceans would be left behind and have to go through the Great Tribulation.

I noticed that the White Horse of Revelation appeared after "*a door standing open*" in heaven (4:1; 5:1-2; 6:1-2). This sounded strikingly similar to Jesus's words to the Philadelphia church.

Jesus identifies himself to the Philadelphia church as he "*who opens*" (3:7). He says to the Philadelphians, "I have put before you *an open door*" (3:8).

The words swirled around in my head: a *door standing open ... an open door ... a door standing open ... an open door ...* and then I realized: the Philadelphia church and its preaching of the true gospel—Herbert Armstrong's trips, in other words—was the fulfillment of the *White Horse!*

I wrote my reinterpretation of the White Horse into a short paper and gave it to Dr. Torrance. My paper was entitled, "Is the White Horse of Revelation 6:2 the Work of God?," dated December 27, 1974. I wrote:

> The rider of the white horse goes forth "conquering." This is the same word in Greek as "overcoming" as when Christ tells the seven churches, "To him that *overcometh* will I give to eat of the tree of life" (Rev 2:7). The rider of the white horse was given a crown. To the Philadelphia church Christ says, "Behold, I come quickly: hold that fast which thou hast, that no man take thy crown" (3:11). The crown symbolizes the reward given to Christ's servants for their righteousness. The rider is pictured as having a bow. The bow is a symbol of the preaching of the truth (Ps 7:11-13; 45:5) ... In Revelation 19 we see Christ pictured as "the Word of God" and riding on a white horse. Would it not make sense that the book of Revelation would begin and end with the truth, both on white horses? The first seal would be the truth going forth (the Word of God) ...
>
> To the Philadelphians, Christ describes Himself as "he that openeth" (3:7). He also tells them, "I have set before you an open door" (3:8). Christ is He that opens, yet what does He open? The next two chapters tell of Him opening the sealed book. It is the opening of the first seal which opens the book. It is as if Christ is telling the Philadelphia church, "I will open the seals of Revelation in your time" ...

Dr. Torrance was impressed with what I had written. He quoted excerpts from my paper in a memo of his own, and, prominently crediting me for the quoted passages, sent his memo out to Pasadena.

Key Events in the 1973-74 Sacred Calendar

The Black Hole

Now this was progress! I had been learning from experience that headquarters didn't seem to bother with submissions mailed in by a mere student. But with *this* kind of high-powered recommendation, at last one of my researches would get some attention!

Sadly, not even Dr. Torrance at Big Sandy could get a response from headquarters. His memo received no answer or acknowledgement—it just disappeared into the black hole of unanswered mail the same as if I had sent it out myself. I suppose it was a small consolation to learn that at least I wasn't the only one who didn't get mail answered from headquarters.

(I had this idea that there was a room somewhere out at Pasadena full of headquarters officials who were charged with advising Herbert Armstrong on important matters and doctrines. An envelope would come addressed to them. Inside would be neatly typed pages representing hundreds of hours of research carefully and humbly prepared for their consideration. But the envelope would bear the telltale postmark, "Big Sandy." At this, the headquarters brass would all cackle with laughter and say, "Can any good thing come out of *Big Sandy??!!??*" Then they would laugh themselves hoarse as they pitched the package sailing through the air unopened into a huge bottomless wastebasket labeled "Black Hole.")

I thought my idea of the White Horse as the proclamation of the gospel by the Philadelphia church had so much promise! Who knows what Herbert Armstrong would have done with this if he had heard of it—this direct identification of himself, personally, as the man on the White Horse whose destiny it was to start the prophecies of the book of Revelation to *happening* for the world?

But it was not to be. The headquarters bureaucracy effectively shielded Herbert Armstrong from New Ideas emerging from too far down in the pyramid.

Key Events in the 1973-74 Sacred Calendar

~ ~ ~

Of course, I wasn't one to let minor bureaucratic idiosyncrasies stop me from being creative or believing in the mission and goodwill of the church. I kept examining the times and the seasons. Before long I had another paper ready to send off to headquarters!

In this paper I correlated significant events in the church with the meanings of the days on which these events happened in the sacred calendar of the past year, 1973-1974. I have already mentioned Herbert Armstrong's first testimonial dinner on Trumpets 1973 and then the Yom Kippur War of the Day of Atonement 1973. Then my faculty friend who taught Hebrew, Mark Kaplan, told me that he had noticed that a meeting of dissident ministers in Pasadena with Herbert Armstrong occurred on the Jewish Feast of Purim 1974. (The Feast of Purim, celebrated by Jews to commemorate the Jews' deliverance from enemies as told in the Book of Esther, was not celebrated by the Worldwide Church of God, but Kaplan, with his Orthodox rabbinical background, noticed it.) To these three I added a few more correlations and collected them into a paper.

This paper was entitled "Key Events in the 1973-74 Sacred Calendar" (March 1975). First I will give a brief summary of the paper. After that I will tell the story of how this paper came within a hairs-breadth of making it all the way to Herbert Armstrong himself.

First was (1) Trumpets 1973, the first of Herbert Armstrong's "testimonial dinners." I cited Ezek 33:3 as showing a connection between the Day of Trumpets and the preaching of the gospel in the end-time.

Second was (2) Atonement 1973, the Yom Kippur War. I drew a connection between Satan being cast down to earth with wrath, of Revelation 12, and "the first people Satan would attack after being cast down to earth would be the Jews, as he hates this people more than any other physical nation on earth."

Third was (3) Feast of Purim 1974. I wrote:

Key Events in the 1973-74 Sacred Calendar

> A challenge to the Armstrongs' leadership unfolded in early 1974 ... Dissident ministers in the United States were invited to Pasadena to meet with the Armstrongs. On Friday [*sic*, Thursday], March 14, Herbert Armstrong met with and spoke to those who came in. Although it seems few are aware of it, this crucial meeting between Mr. Armstrong and many of the dissenting ministers, prominently reported in the *Worldwide News*, occurred on the Feast of Purim ... The attempt to oust the Armstrongs failed. The Feast of Purim (described in the book of Esther) pictures the deliverance of God's people and the destruction of their enemies.

Next was (4) the Wave Sheaf Sunday evening, April 7, 1974, the opening night of the Ambassador Auditorium. I wrote:

> The Auditorium has often been likened to a modern house for God ... On the Wave Sheaf Sunday evening the disciples saw the risen temple of Christ's body (John 2:21) for the first time as an assembled gathering ... The Auditorium's opening night (and dedication) had been scheduled for the evening following the first day of Unleavened Bread, April 7. But the Wave Sheaf Sunday (the beginning of the count to Pentecost) was originally thought to be the following Sunday, April 14, one week later. It was only a short time before the spring festival season that the truth was recognized and accepted by God's Church concerning which Sunday is the correct Wave Sheaf Sunday on years when Passover falls on a Sabbath. It was this new understanding which virtually at the last minute moved the Wave Sheaf day ahead one week to Sunday, April 7, the evening of the Auditorium's opening night.

Next was (5) Second Passover 1974. Unforeseen construction delays forced a month's postponement in the actual dedication of the Ambassador Auditorium (distinct from the "opening night"), which occurred May 6, 1974. On this date a ministerial conference was held, a change in the doctrine on divorce and remarriage was announced, and the Auditorium was dedicated to God. By coincidence, May 6 happened also to be the day of the "second Passover" (Num 9:10-12). Biblically the second Passover was held a month later for persons who had been unable or unworthy to partake of the first Passover. The

Key Events in the 1973-74 Sacred Calendar

dedication of the Auditorium and ministerial conference was originally planned for the first Passover season, but instead had been postponed until the second Passover. I asked: "Did God cause the dedication of the Auditorium and the ministerial conference to be delayed as a symbol for us? Was God's Church in some way unworthy or unready at the time of the first Passover?"

Sixth was (6) the day of Christ's ascension and giving of the Great Commission. The first of Herbert Armstrong's public appearances before *large* audiences in foreign nations took place in Manila, the Philippines, May 17-19, 1974. This had been rescheduled for those dates after an uprising of dissident ministers in the United States had forced a sudden cancellation of an earlier scheduled campaign in Manila two months earlier. Previous to that, a scheduled campaign in Saigon had been cancelled due to a North Vietnamese offensive. But this third attempt for a first such overseas campaign happened in Manila as planned. I noted that "Mr. Armstrong delivered his first message in Manila on Friday evening, May 17, 1974, forty days after the Wave Sheaf Sunday (April 7). It was forty days after the Wave Sheaf Sunday of Christ's resurrection that Christ commissioned His disciples to go into all the world and preach the gospel 'even to the remotest part of the earth' (Acts 1:3, 8)."

And finally, (7) Pentecost 1974. "Pentecost 1974 might possibly be considered another noteworthy item in the 1973-74 sacred calendar, making seven in all, in that it was the first Pentecost observed by the Worldwide Church of God on the correct day (Sunday) after forty years of error (Monday)," I wrote. I concluded:

> What is meant by the unusual synchronization of key events with significant days in God's calendar? The fortieth year of the Work, 1973-74, has certainly been an unusual year. Will we witness in coming months and years the same remarkable precision of significant events in God's plan falling on particular days in God's calendar relevant to those events? Christ said the wise would be

Key Events in the 1973-74 Sacred Calendar

watching, discerning the times and the seasons. Will we someday understand what has been taking place this past year?

I showed copies of this paper to several students and faculty friends at Big Sandy. There was praise for my paper from all around. So, forgetting about my past experiences with the black hole, and brimming with optimism and goodwill, I submitted it to several sources at Pasadena.

A letter from Stanley Rader

A couple of months went by and nothing happened. Just as I was resigning myself to another forgotten paper receiving no response or interest, something happened. To my utter astonishment, I received back A Response! It came in the form of an official-looking business-size envelope from Pasadena in my mail one day in June 1975. I saw from the outside of the envelope that the letter was from Stanley R. Rader, personal assistant to Herbert Armstrong, lawyer, treasurer, jet aircraft part-owner, and a few other things for the church.

Stanley Rader (1930-2002) was the brains behind Herbert Armstrong's meetings with world leaders. Rader was rapidly becoming the second most powerful man in the Work, surpassing even Garner Ted Armstrong. Because my paper dealt with the travels of Herbert Armstrong in which Rader was so closely involved, he was one of the persons to whom I had sent my paper. (It had not occurred to me to try that route to Mr. Armstrong's attention before.)

With hands trembling at the very thought of a reply from headquarters—*a first!*—I opened the envelope. Inside was a courteous personal letter from Stanley Rader. Mr. Rader thanked me for my article. He said he found my article of great interest and planned to show it to Herbert Armstrong!

Key Events in the 1973-74 Sacred Calendar

Worldwide Church of God
World Headquarters
Pasadena, California

Office of Stanley R. Rader, General Counsel
June 19, 1975

Dear Mr. Doudna:
    I want to thank you for the article which you have sent me last month. I have just received it in Tokyo, as I have been out of the States for almost eleven weeks with only one day in Pasadena during that time.
    I find the article of very great interest and I intend to bring it to the attention of Mr. Armstrong and others as soon as possible.
    My kindest personal regards.
    Yours truly,
    Stanley R. Rader

~ ~ ~

I couldn't believe it!

Stanley Rader's letter being the most direct answer I had received from Pasadena to the repeated submissions I had been making, at times I felt like *framing* it. My existence had been acknowledged! (Naturally, my respect for Stanley Rader's theological acumen also just soared.)

I basked in the glow of Mr. Rader's words. My humble patience had paid off. Now, at last, my previous two years of meekness and dedicated study were about to bear fruit.

I noted with irony that Stanley Rader was not an ordained minister. Come to think of it, he had been a member for only a few weeks when he wrote me. (Rader was baptized by Herbert Armstrong in March 1975 in a hotel bathtub in Hong Kong.) Yet, babe in Christ though he may have been, newly converted Stanley Rader seemed to be about the only person at Pasadena who answered his mail. I concluded this was because he was not ordained. He was simply an average, normal, everyday fellow member—just like us. I liked Stanley Rader.

Key Events in the 1973-74 Sacred Calendar

~ ~ ~

With much excitement, I waited eagerly for the effects of my article to begin appearing in Herbert Armstrong's writings and sermons. There wasn't the slightest doubt in my mind that when Stanley Rader told Herbert Armstrong about my article that Mr. Armstrong would like what I had written. After all, my paper did not just show relationships between world events and the holy days. My startling parallels furnished original, unmistakable evidence of Herbert Armstrong's *personal* place in history. Everybody knew this was Herbert Armstrong's favorite topic.

Maybe Herbert Armstrong would mention some of my parallels in one of his co-worker or member letters or in a sermon. I wondered if any day now one of Mr. Armstrong's letters to members might read something like this:

> Brethren, I wrote you some time ago about Robert Kuhn, a brain researcher who, independently of what was being revealed to me through the Word of God, proved through advanced scientific brain research that there is a non-physical component which makes the human mind different from the animal brain.
>
> Now, brethren, I am happy to report that on a different matter the same kind of thing has happened again. A Big Sandy student's independent research proving my place in history has recently come to my attention ... At last I've finally come to see that that campus is good for something after all ...

I savored the day with anticipation. When this came out, all those *bureaucrats* at Pasadena who had been *ignoring* the submissions of me and others at Big Sandy would just have *egg all over their faces!* This would *show them!* This would get Big Sandy a little respect for a change out at headquarters. I could hardly wait.

~ ~ ~

But alas, it was not to be. I don't think my paper was ever brought to Herbert Armstrong's attention.

For one who saw himself personally referred to by name when Isaiah said the Lord would rule earth with "the *arm* of his *strength*" (Isa 62:8; 40:10), as well as seeing himself as a modern-day Elijah, Moses, David, John the Baptist, Paul, et al, as did Herbert Armstrong, the material in my article would have fit perfectly. But none of the coincidences of my paper ever appeared in Mr. Armstrong's writings and sermons. I believe this to be most reasonably accounted for by his never having become aware of them.

And so my sounder papers in which I had put so much work and submitted so carefully through all the proper channels were ignored. It was *this* paper which soared to the top of the pyramid almost to Herbert Armstrong's very doorstep! It came *so close!*

(I'm still trying to figure out the lesson and the irony in this.)

~ ~ ~

Not every reaction to my paper was as favorable as that of Stanley Rader. I also sent my paper to a recent graduate from Ambassador College, Big Sandy, two years ahead of me as a student. He had become a dissident during his senior year. I wondered how a dissident would answer all of the clear evidence of Herbert Armstrong's prophetic significance that I had collected. My paper got a reaction. I promptly received back the paper with scathing handwritten comments and exclamation points peppering its pages, a few milder excerpts of which I quote here.

> Unlike your other two papers, I personally have no interest in this one, which is a nice way of saying that I don't think it was worth the effort ... I would doubt whether the so-called "top-down" method of warning is a valid means to "teach all nations" ... "The Auditorium likened to a modern house for God"—a bit presumptuous I would say ... "New understanding on Pentecost"—B.S.! This "new" understanding had been around for 14 years! Dr. Martin had it nailed down for that long but it had been lightly dismissed. HWA's temperament and personal schedule overcame the truth for 14 years

Key Events in the 1973-74 Sacred Calendar

> ... "Second Passover"—what happened to first Passover? Nothing to read into it? ... Following your pattern I could rig up something along the same line, but with a different point of view. For example on March 25, 1974—the daylight portion of the first day of Nisan, the new year—20 students at Big Sandy were arbitrarily fired on religious grounds (illegal, by the way). It was a turning point for many—a rebirth on the day of the birth of the new sacred year. If I had a more detailed history of the hassle I could do many more ... Your comparisons are not logically valid, or at least they are no more logically valid than any I could readily make in favor of the dissidents.

These comments, written as they were with the style and grace one uses to let a friend know that he's gone completely bonkers, I *entirely* agree with today.

~ ~ ~

Of course, all of this is obsolete now. The year 1977 is history. The world continues and the millennium, surprisingly, is not here. But at the time, as these things unfolded before my eyes precisely 5997-1/2 years after the presumed start of human history, they made life meaningful and prayers of heightened passion. Others find meaning and archetypical relevance in such things as the I Ching, the courses of the planets through the heavens, "numerical time-squared economic cycles," or a thousand other means of divination ancient and modern. At Ambassador College I found meaning in the richness of biblical prophecy, symbolism, and numbers, combined with active prayer and a heartfelt desire to *know*.

How is it that coincidences and meaning seem to so dramatically multiply in the directions in which we look for them? Some insightful studies of this phenomenon are G. Spencer-Brown, *Probability and Scientific Inference*,[170] F. David Peat, *Synchronicity*,[171] and Rudy Rucker, *Infinity and the Mind*.[172]

---

[170] G. Spencer-Brown, *Probability and Inference* (London, 1957).
[171] F. David Peat, *Synchronicity* (New York: Bantam, 1987).

354
Key Events in the 1973-74 Sacred Calendar

In *The Roots of Coincidence*, Arthur Koestler argued that there was more to clusters of startling daily coincidences—which everyone has experienced—than mere chance.[173] Perhaps there was some not yet understood "integrative tendency" operating, Koestler suggested. But popular American science writer Martin Gardner didn't think much of Koestler's suggestion. Gardner explained:

> The number of events in which you participate for a month, or even a week, is so huge that the probability of noticing a startling correlation is quite high, especially if you keep a sharp lookout ... I urge Koestler to make the following simple experiment. It was invented by A.D. Moore, professor emeritus of electrical engineering at the University of Michigan. He calls it the "nonpareil mosaic" because he uses large quantities of tiny colored balls of nonpareils, a sugar candy made in Milwaukee. Fill a beaker with thousands of the little beads, half of them red, half green. Shake thoroughly, then inspect the beaker's sides. Do you see an intimate, homogeneous mixture? You do not. You see a marvelous mosaic: irregular large clumps of red interspersed with similar clumps of green. The pattern is so unexpected that most physicists, when they see it, suspect an electrostatic effect ... Nothing is operating here except elementary laws of chance ... I do not believe that integrative tendencies were at work when the APollo 16 crew left for the moon on APril 16 from CAPe Kennedy, there being exactly sixteen letters from *A* to *P* inclusive.[174]

What is the lesson? Synchronisms can prove many things. We tend to see what we desire to see. We draw out of the universe what we pray for. Life itself is a miracle of synchronisms which we call by other names. As Spock on *Star Trek* used to say, "There are always possibilities."

---

[172] Rudy Rucker, *Infinity and the Mind* (New York: Bantam, 1983). Includes a rare personal interview with the brilliant, reclusive mathematician Kurt Gödel (1906-1978).
[173] Arthur Koestler, *The Roots of Coincidence* (New York: Random House, 1972).
[174] Martin Gardner, review of Koestler, *The Roots of Coincidence*, in *World* magazine, Aug. 1, 1972.

CHAPTER 16

HEADQUARTERS IN PROPHECY

Usually, the future "Beast" of Revelation is understood to be someone like the Pope, a European political leader, a figure in the Middle East, or whoever. In any event, it is generally agreed that he will be a fearsome (though, to the world's eyes, an acclaimed and popular) world dictator, prophesied to head a world government which will exterminate true Christians. With variations, this is the approximate picture of the near future held by millions of evangelical Christians.

The Worldwide Church of God held substantially to this picture, though with the following modifications:

(1) The Tribulation was expected to last 3-1/2 years, instead of 7 years.

(2) Instead of being raptured to heaven to avoid this Tribulation, faithful church members would be taken miraculously to a physical place of safety on earth where they would be divinely protected.

(3) The Beast was expected to most probably be a German.

However, for reasons to be explained, I became convinced that the future Beast was some as-yet-unknown person in high position at headquarters at Pasadena. He would likely be someone we all knew. An unsuccessful attempt to enrich himself would result in his being ignominiously kicked out. He would, metaphorically speaking, be "mortally wounded." But, to everyone's astonishment, he would turn up next as a European Beast and world dictator. Then he would wreak vengeance on the true church and declare war on his former associates—God's faithful witnesses Herbert and Garner Ted Armstrong.

~ ~ ~

I have to credit the inspiration for this amazing idea to the crusty registrar and director of admissions at Big Sandy, Lynn Torrance (the survivor of Bataan in World War II). Dr. Torrance took keen interest in my researches and papers, and for a while was my closest faculty friend.

Like most of the veteran faculty members at Big Sandy, Dr. Torrance had a strong loyalty to the Armstrongs. He told me it was he who "blew the whistle" on the dissident minister uprising in 1974. He told me how that happened. Torrance's office in the library in the Redwood Building happened to be next to that of Howard Clark, the colorful and popular speech instructor. Clark's naturally booming voice, which could usually be heard half a mile away and that's when he wasn't trying, boomed no less when he talked on the phone. Torrance explained that he simply sat in his own office one evening listening to Clark's half of a long-distance telephone conversation which carried through the inadequately insulated adjoining wall. In this way Torrance learned of the existence of dissident ministers and their plans. Torrance reported this shocking development to Garner Ted Armstrong, who then took action. Surprisingly, although Clark was the leading figure on campus identified with dissident students, and Torrance in his outspoken way had nothing good to say about dissidents, Clark and Torrance were old friends, got along well, and would play racquetball together.

Torrance and his wry, quotable aphorisms were well-known among students. What was not so widely known was Torrance's degree of study into certain things in the Bible. At times this aspect of Dr. Torrance amazed me. We had countless talks. He took a personal interest in my welfare, showed me kindnesses, and generously made available to me his office and typewriter many nights and weekends. That is where a number of my papers were typed in the December 1974 to May 1975 period.

The idea for the paper to follow began when Dr. Torrance pointed out an interesting fact to me.

Actually, Torrance's manner of conversation was more indirect, when it came to matters of innovative and potentially controversial biblical interpretations, than the words "pointed out" would indicate. Dr. Torrance had a unique style. His manner was to hint at or "wonder" about this or that, while he frowned in deep puzzlement and looked at you. If you didn't pick up on the point, he would drop it, but then next time "wonder" again about the same thing. After several times of this he would succeed in getting you to "wonder" about it too. Then he would act completely stunned and surprised when you stumbled on to discovering the obvious fact that he wanted you to discover. Years of experience with students had honed his skills in this area to a fine art.

In his oblique way, Dr. Torrance kept pointing me to a passage in 2 Thessalonians 2 wherein a figure known in the King James Version as a "Man of Sin" is described. This Man of Sin is called by the same title as Judas Iscariot—"son of perdition." Dr. Torrance would always comment, with a puzzled look on his face, that the Man of Sin is mentioned in a context of a falling away from the truth. Torrance kept returning me to this topic. He kept suggesting that there must be something significant there. I took a closer look. I examined the words forward, backward, and upside down.

One day, like a light bulb going on, it struck me. "Dr. Torrance," I said. "If the Man of Sin falls away from the truth, then this means he is going to come out of the True Church!!!"

Dr. Torrance looked stunned and surprised. He asked me to elaborate.

Excitedly, I explained to him my reasons for "my" startling discovery. I added the innovation that my studies showed that the prophesied Man of Sin was, in fact, none other than the figure of the Beast himself. (The Worldwide Church of God believed the

Man of Sin was another prophetic figure known as the "false prophet.")

With the support of Dr. Torrance I wrote a paper developing these themes. We both thought it was an important paper. In fact Dr. Torrance helped edit it. It was titled, "Will the 'Beast' of Revelation Come Out of the True Church?" (May 2, 1975).

How I argued that the Beast of Revelation would come out of the True Church

Here is how I did it. First, I argued that the "man of sin" of 2 Thessalonians 2 was the Beast of Revelation, not the false prophet as was taught in our classes at Big Sandy. I wrote:

> Paul says this Man of Sin or "son of perdition" sets himself up in the temple and claims to be God. Here Paul directly quotes a verse from Daniel relating to that wicked person known prophetically as "the Beast"—not the false prophet. It is the Beast, not the false prophet, which Daniel was told would "exalt himself and magnify himself above every god" (Dan 11:36). In Revelation 13, which describes the Beast and a second beast which we may safely assume to be the false prophet, it is *the Beast*, not the false prophet, who is worshiped (Rev 13:4; 14:11). The false prophet causes the whole world to worship the Beast (Rev 13:12).
>
> Paul said this wicked person would set himself up in the temple to be worshiped as God (the abomination of desolation of which Christ warned, Matt 24:15). He cites Daniel 11:36 which is recognized to be a reference to the Beast. And when Revelation informs us it is the Beast, rather than the false prophet, who is worshiped by the world ... can there be any doubt that 2 Thessalonians 2 is a discussion of *the Beast, not the false prophet*? ... The Man of Sin of II Thessalonians 2 is called "son of perdition," a title also applied to Judas. It is the Beast which at the end "goes to *perdition*" (Rev 17:11). This is why the Man of Sin—the Beast—is called the "son of perdition"—because perdition is where he is headed.
>
> The Greek for "perdition" is *apoleia*. It means destruction, damnation, perishing, waste, utter ruin. It is often used in the New Testament in reference to individuals who have fallen away from the truth (Matt 7:13; Phil 3:19; 1 Tim 6:9; Heb 10:39; 2 Peter 2:1; 3:7). This is further confirmation of the true origins of the Beast.

I argued that the Beast would have a two-stage life-history. First in the true church, and second as world-ruling Beast.

> Biblical types of the Beast seem to follow two themes. One theme is personified by Judas and Ahithophel—a traitor from among the people of God. The second theme is personified by Pharaoh, Nebuchadnezzar, the prince of Tyre, the king of Babylon, and Herod ... a powerful political ruler ... There is at least one example of a biblical type of the Beast in which both themes exist in the same person. *Cain* was among the people of God, iniquity entered his heart, he murdered his brother Abel (a type of Christ), and he was ignominiously exiled, whereupon he went out and *established his own kingdom* (Gen 4:17; Jude 11) ...
>
> When we put the types of the Beast together with the basic example of Satan who sets the pattern, we see the following scenario shaping up: someone among the people of God for whatever reason or reasons (love of money? John 12:6; 1 Tim 6:10) becomes offended and betrays the saints. His betrayal, however, does not quite turn out like he had hoped, he receives some kind of "mortal wound" (Rev 13:5), and is cast out from among the people of God in ignominy. But his "mortal wound" is healed. At some point later he emerges as a powerful world political leader, heading a resurrected Roman Empire ...

Then I took up the question of the mysterious "restrainer" holding back the revealing of the "man of sin," to which Paul alluded. I argued that Paul saw himself as the restraining influence—the "he who now restrains." I cited Acts 20:29-31, discussed the role of Paul in the Book of Acts and that book's abrupt ending, and a few other things to make the case that Paul was the restrainer, and that when he was gone evil increased, and that that was a type of what would happen with the church in the end time. I concluded the paper:

> In this paper I have hoped to contribute to a true understanding of 2 Thessalonians 2 and the subject of the Man of Sin. By examining historical applications of scripture we may gain greater insight into their significance for us today. I have developed these three points:

(1) The Man of Sin is the Beast, not the false prophet.
(2) Paul may have viewed his own life's work as the force restraining the working of the Man of Sin.
(3) The Man of Sin will come out of God's own people.

The first and third I consider certain, based on the evidence. The second I consider an interesting possibility, but not yet proven. The most radical conclusion is of course the third. The shocking truth is that the Beast's origins—where he originally came from, what he fell away from—will be one of the strongest proofs or confirmations of where God's saints have been on earth today.

The paper is submitted to headquarters

Dr. Torrance and I had high hopes for this paper. Eager to warn headquarters of what was coming, and with Dr. Torrance no less interested in the outcome, I submitted my paper to the deputy chancellor at Big Sandy and to the director of the Theological Research Project in Pasadena. Alas, no responses were ever received.

~ ~ ~

I considered also sending the paper to Stanley Rader, Herbert Armstrong's brilliant attorney, whose expression of appreciation for my previous paper on "Key Events" had so favorably impressed me, so that he could help Herbert Armstrong be on the lookout for the person to emerge at headquarters who would love money more than the truth. But, sadly, I never quite got around to it. Too bad. I wonder what Rader would have thought or have done if I had done so.

The amazing Stanley R. Rader (1930-2002)

The mysterious pencil-moustached, monotone-voiced, dark sunglasses-wearing lawyer Stanley Rader, Herbert's right-hand man, with his web of financial contracts, legal paraphernalia, shell companies, contacts with foreign dignitaries, and growing rival to Garner Ted Armstrong for the succession, was on Torrance's and other people's minds at Big Sandy. Not to put too fine a point on it, a lot of people at Big Sandy and in the church thought of the mysterious Rader as a shady character of somewhat dubious spirituality and increasing power over everything financial in the church.

For starters Rader had a whopping $3.5 million employment contract ($200,000 a year for seven years—this is 1970s dollars remember—plus $100,000 a year until the year 2003).[175] However that was only the beginning. Like his mentor Herbert Armstrong, Rader too believed in God's way of beauty and quality. Newly converted to the simplicity of Christ after being baptized by Herbert in 1975, Rader lived in a Beverly Hills home worth nearly two million dollars. The church paid for his mansion in addition to his $200,000 a year salary. Rader decided it was his home and not church property when he later sold it for over a million dollars profit. Rader (who was both a lawyer and an accountant) was a member of the accounting firm of Rader, Cornwall, and Kessler, and the legal firm of Rader, Helge, and Gerson. Both firms represented the church. The accounting firm audited the church's books. Sometime around 1975 lawyer Rader conveniently became treasurer of the Worldwide Church of God, controlling how its millions of dollars were spent. Treasurer Rader said he dropped his official involvement with the accounting firm that still bore his name and which audited the church's books. He said he had sold his interests to his partners. Jack Kessler (one of the partners in Rader, Cornwall, Kessler, and Pallazo) testified in court that the firm had been purchased

---

[175] Information in this section is from *Ambassador Report* (back issues online at http://www.hwarmstrong.com/ambassador-report.pdf); John Tuit, *The Truth Shall Make You Free* (Feedhold Township, N.J.: The Truth Foundation, 1981); Henry Goldman, "The Devil and Stanley Rader," *The American Lawyer*, August 1979 (http://members.tripod.com/gavinru/rader.htm); and Stanley R. Rader, *Against the Gates of Hell* (New York: Everest House, 1980 [online at http://www.destiny-worldwide.net/rcg/history/gateshell/ghell0.htm]).

from Rader for a surprisingly low price—no money at all. Kessler explained: "We promised him to service his clients to the best of our abilities ... and he promised us not to compete with us and that we could use his name."

The church's advertising was handled through a firm called Worldwide Advertising. This was a corporation controlled by Rader and Henry Cornwall. Cornwall happened to be one of the partners in the accounting firm which audited the church's books. (The accounting firm was the one which bore Rader's name.) Treasurer Rader decided that Worldwide Advertising, of which he was half-owner, was obviously the best-qualified agency for the church to hire to make its media purchases. Worldwide Advertising, of course, took a percentage of the several million dollars per year of radio and television time it bought for the church.

Rader was involved in Currier Insurance Company, which treasurer Rader decided was the best place for the church to place its insurance business. Rader was instrumental in the formation of the Ambassador International Cultural Foundation which scheduled celebrities to perform at the Auditorium on campus. Rader was closely involved in starting *Quest* magazine. (This was a glossy yuppie publication in New York City which had nothing to do with religion, which Rader decided Worldwide Church of God tithe-payers should subsidize as a public service to the tune of several million dollars annually during its first years to help it get on its feet; a few million dollars later Herbert Armstrong was sorely displeased to discover he could not get one of his own articles published in it.) Rader also had leasing companies which owned jet planes leased to the church. The biggest jet owned by a company controlled by Rader and his partners was Herbert Armstrong's $3.5 million personal Gulfstream II. Armstrong and Rader flew around in this one all over the world. Rader orchestrated Herbert Armstrong's many trips to dignitaries around the world and gave away lots of church money to overseas charities. To say lawyer Rader had a long web of financial ties around the church is an understatement. Several years later, at a hearing before a Pasadena judge in January 1979, attorney Hillel Chodos described the situation succinctly:

> Now, Your Honor, the problem in this Church is that nobody but Mr. Rader ever reviewed Mr. Rader's transactions. When Mr. Rader wants some money, he draws up an agreement or has his long-time counsel, Ervin, Cohen and Jessup draw up an agreement. He takes it to the Church, presents it, and shifts to the other buttock and signs it. Mr. Rader has twelve hats in this Church and every time he changes hats, makes a few bucks. And that is what has happened for the last I don't know how many years.

Dr. Torrance told me that once he had been in a meeting at Pasadena. According to Torrance, church personnel kept saying one idiotic thing after another. Then Rader spoke and he was the only one that talked any sense. Torrance told me he knew then the church was in for problems when the only one with any brains wasn't even a member. (This was before Rader was baptized in 1975.)

Stanley Rader had a man working for him named Osamu Gotoh of uncertain Japanese origins. He was said to be from elite, upper-class circles in Japan. What was known was he had been a cabdriver in Tokyo at one time, some kind of radio evangelist at another, and he knew the brother of Emperor Hirohito. Beyond that, nobody at Big Sandy seemed to know a lot about him. He flunked out of Ambassador College, Pasadena, in 1967. After this unsuccessful bout with his schoolbooks he was named head of a newly created Japanese Department at Ambassador College, Pasadena. Later it was discovered he had submitted a forged transcript in his original student application to Ambassador College and had no degree. Nevertheless Gotoh was promoted to full professor at Ambassador College and was now "Professor Gotoh."

Gotoh became an advance man for Herbert Armstrong's trips. True, he could burn through a lot of money in the process going to who knows where, and in June 1975 he was apprehended by

U.S. customs authorities in Los Angeles trying to smuggle in what was described as a substantial quantity of undeclared jewelry (Rader somehow got the charges dropped). But these details aside, Gotoh got results—a stunning series of invitations for Herbert Armstrong to meet important people.

Herbert Armstrong condemned any criticism of Osamu Gotoh. "He is part of my *team*, brethren!" Herbert would thunder. Church members were told the invitations for the meetings of Herbert Armstrong and Stanley Rader with world leaders were because these leaders liked Herbert Armstrong so much. I remember Herbert Armstrong telling us at the Feast of Tabernacles in the late 1960s: "I didn't *ask* for these meetings! They just came to me! Brethren, God is giving me favor in the eyes of world leaders!" It was rumored that God was assisted in this by Osamu Gotoh's profligate gift-giving setting up these appointments. Gotoh frequently carried $25,000 in cash in his briefcase going out the door on these trips, according to later reports.

From the rural setting of Big Sandy, I and others did not know most of these things. But Torrance heard glimpses and rumors of things of this nature, some of which Torrance would pass on to me. I wondered what was ahead for the church.

Fevered eschatological expectations, continued ...

After writing my paper, my thinking continued concerning the Beast as emerging from the true church. Now I went one step further. I came to believe that not only would the *Beast* come on the world scene after having been active among true Christians, but that *"Babylon"* of Revelation 17 itself—prophesied to persecute the saints—would be the organization of the true church gone corrupt.

I noticed that in Rev 12:14 there is a woman in the wilderness who is the true church. I noticed that nothing further is said of this wilderness, or the woman there, until chapter 17. In chapter 17 John is taken in vision to the same wilderness. But now, where formerly there was the woman who was the true church, John sees "a woman sit upon a scarlet colored beast ... and upon her forehead was a name written, 'Mystery, Babylon the Great, the mother of harlots and abominations of the earth.' And I saw the woman drunken with the blood of the saints, and with the blood of the martyrs of Jesus" (Rev 17:3-6). As I flipped back and forth from the one passage in chapter 12 to the other in chapter 17, I wondered: why is the woman who is the true church missing in chapter 17? But the woman who *is* there, where the true church was last seen, is the harlot "Babylon." I wondered: was this an image of a transformation in which what had been the true church in some sense had become, in its outer form, Babylon?

In my notebooks I wrote things like: "God's house was a house of prayer, but it became a den of thieves. Will this happen to us?" I thought on the "abomination of desolation" (as the King James Version calls it) which was prophesied, by Daniel and Jesus and then by Paul, to emerge in the midst of the temple (Dan 11:31; Matt 24:15; 2 Thes 2:3-4). This was normally understood in the Worldwide Church of God to refer to a future literal holy place in Jerusalem. But I wondered if it might, instead, refer to an abomination emerging within the church of God, since the New Testament calls God's people his temple in this age (2 Cor 6:16).

Of course the mid-1970s Worldwide Church of God with its 60,000 members, $60 million annual budget, and no political involvement was a far cry from being a world-ruling political power. The outside observer might see this image of the future as just slightly unrealistic and hallucinatory. But to the eschatological mind, the objection of realistic expectations is of less consequence than it might seem. Dr. Torrance speculated to me about breathtaking, phenomenal growth that could be ahead, tremendous breakthroughs, millions of Americans joining the church and millions more worldwide. And then there were all of those world leader contacts of Herbert Armstrong and Stanley

Rader. What was that all about? Who knew how that would all turn out in the end?

All of these speculations for me were cast in terms of post-Herbert Armstrong. Herbert Armstrong was like the apostle Paul whose presence, as long as he stayed alive, restrained the bad things from happening. When Herbert Armstrong died, was removed out of the way, then the bad things would come to pass. I don't think it occurred to me that the real bad apple at headquarters of the Worldwide Church of God might be not someone close to Herbert Armstrong, but Herbert Armstrong himself.

These prophetic speculations were sort of like Rorschach inkblots—what you see is shaped by what you look for. You look hard enough for something in a Rorschach inkblot, or in cryptic words in ancient prophetic texts (and the Bible has a huge tapestry of words and images and double-entendre wordplays coursing through its stories and images, so is fertile ground for this sort of thing) ... and pretty soon you start seeing things. Later when I came to study the Qumran *pesharim* (ancient biblical commentaries) from over two thousand years ago, I saw that the authors of those texts were doing much the same thing: they were interpreting biblical texts like Habakkuk and Nahum and Isaiah as relevant to *their* current enemies and issues of *their* time, over two thousand years ago. The ancient authors of those texts found meaning in wordplays, puns, and images in the biblical texts brought to life in present crises. They hallucinated imminent catastrophes and doom upon their enemies; they imagined imminent deliverance for themselves and a wonderful world tomorrow, all based on their divination of ancient prophetic texts which they believed were written for *their* time, the *end* time. When I studied the Qumran commentaries of Nahum and Habakkuk I felt a glow of recognition. I felt I had some glimpse of insight into what was going on in the thinking of those ancient authors. For I had been there, I had done it myself. I know how the thinking in the world of these texts can operate, and how creative and hallucinatory it can be.

... and then there is reality

Of course time went on and although there were surprises—the collapse of credibility of both Armstrongs, now both dead; the meltdown of the Worldwide Church of God in the 1990s in the wake of its leaders' repudiation of Herbert Armstrong and its transformation into a Sunday-keeping evangelical church—they were not the surprises *I* had anticipated.

The very notion of a "Beast" is dependent on a belief that the future is foreordained and was written in code long ago, and that through the right oracular keys—in this case correct decipherment of ancient prophetic riddles—one can know what is to come in one's own time, in a way that a blinded world cannot see. But at some point one wakes up and comes to one's senses: the future *isn't* known in these ways. Divination of the future by exegesis of ancient written texts has no better track record, and no more merit, than reading animal entrails or the positions of the stars or a hundred other methods of divination from a pre-scientific world.

And it is not healthy to look for and see "Satan" in other people, in events of the world, or in struggles internal to one's group. It is like witchcraft accusations of old revived. Attribution of physical illnesses, lightning, personality disorders, epileptic fits, and so on, to "demons" was part of the cultural world in which the Gospels were written. There is no good purpose served by continuing to use those notions and language today. This is one area of biblical language that definitely needs deconstruction and demythologization.

CHAPTER 17

THE MOST IMPORTANT HOLY DAY

With all of the attention devoted to the biblical holy days in the Worldwide Church of God, it may seem difficult to imagine that a lowly student at Big Sandy in the 1970s could discover an annual holy day in the Bible that nobody previously had noticed, neither senior researchers at headquarters nor dissidents critical of the church. Well, I did. In my studies I discovered a real, live, overlooked biblical annual holy day. And this wasn't some obscure or marginal holy day—this looked like it could be the most important one of all.

I refer to the annual occasion in the holy day system of ancient Israel when a first sheaf of the spring harvest, the barley harvest, was raised over the altar in the temple by the high priest. For lack of a better term, this was the Wave Sheaf Sunday, an annual day in the Jewish calendar every spring.

Although this day is named in Leviticus 23 with the rest of the holy days, it is not called an annual "Sabbath" nor is a convocation on this day directly commanded. But then neither does Leviticus 23 command a convocation on the Passover. But the church considered it important to observe Passover, using the symbols Jesus gave in the Gospels, of bread, wine, and washing of feet.

Yet although the church considered it important to observe Passover to commemorate Jesus's *death*, the day in the holy day system corresponding to Jesus's *resurrection* was given no commemoration of any kind in terms of a meeting, gathering, or formal observance.

When I say the Wave Sheaf day was "overlooked" at Ambassador College and in the church, obviously ministers and members read the words in Leviticus 23 about the day of the Wave Sheaf. And in articles, and in sermons on *other* days, the ministers would explain how Jesus fulfilled the meaning of the Wave Sheaf. It was not unnoticed in that sense. What I mean is the idea of observing or meeting on this annual holy day, as part of the holy day system, was something that had not previously occurred to anyone in the history of the Worldwide Church of God, so far as I could tell.

And yet from the point of view of the New Testament, this particular day in the holy day calendar of Israel looked like it might be the most important annual holy day of all. Not only do the Gospels tell of a meeting of Jesus's disciples on the Wave Sheaf Sunday of Jesus's resurrection, but later meetings of Christians on this occasion seemed to be mentioned other times in the book of Acts, suggesting a recurring annual celebration.

If it seemed odd that this day was not observed by the church, it seemed odder still that, so far as I knew, no one had even thought of doing so. This day seemed to be right there in the center of the New Testament, and yet it was somehow invisible to people who cared very much about observing the seasonal celebrations in the holy day system of Israel.

Rushing to get word to headquarters

Excited but sobered by this discovery, I told my Pasadena friend Russ Gmirkin about it, and he became convinced too. Gmirkin had taken a bus to Texas in March 1975 to visit me. Having recently flunked out of Ambassador College in Pasadena for a second and final time (he had become bored with his classes again), he had time free for this trip.

We thought this could be big. We wondered what it could mean if Herbert Armstrong adopted this missing centerpiece to the holy day system of Israel. What would be the implications?

Most Important Holy Day

Since the Wave Sheaf occurred in the spring holy day season, and since that was only a month or so away, we believed we needed to get word of this to Pasadena immediately so that headquarters could get right on it. We prepared urgent letters to Dr. Dorothy, the head of the Theological Research Project in Pasadena, to whom I had already been sending papers. Unlike me, Gmirkin knew Dr. Dorothy personally and Dr. Dorothy liked him. Here were our letters.

> March 13, 1975
> Dear Dr. Dorothy,
>
> I have something I feel I must get to your attention before the spring holy day season. In your experience, has anyone suggested an annual observance of Christ's resurrection? ...
>
> Acts 20:7 is a distinctive Christian meeting on the Wave Sheaf ("first of the weeks"). Paul preached a sermon and someone was raised from what was thought to be death. In our literature on Sunday-keeping, we explain what this doesn't prove, but my question is why is this recorded in the first place. Did the early Christians celebrate Christ's resurrection annually on the first day of the weeks?
>
> Christ said he would be in the heart of the earth three days and three nights. Luke 23:54 seems to indicate he was placed in the tomb at sunset Wednesday evening, meaning he would come out of the tomb at sunset Saturday evening—the beginning of the Wave Sheaf Sunday.
>
> When Christ appeared to the gathered disciples Sunday evening after his resurrection, this may have been the beginning of what became an annual observance in the New Testament church. Acts 12:12 may also be a reference to Christian annual observance of the Wave Sheaf Sunday. In Leviticus 23, observance of the Wave Sheaf Sunday is commanded forever. We commemorate Christ's death. Why do we not celebrate his resurrection? ...
>
> In the sacred calendar there are seven annual sabbaths plus Passover (Christ's death) and the Wave Sheaf (Christ's resurrection). Christ may have changed both, but perhaps both should be kept ... it seems to me that keeping the days of Unleavened Bread without noticing Christ's resurrection pictures salvation by works. The Wave Sheaf Sunday when the disciples were gathered and Christ appeared was the happiest time for them. It would be the happiest time of the year for God's people today ...

Most Important Holy Day

The Auditorium was opened, apparently unwittingly, on the Wave Sheaf Sunday evening this past year (1974)—the very anniversary of the Wave Sheaf Sunday evening when Christ (the risen temple of his body) appeared to the gathered disciples.

Have we been neglecting the most sacred day of all in God's calendar? Are we as the Church of God missing out on blessings—like Thomas, who wasn't there—by not keeping the Wave Sheaf day? Would Christ open our minds to the scriptures as He did then, would we rejoice and forget our sorrow that was part of Christ's death, would our minds be on Christ resurrected rather than our own works (on which the days of unleavened bread focus our minds)? There is currently a theory in scholarly circles that "the Lord's day" of Revelation 1:10 is a reference to the *annual* day Christ was resurrected. It would fit the context of the appearance of the living, glorified Christ to John.

In the Jubilee cycle both the first and fiftieth years are observed. This could be a parallel to observance of both the Wave Sheaf Sunday and Pentecost Sunday.

The Wave Sheaf Sunday could be the specific annual occasion in the cycle of holy days when the following verse is fulfilled both literally and in its meaning: "If you confess with your lips that Jesus is Lord and believe in your heart that God raised him from the dead, you will be saved" (Rom 10:9). We are now keeping holy days picturing all aspects of God's plan except the most important—Christ's resurrection. My suggestion of keeping an annual celebration of Christ's resurrection does not challenge one thing we already believe—but what it adds!

Sincerely yours,
Greg Doudna

PS: I am living in Longview and working, and also taking one class at AC in Big Sandy. Russell Gmirkin is here with me right now for a couple weeks. We will have some more things for you in the weeks and months ahead.

March 13, 1975
Dear Dr. Dorothy,
This is a kind of PS to Greg's letter on the Wave Sheaf. The key to the problem of its observance or non-observance seems to me to be the fact that the days of Unleavened Bread, in which the Wave Sheaf figures prominently, symbolize the *conversion process*.

Most Important Holy Day

Israel ate unleavened bread seven days, and in the night of the eighth day was "baptized" in the Red Sea; this represents repentance and baptism. The days of Unleavened Bread do not merely picture "putting out sin."

This important fact (which for all I know may be already understood, but I have never heard it preached) sheds light on the significance of the Wave Sheaf offering.

The point is this: the conversion process is not merely repentance and baptism. You must "repent, *believe*, and be baptized." Believe in what? The New Testament is full of references to confessions by Christians that Jesus Christ was Lord, which confession was considered to be equivalent to admission that Christ was resurrected from the dead!

Repentance, and confession of Christ (his resurrection)—these are the two New Testament prerequisites for baptism. At such point as a person had faith that Christ was resurrected, God worked with him and granted him the *gift* of *true* repentance—even repentance is a gift of God. Is it possible that by omitting the celebration of the Wave Sheaf offering we are leaving out both faith and God—excluding them from our yearly celebration of conversion? Would this not picture salvation by works and not by faith? It may well be that the holy day of the most personal significance to individuals is the Wave Sheaf, representing a key phase in the process which symbolizes *our own* conversions.

I hope this supplement to Greg's research will be of use in your study of the subject.

Respectfully yours,
Russ Gmirkin

Attached to these typed letters I included photocopies of supporting materials such as abstracts of scholarly articles I had found arguing for an annual Lord's day interpretation of Rev. 1:10.

Our research is processed at headquarters

Our haste was entirely in vain. There was no response or answer received to our letters, then or later. Our contributions just dropped into the bottomless maw of headquarters without a trace.

Further development of the idea

Although our letters and attachments on the meaning of the Wave Sheaf received no response, I was undeterred. I continued thinking and reflecting. A few months later I wrote up a fully developed paper, "Are We Missing Out On the Most Important Holy Day of All?" (August 31, 1975). It built on the earlier letter and abstracts I had sent to Dr. Dorothy. I wrote:

> Revelation 1:10 says John was in the Spirit on "the Lord's Day" when he received the revelation of Jesus Christ ... What would be more natural than early Christians terming the day of the year commemorating Christ's resurrection their *Lord's Day*? Later, it became corrupted into Easter ...

I also focused on parallels between Peter's release from imprisonment of Acts 12 and Jesus's resurrection of the Gospels. In both cases Jesus and Peter went to meetings of disciples after their respective releases from the grave and prison. The meeting of Jesus and the disciples in the Gospels was on a Wave Sheaf Sunday. If the analogies between these passages were further extended, I argued, the gathering of disciples of Acts 12 may have been a Wave Sheaf Sunday too. I wrote:

> There are typological similarities between Peter's release from prison and Christ's release from death. Peter was asleep; Christ was dead. The angel said to Peter, "Get up quickly!"; Christ rose from death. Chains fell from Peter; chains of death were broken by Christ's resurrection. Peter went to a house where the disciples were "gathered together" (Acts 12:12); so did Jesus (Luke 24:33). Peter was first seen by Rhoda, a woman who told the others; Christ was first seen by a woman, Mary Magdalene, sent to tell the others. "Go, tell his disciples and Peter," Mary was told (Mark 16:7); "Tell this to James and to the brethren," said Peter (Acts 12:17). The women told the disciples Christ was risen, but "these words seemed to them an idle tale, and they did not believe them" (Luke 24:11); Rhoda reported that Peter was at the door, but the disciples told her, "You are mad" (Acts 12:15). There was "no small stir among the soldiers" over what had become of Peter (Acts 12:18); there was a disturbance

among the soldiers guarding Christ's tomb (Matt 28:2-4). Peter's reaction to hearing of Christ risen was he didn't believe it (Luke 24:11); the disciples wouldn't believe Peter was released. Peter departed for "another place"—we are not told where (Acts 12:17); Christ "vanished out of their sight" (Luke 24:31). With all of these other parallels, perhaps Peter's release, like Christ's resurrection, also occurred on a Wave Sheaf Sunday.

There was other argument and analysis. I closed with:

> What happened on the Wave Sheaf Sunday? The power of death was broken. Christ became the firstborn of many brethren. Christ was raised by the Spirit of the Father, as we shall be. The disciples' sadness was turned to joy and rejoicing. Christ breathed on the disciples and said "Receive the Holy Spirit." The emphasis of the Gospels is on what happened on this day, the apostles preached what happened on this day ... The anniversary of Christ's resurrection passes us by as a church and we pay no special attention to it ... It has been noted that people understand those aspects of the plan of God pictured in the holy days which they keep ... Will this also be seen to be true of the day commemorating Christ's resurrection? ... We are exhorted many times in the New Testament to follow the apostles and their teaching and example. Instead of calling it the Wave Sheaf Sunday we could call it the First Day of Weeks or "the Lord's Day" ...

An annual "Lord's Day"

What started it all for me in those days was when I encountered by accident in a library a scholarly discussion of a possible annual meaning of the "Lord's day" of Rev. 1:10.

The "Lord's Day" of Rev 1:10 is a key verse long used by Sunday-keepers in support of weekly Sunday observance. The argument is very simple: (a) There is indisputable testimony in early Christian writings that the expression "the Lord's Day" was used with reference to weekly Sunday meetings of Christians. (b) The identical expression occurs in Rev. 1:10. Therefore (c) the custom of weekly Sunday meeting finds allusion in the New Testament.

Of course this was not the interpretation of Rev 1:10 we learned at Ambassador College. In our classes at Big Sandy it was taught that the "Lord's Day" of Rev. 1:10 was the eschatological "day of the Lord" at the end of the age—not a day of the week.

But there was a problem with the church's explanation. The Greek expression of Rev. 1:10, *kuriakei hemerai*, "Lord's day," is not the Greek *hemerai kuriou* ("day of the Lord") which would be expected if the eschatological day of the Lord was meant. But *kuriakei hemerai* of Rev. 1:10 *is* the known technical expression used in early Christian sources for the weekly Sunday. The Sunday-keepers' argument seemed to have the edge here, if these were the only two alternatives.

But I was surprised to discover a third alternative: scholarship that argued that the "Lord's day" of Rev 1:10 refers to the *annual* day of Jesus's resurrection, the Wave Sheaf Sunday.

An article by a C.W. Dugmore in 1962 argued that early "Lord's Day" allusions in *Didache* 14:1 and *Apostolic Constitutions* 7:30 could be taken as referring to an annual rather than weekly Sunday.[176] These arguments were further developed in an article by Kenneth Strand.[177] It was Strand's article that was my first awareness of this discussion. In answer to an objection that had been raised against Dugmore's thesis, Strand argued that a passage in second-century Ignatius, *Magnesians* 9, reads better as "Lord's life" instead of "Lord's day."

Lawrence Geraty in 1965, meanwhile, considered the statement of Pliny, governor of Bithynia (AD 110-113), that certain former Christians had confessed "the whole of their guilt,

---

[176] C.W. Dugmore, "Lord's Day and Easter," in the Oscar Cullmann Festschrift volume *Neotestamentica et Patristica* (Supplements to Novum Testamentum 6; Leiden: Brill, 1962), 272-281.

[177] Kenneth Strand, "Another Look at 'Lord's Day' in the Early Church and in Rev. i. 10," in K. Strand, *Three Essays in Early Church History* (Ann Arbor, Mich.: Braun-Brumfield, 1967). See also Kenneth Strand, "How Sunday Became the Popular Day of Worship," http://www.biblehistory.com/The%20Origin%20of%20Sunday%20Worship.html.

Most Important Holy Day

or their error" to have been that "they were in the habit of meeting on a certain fixed day before light, when they sang in alternative verses a hymn to Christ, as to a god."[178] Pliny's letter does not say that it is Sunday morning, but that is what has usually been thought. However, Geraty argued that the reaction of the Romans, the time of the meeting, and the content of the service seemed to indicate an annual, rather than weekly, Sunday celebration. All of these articles just named I found in my Big Sandy days, and I had sent abstracts and/or photocopies of them with the letters from me and Gmirkin to headquarters in Pasadena.

Later I obtained a 1961 study of J. van Goudoever, *Biblical Calendars*, which provided extensive further background information on the Wave Sheaf day in Israelite and Christian tradition.[179] Among other things Van Goudoever argued that the Rev. 1:10 "Lord's Day" corresponds to the Wave Sheaf day due to references to a wave sheaf harvest in Rev 14:14-16 as well as the Passover Lamb, plagues, exodus, the Song of Moses celebrating crossing the Red Sea, 144,000 "first fruits" (14:4), and so on.[180]

Now it is only fair to say that there is a scholarly literature that disputes this argument concerning an annual Sunday interpretation of "Lord's day" of Rev. 1:10. Many New Testament scholars argue that "Lord's Day" meant weekly Sunday from the earliest use of this term in texts, and they claim that no evidence, as distinguished from an argument of possibility, has shown that

---

[178] Lawrence Geraty, "The Pascha and the Origin of Sunday Observance," *Andrews University Seminary Studies* 3 (1965): 85-96. The reference in Pliny is *Letters* 10.96.

[179] J. van Goudoever, *Biblical Calendars* (Leiden: Brill, 1961).

[180] Goudoever, *Biblical Calendars*, 164-194. For a more recent statement of the argument that Rev. 1:10 "Lord's day" is the annual Wave Sheaf Sunday see R. Clover, *The Festivals and Sacred Days of Yahweh* (Garden Grove, Calif.: Qadesh La Yahweh Press, 1998 [http://www.yahweh.org/PDF_index3.html]), chapter 22, 348 n. 62 (as well as throughout chapter 22 and in other parts of that study).

there was an earlier stage at which the meaning of the term was annual before it became weekly.[181] Due to the paucity of evidence the matter remains ambiguous. Both sides argue by inference in the absence of hard information, on this point. (However, for reasons which I won't go into here, I believe the annual "Lord's day" interpretation of Rev 1:10 has additional argument in its favor that has not yet entered into scholarly discussions.) But to continue ...

Did Christ fulfill the Wave Sheaf by going to heaven?

One of the novel points of Worldwide Church of God teaching was that Jesus went to heaven and returned back to earth the same day the tomb was discovered empty. This journey by Jesus to heaven to appear before the Father, it was believed, fulfilled the typology of the Jewish ceremony of the Wave Sheaf. The annual Jewish Wave Sheaf ceremony took place in the morning. The previous evening, the first sheaf of barley for the season was cut just after sunset. Then, the next morning, this sheaf was lifted in the air before God by the high priest.

Evidence for such a round trip to outer space and back again by Jesus, corresponding to the wave sheaf ceremony in the temple, was claimed from John 20:17. According to this verse, the risen Jesus told Mary Magdalene on Sunday morning, as the King James Version has it, "Touch me not; for I am not yet ascended to my Father."

---

[181] Willy Rordorf, *Sunday*, trans. A.A.K. Graham (Philadelphia: Westminster, 1968), 207-215; Samuele Bacchiocchi, *From Sabbath to Sunday* (Rome: Pontifical Gregorian U. Press, 1977), 118-123; R.J. Bauckham, "The Lord's Day," in D.A. Carson (ed.), *From Sabbath to Lord's Day* (Grand Rapids, Mich.: Zondervan, 1982), 222-49. Henry Sturcke, *Encountering the Rest of God. How Jesus Came to Personify the Sabbath* (Zurich: Theologischer Verlag Zurich, 2005), dismisses the Dugmore-Strand annual Lord's day hypothesis in two sentences without discussion: "C.W. Dugmore contends that this and other early uses of the phrase ["the Lord's day" of Rev 1:10] refer to Easter, rather than Sunday. This view has not won a wide following" (p. 336 n. 6).

But that evening—later the same day—Jesus instructed his disciples to touch his hands and feet and feel his wounds: "handle me, and see; for a spirit has not flesh and bones, as you see I have" (Luke 24:39). The conclusion, it was explained, is that in the intervening time Jesus had gone to heaven, untouched and uncontaminated by human hands, and fulfilled the Wave Sheaf by being presented before God in heaven. Then he returned to earth again, the prohibition on touching him now removed.

I realized early on that this teaching had some problems. Apart from the fact that this excursion to heaven and back is nowhere mentioned directly, there is an even more basic problem with this interpretation—which also serves as a good illustration of the way use of the King James Version can lead to unconscious errors. For Mary Magdalene of the story *did* touch Jesus, contrary to what was assumed. Most modern translations correctly render Jesus's words in the sense of, "*Stop* cling*ing* to Me" (John 20:17, New American Standard Version). When Mary Magdalene recognized Jesus was alive, she embraced him. Jesus (who had been through worse than a bad sunburn) told her to *cease* embracing him. She was touching him and Jesus was telling her to stop. The King James Version mistranslated the sense—and a Worldwide Church of God doctrine was based on the mistake.

The typological fulfillment of the Wave Sheaf was the resurrection itself, I saw—not an ascension hours later. Paul said, "Christ has been raised from the dead, the first fruits of those who have fallen asleep" (1 Cor 15:20, 23). The Wave Sheaf was the first fruits of the harvest. The early Christian belief was that Jesus's resurrection, not something later or other than this, fulfilled the Wave Sheaf.

The Wave Sheaf day and the rejection of Caesar as Lord

In sermons and classes at Ambassador College it was always said that other Christian churches did not understand those aspects of the divine plan of salvation which were taught, in symbol, by holy days which were not kept. I asked myself, could that be the case here?

I wondered: what in the Worldwide Church of God was being overlooked that corresponded to the non-observance of the Wave Sheaf day?

It dawned on me: it was the confession that "Jesus is Lord," so central in the New Testament, and so clearly associated with the Wave Sheaf day in the New Testament. In my notebooks of the time, I thought about the connection between Christ's resurrection and the early Christian profession "Jesus is Lord" (Rom. 10:9-10; 1 Cor. 12:3). It seemed to me that the earliest Christians collectively and publicly professed "Jesus is Lord" on this day, the Lord's Day or Wave Sheaf day (John 20:9-19; Acts 2:31-36; Rom. 1:4; Phil. 2:8-11; Rev. 1:10-18). This was the first Christians' most basic profession of belief. It was at Christ's resurrection that he became Lord (Rom. 1:4; 14:9; Eph. 1:20-23). *This* was the meaning of the Wave Sheaf day.

The expression "Jesus is Lord" in its original context was far more explosive than commonly realized. It was in contrast to "Caesar is Lord." The early Christians proclaimed an alternative allegiance than to Roman authority. The sense was not Caesar *and* Jesus were lord, but Jesus *instead* of Caesar was Lord. The sense was not that Jesus was Lord in heaven and Caesar was lord of earth. The sense was rather that Jesus was lord of both heaven and earth instead of Caesar. I remember thinking in those days that it would be as if Christians in America today refused to pledge allegiance to the flag, on the grounds that Jesus is Lord. There was more to the ancient Christian "Jesus is Lord" than meets the eye.

The Worldwide Church of God did not keep the Wave Sheaf day, did not formalize a confession that Jesus was Lord, and its members participated in allegiances to earthly flags and the national states for which they stand. I saw these as interconnected.

CHAPTER 18

FAITH HEALING AND DOCTORS

When I first began attending Worldwide Church of God services at age thirteen in Akron, Ohio, one of the first persons I met was a pretty, effervescent girl the same age who happened also to go to my school. Her name was Debbie. I was very shy and therefore never told her what effect her smiling personality had on me, which was to make me imagine for the first time that I was in love. We grew up. After graduating from high school I went away to Ambassador College. She remained in Akron.

During the first semester of my freshman year, in the fall of 1972, I received a long distance phone call at Big Sandy. I will never forget the shock and sadness I felt upon learning that Debbie, my thirteen-year-old love, was dead at age eighteen. Her death was unnecessary. She had developed diabetes. In compliance with church teaching, her family had trusted in divine healing and had forgone the elementary medical treatment (insulin) which would have made possible the promising life she had ahead. Without insulin, Debbie had gone into a coma and died. I heard that it absolutely devastated her mother, who soon left both the church and her husband and was reported to be "bitter" towards God's Truth.

Debbie's death was the result of the church doctrine on healing. This belief was based on God's promise to heal "all your diseases" (Ps 103:3). Certain biblical promises, such as the promise that the gospel will be preached for a witness (Matt 24:14), were believed to be accomplished through human instruments. But when the Worldwide Church of God read *other* promises in scripture, such as the statements that God heals, those promises were *not* regarded as coming about through human instruments. The promises of healing were understood to mean without doctors—miraculously, like magic. Such healings would be beyond the ability of doctors to explain, just like the miraculous healings of the Bible.

The medical system with its drugs was condemned for having originated out of paganism. As it was explained in the church, violation of spiritual laws (the Ten Commandments) brings the consequences of spiritual death. In the same way, the theory went, violation of physical laws (lack of sleep, bad diet) brings about physical illness and death.

The atoning death of Jesus Christ was believed to pay the penalty for our violations of both these spiritual and physical health laws. The blood of Christ (symbolized by the wine at the Passover memorial) paid for spiritual sins. The broken body of Christ (symbolized by the bread), on the other hand (so the theory went), paid for the physical things we did or inherited which made us sick. Somehow it was overlooked that nowhere does the Bible define the alleged concept of "physical sin" in the sense of health rules. Nor was it explained how Jesus could unhealthily go without sleep the night before his crucifixion yet be said to be "without sin."

In practice, there had to be lines drawn between what was considered acceptable and what wasn't. Setting broken bones and dental treatment were fine. Eyeglasses and contact lenses were fine. Natural fasting and diets were recommended. Chiropractic treatment was fine. But surgery, vaccinations, and drugs crossed the line of acceptability. Surgery, vaccinations, and drugs were objectionable because they came from the pagan medical system based on drugs. To undergo medical treatment which involved surgery or drugs was regarded as denying God's healing power and even blaspheming God's name as Healer. The person with true faith in God would trust in divine healing through prayer alone.

Faith Healing and Doctors

But what about the borderline cases? A leading evangelist in the church had a cataract removed from his eye. This was decreed acceptable because it was "repair surgery." "Repair surgery" was acceptable. (It was never precisely clear where "repair surgery" ended and "non-repair surgery" began.)

~ ~ ~

"So the child is a vegetable and can't move anything except her eyes and is lying there when she could have had a normal life. It's too late. You can't go back and change that. Now, does God lay that at the door of the entire church? Is that Mr. Herbert Armstrong's fault?"
   -- Garner Ted Armstrong, ministerial meeting, 1974[182]

"And while we have been practicing healing and we've had some miraculous examples of healing, for every one of those, I don't know whether there have been 10 or 100 others where we have not had it."
   -- Herbert Armstrong, ministerial meeting, 1973[183]

"I can specifically recall one case that plagues me even yet and that's ____'s little boy, five years old, who had spinal meningitis. Dr. McReynolds, the Seventh-day Adventist doctor who worked with the church, was advising them to take the child to the hospital and try a new treatment that was 90% to 100% effective. The people asked me what they should do, and I kept saying, 'Read the booklet [Herbert Armstrong's healing booklet], follow God, and have faith.' So they did. They remained faithful to the doctrine of the church. I didn't tell them to do it, but I sure encouraged them. And the little boy died. I remember it so well because it was such a tragic incident, and Dr. McReynolds was so angry. He just flailed at me and said, 'That's just an absolute waste of human life, and there's no reason for it,' and he just let me have it. I know of literally scores or hundreds of cases like this. There's no way to determine the exact number of people who were affected. We're talking abut a forty-year period. I think thousands actually died over the years as a result of this doctrine."
   -- former WCG evangelist Charles Hunting, 1977[184]

---

[182] Quoted, John Trechak, "Modern Moloch. Human Sacrifice in the Armstrong Church," *Ambassador Report* 1977.
[183] Quoted, Trechak, "Modern Moloch."
[184] Quoted, Trechak, "Modern Moloch."

The Worldwide Church of God was extremely sensitive about the manner in which its doctrine of divine healing without doctors was applied. Such doctrines can lead to lawsuits, particularly when children are involved. About the time I started attending church (late 1960s), word went out from headquarters to all pastors that under no circumstances were people to be commanded not to go to doctors. All congregations were told from the pulpit that this doctrine (unlike the others) was strictly a matter of personal choice and conscience. No one would be expelled from church fellowship if they were weak in faith and chose to receive medical attention. Members were instructed that the decision was up to them. If members had enough faith in God to refuse medical treatment for themselves and their children, they should not broadcast the fact to newspaper reporters. If reporters did come around asking questions about, for example, a dead child, members were told they should take personal responsibility for the lack of medical treatment and not mention the name "Worldwide Church of God." If any member didn't have enough faith to trust God and buckled under, and out of weakness blasphemed God's name by obtaining medical treatment, no one was supposed to judge or condemn them.

~ ~ ~

Not surprisingly, the doctrine left a string of dead bodies in its wake. Debbie was but one of many. There is hardly a Worldwide Church of God member of that era who did not know cases personally. The casualties were accepted as the divine will. Those who died would be healed in the resurrection. They were idealized because they had died in faith (and had been spared the terrible things to come in this world). What did mere human life, which is a wisp, compare with the glories of the kingdom to which they were now assured?

~ ~ ~

Faith Healing and Doctors

Fortunately, I enjoyed good health and never faced a test on this doctrine. The same, thankfully, was true of my father and brother. There were a couple of incidents. Shortly after starting to attend church services, my eleven-year old brother was bit by a neighbor's dog. My mother (not part of the Worldwide Church of God) normally consulted with my father about such things, as he did with her. But this time she did differently. She waited until my father left for work, then quickly hustled my brother to a doctor who gave him a shot. She told my father about it after the fact was accomplished so that it could not be undone.

There was another time when I was in high school and I got a splinter embedded in a finger, that required going to a doctor to have it removed. I knew the doctor was going to want to use an anesthetic, which was a drug and therefore, I thought, objectionable. I decided I would tell the doctor to just cut it out without an anesthetic, and I would heroically take the pain, like in the western movies where the hero grits his teeth and beads of sweat appear on his forehead (although sadly I would have to do without the lovely woman holding my hand like the heroes in the movies always had).

Primed to take the pain, I told the doctor I wanted him to cut it out without an anesthetic. The doctor explained how simple and uncomplicated the local anesthetic would be, and that he was not willing to start cutting into my finger unless I did so. I relented and decided maybe that was sufficiently minor that it would be within the bounds of what God would accept.

~ ~ ~

Herbert Armstrong adopted his convictions on healing in his early days. It started in 1927 when he thought he almost lost his wife Loma to blood poisoning. As Herbert told the story in his *Autobiography*:

Faith Healing and Doctors

Along about early August 1927, a series of physical illnesses and injuries attacked Mrs. Armstrong. First, she was bitten on the left arm by a dog. Before this healed over, she was driven to bed with tonsillitis. She got up from this too soon, and was stricken violently with a "backset." But meanwhile she had contracted blood poisoning as a result of being struck with a rose thorn on the index finger of her right hand. For two or three days her sister and I had to take turns, day and night, soaking her right hand in almost blistering hot Epsom salts water, and covering her wrist and forearm with hot towels, always holding her arm high. The backset from the tonsillitis developed into quinsy. Her throat was swollen shut. It locked her jaw. For three days and three nights she was unable to swallow a drop of water or a morsel of food. More serious, for three days and three nights she was unable to sleep a wink. She was nearing exhaustion. The red line of the blood poisoning, in spite of our constant hot Epsom salt efforts, was streaking up her right arm, and had reached her shoulder on the way to the heart. The doctor had told me privately that she could not last another twenty-four hours. This third sleepless, foodless and waterless day was a scorching hot summer day in early August.[185]

Evidently the doctor did not insist Loma be taken to a hospital, nor does Herbert report that as having occurred to him. (Herbert and Loma had gone to hospitals when needed before.)

As Herbert tells it, on the third day of Loma's ordeal (the third day, after the three days and three nights), a neighbor lady offered to ask a Pentecostal minister and his wife to come over to pray for divine healing. A distraught Herbert was willing to try anything. The couple arrived and prayed a simple, earnest prayer, claiming God's promises of divine healing. That night Loma slept well and woke up refreshed and completely recovered. Herbert Armstrong believed in faith healing from that point on.

This story of Loma's miraculous healing became a Worldwide Church of God "foundation story." In innumerable sermons and articles and counseling sessions, this story was told and retold, how God had healed Loma of blood poisoning in 1927, when

---

[185] Herbert Armstrong, *Autiobiography of Herbert Armstrong*, vol. I, chapter 18 (http://www.getbackontrack.org/content/autobiographyVolume1 Index.htm).

Faith Healing and Doctors

"the doctors had given her only 24 hours to live." It was miraculous, just like the miraculous healings in the Bible. This was what God promised all of His people provided one had faith. For example (picked at random):

> Mr. Herbert Armstrong learned that God heals, in the summer of 1927. His wife, Loma, was miraculously healed of several ailments, though the doctors had given her only 24 hours to live.[186]

> Herbert W. Armstrong learned the lesson of divine healing shortly after he was baptized in 1927 ... Mrs. Armstrong had a series of afflictions, and had contracted blood poisoning as a result of a rose thorn. For three days and nights, she was unable to swallow a drop of water or a morsel of food. The doctor told Armstrong she could not last another twenty-four hours. ... They believed, and Mrs. Armstrong was dramatically healed. Even the doctor was astonished.[187]

And on and on, told and retold ... blood poisoning ... twenty-four hours to live ... healed completely ... because they had believed God's promise ... *healed completely* ... twenty-four hours to live ... *healed completely* ...

~ ~ ~

I did a little checking. I found that the description of Loma Armstrong's condition matches that of "cellulitis." Here is what medical information sources say:

> Cellulitis ... sudden tenderness, swelling, and redness in an area of the skin. A thin red line often extends from the middle of the cellulitis toward the mid-line ... Therapy entails: Rest. Elevation. Massive hot wet packs or warm water soaks. Antibiotics ... Rest in bed until fever disappears and other symptoms improve ... Possible

---

[186] Jamie McNab, "The Healing Doctrine," a report given at a Church of God conference in 2001 (http://www.t-cog.net/The_Healing_Doctrine.htm).
[187] Richard Nickels, "Appendix B. Comments by Richard C. Nickels" (http://www.giveshare.org/library/hwa/appendixb.html).

complications: blood poisoning, if bacteria enter the bloodstream ... Prognosis. Usually curable in 7 to 10 days with treatment.[188]

Cellulitis refers to an infection of the tissue just below the skin surface ... The body's reaction to damage is inflammation which is characterized by pain, redness, heat, and swelling. This red, painful region grows bigger as the infection and resulting tissue damage spread ... A normally healthy person is usually not hospitalized for mild or moderate cellulitis. General treatment measures include elevation of the infected area, rest, and application of warm, moist compresses to the infected area.[189]

Today cellulitis is treated with antibiotics, but 1927 was before antibiotics. I wondered what the prognosis for cellulitis usually was before antibiotics. I found this (speaking of cellulitis before the advent of antibiotics):

Cellulitis can range from mild to serious. Without treatment, a "battle" is fought between the immune (defence) system of the body and the invading bacteria. Often the body would fight off the bacteria and the infection would clear ...[190]

The point here is that Loma's recovery was within the range of known human responses to the ailment she had. There is no evidence that it involved supernatural intervention or that something medically impossible had occurred. There is no evidence Loma had blood poisoning. What happened was Loma was sick and then she recovered, as people who have fallen ill have done on innumerable occasions in history and do today all over the world. In this case, the recovery was credited to God, and in particular to the faith healing prayer which preceded the recovery.

Yet this "foundation story" of Loma Armstrong's healing when she had "only 24 hours to live" was used to illustrate that God would intervene in ways that could *not* be explained, that

---

[188] http://www.rxmed.com/b.main/b1.illness/b1.1.illnesses/cellulitis.html.
[189] http://www.healthatoz.com/healthatoz/Atoz/ency/cellulitis.jsp.
[190] http://www.patient.co.uk/showdoc/23068991/.

were medically *not possible*. People would forgo medical treatment for their own conditions in favor of trusting in the promised miraculous intervention on the basis of this "foundation story" of Loma's healing. Yet there is no evidence that Loma's recovery differed from the normal range of human responses to the condition she had.

The healing doctrine in a nutshell

It was a psychologically powerful mixture of *suspicion* toward mainstream medical science, and a *superstitious* view toward faith healing. For those caught up in the mindset, it was not easy to untangle the two.

The suspicion toward mainstream medical science is its own set of issues. Here not everyone is going to think alike, and not necessarily for the same reasons. A large number of human ailments get better by themselves, even if one does nothing at all. But while that typically is the case with colds, flus, many muscle pains, and so on, it is not the case with things like appendicitis, diabetes, or muscular sclerosis. The problem was Herbert Armstrong's system made no distinctions. The idea was God had promised to heal *everything, whatever it was*, miraculously, from the mundane to the terminal leukemia patient hooked up to tubes in a hospital with the proverbial only 24 hours to live.

But there are classes of medical conditions that involve the choice of (a) medical treatment (which typically has certain clinically demonstrated efficacy, along with side effects); (b) alternative treatments (which typically have glowing anecdotal testimonies and no clinically proven efficacy); or (c) death or impairment with no treatment. The problem was when medical treatment was forgone in these serious cases.

Faith healing, the way Herbert Armstrong had it, worked like this: you had this belief that God had guaranteed to make you well. However this guarantee came with a condition. If would work every time, *guaranteed*, if you kept to this single condition.

That was you had to *believe* it, to claim it in faith, to present God's check to the bank (as Herbert Armstrong put it).

After you did this, then you just, so to speak, closed your eyes and *thought real hard* that God *has made you well*, and *believe* it never for one moment doubting. Then God would do His part (which He had promised). He would make your outward physical form in agreement with your inner faith, and you would be whole and well.

But there was a basic problem in this whole system. Most of the time, no matter how hard one closed one's eyes and *believed*, healing either happened or did not happen (as the case may be) about the same as if one had not appealed to God for faith healing. In serious conditions that meant death without treatment, God just didn't seem to intervene very many times in those situations. (More below on the occasional claims of interventions in these cases.)

But you weren't supposed to look at it empirically. As Herbert Armstrong taught it, if you *doubted—that* would be why the whole thing didn't work! It was *your* fault you weren't healed—because you had doubted that you would be healed.[191]

So not only did the person not get healed, but they had themselves to blame, because they had let themselves doubt that they would be healed. It was just perverse.

---

[191] Herbert Armstrong: "I have answered the call of thousands, who have come to me for prayer for healing. Many HAVE been healed—miraculously—of even cancer and an advanced case, in a hospital, of leukemia. On the other hand, many HAVE NOT been healed. Yet I have prayed with the same faith for the one as the other. WHY are many not healed? Jesus said it is ACCORDING TO YOUR FAITH. Perhaps they did not fully believe. Perhaps they were not obedient. Perhaps they should read James 4:3, where it says: 'Ye ask, and receive not, BECAUSE …' And you may read the answer yourself ['because ye ask amiss, that ye may consume it upon your lusts'] … I DO NOT KNOW whether YOU will be healed by God—because I cannot know whether you have the faith, are conforming to God's conditions, have really repented and turned from violating God's laws …" (Herbert Armstrong, *Plain Truth* Personal column, December 1967).

Faith Healing and Doctors

As an earlier quotation from Herbert Armstrong indicated, faith healing in the Worldwide Church of God empirically worked, in Herbert Armstrong's estimation, maybe between 1% and 10% of the time. But it is all a matter of definition. In cases where a person's faith was right, the track record was 100%, said Herbert. The 90-99% of cases which did not work out so well were not because faith healing did not work, but because of humans doubting the 100% effectiveness of God. In this system God never failed. Only human faith fell short (about 90-99% of the time).

Now it should be mentioned that there was actually another category which Herbert worked into this system, in which a person with complete faith of the right kind nevertheless died from an illness. Herbert conceded that certain of these cases existed, but he explained that in these cases they would be healed in the resurrection, and so that was included in the promise that God's healing would work every time. (Don't try to make this all logically consistent. You can't do it.)

This belief about how faith healing worked was mixed in with suspicion of medical science. The argument went: look at exhibit A, B, and C, which would be this or that scandal in medical science. *Therefore*, the logic follows, God's way of divine healing is proven right. That doesn't logically follow. These are distinct issues. But it was hard for many people in that manipulative environment to get things distinguished.

What about the anecdotes of miraculous healing? Every faith healing system has them, and so did the Worldwide Church of God. In principle, they are the same in genre as anecdotes one can read for health remedies advertised for sale or for exotic alternative treatment clinics. Testimonials are easy to come by. Faith healers know, for example, that one of the most common types of ailments, lower back pain, typically ebbs and flows. It is not hard to get a gullible person in the normal shift of the level of pain to connect that shift with the faith healer and be convinced that the faith healing did it.

Faith Healing and Doctors

In the Worldwide Church of God there were testimonials of miraculous healings, as well as testimonials of God's blessings for tithing (stories of unexpected pay bonuses shortly after mailing one's tithe to Pasadena, and so on). The foundation story of Loma Armstrong's healing in 1927, proving that God intervenes when humanly all hope is lost, was just one of many.

Nearly all of these Worldwide Church of God healing testimonials were cases in which someone recovered from being sick in ways that were within the normal range of human responses, and credited the faith healing for it. Of course there were occasional more unusual stories of healings that did not seem explicable in natural terms. But these were considerably rarer. A typical member might be able to tell you of one or two such stories they had heard about, but not dozens or hundreds.

The more amazing of the Worldwide Church of God healing stories, as in the literature concerning UFO sightings and abduction claims, tended to feature certain key themes, like a repeated literary genre. There is the ubiquitous worried doctor who solemnly proclaims "only twenty-four hours to live." There is the florid description of some impossible weight, temperature, or physical limitation which is miraculously transcended. There is the astonishing discovery of the disappearance of the medical condition which was so threatening only hours earlier. There is the dumbfounded doctor shaking his head saying he had never seen anything like it and there was just no medical explanation. There is the humble gratitude to God Almighty in heaven for His mercy and love, for having once again heard the pleas of his children on earth.

Herbert Armstrong's healing of a woman with terminal leukemia

Herbert Armstrong made repeated mention through the years of a case in which he says he entered a hospital room in which a woman had terminal leukemia. The woman was hooked up to tubes. She apparently had less than twenty-four hours to live. Herbert Armstrong had the nurses leave and anointed and prayed

Faith Healing and Doctors

for the woman. The woman was instantly healed, and left the hospital completely well the next day.

> "Some with cancer in an advanced stage were HEALED—while others at this stage were relieved of the intense pain, though they died and will have their healing IN THE RESURRECTION ... One woman with leukemia in the hospital with apparently less than 24 hours to live, and with tubes in her ankles for blood transfusions, tubes in her nostrils—a horrible sight—was healed instantly when I anointed and prayed for her (after putting all nurses out of the room). She left the hospital the next day."
> -- Herbert Armstrong, *The Plain Truth About Healing*, 1979[192]

> "In my ministerial experience over forty years, literally thousands have been healed—of almost every disease or sickness, including cancer and leukemia—by my prayers, and those of God's ministers in this Work associated with me."
> -- Herbert Armstrong, Co-worker letter, Feb. 27, 1967[193]

> "I have answered the call of thousands, who have come to me for prayer for healing. Many have been healed—miraculously—of even cancer and an advanced case, in a hospital, of leukemia."
> -- Herbert Armstrong, "The Key to RADIANT HEALTH" (date unknown)

The story is florid and sensational. There was no case cited by Herbert Armstrong that is more impossible to explain humanly. But I noticed something. I noticed that Herbert Armstrong never told the location of this healing, the city, the name of the hospital, the name of the woman, or even the year this happened. There was absolutely no identifying information, in the many times Herbert told this story. I could not find this story in Herbert Armstrong's *Autobiography* where it might be dated and perhaps identified. The story seemed to be free-floating, undocumented, timeless and transcendent, without means of verification or falsification. Then I found this, in a 1954 co-worker letter:

---

[192] Herbert Armstrong, *The Plain Truth About Healing* (1979 edition); Sept. 11, 1978 *Good News/Worldwide News*.
[193] http://www.hoselton.net/religion/hwa/booklets/auto/ch74.htm.

> "Oh, yes, before I close—I'm going to reprint for you [in 2-3 weeks] many letters from listeners who have been HEALED of many sicknesses and diseases—even cancer, leukemia, and other incurable diseases."
> -- Herbert Armstrong, Co-worker letter, Aug. 9, 1954

There is the "leukemia" allusion again. The date indicates the "leukemia" healing predates the writing of that letter in 1954. There is one further detail of interest: it may be that Herbert Armstrong's information concerning the outcome of his prayer for this woman came in the form of a letter from the woman. I was not able to find the later co-worker letter in which Herbert Armstrong promised to publish the healing testimonial letters, in which possibly the "leukemia" woman's letter might have been quoted.

Did the woman really have leukemia? And then there was no more leukemia? How much longer did the woman live after leaving the hospital? Did the leukemia ever return? Did the woman join the church of Herbert Armstrong whose prayer had "instantly and completely" healed her of terminal leukemia? All of this is unknown. These details, apparently, were not considered important to the story, as it was told and retold, year after year, decade after decade, timeless and forever ...

~ ~ ~

I once heard the late astrophysicist Carl Sagan lecture about UFO (Unidentified Flying Object) sightings. He made the point that the sightings are either well-verified but difficult to rule out natural explanations (such as the unexplained light low in the horizon that a hundred people testify simultaneously to having seen), or impossible to explain through natural means but not well verified (such as the saucer that lands and little green men come out, seen by only one person). You could never seem to get, in this kind of story, Sagan lamented, the two *together*—the saucer with little green men coming out *and* the strong

Faith Healing and Doctors

verification of one hundred simultaneous witnesses. Researchers have shown how UFO stories come in cycles, like literary genres, with common features and motifs, which adapt and morph along with the culture.[194]

In the same way, the occasional sensational healings in the Worldwide Church of God, the ones that allegedly flouted natural law in impossible ways, tended to be impossible to document other than through the testimony of the ones who said they experienced it. There was not a single case, to my knowledge, in which medical doctors published affidavits documenting the facts in these cases. In fact, the Worldwide Church of God was consciously opposed to making an organized effort to forensically document such cases.[195]

The old rule applies: the more unusual the claim, the higher the standard of evidence that should be required before believing. But now, return with me to 1970s Big Sandy.

~ ~ ~

I came to see clearly during my studies in my Big Sandy days that the church doctrine on healing was scripturally without basis or foundation. The way I came to see it, there were two key problems with the doctrine as it was taught in the church. First, there was no separate category "physical sin" as opposed to "spiritual sin" in the Bible. You couldn't get that from the Bible. This was very important. It meant physical healing was not in the atonement (forgiveness of sin) of Christ. And second, there was

---

[194] See the excellent study of UFO abduction cults of Brenda Denzler, *The Lure of the Edge* (Berkeley: University of California Press, 2001 [http://www.ucpress.edu/books/pages/9018.html]). Brenda Denzler, formerly Brenda Reser, was a student at Ambassador College Big Sandy 1971-75, before going on to obtain a PhD in Religious Studies at Duke University.

[195] On the Howard Clark healing of 1958 in which a paralyzed Clark got up out of his wheelchair and regained the use of his limbs (considered one of the most outstanding miraculous healings in the church) see further at the end of chapter 24 of the present book.

no contradiction between asking God to heal and getting appropriate medical attention. It wasn't one or the other.

These two points went to the heart of the matter. They weren't original with me. But I came to see both of these points crystal clear for myself as the heart of the issue. I thought I could express these two points in a paper better than I had seen expressed before.

I put my heart into writing the best paper I was capable of writing in an attempt to correct this horrible error. I was dead serious on this one. This doctrine was killing people. When I finished, I had a 17-page, single-spaced paper entitled "Healing in a New Light" (May 3, 1975).

I submitted this paper to Ronald Dart, deputy chancellor at Big Sandy and personally close to both Armstrongs. And I submitted the paper to Dr. Charles Dorothy at Pasadena, in his capacity of being responsible for preparation of the previously-mentioned Theological Research Project. I heard nothing from Pasadena. I heard nothing back from Mr. Dart either. No reaction at all, nothing.

And the doctrine remained, and more people died.

Like the rest of my papers, this one seemed in retrospect to have had all the effect and impact of if I had mailed it instead to the North Pole.

First postscript

> "Now suppose a member thinks he or she has found an error in our doctrines. How must you proceed? If you have found truth, we all want to know and embrace it! But how MUST you proceed? *NEVER* by trying to convince another member of your 'finding' ... Take it to your local minister or write to headquarters ... If it is felt to be a valid truth, it will be brought to me personally, and the LIVING CHRIST will make it clear to my mind!"
> -- Herbert Armstrong, April 1979 *Good News*

> "I know many will say Herbert Armstrong is human and subject to being prejudiced or close-minded. I am human all right, but the living CHRIST has chosen me and MADE ME HIS APOSTLE. He

Faith Healing and Doctors

> is the DIVINE Head of this Church. Do you not think *HE*, the ALMIGHTY Christ, has power to see that my mind will be opened to either new truth or to correct error? Otherwise you QUESTION JESUS CHRIST!"
> -- Herbert Armstrong, June/July 1979 *Good News*

Unknown to me, Dr. Dorothy, to whom I submitted my paper at Pasadena, and many others at headquarters, valiantly attempted to modify Herbert Armstrong's views on the healing doctrine during the same period of time that I submitted my paper. But it was to no avail. What Dr. Dorothy and others wrote about healing (which later became adopted by the Worldwide Church of God point-by-point) led to Herbert Armstrong's public excoriation of dedicated ministers and teachers who had served him loyally for decades.

In 1978 Dr. Dorothy assisted Robert Kuhn and others at headquarters in producing what was called the Systematic Theology Project (STP). Significantly, the STP changed the healing doctrine on these two key points: healing was not in the Atonement, and there was no theological reason not to use medical treatment that was otherwise effective. (Exactly what my 1975 paper argued.)

Ministers from headquarters took the finished Systematic Theology Project manuscript to Herbert Armstrong in his home in Tucson. They walked him through it page by page, explained it and had it approved by him. Or so they thought.

In January 1978 this Systematic Theology Project, in a notebook binder, was distributed to the ministers at a conference in Pasadena, a few hours after Herbert Armstrong left for an overseas trip. But such a good thing was not to be. Herbert Armstrong became enraged when he learned what had been distributed. He said he'd never been told. He publicly blasted the hapless ministers who had worked so hard on the project, declared it was a conspiracy and that Satan (who else) was behind it. Herbert canceled the Systematic Theology Project, had all copies recalled, and consigned it to everlasting oblivion. In 1978, serialized in articles, and in 1979 in booklet form, Herbert

Armstrong's own revised healing booklet came out: *The Plain Truth About Healing*. Herbert Armstrong was on the warpath. This booklet reemphasized the old hard-line doctrine of faith healing, while carefully incorporating legal deniability by telling readers they must decide for themselves whether to obey God or to deny God, to trust in divine healing or lack faith and go to a doctor, in this *personal* choice for which the church was not going to interfere.

Although Herbert Armstrong's booklet emphasized that the choice was freely up to the member, Herbert could not help interjecting that he, and no doubt Christ as well, were indignant that some people might choose one of the two alternatives open to the members' free choice, that of medical treatment.

> Frankly, it makes me a little indignant, as I fully believe it does the living CHRIST, to find people exalting the advances and "expertise" of medical doctors, while at the same time denying that God's PROMISES are promises—discrediting faith in God, excusing their lack of trusting GOD while they argue for trusting MAN!

(The absolutely blatant hypocrisy of this, when Herbert Armstrong himself had around-the-clock medical attention, drugs, the works, toward the end of his life, is another story.)

In retrospect, if long-time evangelists and ministers who knew Herbert Armstrong could make no headway, it was naive for an unknown sophomore student like me, typing away in east Texas, to think my paper would make much of a difference. But I didn't know I was naive. With Debbie on my mind and with tears in my eyes I gave it my best, and tried. (See the impassioned plea with which my paper ended.)

Second postscript: repudiation of the healing doctrine by the Worldwide Church of God in 1987

In March 1987, a year after Herbert Armstrong's death, Joseph Tkach, Sr., successor to Herbert Armstrong, ended the

Faith Healing and Doctors

Worldwide Church of God's nightmarish doctrine concerning medical treatment.

Tkach, Sr., claimed that before he died, Herbert Armstrong had urged Tkach, Sr., to do this. The only witness of this appeal of Herbert Armstrong to change the healing doctrine was Tkach Sr. There was no corroborating evidence or testimony from any other source that that was Herbert Armstrong's wish. According to Tkach Sr., Herbert Armstrong refused Tkach's request for Herbert to have himself taped saying this, telling Tkach Sr. that the members would have to take Tkach's word for it "on faith." Nor was it clear why Tkach Sr. waited a whole year to carry out what allegedly was Herbert Armstrong's wish, and to report to the members the existence of this expressed wish of their departed Apostle.

But however it came about, the fact is that in 1987 the doctrine of the Worldwide Church of God came to be practically identical in all particulars with the argument of the paper I wrote as a student at Big Sandy in 1975.

~ ~ ~

Unfortunately, there is no record that the Worldwide Church of God, either in 1987 or later, ever lifted a finger to attempt restoration or assistance to the past broken lives from the doctrine on healing. They probably reasoned that to admit liability in any case would open them up to legal liability in more cases, and bankrupt them.

~ ~ ~

Here is a condensed version of my paper from that time, which you can either read or skip over.

Faith Healing and Doctors

"Healing in a New Light"
Greg Doudna
May 3, 1975

There are certain glaring inconsistencies in both the traditional and present church teaching on healing. The doctrine as presently understood is patently untenable, and raises questions to which no one yet has offered answers.

The doctrine of the church has been that God has promised in His Word to heal our physical infirmities, and that if we claim His promise in faith, He must heal us.

The basis for this doctrine is the belief that Christ's sacrifice paid the penalty for all spiritual and physical sins. That is, Christ's shed blood paid the penalty for spiritual sins, whereas Christ's body paid the penalty for physical sins—"By his stripes we are healed." Upon this premise it is taught that upon claiming Christ's sacrifice in faith not only will every spiritual sin be forgiven, but also every physical sin and resulting penalty....

That Christ's shed blood paid the penalty of eternal death for spiritual sin is the plainest of teachings in the New Testament.

I wish to emphatically challenge, however, the concept that Christ's broken body or shed blood in *any* way paid the penalty for *physical* sin. Instead, both paid the penalty for spiritual sin, and "by his stripes we are healed" refers to *spiritual, not physical*, healing.

In other words, the fundamental premise, the trunk of the tree on which the entire teaching is based, I am saying is in error.

Inherent contradictions

Why are true Christians today not healed instantly, always, without fail? Let us examine the answers traditionally given. None stand, none are tenable. All break down completely under rather elementary analysis.

"The individual must have lacked faith (he wasn't healed)." What about Christians who die from various diseases? Did they all lack faith? Christians become sick just like those in the world apart from God. There is no difference. The psychological damage done to individuals who believe they will be healed, then when they are not are led to believe it must of necessity be because they lacked faith, is monumental.

"God heals, but we do not know when He will choose to do so." Here is the reasoning: "If I pray in faith for healing, and God does not heal me instantly, and perhaps I even die from my disease, that

Faith Healing and Doctors

does not mean God's promise has failed! It means God will heal me in the resurrection!" This is absurd. When I am born into God's family at the resurrection as a spirit being I will have no need of physical healing. How can God heal me physically when there is nothing physical to heal?

Healed spiritually, not physically

Christ came into this world offering the forgiveness of *spiritual sin*, not physical sin. Let us draw the analogy of the physical to the spiritual.

Type	*Antitype*
physical life	spiritual life (begettal, birth, all over again)
physical sickness	spiritual sickness (Christ's stripes heal)
physical death	spiritual death (Christ's blood redeems us)

Adam's sin brought physical death into the world (Romans 5). Christ's victory brought spiritual *life* into the world. God not only is Life-giver, but He also is Healer—He forgives spiritual illnesses!

> "But he was *wounded* for our transgressions, he was *bruised* for our iniquities: upon him was the chastisement that made us whole, and with his *stripes* we are healed." (Isa 53:5)

> "He himself bore our sins in his body on the tree, that we might die to sin and live to righteousness. *By his wounds you have been healed.*" (1 Peter 2:24)

The context of both references to being healed by Christ's stripes shows that His suffering and death paid the penalty for spiritual sin, not physical sin! Why should it seem surprising that God would heal spiritual afflictions? The Bible uses healing in this sense repeatedly. Examples:

> "As for me, I said, 'O Lord, be gracious to me; *heal me*, for I have sinned against thee'" (Ps 41:4)

> "He *heals the brokenhearted* ..." (Psalm 147:3)

> "Return, O faithless sons, I will *heal your faithlessness.*" (Jer 3:22)

> "The weak you have not strengthened, the sick you have not *healed*, the crippled you have not bound up, the strayed you have not brought back, the lost you have not sought, and with force and harshness you have ruled them." (Ezek 34:4)

> "I will *heal* their faithlessness; I will love them freely ..." (Hosea 14:4)

> "He has blinded their eyes and hardened their heart, lest they should see with their eyes and perceive with their heart, and turn for me to *heal* them." (John 12:40)

> "But he was wounded for our transgressions, he was bruised for our iniquities; upon him was the chastisement that made us whole, and with his stripes we [the nation of Israel] are *healed*." (Isa 53:5)

These are only a few of *many* instances in which "healing" is used in imagery or in a spiritual sense. Israel is pictured as a sick man in Isaiah 1. "They have healed the wound of my people lightly, saying, 'Peace, peace,' when there is no peace" (Jer 6:14). The sins of the nation of Israel were placed on the Servant of Isaiah 53, and the nation of Israel was healed by the stripes laid on him. Here is what Christ brought to this earth.

> "The Spirit of the Lord is upon me, because he hath anointed me to preach the gospel to the poor; he hath sent me to *heal* the brokenhearted, to preach *deliverance* to the captives, and recovering of *sight* to the blind, to set at *liberty* them that are bruised ..." (Luke 4:18, KJV)

Christ literally performed the physical acts of healing, giving sight to the blind, etc. during his earthly ministry as *types* of the *spiritual* healing, *spiritual* eye-opening that he offers to *all humanity*. This is the true healing Christ offers.

Physical healing is the exception, not the norm

God offers forgiveness of spiritual sin to all men. "Whoever calls on the name of the Lord shall be saved" (Acts 2:21). Physical healing, on the other hand, is not universal. It is a special gift from God, not available universally.

Faith Healing and Doctors

> "To one is given through the Spirit the utterance of wisdom, and to another the utterance of knowledge according to the same Spirit, to another faith by the same Spirit, to another *gifts* of *healing* by the one Spirit, to another the working of miracles, to another prophecy" (1 Cor 12:8-10)

The healings in the Bible, like the resurrections from the dead, were signs or miracles. The dramatic healings in the Bible are no more the promised *normal* experience of all believers than are the resurrections from the dead or speaking in tongues. Periods of miracles come and go. John the Baptist did no miracle (John 10:41), yet he was the greatest prophet, Christ said. Miracles such as healings are the exceptions, they are signs, not the constant such as forgiveness of spiritual sin through acceptance of Christ as Savior.

The bread and wine at Passover

The bread and wine represent Christ's blood and body. They are not the payment for physical and spiritual sins. They are the payment for spiritual sins only.

Christ did not remove the curse of physical death from mankind or from His followers. Neither did He remove the curse of physical afflictions and maladies. Paul had an affliction in the flesh. Paul said he left Trophimus at Miletus sick (2 Tim 4:20). Paul mentions Timothy's "often infirmities" (1 Tim 5:23). Notice the references Christ makes to His body and blood. They are both of distinctly spiritual significance.

> "I am the living bread which came down from heaven; if any one eats of this bread, he will live for ever; and the bread which I shall give for the life of the world is my flesh." (John 6:51)

> "He who eats my flesh and drinks my blood has eternal life ... and I will raise him up at the last day ... He who eats my flesh and drinks my blood abides in me, and I in him." (John 6:54-56)

Notice how Christ says *both* His body and blood give eternal life. *Not one scripture* states that Christ's broken body paid the penalty for physical sins (as opposed to spiritual sins). Christ's own explanation of the symbols of the bread and wine give no hint that one paid the penalty for spiritual sin and the other for physical sin.

Faith Healing and Doctors

"This is *my body* which is *given for you* ... This cup is the new testament in my blood, which is *shed for you*." (Luke 22:19-20, KJV)

In 1 Corinthians 11:29-30 Paul states that some in Corinth were eating and drinking unworthily, not discerning the Lord's body, and that for this reason many were weak and sickly, and many had died. These verses do not say that through Christ's broken body Christians are guaranteed healing of physical afflictions. Instead, Paul seems to be saying (although there may be more to it than this) that God had specially afflicted some with physical ailments who were taking the Passover unworthily. But it cannot mean that all who are weak and sickly and dead must necessarily have taken the Passover unworthily—else Paul, Timothy, Trophimus, Epaphroditus (Phil 2:25-27), and all Christians have taken it unworthily. What happened *physically* to the Son of God enables spiritual things to happen to us. The parallel is destroyed if Christ's physical sufferings paid for physical penalties.

Christ's *physical* death ...   substitutes for *spiritual* death
Christ's *physical* sufferings ...   substitutes for *spiritual* suffering

Neither physical sickness nor physical death was removed by Christ's sacrifice. Both spiritual sickness and spiritual death were. In examples where Christ would heal and say, "Your sins are forgiven," he was forgiving *spiritual* sins, and accompanying this forgiveness with physical healing as a *sign*. "Flesh and blood cannot inherit the kingdom of God" (1 Cor 15:50).

Implications of the present doctrine

The implications of our present teaching are disturbing. Those who are not healed (who happen to be in the majority) ask "why?" and what satisfactory answer is there, when they have been told God promises to heal. Will they not also be led to question whether God has likewise delayed forgiving their spiritual sins also?

Those who have not been healed often feel something must be wrong with them. They are led to doubt, to wonder "why" and there are no answers. This could all be avoided if we recognized the true scriptural teaching that Christ's death left physical life and death untouched, that it was wholly concerned with paying penalties for spiritual sin.

Faith Healing and Doctors

"Trust in God for healing, or trust in medical science—which?"

Where oh where is the teaching derived from God's Word that availing oneself of the full range of medical services in *any* way shows a lack of trust in God? This is a second *assumption*, without one iota of scriptural backing, which has led to all manner of error and needless tragedy.

How often have we heard the contrast drawn between "trusting in God, or trusting in doctors," or, "It is up to you whether you have faith enough to trust completely in God—if not, by all means go to a doctor." In other words, going to the medical profession is at worst a total renunciation of faith in God and blasphemy to His name, or at best shows "less" faith than one who voluntarily abstains from medical help. We have been taught this contradiction, this dichotomy, for so many years, that if we are sick we must "choose," that it cuts across the grain to realize that when we look to the Bible this concept vanishes into thin air!

There is *no* biblical praise for forgoing available help. There is a comment made of one of Israel's kings that he trusted in the physicians and not in God. The point is that he was not trusting in God. The Bible itself makes it abundantly plain that God is not against physicians. In fact, He is one Himself. James 5:14 says if one is seriously ill he should call for the elders of the church to pray for him. The implication is that all hope is gone for him, that he is about to die, but that if the elders and his brethren will pray for him the prayer of faith shall "raise him up." Nothing is said about not going to a doctor or about refusing the help of medical science. Is there any reasons why one could not both be anointed and prayed for, and have an operation? Here is a plain, simple statement from Christ:

> "Those who are well have no need of a physician, but those who are sick." (Luke 5:31)

Christ said the sick need physicians. When afflicted persons came to Him for healing, not once did he tell them they must renounce all doctors and drugs, that a "choice" must be made. There is absolutely no spiritual reason, no scriptural reason, for refusing available medical help! We should be thankful for what medical science has to offer us, not condemning of it!

This is a second premise which is in error, upon which a doctrine has been based. These are the two premises: (1) Christ's broken body paid the penalty for physical sins (in reality it paid for spiritual sins), and (2) a choice must be made between trusting in God and going to medical science.

There is perhaps one possible valid reason for forgoing the help of medical science. That would be if one sincerely objected to it on the grounds that drugs, etc. were not natural, that perhaps naturopaths, etc. were closer in tune with the way things should be. That would be a personal decision, but one could not claim biblical command, precedent, principle, intent, example, or suggestion that such was God's law.

What about the pagan origins of medical science? The physicians Christ commended were of the same pagan system. There is no evidence that Luke was different from any other physician. Our modern educational systems are of pagan origin, yet there is much that can be learned from universities. The whole world is based upon pagan systems. We cannot withdraw from it. Christ did not teach asceticism. Medical science has made many advances. We can rejoice in them just as we rejoice in technological achievements, breakthroughs in any field of human knowledge.

When Paul learned of Timothy's many infirmities, he advised him to take some practical action. He told him to take a little wine for his stomach's sake. The wine would have a therapeutic effect. Why did not Paul put the choice to Timothy—"Timothy, you can either trust in God to heal you, or you can trust in wine if your faith is weak, but you must choose." Have we imposed our predetermined beliefs and mores onto the Bible and said "God says" when in fact God hasn't said?

Conclusion

The fundamental premise of the doctrine on healing has been the assumption that "by his stripes we are healed" refers to physical healing. Instead the context of Isaiah 53, the context of 1 Peter 2, the usage of "healed" throughout the Old Testament when applied to nations (such as Isaiah 53 is written about Israel), show that it is a *spiritual* healing which is intended. Not once do we find the doctrine stated that Christ's broken body paid the penalty for physical sins.

Physical healings during Christ's ministry were seen to be signs (like resurrections and tongues-speakings), not the normal everyday experience of all believers throughout history. Psalm 103:3 becomes understandable when realizing the concept of spiritual healing (David himself had many diseases and infirmities when he wrote this Psalm).

Faith Healing and Doctors

The fact that true Christians seem to pick up diseases and infirmities and die from them right along with the rest of mankind—it all becomes explainable. What Christ came to offer to mankind in no way changed his physical state—instead it was, as He told Nicodemus, a new birth process all over again.

This understanding of Christ's sacrifice as it relates to healing, as presented in this paper, challenges nothing central to the gospel. Instead, it adds to the impact of the gospel rather than detracting from it—to realize Christ brought spiritual healing instead of physical healing. What this understanding would mean, as well as a further growth into *truth*, would be an end to a *wrong* doctrine which has resulted in some cases in terrible tragedy and trauma in the very real lives of very real people.

If the present church teaching on healing is wrong or in any way not in exact accordance with the revealed will of God it is important and urgent that we fully and openly repent as a body. Any delay or obstinacy on our part, if we are indeed teaching a doctrine which is in fact without foundation in God's Word, may be held accountable to us by God. If we are wrong, the blood of thousands is on our heads. Perhaps God in His mercy will forgive us of the mistakes and tragedies of the past if we repent from our hearts! May God have mercy on us all! [*End of 1975 paper*]

Third postscript

And a third postscript: our very world today is in danger of death, just like critically ill Debbie. Millions of Christians trust in divine intervention for the world's salvation and ridicule attempts at human solutions. Medical help for Debbie was likewise regarded as a "human solution" contrary to the will of God, by many of her fellow Christians.

But just as the misguided ideas of Debbie's fellow Christians played a role in that sweet girl's untimely death, so the misguided ideas of Christians in America today may play a role in the outcome of our world's crisis of survival.

The issues are parallel. The plight of our world—global warming, nuclear proliferation, misuses of resources, and so on—may be likened to that of a sick person. In both cases—for individuals and for the world as a whole—there is biblical

Faith Healing and Doctors

language of promises of divine relief and healing. In each case these promises have been interpreted as denying the necessity of effective, appropriate human action. May the tragedy of Debbie be a lesson for those with ears to hear not to repeat the same mistake with respect to the plight of our world.

CHAPTER 19

CREATION AND ORIGINS

It was basic to Herbert Armstrong's message that evolution was not simply factually wrong. It was *willful* ignorance on the part of the vast majority of the world's scientists who, against all reason, *chose to reject God.* This message was emphasized in the "World Tomorrow" broadcast, the *Plain Truth* magazine, and other church literature and sermons. Just as the choice was set up with the healing doctrine, choose faith in God *or* choose to go to a doctor, so it was with evolution: either God created *or* there was evolution. You can have one or the other but not both. And, it was darkly pointed out, the world had chosen to believe in evolution, and *just look what has resulted* (insert list of social ills here).

Garner Ted Armstrong would spend countless radio and television programs presenting what he said were claims of the theory of evolution, and then debunk them. The church held to a "gap" theory of Gen 1:1-2 which allowed for an old earth prior to a "re-creation" 6000 years ago which produced all humans and present-day life-forms. So the age of the universe and dinosaur fossils were no problem. But evolution was believed to be untrue and against all reason. Garner Ted would ridicule things that scientists said. He would paint pictures in words of dead proto-woodpeckers littering forest floors because they could not survive without having fully developed abilities. Yet fully-developed woodpeckers do exist, even though (as he had just conclusively shown) they could not have come about through evolution. After showing evolution to be impossible through illustrated case examples such as this, Garner Ted would give the only logical conclusion: since there was no natural explanation, the diverse life-forms therefore came about by special creation, just as in Genesis chapter one. When Garner Ted contrasted the claims of scientists against common sense and logic in this manner, the scientists just came out looking like idiots.

This was drilled in as basic, like programming, like teaching Pavlov's dogs to salivate at the ring of a bell.

At some belated point an elementary question dawned on me. If evolution had so many glaring fallacies and was so obviously impossible, why did so many biologists (just about 100%) not think it was ridiculous? What was the *biologists'* explanation in their own words, instead of the caricatures presented in *Plain Truth* articles?

I realized that my honest answer to this question was: "I don't know." I took the fateful step, one day in the fall of 1975 toward the end of my Big Sandy days, of deciding to find out. I pulled the *Encyclopedia Britannica* off the shelf of the library in the Redwood Building and looked up an article entitled something like "Evolution, Evidences for," photocopied it and studied it carefully.

What I found was eye-opening. There were five distinct evidences for development of earth's various life forms from common origins discussed in this article. To my surprise the case was quite convincing.[196]

---

[196] "Evidence Supporting Biological Evolution" at http://newton.nap.edu/html/creationism/evidence.html looks similar in form to the *Britannica* article I read at Big Sandy. Also compare Chris Colby, "Introduction to Evolutionary Biology," http://www.talkorigins.org/faqs/faq-intro-to-biology.html, and J. Richard Wakefield, "Biological Evolution. An Overview of Mechanisms and Evidence", Oasis Supplementary Monograph #1 Biological Evolution Overview, http://www.skepticfiles.org/evo2/bioevo.htm. (Note: The author of this last study, J. Richard Wakefield, is not the Ambassador College, Big Sandy, biology instructor Richard Wakefield of the 1970s whose class I took in 1973. I have verified that these are not the same persons and that the identical names are coincidence. What are the odds of this happening by chance? Yet it is so.)

Creation and Origins

In church literature it was taught that the whole range of life-forms on earth today were created as full-blown species in six days, 6000 years ago. Other interpretations of Genesis 1 were condemned. It was said as a mantra, "there is no contradiction between the Bible and *true* science." *True* science, it was explained, could be known by this criterion: it was consistent with the correct interpretation of the Bible (which in the case of Genesis 1 was creation of earth's life-forms by the spoken command of God and *not* evolution). True science most certainly was not what a consensus of scientists published in peer-reviewed scientific literature said. (On some matters, like the true scientific explanation of human origins as created six thousand years ago, Satan had brainwashed nearly all practitioners of the various scientific disciplines on earth.)

I began to suspect there might be something wrong with this picture. I considered that no one, not even the most literal-minded fundamentalist, takes the Bible literally on *everything*. (If so, we'd believe the earth has corners, that God has wings, that the earth rests on pillars holding it up, and so on.) This is not to say the authors of Genesis necessarily read their own words as metaphor. The authors of Genesis probably did believe in things like a physical "vault" over the sky (which could be attained if one built a tower or a ladder tall enough), i.e. earth as a flat circle with a giant dome over it. There are repeated biblical allusions to "foundations" or pillars upon which the earth rests. Few today have problems reading those as metaphor, but the ancient authors probably believed those pillars were as real as the six days of creation. There is no sign the authors of Genesis had any idea of the billions of years that actually are involved in earth's history.

Of course there was the theological question of how did the first humans receive the potential to become divine. This was supposed to be an objection to humans' descent from earlier primates. If so, it meant that at some point hominids became able to receive the spirit of God with potential to become divine, but their ancestors—their parents—were not. Well, I considered, yes, that did logically follow. But that brought up the whole question of the animal world. The church generally thought that all animals, once they died, were dead forever, unlike humans who have a role in the world to come. But there were always a few in the Worldwide Church of God here and there (occasionally I ran into such people) who pointed out that Rom 8:19-21 says *all* creation has a role in the world to come. In this view, we may not know exactly how it works, but the animals, and the first humans' parents, will have a role in the world to come too.[197]

~ ~ ~

Dennis Dietz, Ambassador College Big Sandy's instructor in physics whom I have mentioned earlier (in chapter 3), had scientific training (PhD in physics), an active mind, and was dedicated to the church. As I remember, it was after I had looked up the *Britannica* article and done my own thinking that I talked with Dietz about it. I was surprised when Dietz told me that he saw no conflict between evolution and the Bible, and that in his opinion the claims in church literature that there was such

---

[197] One scripture cited in Ambassador College classes to supposedly show a difference between humans and animals in the hereafter was Eccl 3:21, "Who knows (if) the spirit of man really goes upward, and the spirit of the beast really goes downward to the earth?" However, occasionally someone would correctly point out that that verse is a question and actually is stating the opposite, that there is no difference between the fates of humans and animals. Pointing this out could be hazardous, though, as one unknown student at Pasadena learned according to this report: "[O]ne student wrote a research paper for an Ambassador theology class, claiming that the scriptures speak of a spirit in animals as well as a spirit in man. He provided considerable evidence to support his contention. Upon presenting the paper to his instructors, the student was urged to keep his ideas to himself. It seems the spirit in man and the idea that animals differ from man is a pet concept of Mr. Armstrong's, and the theology instructors were afraid to present the student's findings to him. The following semester the student was not allowed to register for classes and was expelled from the college. He was charged with the crime of 'highbrowing the ministers,' whatever that means" (Harry Eisenberg, "Executive Action," in *Ambassador Review*, June 1976). I don't know who this student was; I wish I did.

a conflict was a mistaken path to go. He described several examples to me of creationist literature making incorrect representations and flawed arguments.

Dietz explained his thinking to me this way. If you take Genesis 1 at face value, he said, it *sounds* like earth was created a few thousand years ago. Of course there are ways of explaining it differently, such as the "gap" theory between Gen 1:1 and 1:2, and so on. But when all is said and done, those have the feel of special pleading. The most uncomplicated reading of Genesis 1 is a short history of the universe in which everything is only a few thousand years old. But all natural evidence—stratification, radiometric dating, and so on—indicates an earth and universe far older than the few thousand years suggested by Genesis. Of course one can say God created the appearance of age. But would God give us minds, then set everything up to deceive humans into thinking there was great age when there really wasn't? Therefore there is a paradox: Genesis 1 suggests a young earth, whereas scientific methods indicate an old earth. This suggested to Dietz that maybe the meaning of Genesis was something other than what people were assuming. Maybe Genesis was not about telling the age of the universe in the literal sense, but was conveying some other point. This was Dietz's reasoning.

I also sought out Donald Deakins, head of the science department at Ambassador College, Big Sandy, for a talk. Dr. Deakins' training and degree was in biology, right at the heart of the issue. I asked Deakins if it was true, as the illustrated booklets from headquarters said, that new species (Genesis "kinds") coming about through natural selection were impossible. Deakins answered by recounting Darwin's observations of geographic distributions and separate species from common ancestors that—cut off from one another by oceans or mountain ranges—separately developed to the point where they no longer could interbreed and are distinct species today. For church literature to say this could not happen was wrong; it had happened, Deakins explained. (However Deakins suggested this could still be part of a wider definition of "microevolution" which is permissible within creationism.) Deakins said the arguments published by the church on evolution were not scientifically sound. Once life started, he said, there was no *scientific* reason why the evolutionary process could not have happened—the various species, development of organs such as eyes, the whole works. Deakins told me he still rejected evolution for theological (rather than scientific) reasons. But he was straight with me about the science. That was like a breath of fresh air.

So both Dietz and Deakins—the two leading scientists on the faculty at Ambassador College, Big Sandy, and both in good standing with the church, independently told me, directly and matter-of-factly, that church literature on evolution emanating from headquarters was filled with misinformation.

The "gap" theory

In classes and sermons at Big Sandy we learned a "gap" theory of Gen 1:1-2 which allowed for billions of years of history of the earth and the universe before a seven-day re-creation week, about six thousand years ago.

The biblical argument for this "gap" went like this. Gen 1:1 says "In the beginning God created the heavens and the earth." Here is the key point: in the next verse, Gen 1:2, it says, "And the world was without form and void." The Hebrew for "without form and void" is *tohu* and *bohu*, two Hebrew words every Ambassador student of those days knew, because they were explained so often. The general sense of *tohu* and *bohu* is "wild, unordered, chaos." (There are arguments over nuances, but this is close to the sense.) But Isa 45:18 says, "God himself who formed the earth and made it—he established it, he created it not *in vain (tohu).*"

That is, God did *not* create the world *tohu*, says Isaiah. But Gen 1:2 says after God created, the world was *tohu*. See? Smoking-gun proof that something happened between verses one

Creation and Origins

and two of Genesis 1. What happened, it was explained, was a vast pre-Adamic age of Lucifer and his angels, put on earth to prepare earth for human habitation, but Lucifer rebelled to become Satan. The dinosaurs and the life-forms before Adam were from this former era, which lasted hundreds of millions or billions of years. There was a major cataclysm about 6000 years ago which caused God's creation of Gen 1:1 to become *tohu* and *bohu* of Gen 1:2, followed by the seven days re-creation. Gen 1:2 therefore had the sense, "And the earth *became* without form and void." Now there was no problem with the evidence for an ancient earth, the dinosaur fossils were explained, and there was no contradiction between Gen 1:2 and Isa 45:18.

I came to a different reading of Gen 1:1-2 in my Big Sandy days. The way I came to read it, verse one was like a title or section heading: "In the beginning God created the heavens and the earth." That was the *title*. The creation had not happened yet. Starting with the next verse and going on for the rest of the chapter, the text describes the creation. The *tohu* and *bohu* of Gen 1:2 was the condition of the universe *before* God started creating. The creation of Gen 1:1 *was* the six days of Genesis 1 which started from an original state of *tohu* and *bohu*.

In this reading of Gen 1:1 as a title (and the six days as the creation of Gen 1:1), there was a corollary: the creation of God of Genesis 1 was not, as often assumed, *ex nihilo* in which matter was brought into existence where before there was empty space or nothing. Rather, the *tohu* and *bohu* description of Gen 1:2 was the description of the pre-creation state of things. Before God created, it was not that there was nothing. There was chaotic wilderness-like stuff already in existence. God's creation (in terms of the text) was when an intelligent mind introduced order into the chaos, engaged the chaotic wilderness and out of the raw stuff of that chaos created design and beauty.

Of course some might object that this leaves unexplained where the wild, unordered matter came from. In this reading of Genesis that indeed is left unexplained, just as where God came from and what he was doing before the creation also is left unexplained. But think: which is harder to explain: the existence of chaotic matter in space before God creates, or the existence of totally empty space before God creates? When I thought about it, both seemed equally paradoxical. It was not as if limitless empty space as the pre-creation state was somehow less paradoxical.

A second corollary to this reading was that Genesis indeed was a picture of an earth and universe only a few thousand years old. The "gap" theory was an attempt to remove some of the scientific conflict with a literal reading of Genesis 1. But it wasn't what Genesis 1 was saying. Genesis 1 was telling of a six-day process of creation, which if one takes the Bible literally, was only a few thousand years ago.

On scientific grounds there is an ancient universe and development of earth's various life-forms over time from common origins. I came to see at Big Sandy that Genesis 1 should not be a basis for objection to this, any more than the biblical "pillars" upon which the earth rests should be a basis for objection to scientific explanations of the earth which do not involve being supported on pillars. The problem was not with the scientists who encountered, and with much struggle, worked out natural explanations for these processes, I thought. Scientists should be regarded as searchers into the mysteries of God, of what makes the universe *tick*—which is slowly uncovered by means of the scientific method. The way I came to see it at Big Sandy, science is a *window* into the very *soul of God*. I liked these two quotations:

> "It is the glory of God to conceal a thing
> But the glory of kings is to search out a matter."
> -- Prov 25:2

> "Nature and Nature's Laws lay hid in Night
> God said, Let Newton be!—And all was Light."
> -- Alexander Pope

Creation and Origins

Dr. Hoeh's amazing student forum at Big Sandy

Another person who was not happy with the way Genesis and natural history were understood at Ambassador College was the leading theoretician in the church on such matters: Dr. Hoeh.

In March 1975 Dr. Hoeh gave an address at a student forum at Big Sandy which was very odd.

Student forums with special speakers were held weekly in the Field House on the Big Sandy campus. Attendance was compulsory for all students. About two-thirds of the time the guest speaker would be someone from the outside with some interesting topic. Other times the speaker would be a member of the Ambassador College faculty presenting some area of research or subject matter to the wider student body. On this particular occasion Dr. Hoeh from Pasadena was the speaker. His talk was about geology and creationism.

In his address Dr. Hoeh said the church had no answers on basic questions concerning radiocarbon dating, the Flood, prehistoric humans, and so on. It was odd because few other sermons or messages took the theme of despairing at what was unresolved with no solution given at the end. But that was Dr. Hoeh's message to the faculty and students that day. He said: we criticize the world's scientists and historians, but *we don't know what happened, we don't have answers*. He just spelled it out: *we don't know what we are talking about*. Hoeh said plainly that a large part of what Ambassador students sitting in that forum had learned in their Ancient World History and Systematic Theology classes relating to Genesis and the Flood—based in large part on Hoeh's articles—was worthless. And he offered nothing better in its place. It was one of the most unusual, amazing, self-revelatory public statements of a leading church figure I ever heard.

It was so odd, so out of key with what sermons and messages normally were, yet Dr. Hoeh had so much stature and reputation (including his iconoclasm) that he could get away with giving a talk like this. I never heard a later comment about it. It is as if it went in one ear and out the other of everyone present, and life went on as if he had never spoken. In later years, I found that other students who must have been present that day did not even remember this had happened. (Did it go right over their heads?)

Here is what Dr. Hoeh said at this student forum at Big Sandy, direct from my notes taken as he was speaking. This was March 20, 1975.

> Is there no disagreement between true science and true religion? What evidence is there then for this agreement?
>
> On origins there is no problem. But it is difficult to reconcile some facts of nature with the Bible from here on. Like what is man, where did he appear historically, and what did he look like? After Genesis 1:1 there are problems.
>
> Our own views were often wrong because of Adventist influence. We followed George McCready Price, for example. The evidence doesn't fit that all geologic evidence is from the Flood. Creationists are as closed-minded as evolutionists!
>
> We are ourselves in disarray about how to reconcile geology and the Bible. We have no voice, no official position at any level. After 25 years we know less than when we started! It is our responsibility to get this straightened out.
>
> *Is* there any way to reconcile present human knowledge with revelation? Do we presume we can know in areas that we can't? Are there limitations to what we can know? Such as the Flood—can it be established to be Late Tertiary? How can we say the world is willingly ignorant when we don't have the answers ourselves? We need to know what can be proved and what can't, what is proof and what isn't.
>
> We don't even know the limits to where we may test the questions! Our own faculty can't answer even the simplest questions. We don't know. No coherent solutions have been proposed.
>
> Will it come down to having two compartments in your mind—science and revelation? Like Benjamin Mazar who says he is a Jew in the synagogue and an archaeologist at the dig site?
>
> Generally our positions are philosophical, not subject to investigation, private positions. If we have no evidence we can't offer a public opinion! Floods today leave things virtually untouched. What *would* a Flood cause? Could the reason the Bible tells of a Flood be because we couldn't know it from geology or archaeology?
>
> Radiometric dating.
>
> If Genesis 1-11 can be proved true and not myth then why hasn't someone come up with the proof yet? Will we have to ultimately

Creation and Origins

say it is a matter of faith? Will we someday be able to define what is a human artifact and what isn't?

That evening Ken Herrmann had been kind enough to invite me and two other students along with several faculty to his home where Dr. Hoeh was visiting and discussing things further. The next morning I wrote a few notes of the evening as I remembered things. No doubt there was more than this, but here are my complete notes:

3/20/75. Evening at the home of Ken Herrmann. Present: Dr. Hoeh, Dietz, Kaplan, Ronish, Anderson, Knauf, Manteufel, Mac Overton, Wes Eccles, and me.

Ken Herrmann: At the exodus Venus was seen. 1487 is very peculiar astronomically. The Israelites worshiped like back in Egypt, Friday, Vendredi. On Tammuz 16 Moses returns and breaks the tablets on the Sabbath.

Hoeh: Jewish tradition says Passover was Thursday and the exodus Friday. The law was given on a Sabbath not Pentecost (Sivan 5), the first Jewish tradition. The covenant was given on a Sunday (Pentecost).

Kaplan: There is a Jewish tradition that Esau killed Nimrod.

Dr. Hoeh: Nimrod was the name of a priestly line. There is another tradition that Nimrod persecuted Abraham's line. So there was another Nimrod. The sacred calendar corresponds to the Babylonian calendar. A statue of Moses shows him to be tall. Radiocarbon dating is valid. Potassium-argon dating can be off due to leaks. No creationist has ever yet defined radiometric dating to know where we're at. We have to live with an apparent contradiction. The data is there, it's the right interpretation of it that we need. What were the "fountains of the deep"? We don't know yet. They were later sealed. They may have been something along the continental shore. The only way for the Flood to cover mountains must have been a change in level of the ocean floor. The ocean floor could have been raised and the mountains lowered by the coast acting like a hinge for both.

From someone: [Tom] Crotzer from this area traveled to see Noah's ark. A government report says there will be no magnetic field in 25 years (or the year 2025).

Dr. Hoeh: We have invented theories to explain away problems.

Postscript: Dr. Hoeh returns to Big Sandy two years later with solutions to the problems

Two years later Dr. Hoeh returned to Ambassador College, Big Sandy, and in a similar address to the faculty and student body announced he had solutions to the problems he had raised in his earlier forum. This address took place March 17, 1977. (This was after I was no longer at Big Sandy.) According to a transcript of his remarks I have recently found Dr. Hoeh opened with the following words:

> Two years ago this month I had the privilege of addressing the Assembly of the Big Sandy campus of Ambassador College. At that time I challenged you to investigate the issues that stood in the way of a proper synthesis of science, history and biblical studies on the nature and purpose of man. By the evening of that day a number of your faculty and students had participated in a series of discussions with me. A breakthrough was apparent. And now, two years later, I want to summarize for you both the causes of our past dilemma and the simple solutions ... [198]

Dr. Hoeh's solution was a theory of multiple trial creations of species including proto-humans, done by God and his angels, in which God and the angels experimented and worked out design problems until God was ready to create Adam and Eve.[199]

---

[198] "Text of the Address Delivered by Dr. Herman L. Hoeh at Ambassador College, Big Sandy Texas Campus, Mar. 17, 1977" at http://www.friendsofsabbath.org/~surfer/HL%20Hoeh/Hoeh_changes.pdf, prepared by Craig White. Other addresses of Dr. Hoeh from the same time period are also at this web site.

[199] Hoeh: "God 'experimented' with life, and with angels to see if they would do his will ... In six days God has the power to recreate the world as we know it. But there is no need to assume He designed it all suddenly. It was not much different from the immediately preceding creation. Perhaps He just modified the creatures slightly. The major effort of creation was the planning and design of the whole thing (not the manufacture) which had been completed earlier than Creation Week. The Devil had led us to believe that God was a master magician who said 'poof' and there it all was. That is not the way it happened" (Dr. Hoeh, sermon, April 1977; see note 198).

Creation and Origins

Sometimes demons were involved too.[200] All of the pre-Adamic hominids, in this theory, including Cro-Magnon man, were without the "spirit in man." They were practice humans before God was ready to go with Adam. All of the practice humans went extinct before Adam, Hoeh said.[201] The chief virtue of this theory from Dr. Hoeh's point of view was it accounted for the fossil finds of early humans without need to challenge conventional scientific datings (which Hoeh had come to accept as accurate). He concluded his 1977 Big Sandy address: "So it is now possible to reconcile Bible, history, and C-14 with a totally new view of the kind of world angels were asked to govern."[202]

---

[200] *Hoeh*: "Prior to Adam, the world was subject to angels. They were placed on earth as a training ground. Were angels there solely to watch over rocks, vegetation, and brute animals? Hardly. The real development of their skills and character could best be tested by being able to work with creatures only partially governed by instinct—as, for example, *homo habilis*. Once we know the biblical account and purpose for angels, it is not difficult to understand the sudden appearance of varieties of pithecines and hominids. It is not a matter of biological evolution, but of the creation of greater physical challenges for the angelic world. The angels were being tested on earth to see whether they would maintain the principles of the government of God in running an ever more complex world. They did not all maintain their loyalty to that government. They, it would seem, are chargeable for the fact that the first forms of art are perverted in usage. Upper Paleolithic art is not sensible art; it is magic, hidden in caves, with one work of art drawn over another. Their mentality was altogether different from humans ..." (Dr. Hoeh, address at Ambassador College, Big Sandy, March 17, 1977; see note 198). "Angels governed the weather as well as life. They apparently also sought to possess the animals. Remember the demons who entered the swine in Christ's day ... Dr. C.P. Meredith once had to deal with a demon-possessed horse—that had more than ordinary 'horse sense' ..." (Dr. Hoeh, sermon, April 1977; see note 198).

[201] *Hoeh*: "Modern man is a refined and reduced Upper Paleolithic hominid. So far as we know, we don't have any fossil [pre-Adamic] hominids alive today—they were all extincted before the Adamic creation" (Dr. Hoeh, sermon, April 1977; see note 198).

[202] See note 198.

Poor Dr. Hoeh. His new theory of trial creations of prehistoric men before a Genesis re-creation week 6000 years ago was no solution. For example, Australian aborigines go back at least 40,000 years without interruption in Australia. American Indians go back continuously at least 15,000 years in North America, and so on. How did Dr. Hoeh get all these peoples wiped out, then the same kind of people migrated right back there again in the same places, with the same customs, tools, and genetic makeup, this time all descended from Adam? (And 1600 years later, wiped out again in Noah's Flood, and then Noah's descendants migrated right back there again.) He never explained that. In addition, according to later reports based on genetic science (e.g. *Science* magazine, Oct. 8, 1999), all humans on earth are descended from a single woman believed to have lived (according to the 1999 estimate) c. 145,000 years ago in southern Africa. Scientists refer to her as "Eve." This is slightly different from Hoeh's theory in which all living humans are supposed to be descended from his Eve 6000 years ago (and Noah's wife 4400 years ago).

Dr. Hoeh never published any of this. And in his entire life he never published any of his scientific or historical theories in any peer-reviewed journal. This was not science. This was pseudo-science. Real science gets published in scientific journals.

A comment from today: the Game of Life

There has been discussion concerning what is called the "Game of Life," or cellular automata. Basically the phenomenon consists of starting out with a dot on a checkered computer screen, followed by repeated running of a program with very simple rules. By running the same simple rules repeatedly amazing things can result—in some cases an evolutionary-like process of complex "creatures" on the computer screen can emerge, which reproduce and take on lives of their own. Some sets of simple rules repeated over and over, of course, produce nothing or

Creation and Origins

gibberish. But other sets of very simple rules, when repeated thousands of times, produce complex forms which look like on-screen "life."

The lesson in this is that there is more than one way complexity can come about. Complexity does not *necessarily* require intelligent design or planning in advance; it can also happen unpredictably by a simple algorithm repeated enough times. The original starting algorithm is not complex. But designs of startling complexity and beauty can result.

You start out with a couple of trivially simple rules at the beginning and repeat often enough, and you could get ... well, you could get something like the universe we see in existence today. This idea has been developed by researchers such as Konrad Zuse and Edward Fredkin—that our universe is explicable in terms of a simple algorithm or a computer program that has produced everything that we see.[203]

Of course such a model leaves unexplained how the starting simple rules came about, and the mechanism by which repeated application of the simple algorithm occurs. It doesn't explain everything. But at the very least such explorations can help break our thinking out of narrow boundaries of "can only be" explanations for the living complexity we see around us. There are, in short, well-known and well-described mechanisms by which complexity can come from simplicity, seemingly spontaneously. And yet, paradoxically, the more we understand the workings of the universe in underlying simple terms, the deeper the ultimate and vast mystery.

---

[203] For more on this see the papers of Edward Fredkin at http://www.digitalphilosophy.org/. There is a web site, "The Notebook of Philosophy and Physics," which explores the idea that the universe is a giant computer program and provides links to relevant scientific articles: http://www.bottomlayer.com/index.html. ("The universe is the manifestation of a computer and its programming. If the universe is a computer running along conventional programming lines, then who are we? And who programmed this virtual reality simulation? And why? That is philosophy, certainly. And it is religion. And it is still science.")

CHAPTER 20

TITHING

The Worldwide Church of God taught its members in the United States that God commanded them to mail in ten percent of each paycheck to headquarters in Pasadena, calculated on gross pay before taxes not net. Members in other countries where taxes were higher were allowed to send in ten percent of their net. But not people in the U.S. God wanted ten percent of the gross from Americans.

Mailing in this percentage to God's Work was called tithing. Tithing was one of Herbert Armstrong's most important doctrines. (Some would say, the most important doctrine.) Herbert Armstrong taught that tithing would bring showers of material blessings. That was one thing Herbert got right, the part about material blessings. Here is a firsthand account:

> It was February 18, 1970. A small group of ministerial students were spending an evening with Herbert W. Armstrong, the founder of the Worldwide Church of God. Those of us who had been invited were given a glimpse of a life-style which in today's world only a very few are able to afford. At his home, a small mansion on Pasadena's South Orange Grove Boulevard (once nicknamed "millionaire row"), we were surrounded by rare antiques, expensive paintings, and Steuben crystal. The carpets were luxuriant; a Steinway grand piano stood in the corner of the drawing room.
>
> The gourmet cuisine served at dinner was excellent as were the European wines—all four of them. We had been shown a large number of expensive paintings and *objets d'art* and, as was his custom, Herbert would relate what he paid for each and what they were now worth. That theme carried over into the conversation at dinner. Then, as the servants began to clear the table, he turned to

one of the guests and said, "What do you think all of these beautiful things on the table are worth?" Of course, none of us had even the slightest idea. And so, he was able to proudly proclaim, "Over $125,000!"

He was quick to point out, however, that art objects of this quality were so rare that they were in fact "priceless." The sculptured, foot-high, solid-gold saltcellars were, for instance, the only known copies of those once owned by Louis XIV. (They had been specially made for Herbert by Harrod's of London.) The crystal goblets were identical to those found on Queen Elizabeth's table. The supremely crafted cutlery was of solid gold. The tablecloth was made of the finest Belgian lace. The gold-covered china was of the finest craftsmanship and formerly belonged to Czar Nicholas II of Russia.

As we sat there sipping our four different wines and eating off the czar's china, I couldn't help but think of the incredible contrast all this presented to the meager existence of so many members of Herbert's church—the very ones who were, through their tithes and offerings, making all this possible. ... As Herbert has often stated, "Tithing pays off!" One of his editorials was once titled, "This is the Life!—Real Abundant Living!"...[204]

Yes, it is good to be a modern Apostle.

Second and third tithe

Actually, Worldwide Church of God doctrine demanded three tithes. The first ten percent, or "first tithe," was the tithe to support the Work and ministry. The members saved the second ten percent—"second tithe"—in their own bank accounts to pay for a trip to the annual fall Feast of Tabernacles held at various U.S. sites and worldwide. The third ten percent—"third tithe"—was paid every third and sixth years in a seven-year cycle, beginning from the time of baptism. Third tithe was sent in to Pasadena for a fund that members were told was for widows and orphans and other hardship cases in the church.

During my second year at Ambassador College, Big Sandy, in late 1973 or early 1974, evidence began to leak out that for a

---

[204] John Trechak, "Fleecing the Flock," *Ambassador Report*, 1977.

number of years the third tithe funds had been dipped into for such things as financing interior decorating of evangelists' homes, overseas junkets for top church officials, and similar purposes. The struggling church members sending in their third tithe checks were told the money was used for charitable purposes. Well, I guess charity begins at home—in this case top evangelists' homes. This wasn't a matter of occasional lapses or tiny amounts involved either. Insiders reported a whopping 60% of third tithe sent in to headquarters was spent on luxury travel and purchases for top ministers, with only 40% of the struggling members' hard-earned third tithe payments actually going to the widows and poor which the members were told was the purpose of the fund.[205]

When these revelations came out, headquarters alternated between defending the practices (on the grounds that helping poor Levites like Herbert Armstrong and the top evangelists was biblically permissible), and saying the improprieties had been corrected. Mainly it was swept under the rug. No one was known to have been fired over this, or to have served time.

On January 3, 1974, Garner Ted Armstrong openly admitted at a ministerial conference that huge amounts of third tithe were being used for purposes other than widows and orphans.

---

[205] "Millions of dollars had been drained from the third tithe account for emergency use which included the jets and other personal needs. There was also a mountain retreat, as well as a Lake Tahoe home—both supported by third tithe—along with other similarly questionable expenditures ... The evangelist in charge of disbursing the third tithe at that time estimated that only 40% of the third tithe was going to the widow, the stranger, and the fatherless. The remaining 60% was going to the "Levite" at the top level" (Paul Royer and Bryce Clark, "The Doctrine of Divorce and Remarriage. How and Why it Was Changed" (http://www.bethelcog.org/Cover_DAndRWhy Changed.html).

> It is true that massive segments of third tithe as it built up in the balances of this work were used both for ministerial homes and for ministerial salaries.[206]

He apparently didn't see any reason to change this. Five months later in May 1974 he repeated it again to the ministers:

> But you know it [third tithe] is still being used for your salaries. It's still being used for church homes.[207]

This was not what the members were told. In the February 1970 issue of *The Good News* (the Worldwide Church of God members' magazine), an article had appeared telling the members about the wonderful benefits of paying third tithe. It was entitled, "How You Can Receive an Extra Blessing!" The article assured the members concerning third tithe distributions: "All those who benefit are genuinely in need … Third tithe help does *not* go to the lazy, idle, shiftless or able-bodied."[208]

Now it is true that "genuinely in need" is a relative matter, subject to some differences in interpretation. Jets genuinely need fuel. Expensive resort homes for top executives genuinely need landscaping maintenance, art on the walls, etc. The hapless members, however, naively thought (because that is what they had been told) that the third tithe they were breaking their backs to send in was going solely to widows and people in hardship.

Ambassador Report quoted from approved and signed third tithe requisition forms from the year 1969, the year before the *Good News* article just quoted. Copies of these internal documents had been leaked to John Trechak, editor of *Ambassador Report*. Trechak noted accurately that "99.9% of the

---

[206] Transcript, ministerial conference, Jan. 3, 1974, quoted in "Fleecing the Flock," *Ambassador Report*, 1977.
[207] Transcript, ministerial conference, May 1974, quoted in "Fleecing the Flock," *Ambassador Report*, 1977.
[208] Quoted *Ambassador Report*, 1977.

Tithing

members were totally unaware" that major portions of the fund were being siphoned off for things like this:[209]

> 1969 (no further date), D. Apartian, Furniture, carpets, appliances, $22,000.
> 1/2/69, Ron Dart, Drapery, $5,000.
> 7/10/69, Ron Dart, All furnishings, interior and exterior, wall coverings, etc., $40,000.
> 11/3/69, R. Plache, Furnishings, upholstery, drapes, carpets, and misc., $25,000.
> 1/21/70, D. Antion, All furnishings, interior and exterior, wall coverings, etc., $40,000.

Trechak reported: "*All* of this money came from the church's third tithe account, and it is so stated on each requisition." (Remember these are 1969 dollars, which would be multiplied about five times over for 2006.)

Korah

The Worldwide Church of God correction of improprieties involving the third tithe account seemed to follow a pattern consisting of this basic sequence: (a) being caught with their hand in the cookie jar; (b) promising that they had stopped doing that; followed by (c) refusal to verify "b"; and (d) new allegations of the same type of improprieties a couple of years later. (Repeat.)

As for "c," refusal to verify or offer accountability to the church members, you might wonder about that. Let me explain. The very fact that you would ask about this at all is because you are infected with the *spirit of suspicion* of *this world*, which is not one of the fruits of the Spirit. The Spirit of God is humble and believes all things (1 Cor 13:7). Even more importantly, it wasn't members' *place* or *duty* to oversee headquarters' use of money. That was up to *God* to handle. Once you put it in the

---

[209] Trechak, "Fleecing the Flock," *Ambassador Report*, 1977.

mail, you had done your part. If something was amiss, *God* would correct it, *God* would see that the situation was handled. It was not for the members to take matters into their *own* hands, like Korah. This was the message repeated in sermon after sermon out in the hinterlands.

Who was Korah, you ask? Korah was the leader of some rebels against Moses and Aaron when the Israelites were wandering in the wilderness. The earth opened up and swallowed Korah and everyone with him. This scary Bible story was quoted in sermons to show the perils of criticizing the apostle whom God had chosen. Do you want the same thing to happen to you?

Second tithe too

Headquarters also looked greedily at the second tithe, which was the one tithe which members controlled and were biblically mandated to spend on themselves. There was a lot of thought at headquarters on how they could get their greedy, grasping paws on that money too.

They were already getting some of it. To start with, members had always been asked to send in a tenth of their second tithe—called "the tithe of the tithe," to pay for festival expenses. That sounded reasonable enough, but that was only the beginning. Members were expected to send in their "excess second tithe" left over after the Feast of Tabernacles was finished, to headquarters. Even better yet, headquarters urged, members should send their *projected* surplus in *advance* of the Feast. (Better to grab it before they spent it.) Members were told the excess second tithe went to financially assist poor brethren to enable them to attend the Feast. Former headquarters Business Office employee from the early 1970s Richard Nickels told how this worthy charitable objective was carried out: "When I worked in the Business Office, I signed hundreds of sizeable second (festival) tithe checks paid to the ministers for their personal use,

Tithing

while at the same time I had to explain to poor members why they could not receive second tithe assistance."[210]

~ ~ ~

A breathtakingly outrageous, naked grab for the members' second tithe money was cooked up in the head of Garner Ted Armstrong around 1975. He got the bright idea that it was a shame for members to just spend all their second tithe money on themselves at the Feast after saving it up all year. Wouldn't the money be much better used by sending all of it in to Pasadena to meet pressing needs there to do the Work? Think of all the good headquarters could do with all that money! Thus was hatched Garner Ted's amazing idea of just canceling the Feast of Tabernacles—after members had saved up their second tithe all year to go to the feast. At the last minute headquarters would tell the members about the latest crisis and to just stay home and mail in their accumulated savings to Pasadena. What a bonanza it would be! Note this would not be members' *excess* second tithe; it would be *all* of the members' second tithe savings bank accounts for the year, harvested just like that! What a way to *really shear those sheep!*

Garner Ted called a meeting at Pasadena to discuss his brainstorm. Ronald Dart, administrator at Big Sandy, was called out for this, and he told the church at Big Sandy about it upon his return. Even faithful Mr. Dart had difficulty putting this one in a good light. Mr. Dart said he had told Garner Ted that his idea might not be the wisest thing to do after members had their hopes up all year long to go to the Feast and hear Herbert Armstrong in person. Apparently, the counsel of Mr. Dart and others carried the day and headquarters was persuaded to cool it on that one.

But still they just *lusted* after that second tithe money. The problem, from headquarters' point of view, was that members

---

[210] Richard Nickels, *Herbert Armstrong 1892-1986* (St. Charles, MO: Giving and Sharing ministries, 1988), 5.

were just wasting too much of that money on themselves. Garner Ted's idea to simply grab all the money, one time, had been considered and reluctantly abandoned. That could kill the goose that was laying golden eggs, as more sensible minds probably pointed out to Garner Ted in words of single syllables that he would understand.

With that brainstorm thwarted, headquarters efficiently implemented a more practical means of gobbling up a bigger share of the members' second tithes. The first I heard of this was an innocuous-sounding announcement sometime in 1975. The announcement was that there was going to be a new focus or emphasis on *the family* this year at Feast time. As part of this emphasis on *family togetherness* at the Feast, headquarters magnanimously and generously announced that there would be fewer "feast transfers" approved.

In earlier years, members had been allowed to attend feast sites away from their home area or overseas upon request. Members did have to go through a registration process to go to different feast sites, but this had been mostly automatic approval, a formality similar to making RSVP dinner reservations, to assist in planning for logistics and facilities. For some members, taking vacations to exotic places was the only way to use up so much money in eight days, other than giving it to headquarters of course. (But this last alternative was exactly where greedy headquarters had set its eyes, and was licking its chops.)

Part of the initial "sell" of the whole tithing-package system to prospective members, in addition to explaining that it was the law of God, was the concept that the second tithe was God's way of ensuring that average people with limited incomes could once a year afford the nicer things in life. Once a year they could eat out in expensive restaurants, go on vacation, etc.—blessings that otherwise would not be experienced.

But now headquarters was pulling a "bait and switch," so to speak. Headquarters saw the members doing exactly what headquarters had told them the second tithe was *for*—God's intent that all people be able once per year to experience quality and luxury for a few days, or as the King James Version of Deuteronomy 14:26 puts it, "whatever thy soul lusteth after, for oxen, or for sheep, or for wine, or for strong drink, or for whatsoever thy soul desireth ... and thou shalt rejoice, thou and thy household." Headquarters never came right out and told members not to live well during the eight days of the feast. But they skillfully found ways to reduce members' spending so that there would be more excess second tithe to turn in.

Headquarters' reasoning was quite logical: if members' trips to overseas sites, or to transfer sites elsewhere in the United States, could be reduced (headquarters just hated to see money wasted), then there would be more unused or excess second tithe to be mailed in.

Actually at an earlier stage, before I started attending church in 1968, members were told they were limited to one overseas transfer every three years, or something like that. That arbitrary rule reduced the ability of the wealthier members to spend large amounts of their second tithe on themselves two years out of three. But headquarters decided that wasn't good enough. So in 1975 members were told that festival transfers should not be requested at all unless cause or need could be shown. Now, members were forced to ask permission and explain themselves, in order to take a trip to a destination of their choice with their own money where festival services were being held. If they could not show a good reason, they would be turned down. The reason for this new policy, of course, was for the members' own good. As noted, headquarters, ever solicitous of the members' welfare, had decided the theme this year would be this new emphasis on family togetherness.

Part of this focus on family togetherness was that "people don't need to be traveling so far away from home." Everyone should stay nearer home and spend more time with their families, instead of blowing huge quantities of money unnecessarily going to, say, Sri Lanka or New Zealand or wherever for the feast, where they probably didn't have any good reason for needing to go that headquarters could see.

Tithing

Headquarters saw that if they reduced this way in which members could spend their accumulated "second tithe," they could get their claws on more of it when members mailed in their excess second tithe. This was carried out. I remember Dean of Students Ronald Kelly explaining the new policy, and how it would allow families to spend more time together, etcetera, etcetera, and he did so with a straight face.

Reflections on the racket

Looked at in retrospect, it was a racket. The church membership—about equal parts struggling middle class and working poor (with a few better-paid professionals and small business owners thrown in)—were the chumps, a cash cow to be milked. And that is how, when you scratched under the surface of the rhetoric, the senior executives at headquarters looked at the members. They didn't respect the members. The members were the peasants or sharecroppers. A member's duty was to work and pay. The ministry and students at Ambassador College were the privileged nobility. There were the top nobles whose duty it was to spend on the very best for themselves (God's way of quality as a foretaste of the world tomorrow) in the process of getting the gospel to the world. And there were the lesser nobles out in what was called "the field" whose duty it was to do the thankless task of shepherding some mighty dumb sheep (as headquarters thought of it). Jesus, amazingly, was believed to have ordained all of this. The hypnotic rhetoric that cast a spell over everything made all this sound completely reasonable.

~ ~ ~

The Ambassador College-trained "field ministers" in most cases had few other good job prospects. Their employment was at will—no contract, no job security, their employment continued entirely at the pleasure of upper management at headquarters and Herbert Armstrong's whim. Headquarters had opted out of the

Tithing

Social Security system for the ministry. (The reasoning was, since the time was so short before Christ's coming it would not be needed.) There was no other retirement program. (It was hoped that if time did go on that long, the church would take care of them in their old age, even without formal obligation.) If any of the field ministers *did* quit or were terminated, they had few easily transferable job skills. Herbert Armstrong was blunt in spelling out what happened to ministers who treacherously abandoned God's Apostle: some of them *now had to work with their hands*. That was Herbert Armstrong's idea of a truly horrible fate. With undisguised satisfaction, Herbert Armstrong wrote:

> "In 1974, some 35 ministers left [the Worldwide Church of God] ... Where are they today? I know many of those former ministers have had to take jobs working with their hands to earn a living. That is JUSTICE!"
> -- Herbert Armstrong, Co-worker letter, July 30, 1978

The ministers, the elite, were like plantation overseers. They had two basic options within this system. They could be loyal up, to their employer (Herbert Armstrong). This would keep their job, their salary, their position and its perks, and their standing. Or, they could be loyal down, to the people whom they were charged with shepherding, God's people. The problem was that standing for the best interests of the people they were shepherding was not always consistent with the agenda of the ones signing their paychecks (headquarters). This was the dilemma. They could carry out the will of headquarters and continue to be part of the oppressive apparatus; they could defend the best interests of the church members and be fired; or they could quit. The last two options involved serious economic consequences and, more often than not, downward economic mobility. (See Herbert Armstrong's gloating over this, above.) In some cases, as Herbert Armstrong pointed out, it might mean having to take a menial job like so many of the tithe-paying church members. And most ministers had wives and children to support.

Tithing

You might ask, where were the ministers' wives in all this? A minister's wife had status in the reflected glory of her husband. It was life as nobility. But it was a noble's life that could be terminated at any moment, if anything went haywire. In light of the vulnerability of the Worldwide Church of God ministers' employment situation, you might ask if some of the wives might not quietly pick up job skills or degrees on the side. Some did. But not with the encouragement of headquarters. In Akron, Ohio, my mother (who was never a Worldwide Church of God member) got to know, on a friendly basis, the young wife of the Akron pastor. At the time my mother was employed teaching young women secretarial skills for a federal government job training program. This pastor's wife talked to my mother privately about her own attempts to acquire employable skills. The pastor's wife told my mother how Herbert Armstrong did not want ministers' wives learning job skills or taking jobs, and of her frustrations with this. This woman's attempt to help herself and her husband become able to support themselves without need of a church salary, if necessary, had to be done almost in secret, furtively, lest headquarters find out and be displeased.

So the life of the lesser nobility or plantation overseers, the ones actually wielding the whip over the serfs and most visible to the serfs, had its own costs. Of course there were some good plantation overseers in the antebellum south, overseers who were kind to the slaves, considerate, who genuinely cared about the slaves' welfare and well-being. Not all were cruel bastards. Similarly, the Worldwide Church of God had ministers who tried to care for the members. But just let a plantation overseer start begin speaking of freedom for the slaves, start teaching slaves to read, or support the slaves if they decided to go on strike. The smiling facade would quickly disappear and the violence of the system would become clear. There are invisible lines in systems that you just do not cross—no matter how good-hearted you are. (And yet the story of hope for the human race is that there always

Tithing

are those who do cross those lines, who say "this is wrong" and who face down the oppressive powers of the world.)

Blood on the floor at headquarters

Given the amount of money the Worldwide Church of God extracted from its members, it is not surprising that the doctrine on tithing came under intense scrutiny. In 1973 a researcher for Garner Ted Armstrong's television program, Harry Eisenberg, turned his research skills to producing a solidly documented paper on tithing. Among other things, the paper traced the history of tithing's inauguration in Christianity to the Catholic Church's adoption and enforcement of the practice in the sixth century. On January 7, 1974 Eisenberg was fired after he showed copies of his research paper to friends and fellow employees.

Shortly after Eisenberg was fired, Ernest Martin, the former head of Ambassador College's Theology Department at Pasadena, published a paper on tithing. Martin showed that tithing in Israel was on agricultural produce only, not money wages. Martin argued that tithing did not apply to Christians today.

The response at headquarters was to tell members not to read anything by Ernest Martin, and the preparation, under the direction and organization of Herman Hoeh, of a collection of pro-tithing study papers from members of the Doctrinal Committee. (This was shortly before Herbert Armstrong axed the Doctrinal Committee out of existence for all eternity.)

These study papers on tithing were distributed to the Worldwide Church of God ministry in September 1974. It happened that I visited Dr. Hoeh in Pasadena just after he had finished his work on this project. He gave me a copy of these ministerial study papers. After reading the collection, I told Dr. Hoeh, "This certainly seems to put to rest the objections to tithing, for anyone whose mind is not already made up." I did not realize then how unbelievably naive on my part that was—or that after further reflection in succeeding months I also would see tithing quite differently.

~ ~ ~

Dr. Hoeh told me on that occasion that he had had problems with other members of the Doctrinal Committee on the tithing issue. (He mentioned David Antion in particular as having been a "problem.") But I did not then realize the appalling extent of the censorship of papers of the Doctrinal Committee members that Dr. Hoeh had carried out. This came out in 1977 in the dissident publication *Ambassador Report*, which gave a glimpse of a titanic internal struggle that had taken place at headquarters over this issue. I had been aware of only faint rumblings. Now I learned that Dr. Hoeh had been the key enforcer carrying out an advance decision made by the Armstrongs that tithing was not going to change. No matter what any researcher on the Doctrinal Committee showed out of the Bible, it did not matter; Herbert and son had already decided.

Mr. Dart at Big Sandy told the members during announcements one sabbath of a meeting at Pasadena in which he had participated, during which the subject of tithing had been discussed. Mr. Dart said that Brian Knowles (editor of the *Plain Truth* magazine) had played the role of "devil's advocate" in arguing against tithing for the New Testament church today. Dart gave the impression that everyone else (or nearly so) in the meeting was in favor of the existing church doctrine on tithing, making it sound as if Knowles was isolated in this (in Dart's view, wrong) opinion.

In fact, *most* of the Doctrinal Committee urged changing the church doctrine on tithing. But this meant nothing since the power was in the hands of Herbert Armstrong, who had delegated it to Garner Ted who told Dr. Hoeh in advance what the committee's conclusion was to be. In this way information was processed, spun, and a ministerial study guide on tithing produced giving a doctrinal committee *imprimatur* on an outcome that had been predetermined, and which was the opposite of what the members of the doctrinal committee believed. Here is how it worked according to one frustrated insider:

> One well-educated member of the Doctrinal Committee ... described the method of ascertaining truth at the meetings: "Mr. Ted Armstrong calls Dr. Hoeh and gives him the subject he wants discussed and proceeds to give him his surmise on the matter. Then the Doctrinal Committee meets. We discuss the subject, all the pros and cons, in many long-hour sessions. When we are all finished, Dr. Hoeh writes a report and submits it to Mr. Ted Armstrong. No matter what is discussed, the report always coincides with Mr. Ted Armstrong's conclusion of the matter prior to the discussion. So what's the use in discussing the question—the doctrine—in the first place?"[211]

Meanwhile back at Big Sandy

Ernest Martin's booklet on tithing would not go away. Students at Big Sandy were passing it around and reading it, albeit clandestinely. I read it; so did many other students and members. Taking the direct approach, Garner Ted Armstrong flew into Big Sandy and from the pulpit ordered students (and everyone else) not to read Dr. Martin's articles. I thought, this is ridiculous. I felt embarrassed that my church was behaving in such an infantile way. Here Garner Ted was acting as if he had the right to control personal reading choices of students in a *college setting* supposedly dedicated to critical thinking.

Our Ambassador College student handbook said that students were "encouraged to question their instructors." I thought to myself: telling people what they may and may not read is what cults do. It is what eastern European communist parties do. It is what George Orwell's *Big Brother* does. Garner Ted did not address the substance of Dr. Martin's article with clear reasoning and argument. Garner Ted's response to Ernest Martin on tithing was *ad hominem*, caricature, bluster, and then finally the mailed

---

[211] Royer and Clark, "The Doctrine of Divorce and Remarriage."

fist: the *command* to college students not to read the forbidden information.

I didn't pay a bit of attention to these proscriptions. Neither did Mr. Dart. Mr. Dart, the resident administrator at Big Sandy, studied Ernest Martin's booklet on tithing and prepared a refutation of Martin's case, which he presented in sermons. Mr. Dart seemed to take the more intelligent approach that the better way to defend the corporation was to answer with information, and address the substance of the issue.

Mr. Dart had decided at some point to become the Worldwide Church of God's leading advocate and apologist for the tithing doctrine. He wrote a sermon on the subject in preparation for what was to be a major 1975 Feast of Tabernacles address he would deliver to the whole United States membership on the subject. A faculty member at Big Sandy to whom Mr. Dart had given an advance draft of the planned sermon allowed me to read his copy.

Crossing the Rubicon: I write a paper challenging the tithing doctrine

After much thinking I came to the sobering realization that the Worldwide Church of God's tithing doctrine was without foundation.

The insight for me was when I thought about the differences between prophets, elders, Levites and priests in Israel. The prophets and elders of old never received tithes in Israel. (The tithe went to the Levites and priests.)

Yet in the New Testament, the evangelists who preached the gospel were in continuity from the *prophets* of old, and the church elders were in continuity from the *elders* of old, none of whom ever had rights to the tithe. The Worldwide Church of God had somehow taken the tithe which went to the Levites and priests of old and—through some exegetical sleight-of-hand—had *redirected it to* the prophets and elders without biblical warrant or precedent. And as part of this sleight-of-hand, the

Tithing

Worldwide Church of God had fallen into the Roman Catholic heresy of denying the priesthood of all believers, which is a basic teaching of the New Testament.

I finally saw this. It took a lot of work and thinking to get to this point. But like many journeys, once one gets to the destination and looks back, it seems so clear in retrospect. From the vantage point of looking back, one wonders why there ever was a problem seeing it.

~ ~ ~

Fully aware of the stakes and risks, but unaware of the cauldron of internal ferment at headquarters already barely suppressed on this issue, I wrote a paper on tithing in hopes of helping the church correct its error ("Tithing," Aug. 17, 1975). I submitted this paper to Mr. Dart in direct response to his defense of tithing. Mr. Dart at this time was giving sermons and Bible Studies at Big Sandy on tithing. He was rehearsing for his forthcoming Feast of Tabernacles address on tithing to the full U.S. membership. He was close to both of the Armstrongs personally and was the leading pro-tithing advocate in the church next to the Armstrongs. What better way to get this information processed and corrected?

Nevertheless, although I had come to see tithing differently, I still remained a loyal and believing member. The way I struggled to explain this to myself and others, tithing was not a fundamental doctrine to the Worldwide Church of God. (On hearing this, one despairing friend at the time just shook his head sadly and told me my naiveté knew no bounds.) That the church was wrong on tithing (as I had now come to see) distressed me deeply. But it did not affect what I regarded as the foundation of the God-family doctrine.

Needless to say, tithing was an extremely volatile topic. Conscious of this, and intent on following proper procedures, I carefully kept quiet on this subject, even to most of my friends. I did not circulate my paper outside of my submission to Mr. Dart.

I kept this paper very much under wraps, neither passing it around nor talking about it, in compliance with administrative wishes for students in cases such as this, particularly on a matter so important to the spiritual health of the church as the extraction of money.

I regret I did not send my paper to Dr. Hoeh as well. Somehow I suspected that my paper on tithing would anger him, no matter how courteously I might attempt a cover letter. (I had developed almost a sixth sense about these things.) Some church officials had a way of ignoring the substance of an argument and focusing on your "bad attitude" instead, if they didn't like what you said. There was no good defense to the charge of "bad attitude." If you tried to argue that you did not have a bad attitude, that would be considered further evidence that you did. I had a weak constitution for that. So out of faintheartedness, I never sent my paper to Dr. Hoeh.

But with great trepidation I summoned up my courage and gave my paper to Mr. Dart, about August 17, 1975.

Mr. Dart's tithing sermon

In the weeks leading up to the Feast I received no reaction back from Mr. Dart about my paper. Several weeks after receipt of my paper Mr. Dart spoke at the 1975 Worldwide Church of God U.S. Feast of Tabernacles sites. He flew to all of the sites in the United States, one after the other, speaking at each one, covering them all in eight days, just like the Armstrongs flew to all of the sites. In this way virtually the entire United States church membership heard a rhetorically powerful pro-tithing argument that was intended to rebut and counteract the influence of Ernest Martin's anti-tithing paper.

Mr. Dart has always been an accomplished speaker. His sermon was powerful and effective in its impact. He argued that the tithe was God's way of financing the Work—the Levites then, God's ministers now. He said: if we can figure out how to give money to God on the holy days, we can figure out how to

Tithing

tithe to God. His sermon was entirely unaffected by my paper. I never received a response of any kind from Mr. Dart to my paper. After the Feast was over and as the weeks continued to roll on, I saw that although my paper had addressed directly and specifically Dart's arguments in his sermon, it had made not the slightest bit of difference. Its impact was the same as if I had never written it.

Defeated

All of the unanswered papers up to this point had taken their toll. I realized with a sinking feeling in the pit of my stomach that I was simply a zero, a nobody, to people like this powerful administrator and the headquarters apparatus he represented. My tithing paper was the last paper I would ever submit to anyone in official position as a student. I was throwing in the towel.

~ ~ ~

The Worldwide Church of God juggernaut rolled on. Sure, there were serious criticisms from within the ranks on this issue. There were intelligent, thoroughly-researched studies from all over the church, at all levels, from ministers in senior positions putting their jobs on the line, to lowly church members typing their hearts out in out-of-the-way places. The papers and research just poured in to headquarters. The problem was that no matter *how* brilliantly such research was expressed, no matter *how* extensive and impeccably it was presented, *absolutely nothing* made *any* difference. In 1977 *Ambassador Report* reported:

> For more than three years the Armstrongs and their evangelists have been deluged with over 40 research papers demonstrating that a Christian is NOT required by the Bible to give God a tenth of his gross (or net) monetary income. Many ministers, top headquarters administrators and department heads have come to understand the Biblical theology of tithing and admit privately that the church has no proof or authority for requiring a tithe on monetary income.

Unfortunately, the WCG leaders have time and again refused to refute the new facts that have come to light, and they attempt to silence those who would spotlight their futile attempts to cover up this important new data.

I wasn't one of the silenced ones. That was because I kept my mouth shut. I don't know what most of these other forty research papers were, but I know my paper was not included in this number, since mine was not circulated anywhere. I followed the Godly procedures of sticking to proper channels. That meant no one saw my paper at all. (Later, I realized that was the whole point of the "proper channels.")

My paper on tithing

Following is a condensed version of the paper on tithing I turned in to Mr. Dart. This paper was concerned solely with the "first tithe." Following this I will turn to the additional tithes, which I also studied during my Big Sandy days.

"Tithing"
Greg Doudna
August 17, 1975

The Worldwide Church of God is one of many churches which practices tithing as its means of supporting its work and its ministry. There seem to be *two false underlying premises* upon which the doctrine of tithing is based.

Is tithing God's means of financing the Work for all time? The most common reasoning on tithing is as follows: Tithing is God's means of financing His Work. In the Old Testament, God gave the tithe to the Levites. In the New Testament, God gives the tithe to the ministry to do the Work. The truth is, whenever God had a Work to be done, it was *never* financed by tithes. The *prophets* did God's work in the Old Testament. The prophets were not supported by tithes. *Elijah* who did the work of God was not financed by tithes. He was helped by a woman who gave to him. *Moses* who led God's people out of Egypt was not financed by tithing. *Enoch* did God's work in the pre-Flood world. *Noah* did the work of God when he

Tithing

built the ark. None of these works of God were financed by tithing. Neither Elijah nor John the Baptist were financed by tithing.

"The tithe went to the Levites in the Old Testament; now it goes to God's ministers in the New Testament." People equate "priest" with a professional minister or clergyman. But this does not come from the New Testament. The New Testament *never* calls its elders or any other office in the church, "priests." Revelation 1:6 says Christ has "made us a kingdom, priests to his God and Father." (The King James Version "kings and priests" is in error.) Every believer is a priest in the sight of God. "You are a chosen race, a royal priesthood, a holy nation, God's own people" (1 Peter 2:9). As priests offered sacrifices, Paul wrote, "I appeal to you therefore, brethren, by the mercies of God, to present your bodies as a living sacrifice, holy and acceptable to God, which is your spiritual worship" (Rom 12:1)—that is, "your priestly function." A priest's duty is to approach God on behalf of humans (Heb 5:1). Paul exhorts that "supplications, prayers, intercessions, and thanksgivings be made for all persons" (1 Tim 2:1). Not once does the New Testament use the word "priest" as a title or designation of an office in the ministry, as a synonym for the ministry as a whole, or other than relating to all true believers.

Every believer is a priest. In John 20:22-23, when Christ was speaking to *all* of the disciples, not just the apostles (compare Luke 24:33), he said to them, "Receive the Holy spirit. If you forgive the sins of any, they are forgiven; if you retain the sins of any, they are retained." This is not saying, as Roman Catholicism asserts, that the forgiveness of *Christians'* sins is dependent on some men (i.e. their priests). It means that every believer is a priest and the *world* will be judged on how it treats true believers in Christ. Examples of this scripture's application are when Stephen asked forgiveness on those who were putting him to death. Every believer prays. The prayers of the saints are like the incense on the altar in the Old Testament (Rev 5:8). Every believer does good works. "Do not neglect to do good and to share what you have, for such sacrifices are pleasing to God" (Heb 13:16).

Tithing had nothing to do with the support of elders in the Old Testament. And there is not a shred of evidence that tithing had anything to do with the support of elders in the New Testament. If *Old* Testament elders were not supported by tithes, what is the authority for saying *New* Testament elders *are*? This is the major cause of confusion and error—equating New Testament elders with Old Testament priests or Levites, when New Testament elders should be equated with Old Testament *elders*.

Tithing

But what about the New Testament principle that ministers should be supported financially by those to whom they are preaching? Christ told the seventy to accept whatever was given to them. Yet when Christ taught this, in the case of the twelve and the seventy, that was done while people were still tithing to the Levitical priesthood. One cannot say Christ's instructions were a replacement for the tithing system to support the Levitical priesthood. Christ's instructions were for freewill offerings *other than* the tithe.

The tithe always went to Christ. Abraham tithed to Melchizedek (Christ). Jacob gave tithes to the Angel of the Lord. According to Malachi, failure to tithe to the Levites was robbing Christ. Here is how one gives to Christ today. This is the *only* New Testament instruction on *how* to give to Christ. "For I was hungry and you gave me food, I was thirsty and you gave me drink, I was a stranger and you welcomed me. I was naked and you clothed me, I was sick and you visited me, I was in prison and you came to me ... Truly, I say to you, as you did it to one of the least of these my brethren, you did it to me" (Matt 25:35-40).

Did the early Christian church tithe to the ministry? The prophets and elders in the Old Testament did not receive tithes. Why then would the New Testament church, which was based on the Old Testament, consider *their* apostles, prophets, and elders as the rightful recipients of tithes? Those who study tithing closely, and the recent ministerial study paper on tithing contains several plain admissions to this effect, agree that the early Christians did not tithe to the ministry before 70 AD. The doctrine on tithing then becomes based on the extremely tenuous assumption that after the destruction of the temple (70 AD) the Christians *transferred* the tithe from the Levites to their own apostles and elders. But is there any *evidence* for this? Where? Even now, with a complete booklet published representing church teaching on the subject of tithing, there seems to be no definitive or universal or acceptable answer to the question of *when* the change in tithing to New Testament apostles and elders took place. If it was clearly understood that all believers are priests, would anyone get tithing out of the Bible as the means of support for New Testament apostles and elders?

Conclusion. The tithe in the Old Testament was given to those who had no inheritance. It was to be shared with the poor, the widows, and the orphaned. The prophets repeatedly rebuked the people for forsaking the poor and those who could not help themselves. Is ten percent the basic minimum each of us should give to poor and destitute persons in the name of Christ? "The poor you have with you always." Is this the lifetime, everyday, continuous duty of the believer? And is support for the preaching of the gospel, support for the work, financed by special offerings apart from this—called for as the need arises, to get a specific job done at a specific time? The principle in the system as regards God's Work seems to be to push mightily to get this done, then push mightily to get that done, then go into something else, which may be distinguished from the continuous lifetime duty of tithing for the poor and our brethren.

The Worldwide Church of God multiple tithing system:
its biblical basis examined

The Worldwide Church of God multiple tithing system came about in this way. Tithing is commanded in the law of Moses in the Pentateuch. In the books of Leviticus (27:30-33) and Numbers (18:21-24), "the tithe" is said to be used one way—given to the Levites. But in Deuteronomy (14:22-26), "the tithe" seems to be used in another way—taken to Jerusalem and eaten there. Scholars say this shows development in how the tithe was used or competing traditions as different portions of the Bible were written and collected. But since it was believed impossible for the Bible to contradict itself, the Worldwide Church of God said these must be two tithes. Then the Deuteronomy tithe description says in the third year the tithe was to be given to the destitute at home rather than taken to Jerusalem (14:28-29). This was interpreted to mean a third tithe.

It is true the Worldwide Church of God did not invent the multiple tithing idea. This multiple-tithe interpretation has a history in Jewish rabbinical sources, in the book of Tobit of the Apocrypha, and Josephus.[212] But as I studied the matter toward the end of my time at Big Sandy, I came to believe that, regardless of what the later traditions said, it all really was the same tithe. I began an entry in one of my notebooks of the time: "Why does Numbers mention what we call first tithe, and ignore

---

[212] At the time of Jesus all contemporary Jewish sources had multiple tithes. Debate centered around whether there were two tithes or three, and the rules by which each tithe was to be used.

the second, while Deuteronomy mentions the second and third, but ignores the first tithe?" Since Deuteronomy is supposed to be a *restatement* of the entire law (*deuteronomos* means "second law"), I reasoned that the tithe in Deuteronomy must be the same tithe referred to elsewhere and earlier in the Pentateuch. The problem was in reconciling how it was used (for I also operated under the belief that the Bible would not contradict itself).

I closely examined the uses of the Numbers and Deuteronomy tithes and found some common assumptions were incorrect. Numbers 18:21-24 says the tithe was given to the Levites. Deuteronomy 14:22-27 *also* says the Levites have no inheritance so don't forsake them. It seemed to me that when Deuteronomy said "the tithe" it was speaking of the same tithe as Numbers.

To my surprise I discovered that there was no explicit statement that the Deuteronomy tithe—the so-called "second tithe"—was to be used for the festivals. It was no more a "festival tithe" than the "first" tithe! I came to see there was no difference between *when* the Numbers ("first") and Deuteronomy ("second") tithes were paid or used. In the one case (Numbers), the Israelite took the tithe to God's place and gave it to the Levites. In the second case (Deuteronomy), the Israelite took the tithe to God's place and ate it there, along with the widow, fatherless, and Levite.

Since the festivals were based around the harvest seasons, and since the festivals were when one went to God's place (Jerusalem), the festivals would be the time when the Israelites would bring the tithe/tithes to Jerusalem. I reasoned: an Israelite would bring the tithe of Numbers to Jerusalem at the festivals, and the tithe of Deuteronomy to Jerusalem at the festivals. I concluded it was the same tithe!

The third year, however, was different. Still talking of the same tithe, Deuteronomy says eat and share the tithe of that year within your gates—at home. The Israelite would not take it to Jerusalem as in other years. I read this as the third year of the seven-year land-sabbath cycle. The sabbatical year was the "seventh year." Here, it is speaking of the "third year." The tithe

Tithing

was to be brought to Jerusalem every year, except for the third year of the seven-year cycle, which was an exception. That year, the tithe was kept at home and the Israelite took a vow that he had given it to the poor and Levites in his own town. In other words, it was the same year for all Israel, midway in every sabbatical year cycle. It was not one year out of three, but one year out of seven.[213] And, it was a different use of the same tithe.

Why was the third year of the land-sabbath cycle different? I wondered if this might have been the year the poor would need it most, as an interim between having debts cancelled. Also, note that personal distribution of the third year's tithe at home did not mean not going to the feasts that year. It meant only that the tenth of that year's harvest and value of livestock was not brought to Jerusalem as in other years. Instead, it was distributed at home that year.

The basic problem seemed to be this: Leviticus and Numbers (as well as Nehemiah 13:10-13 and Malachi 3:8-10) seem to say the tithe was to be given to the Levites one hundred percent to use as they saw fit. But Deuteronomy seems to say the Israelite ate it himself *and* shared it with the Levites. But this did not mean they were two tithes, as I reconstructed it. For Deuteronomy 12:6-12 uses the same language of going to "the place which the Lord your God will choose … and there you shall eat … and you shall rejoice, you and your households …" for *every* form of offering—burnt offerings, the tithe, heave offerings, vows, freewill offerings, firstlings. The Israelite was to bring all of these to God's place and eat them there (except in the third year), rejoicing with his family and with the Levites who had no inheritance. Does this mean there was a "second *burnt*

---

[213] It is true the rabbis said "the third year" meant every third and sixth year out of seven. But I wasn't reading the Talmud, I was reading the Bible. "The third year" seemed to me to be one specific year out of seven, based on a comparison of Deut 14:28, "at the end of every three years," with, just two verses later, 15:1, "at the end of every seven years." I saw an analogy between enumerated years in the seven-year cycle of sabbatical years, and the way Quakers named the days of the week "Third Day," "Seventh Day," and so on.

offering," a "second *heave offering,"* a "second *freewill offering,"* and a "second *firstlings*"—by the *same* logic used to supposedly prove a "second *tithe*"?

It became apparent to me that both Numbers and Deuteronomy were describing the same use of the same tithe. The tithe was taken to Jerusalem. After everyone celebrated and ate of it while at the festival, the remainder would be left with the Levites when the Israelites went home. This was biblically considered "giving it to the Levites." The difficulty seemed to be in understanding how it could be spoken of as "given to God" when some of it was eaten by the Israelite personally. The answer was: in the same way the Israelites offered *sacrifices* to God and then ate of them personally—they ate what remained, that is, after giving the priests the best portions.

It is unlikely that an Israelite family could consume a whole tenth of a harvest in eight days, in any case. How much can a family eat in eight days? Unlike Worldwide Church of God practice in which second tithe was spent on travel *to* festival sites, Deuteronomy explicitly *forbade* spending the tithe *on the way* to God's place. The command was to bring the tithe *to God's place* and any spending of it *before* arrival would have been improper. Upon arrival in Jerusalem, the tithe was not then spent on accommodations—rather, the pilgrims stayed in tents and makeshift dwellings at nearly no cost. But they were allowed to eat of the tithe while at the festival, just as an ox was allowed to eat of the field it was treading.

Again, how much of a harvest tithe could a family personally eat in several days? A family bringing the harvest tithe could eat, be filled, and celebrate, just like the oxen could eat of the field it trod. The Levites and priests would still have almost the entirety of the tithe left when the feast was over. It was all one tithe, not a separate second tithe which couldn't possibly be eaten in eight days, I concluded. There was no need to suppose that Deuteronomy, which repeats the law, inexplicably omitted the "first tithe" of the previous law, while simultaneously inventing a *new*

Tithing

"second tithe" of which the previous law knows nothing. Yet this was the basis for the multiple tithing doctrine.

I never wrote up or submitted this analysis of all three tithes being the same tithe, which is taken almost directly from one of my notebooks of March 1975.

Further comment

The discerning reader may note that, unlike other studies that disagreed with the doctrine of tithing of the Worldwide Church of God, my paper (of Aug. 17, 1975) did not, strictly speaking, argue that tithing does not apply to today. Where my paper differed was in *where* the tithe went, *how* one "gives to Christ." My paper ended up essentially in a "social gospel" position, i.e. the shocking idea that Jesus cared about feeding and clothing the poor of this world in the material sense. My paper ended with the suggestion that tithing was for those worse off—for those unable to care for themselves.

Of course I could have gone further. In many western countries taxes fund welfare systems which fulfill the principle of tithing to help the poor. Even if this were not so there are other issues. Millions of Americans and in other countries are working poor, struggling to pay rent and buy food, living paycheck to paycheck. Other millions of Americans, when hit with unexpected medical expenses or a slight downturn in the economy, use credit cards to stay afloat. Where, exactly, is the "increase" for these people, who may be deeply in debt? Millions more Americans are caring for aged family members who might otherwise be indigent, unable to provide for themselves. Are they already tithing without knowing it? But however tithing for the poor might be understood today, I saw the core principle as being about care for those who have fallen through the cracks of society, so to speak—the widows, orphans, and poor, in the words of the ancients, or their modern equivalents. For if we as a society are heartless to those who *but for the grace of God could be us*, what kind of humans are we?

And the Sabbath too

As I thought further about it, I continued to develop possible meaning not only in the tithe but also the Sabbath. I began to explore in my notebooks the idea that maybe the sabbath was not only for us to *receive* rest. Maybe it was also for Christians to *give rest to the world*. "Rest," I came to think, was meant in the fuller sense of rest from sickness, oppression, hunger, and thirst of body as well as spirit. This was the vision I started to see:

> "Is not this the fast that I choose: to loose the bonds of wickedness, to undo the thongs of the yoke, to let the oppressed go free, and to break every yoke? Is it not to share your bread with the hungry, and bring the homeless poor into your house; when you see the naked, to cover him, and not to hide yourself from your own flesh?" (Isa 58:6-7). The Sabbath, both weekly Sabbath and sabbatical year, frees people from the bondage of economic systems. As Jesus went to the people, so we today ought to go to the people. Luke 4:18 is our commission. The Fourth Commandment is our commission. "The Sabbath is made for man." The Sabbath is a foretaste of the Kingdom of God." (From my journal, Sept 7, 1975.)

I never submitted papers on these reflections to anyone. As I wrote continuing insights in my notebooks, I didn't know what to do with them. It was beginning to dawn on me that submitting things to headquarters, going up the line through proper channels, was not proving effective. I was beginning to realize it was a waste of postage.

CHAPTER 21

BIG SANDY SCHOOL DAYS: 1975

In August 1975 I reentered Ambassador College at Big Sandy as a full-time student and moved back on campus. The semester flew by quickly. It was a time of changes.

It was good to be back on campus as a full-time student again, with old friends and new ones. Faculty and student friends warmly welcomed me back. There were larger numbers of incoming freshmen this year, many on a newly-begun two-year (instead of four-year) Associates of Arts program. As always, a good number of the incoming students had previous college experience. There was a lot of energy among the now-expanded student body.

A lot happened that fall 1975 semester at Big Sandy, and I can only tell a few highlights. Here is one. One day soon after the semester had started a recent Ambassador College, Pasadena, graduate named Mike Eash came through Big Sandy as part of another trip, in order to look me up. He had heard about me from my friend Russ Gmirkin in Pasadena.

Clean-cut, idealistic Eash had come to Ambassador College, Pasadena, from Iowa, from Mennonite farming upbringing. He had graduated in 1975 and was running a successful window cleaning business in Pasadena. Before he had gone to Ambassador he had been trained by and worked for the same Russ Rigdon of Cedar Rapids, Iowa, who had trained me.

I was in the dining hall eating lunch with other students one day when Eash found me. His first words to me were that we had two Russ's in common: Rigdon, and Gmirkin.

Big Sandy School Days: 1975

Eash had read novels by Ayn Rand and recommended them to me. The fact that Ayn Rand was militantly atheist didn't bother Eash. Eash was like me in that way: he could harmonize things. He had the ideas of Ayn Rand harmonized with the plan of God as we understood it.

Eash also got me to appreciate a poem of Walt Whitman: "Passage to India." This poem, "Passage to India," is a soaring, optimistic 19th century vision of a multicultural America building a new nation and a free world, and this vision of America is seen by Whitman as a metaphor for transcendence. The poem *just sings* (its hard to describe). It was how Eash himself viewed the world, too—all the idealism and romanticism of the new American experiment of a former era.

> O my brave soul!
> O farther, farther sail!
> O daring joy, but safe! Are they not all the seas of God?
> O farther, farther, farther sail!

And isn't that what Ambassador College was filled with?—young people with such ideals. Amazingly, Eash still had his idealism intact after graduating from Ambassador College, Pasadena. (Having experienced A.C. Pasadena myself, I can assure you that is no minor accomplishment.)

Eash flew back to Big Sandy later that semester for a return visit for a few days. Russ Gmirkin also came out from Pasadena to Big Sandy for a visit that semester, then took off for Knoxville, Tennessee for a few weeks, then returned to Big Sandy. Another from this group in Pasadena, Dan Pavlik, also came through to visit me. There was a lot of traffic through the Big Sandy campus on my account that semester. My poor roommate in Booth City, Rex Sexton, sometimes didn't know what to make of it. Every time he turned around, it seemed, there was another sleeping bag on the floor. Other students joined in with my visitors and me to talk about exciting ideas, and the energy and optimism were electric.

Big Sandy School Days: 1975

Meanwhile, concerning my papers ...

Although it was exhilarating, as the semester drew on I became restless. A factor was the non-responses to my papers. Of course there was one faculty member at Big Sandy who did show significant interest in my papers, and that was Lynn Torrance (registrar and director of admissions). But although he was an administrator at Big Sandy, he was no minister, and as a non-minister he had no status in the area of doctrine. Torrance, like another old-timer non-minister, Ken Herrmann (one of Herbert Armstrong's earliest students), felt comfortable enough with me to comment to me privately about the distasteful caste system of ministers versus non-ministers. It endeared me to Torrance when he described once, in his crusty way, the deference that some ministers expected toward their office and position. He pretended he was addressing one of them: "Oh Most High Mister Pompous Ass," and the way he said it had cracked me up laughing. This was Torrance's true feelings toward ministerial arrogance (except he was fiercely loyal to the two Armstrongs, sort of like Britons I have met in pubs who were irreverent toward authority but fiercely loyal to the queen, at the same time).

At some point midway through this fall semester of 1975, however, Torrance "dropped" me. He didn't say so; he just did it. I just noticed that he was busy, wasn't talking to me (although he would smile and say hello), and had basically cut me off. When I asked him if something was wrong he denied anything had changed. And yet it had changed. And that was the end of the talks with Torrance, and his interest in me or my papers.

I don't know what happened. Perhaps something about my research had crossed a certain line in his mind and he got spooked. Or maybe someone had said something to him. Who knows. I never knew, and it quickly became clear that Torrance wasn't going to level with me. The reason he wouldn't talk openly about this change I chalk up to bureaucratic survival skills. (Torrance was a long-time survivor.)

Big Sandy School Days: 1975

Torrance had done too many genuine kindnesses for me to really be angry with him. He didn't do anything against me. He just cooled without explanation, and I didn't understand it. It was disconcerting.

Friendships inside a group like this can be a transitory thing. Torrance was good to me for a while, and then as mysteriously as can be it vanished.

Anti-intellectualism and "Animal Farm"

> "If you feel you won't do anything or believe anything unless its proven in your own mind you've made your mind your god."
> -- Dean Blackwell, April 19, 1975, men's 3rd year speech class, from my class notes

On the one hand there were young faculty at Big Sandy with degrees from outside universities, usually dedicated church members, encouraging intellectual curiosity and learning. On the other hand there were "old school" faculty, often whose only educational credentials were from Ambassador College itself, who tended to be suspicious of "scholars" and "intellectuals." Their idea of intellectual growth was to fear one's own mind and follow the leading of God's ministers. It was an uneasy mix, with a lot of clashing at the edges between these two basic schools of thought.

Everyone who came into the church from the outside world, i.e. "first-generation" converts, had been reached with a public message that challenged people to "prove things out of your own Bible for yourself." And people who grew up with childhood messages about believing the Bible and had never really questioned what they had been raised with, would be grabbed by this message. They might react at first with disbelief or anger. But then they would look up something from the *World Tomorrow* broadcast or *Plain Truth* magazine, and to their amazement it would check out. They would write in for more literature, and at some point get started on the Bible

Big Sandy School Days: 1975

Correspondence Course which was a sort of programmed learning. The basic appeal was a pseudo-rationalism, in which people were urged to prove things *for themselves*. In this way people would be shaken from traditional beliefs, to see things in a new way.

But after people came into the church, including at Ambassador College, there was supposed to be a shift. Now, you were supposed to *follow the ministers*.

~ ~ ~

In some ways it was like something out of *Animal Farm*. That is the title of George Orwell's classic fictional tale of a revolt of barnyard animals against the rule of cruel farmers. In this story, the animals' revolution starts out with high hopes. The different kinds of animals all cooperate to chase the evil farmers away. The big animals help the little animals and everyone has a part. The farm is theirs and they are now free. The animals all rally around a set of rules they post which will guarantee their freedom from being oppressed again. These rules (from the animals' point of view) include things like "all animals are equal," "four legs good, two legs bad," and so on.

But alas, the revolution, founded in idealism, goes awry. Among the animals there are some evil pigs who use their intelligence to make themselves into a non-working elite living off the work of the other animals, with themselves in authority. These ruling pigs lie and cheat and exploit the other animals, becoming as corrupt and as oppressive as the human farmers were.

The story tells how these clever pigs make each element of their growing power sound logical to the hardworking, but less-quickwitted, other animals. Each of the idealistic slogans of the animals' revolution is turned into its opposite meaning, as the corrupt ruling pigs reinterpret the words. The rule "All animals are equal" has words added to it, *"but some animals are more equal than others."* The rule, "Four legs good, two legs bad" becomes, when chanted, *"four legs good, two legs ba-a-ader ... two legs be-e-etter!"* And so on. The ruling pigs at the end stand on their hind legs and carouse with the farmers. In a climactic final scene drunken farmers and drunken pigs are indistinguishable.

Similarly the very scriptures quoted to the outside world by the Worldwide Church of God to encourage people to question what they had always been taught and to prove things for oneself, were transformed to mean "follow the ministers" and "don't trust your own mind," after one crossed the threshold into the group.

For example, one scripture was Acts 17:11-12, in which the people of Berea are said to have been "more noble than those in Thessalonica, in that they received the word with all readiness of mind, and searched the scriptures daily, whether those things were so. Therefore many of them believed ..."

To the *public*, this was cited as a worthy example of studying for oneself, not taking other people's word on things. But to *members*, this was given a different spin. I remember sermons explaining that the noble Bereans did not try to prove things *weren't* so (like some dissidents were doing). Rather, the Bereans studied to prove the things being taught *were* so. And the lesson was: this should be the members' attitude, to study to prove the things being taught *are* so.

A frequent motif in sermonettes and sermons was "lean not to your *own* understanding" (Prov 3:5). And another favorite: "In those days there was no king in Israel, and every man did that which was right in his *own* eyes" (Judges 21:25). (Are you attempting to do what is right in your *own* eyes—instead of God's?)

Dean Blackwell, the amiable, party-line old-time conservative minister who had baptized me, would speak with scorn in sermons of "independent" Christians who believed in, as he put it, "studying their own Bible, just me, myself, and I, under my own apple tree." This kind of "independent" Christian (scornfully expressed) was associated, it would be explained, with an

Big Sandy School Days: 1975

attitude of (pause, with emphasis) "you can't tell *me* what to do." That kind of attitude came from human *self*-will, not the Spirit of God. The Spirit of God was yielded and obedient and eager to see things from *God*'s point of view. *That* was the way to peace and happiness. God's way was not that of the "*independent* Christian." Going one's own way independent of the church was disrespectful to our spiritual mother. Rebellion was as the sin of witchcraft (1 Sam 15:23). Over and over and over, these messages were repeated.

You say these kinds of things enough, and get members to repeat them in their own prayers, and it shapes their views on life. This is how programming works. The basic message was to distrust one's own mental processes, or rather shape them in the right directions.

Not every minister talked like this. But the "old school" type of ministers would.

On the hazards of thinking for oneself

Personal Bible study was encouraged, but it was not supposed to result in conclusions different from church doctrines. If one did arrive at conclusions at variance with church teaching there could be big problems. For starters, one was forbidden to speak a word of such findings to another church member (including one's closest friends), under threat of being disfellowshipped, marked, and ostracized, if it was reported. Speak against what were considered key doctrines (such as tithing, to name one at random) and you could be executed. Disappeared. Taken out back and shot. (Metaphorically speaking.) Obviously this was not enforced 100 percent, since people did talk to one another. Ministers made judgments on when to make an issue of members' talking to one another. But this power of the ministers was always in the background of any member-to-member or member-to-minister conversation, even in cases where the minister allowed some latitude.

Big Sandy School Days: 1975

The recommended course for members, it was explained, was to let go of the idea that *everything* had to be proven. Those "in the world" needed to prove enough to themselves to establish that this was God's True Church. That could take time. The ministers would not rush this in a person. But at some point if the person was truly ready to make the commitment, to yield their heart and spirit over to *God* (i.e. the doctrines and authority of the church and its ministry), then they would be invited to attend church services, and after a reasonable interval, counseled and baptized as a member.

The idea being: this was a one time process. Once the key point about where God's Church was established and settled, then barring extremely unusual circumstances (the thinking went), there was no good purpose served by reopening or revisiting such basic questions again. You were supposed to take the things you could prove on your own, along with the basic realization that this was God's church, and allow *God*, through his ministers, to lead you in the remaining areas where, due to being new in the faith, maybe you didn't personally yet understand.

You weren't supposed to question the ministers or church teachings. You weren't supposed to trust your own mind.

I found such views toxic. The only way I could deal with such attitudes was to try to ignore them. This was possible, since not everyone in the early and mid-1970s at Big Sandy was like that. This was a "liberal" period (relatively speaking) when it was possible for independent thinkers to exist in the church and college without being forced completely underground. This was before the aged Herbert Armstrong took back personal control in the late 1970s with a vengeance, carrying out bloody purges against "intellectualism" and putting the Worldwide Church of God through its own Cultural Revolution. It was like the old Soviet Union with its alternating periods of repression and liberalism within the ruling Communist Party, depending on which faction had the upper hand. There was the monstrously brutal Stalin, followed by the thaw of the more liberal

Big Sandy School Days: 1975

Khrushchev era, under whom Russian writers and dissidents could breathe a little, and some recent history could begin to be written and discussed truthfully. But then Khrushchev was ousted (for being too liberal), the air became chillier, and there was a swing back in the other direction: this was the long, stale, oppressive Brezhnev era.

Ambassador College, Big Sandy in the early and mid-1970s was liberal compared to what came before and after. Nevertheless, there was always the sense of being a little squeezed. You step out of line very much, and it could become severe compression, real fast.

Certain Worldwide Church of God ministers had identified what one friend from those days called a "domino theory of new ideas." If you question one thing, then you'll question another, and then another. Before you know it you'll be questioning *everything* and could end up *right out of the church*. To prevent this horrible scenario from becoming reality, the recommended solution was to nip the *first* question in the bud.

A friendly warning

A fellow student who had transferred to Big Sandy from Bricket Wood (after Bricket Wood closed in 1974) out of the blue one day, during that fall semester of 1975, suggested he and I take a walk. As we walked it became clear he had a message for me. He wanted to talk to me about all the ideas I was coming up with. He said that was *good,* but it could be *dangerous*. He cited Dr. Hoeh, who he was sure had to be *extra careful* with his research that it did not lead him astray. Just as Dr. Hoeh no doubt had to *pray extra hard* and be *extra careful* because of the increased risk of going astray that his studies meant for him—*I* (who maybe did not have the experience of Dr. Hoeh, he gently suggested) should be on guard *even more*.

Puzzled, I asked if he saw something wrong in anything I was studying or had talked about. "Oh no," he said, it was simply that I should be *careful*. Was there anything specific he had in mind?,

I asked. No, nothing specific, he replied. Did he see me going in a wrong direction with anything? "Oh no," he said. It was just as a friend he thought my studying could have *the potential* to cause problems. (Except he wasn't exactly a close friend; I knew him, but we weren't close.) There were no specifics. It was simply a general warning: *be careful*. It was *good* that I was studying things, but *beware*.

I didn't know quite how to respond to this, since there was absolutely nothing tangible, nothing specific. He was charming and friendly throughout, as he delivered what was obviously a prepared message. Not knowing what else to say, when we ended our walk I thanked him for his encouragement to me to continue my studies. This was responding to his words at face value, since that is what he said. But it was clear that that was not quite the reaction he was looking for.

Had he spoken on his own, or was he acting as a spokesman for some larger concerns about me (and by whom)? It was the same question I had when I was accosted by Richard Ames on the sidewalk a year earlier and told not to discuss my Ephraim/United States idea any further (chapter 6). Had Ames acted on his own, or was Ames carrying out something cleared from higher up? One could go crazy speculating on things like this. In this case, my fellow student told me he was speaking on his own and I had no actual indication otherwise, so I decided to believe him and forget it.

But this was how it was. *Be careful*. Of what? *Oh nothing specific. Just be careful*.

It is how institutions and the human carriers of institutional mindsets express discomfort with people and ideas who aren't quite fitting in. It's an early warning sign. The wise learn to back off, take the subtle cues, get in line. The unwise, or the socially inept, miss these signals and keep blundering forward. You blunder enough in settings like this, and sooner or later you run into a mailed fist.

Big Sandy School Days: 1975

Reading about Soviet dissidents

At some point in here I read a volume of what Russian dissidents called *samizdat*, or covertly circulated underground essays, titled *From Under the Rubble*, which had an impact on me. From these impassioned essays I gained a glimpse of what it was like to exist in a society in which there is a single ruling party and top-down government. I couldn't avoid seeing parallels with the Worldwide Church of God (except of course the Worldwide Church of God thankfully never had civil or police powers).

The Soviet Union had its *Pravda*. The Worldwide Church of God had its *Worldwide News*. (And the U.S. had its *Time* magazine, it might also be added, though that is another topic.)

I remember in particular one essay discussing how dissidents in the Soviet Union would learn to whom they could talk, and how they could talk quite freely among themselves. As long as they did not speak the wrong things to the wrong persons, they could function that way indefinitely in such a society. *They just couldn't be public about it*. Wasn't that how it was in the Worldwide Church of God? And I started thinking about the way one-party regimes outlaw opposition parties. Similarly, at Ambassador College, Big Sandy, any independent student publication or organization was strictly forbidden. (That was explicit and in writing.) In the Worldwide Church of God at large, any independent members' organization was inconceivable.

And in the wonderful World Tomorrow, as envisioned in church sermons and literature, there would be only one all-seeing ruling Party—members of the True Church of this age led by Christ, along with resurrected patriarchs, ruling the whole world with central planning. No opposition parties and no dissent (and for sure no women's lib), everyone doing their assigned job cheerfully. So long as the people living in this millennium *obeyed,* they would be deliriously happy. But any resistance would be swiftly crushed. (And Jesus Christ, the power of the universe, when he comes back to rule earth, it hardly needs to be added, believes in *capital punishment*. Gerald Waterhouse and other Worldwide Church of God evangelists made that point very clear.)

Roderick Meredith would talk about how God was soon going to *spank* the people of the world in *righteous anger* (for the world's good of course). Garner Ted Armstrong would paint word pictures about *rebellious* peoples shaking their *puny fists* defiantly in God's *face*, and how these *rebellious* people would either bow before Christ willingly or God would *break* those people's knees and *force* them to bow before Jesus Christ. Herbert Armstrong would talk about people being forced to be happy.

(You can only imagine how this kind of language played out in the raising of children. I won't go into it here, but some of the stories are almost unbelievably sad.)

It was an envisioned future in which the lunatics (the ministers and members who believed this interpretation of the Bible) would be in charge of the asylum. I decided that these visions of the future were caricatures and distorted. But the cognitive dissonance was increasing.

Transfer to Pasadena

In January 1976 I bailed. I transferred to the main campus at Pasadena, California: headquarters itself.

The total amount of time from when I first thought of transferring to Pasadena, wrote out lists of pros and cons on paper, thought hard for a few hours, decided to do it, packed and loaded, took care of practical matters, said goodbyes to friends, and pulled my car out on Highway 80 headed to California, was about 24 hours. That is how fast the idea developed in my mind and was implemented. Arriving in Pasadena during winter break, I talked to the admissions and housing people and received approval to be a transfer student to Pasadena, with space in a dorm on campus.

Despite the speed with which I did this, it was not because there was any suggestion from anyone at Big Sandy that I

Big Sandy School Days: 1975

transfer, nor was I running from anything. There were two main factors which made the move seem like a good idea. One was that the friends with whom I could best talk were at Pasadena. Another was that employment prospects in the Los Angeles area seemed more promising than in the Big Sandy area as I looked ahead to life post-AC.

So I said goodby to Big Sandy, where I had so many good memories. There were tears in my eyes as I drove out and away from the familiar east Texas sights and sounds and smells that would never be home to me again. At the same time I felt excitement in wondering what would be ahead in Pasadena.

It was like jumping from the frying pan, one might say, right into the fire.

PART THREE

DENOUEMENT

CHAPTER 22

AMBASSADOR COLLEGE, PASADENA: 1976

Pasadena, located in the Los Angeles area, was a different atmosphere from Big Sandy. In contrast to Big Sandy's naive, refreshing, rural atmosphere with its east Texas sunsets, open spaces, and pine woods, Pasadena was crowded and smoggy.

The Ambassador College campus was located near Pasadena's Orange Grove Boulevard. It was on the route of the annual Rose Bowl Parade. Herbert Armstrong had built the campus by purchasing millionaires' mansions in the early days, turning them into student residences and classroom buildings. Over the years more buildings were built. The headquarters Ambassador College definitely was not operating out of temporary, portable classroom buildings as was the branch at Big Sandy. Ambassador College, Pasadena, was on its way to becoming a respectable small college with modern facilities and a quality faculty. The college almost certainly would have become accredited within a couple of years after I was there if Herbert Armstrong had not axed that idea just as it seemed about to happen. Herbert Armstrong felt accreditation involved just too much compromise with the world. One of the things the accreditation committee required, for example, besides a bigger library and an upgrading of faculty credentials, was an elected student government. At Ambassador College, student representatives were always *appointed* by the administration (God's way), never elected by the students themselves (which was the way of man's *self*-government). This was a major sticking point.

~ ~ ~

I was at headquarters. Here was the brand-new Ambassador Auditorium, one of the most beautiful buildings in southern California, and host to a series of star-studded concerts and performances. Next to the Auditorium was the four-story Administration Building, the nerve center of the Work. Here the various officials and department heads had their offices and secretaries in various levels of status depending on which floor they were situated. The fourth floor, where Herbert Armstrong had his office, was the highest status. The various levels of officialdom continued in descending positions in the divine pecking order down to the first floor, the level where the members walked in and out the door.

Just as at Big Sandy, the grounds were immaculate. (The Pasadena campus won many awards for its landscaping.) Beautiful gardens graced the lawns, and streams cascaded between the mansions. If it wasn't for the smog so thick you coughed from just breathing on some days, it would be about perfect. There were mountains nearby. Unfortunately, the mountains often couldn't be seen because of the smog. I definitely didn't like what was in the air at Pasadena.

Herbert Armstrong's sermons

One of the things I had looked forward to when I came out to Pasadena was being able to hear Herbert Armstrong in person. Gradually I learned that Herbert Armstrong had one basic sermon. He would give this one sermon, with variations, every time he spoke. Every year or so he would develop a new sermon which he would then give, with variations, every time he spoke. This was not the same sermon given to different congregations. He gave the same sermon time after time to the same audiences.

Ambassador College, Pasadena: 1976

Most members of goodwill learned to make allowances for the degree of repetition in our aged pastor general's sermons. After all, he was in his mid-eighties.

One of Herbert Armstrong's favorite passages was Genesis 1:1-2. He would say, as if it was new to everyone in the congregation, "Now, brethren, let's turn to Genesis one, verse one." Everyone would open their Bibles and hunt up Genesis one, verse one. Herbert Armstrong would read the verse, then emphasize, "And the earth *became* without form and void." He would explain (for the thousandth time) that the Hebrew word for "was" could be translated "became," meaning God's perfect creation had been marred by Satan's rebellion.

Satan was one of Herbert Armstrong's favorite topics. Satan's rebellion was the ancient archetype of current malcontents challenging Herbert Armstrong's authority. Hardly a sermon went by without Herbert Armstrong referring to Satan's attacks on the Work, by which he meant the attacks of dissidents. People rebelling against Herbert Armstrong's authority were, of course, rebelling against the government of God. (The government of God on earth was headed by Herbert Armstrong, "under Christ." Herbert Armstrong did not ask for this honor. He humbly accepted it when it became evident.)

In Herbert Armstrong's world, it was obvious that the dissidents were Korahs rebelling against the authority of Moses. (They were not Gideons overthrowing tyrants.) Those who rebelliously questioned Herbert Armstrong's luxurious lifestyle were just like Satan becoming envious toward the luxury of heaven. (They were not expressing the words of James 5:1, "you rich, weep and howl ...") And on it went. Everything in the Bible about Satan was applied by Herbert Armstrong to his enemies. It was all completely clear in the mind of Herbert W. Armstrong. Others who hold identical ideas have found themselves institutionalized. Herbert Armstrong had 100,000 people believing and extolling him.

Herbert Armstrong could certainly communicate with an audience where he stood on matters.

Ambassador College, Pasadena: 1976

Brethren, *whom has God chosen??!* He chose me! Over forty years ago He *chose* me for this great work. I didn't *want* to be chosen. But, brethren, He *chose* me! And he called you to hold up my hands! Brethren, *are you behind me?*

Brethren, these trips are carrying the true gospel to the whole world for a witness for the first time in over nineteen hundred years! Let me tell you, these trips are no joyride! But some of you *criticize*. Some of you want me *out*. Well, I'm not going out.

And as I was saying to my good friend the other day, uh—oh, what's his name? I know it as well as my own—uh ... *BUNSEI SATO!!*

And I was greeted in Japan by eight members of the Japanese Diet. That's like our Congress, you know. They call themselves my Japanese "sons."

(Herbert Armstrong would always beam when talking about his Japanese "sons.")

And so on. Herbert Armstrong's voice, mannerisms, and favorite sayings lent themselves to imitation. I could do an almost perfect Herbert Armstrong-sounding "Greetings, brethren!" followed by sound bites in his voice, such as Herbert's complaint once about being in a foreign hotel room that had "one of these air conditioner *CONTRAPTIONS* in the window" that was noisy and made a draft.

Culture shock: an innocent in Babylon, or,
how I came to headquarters and lost my faith

I experienced a culture shock at Pasadena. In contrast to the down-to-earth, uncomplicated directness which I remembered at Big Sandy, the atmosphere at Pasadena was jaded. (At least it seemed so to me.) There was a gap between the impression of headquarters held by church members in outlying areas and the reality. Here at headquarters, in the drive to upgrade Ambassador College's standing in the eyes of the accreditation committee and

Ambassador College, Pasadena: 1976

the southern California arts patrons, image reigned supreme. But underneath the glossy exterior, there were more scandals, coups, and counter-coups among leaders jockeying for position and vying for control than could be imagined. Phones were tapped. (It was a standard joke among students to pick up the saltshakers in mock inspection for electronic listening devices when sitting down to eat lunch.) Money flowed lavishly in some areas (Herbert Armstrong's traveling entourage, for example), while long-time, hard-working, faithful employees in other areas were let go in middle age to fend for themselves, because of budget cuts. (And of course the brethren out in the hinterlands were always urged to sacrifice further because of the great need.) If a church organization could be likened to a person, Worldwide Church of God headquarters was like a spoiled brat become a teenage adolescent with too much money to flash and a penchant for juvenile delinquency.

Meanwhile, I was changing. It had taken a while, but it was finally beginning to dawn on me that the church was not *interested* in growing in spiritual truth. Rather, the church was more interested in business management growth charts and image to the world. Wealth and bureaucracy had triumphed.

There were also a raft of continuing revelations coming out about misuses of funds, hypocrisy of top ministers, and sordid spy-novel-type chicanery. The Edenic paradise which Ambassador College had seemed in its brochures and which, like a dream too good to be true, had beckoned ahead as I saved money from my junior high and high school jobs ... had changed, or was it I? The church wasn't a divine organization at all, contrary to what it claimed. It was an institution built on money and broken souls. I was disillusioned, and it just shattered me inside. The preaching of Herbert Armstrong on the destiny of humans to become born into the family of God kept me a little longer. But I did not continue as a student at Ambassador College beyond that semester ending June 1976.

Ambassador College, Pasadena: 1976

Giving generously

One time, weary to death of hearing emphasis upon figures of money and percentages of growth in Sabbath services, I turned in a check made out for $150,000 as my offering on one of the holy days. Every holy day, an offering would be taken in the morning after an exhortation to be generous. The money would be counted over lunchtime. Then, the total collected would be announced in the afternoon service with an "average per person" figure for the congregation. This "average per person" typically might range (in those days) from $15 to $30 per person (men, women, and children). Inspired by the plea from the pulpit to give liberally, swept away by the eloquence of the appeal, I wrote out my personal check for $150,000, to see if I could do my small part in helping to boost that day's "average per person" figure. It is true that this was several thousand times more than I had in my account. But I've rarely *felt* so magnanimous. Much to my regret, the afternoon announcement of the average take per person was no higher than normal. I don't know what they did with the check. It never came back to my bank or me.

Ambassador College mail censorship

A primary means by which Worldwide Church of God headquarters' credibility came to be seen as tarnished (some might say, shot to pieces) was the action of several ex-Ambassador students at Pasadena who, in the spring of 1976, put together a publication called *Ambassador Review*. (This was the forerunner of *Ambassador Report*.) It read like a cross between the television program "Sixty Minutes" and the tabloid *National Enquirer*. It contained a wealth of stunning investigative journalism type stories about Worldwide Church of God scandals which were not being adequately reported in the official church publication, *The Worldwide News*.

There were rumors that the publishers of *Ambassador Review* intended to mail copies to students on campus. Headquarters

Ambassador College, Pasadena: 1976

officials moved quickly and efficiently to prevent students from receiving this report. All students received a memo which explained that: (a) student mailboxes were a service provided by the college and not a right, (b) there had recently and suddenly been a "pornography" problem of unsolicited mail to students, and (c) to helpfully deal with the problem of students receiving pornography in the mail, an enclosed legal release had to be signed and returned within *forty-eight hours* allowing college officials to censor mail distribution to students *at their discretion*. Mail withheld from distribution to the student boxes could then be obtained by making special request for it at another office on campus, if the student insisted. If the enclosed legal release wasn't signed and returned, this nasty little note said, we would have to arrange to get our mail at an outside post office off campus. Ambassador College would simply refuse to provide mail service to students who did not sign. The memo was from, it said, an official in the Office of Communication Services (the department that handled the campus mail).

I received this legal sounding document along with all the other students. It was a hot topic of discussion at lunch that day. Many students were in an uproar over it. The "pornography" issue was puzzling, since no one knew of any pornography being mailed to students. Some students darkly suspected that that was a non-issue and that the true purpose was to enable the college to censor *Ambassador Review* and other dissident literature.

(Actually, it's not entirely accurate to say the pornography issue was a non-issue. It turned out later that part of what prompted the reaction from on high was rumors that an article would be featured in *Ambassador Review* in which one of Garner Ted Armstrong's ex-girlfriends was going to tell all. The story, entitled, "In Bed with Garner Ted," didn't appear until the next issue, but it didn't leave much to the imagination. Garner Ted Armstrong was now president of Ambassador College.)

At my lunch table, one student had called the church's Legal Department to protest the censorship memo. Another student had phoned the official identified on the memo as its author, Fred

Ambassador College, Pasadena: 1976

Gilreath, to find out what was going on. He reported back a very strange outcome to his phone call. Gilreath—whose name was typed *on* the memo as the memo's author—denied knowledge or authorship of the memo, and said to just ignore it!

But the memo was no hoax. Apparently, in high-handed manner it had been decided and written higher up. The hapless employee Fred Gilreath's name had been put on it so that he would take the heat for it, instead of the invisible higher-ups who had actually made the decision. In the rush someone forgot to tell him about it.

A number of students expressed their intentions not to sign the censorship permission. I didn't know anything about *Ambassador Review* and had no plans to support or encourage their publication. But I was reluctant to grant unchecked permission to arbitrarily interfere with my mail delivery, even to the most saintly of officialdom. On the other hand, I felt in a bind. The document itself was intimidating. I didn't want to drive off-campus every day in Pasadena's traffic to pick up my mail, and even worse, have to notify everyone of a change of address. But that was *promised* as the consequence if the document was not signed and turned in by the very short deadline. I signed and returned my release form, with the words "I object to and protest this action," written over my signature.

My response was mild compared to some others. According to *Ambassador Review*, some students turned theirs in with swastikas drawn on them, and "even the *Portfolio*, the official [student] newspaper of the college, posted a copy of the memo on its office bulletin board with mocking additions made to its contents."

~ ~ ~

Only about sixty or seventy percent of the students complied with the demand to turn in the signed legal forms. The next sabbath I watched in amazement as our occasionally-less-than-dignified college president Garner Ted Armstrong lost his temper

Ambassador College, Pasadena: 1976

in his sermon when discussing this new first for Ambassador College: a real, live, grassroots student rebellion.

"I've been hearing a lot of talk about *'individual rights'!!*," raged Garner Ted, his voice dripping with scorn. "Well, *institutions* have *rights too!!* We are not going to *censor* anybody's mail! Any student who wants to avail himself of the *slop and garbage* some dissidents want to mail onto *this campus* is *free to do so!!!* We'll have all the trash mail put in one big barrel and take photos of the rear ends of students leaning over into the barrel sorting through it to find their very own package of garbage addressed to them!"

With students continuing to dig in their heels and large numbers refusing to turn in their forms, the administration backed off from its threat of denying student mailboxes to non-signing students. Instead, carpenters quickly constructed walls around the student mailbox area with a locking door entrance. No longer were we able to get to our mailboxes at any time. Restricted hours were established when students could pick up their mail and there was a guard at the door. Since student mailboxes up to that point had been open and unlocked, the purpose of this seemed to be to prevent dissident literature or any other type of unapproved student communication from being stuffed in the students' boxes. The guard would observe the mailboxes and all persons entering the area. All other hours the door was locked so no one could get to their mail.

This was an inconvenience at best, since there was usually a line to get into the cramped room to pick up mail, and the hours were restrictive. But the walls hastily built around the mailboxes did not go all the way to the ceiling (which was very high). Some students figured out how to scale the walls, drop down inside, get their mail, open the locked door from inside, let their fellow students in and themselves out, then the last one out lock the door as before. Numerous students did this in broad view in the student center. The walls were a joke, with students scrambling over them like monkeys to get to their mail.

Ambassador College, Pasadena: 1976

~~~

Here is the press release from *Ambassador Review* that prompted the administrative reaction.

> AMBASSADOR REVIEW is a brand new, frank but exciting publication published by alumni and students of Ambassador College. It will dare to stand up for truth and honesty and report the facts ... The publishers of AMBASSADOR REVIEW intend to make our voices heard by both the Administration and the local community—and will, if necessary, undertake direct mail campaigns to newspaper editors, columnists, and freelance writers, radio and television producers, civic leaders, foreign embassies, educators and other organizations ... The publishers and editors of the REVIEW, however, always intend to keep the above actions at the highest levels of honesty and integrity ... in the first issue, you'll read about:
>
> - THE UNCOVERING OF THE SECRET STRATEGY OF A.I.C.F. OPERATIONS
> - THE INVASION OF PERSONAL PRIVACY
> - THE EXISTENCE OF SWISS BANK ACCOUNTS FOR EXECUTIVES
> - SEX SCANDALS
> - INTERNATIONAL SMUGGLING
> - THE CONTINUED RAPE OF CONTRIBUTORS
>
> Such things have been and are being conducted by administrators and members of the Board of Trustees still in office at Ambassador College. We intend to publish their names in AMBASSADOR REVIEW ...

This was what was behind the attempt to force students to "voluntarily" sign over legal rights to church officials to decide which U.S. first-class mail could be withheld from routine delivery, with records and signatures required for receipt, i.e. surveillance and dossiers on every student who received mail from certain sources. If the students had gone along with this, for all I know it might even have been legal. Only resistance and disobedience on the part of students stopped this Orwellian move.

Ambassador College, Pasadena: 1976

To tell the truth, *Ambassador Review* must have scared the living daylights out of headquarters officials. The problem was, everything *Ambassador Review* was claiming was true, and everyone in high position at headquarters knew it.

This all happened within several weeks of my transfer to Ambassador College, Pasadena. I asked myself: what had I gotten myself into? Had I stepped into the Twilight Zone? What kind of looney-bin was this place? And before long, another question: How do I get out of here?

Sometimes I would wake with a start, thinking, "What am I doing here? This isn't where I belong." I was also beginning to realize that I no longer believed key elements of the fundamentalist world view which formed the intellectual setting or landscape of the church. I could no longer make the kinds of leaps of faith and reasoning required to make everything fit together. Like a baby bird pecking its way out of its shell, I was outgrowing the matrix of social and mental attitudes that made up the Worldwide Church of God.

What headquarters thought of Big Sandy

I learned that Ambassador College, Big Sandy did not have the highest reputation for academic excellence among the administration at Pasadena. In fact Ambassador College, Pasadena, refused to accept any of my academic work done at Big Sandy as fulfilling any of Ambassador College, Pasadena's requirements for graduation! This was the conclusion of a series of memos I received from the Pasadena registrar's office.

At first I wondered if it was a joke. The first memo, which came like a bolt out of the blue, said they had no record of my graduating from high school. It said they needed this evidence for their records. I had graduated from high school in Akron, Ohio, and had furnished everything requested (or thought I had) when I applied to Big Sandy four years earlier. In all my time at Big Sandy I had never been asked for anything further. I had no idea why I was being asked for this now. I ignored the memo.

Ambassador College, Pasadena: 1976

A second memo dutifully arrived from the registrar's office. It said I *must* furnish them with evidence that I had graduated from high school, or else I could not be a properly admitted student and I would not receive credit toward graduation for any work done at Ambassador College so far! I didn't know what the mistake was, but I wasn't enamored with going through the nuisance of making long-distance phone calls to Ohio to learn the address of my old high school, then writing to request a transcript be sent to Pasadena. It amazed me that what was accepted at one Ambassador campus was not transferable to another Ambassador campus. By now I was not planning to continue as a student beyond that semester. I felt little motivation to prove I had graduated from high school and was therefore retroactively qualified to have undergone the previous two and one-half years of academic work at Ambassador College, Big Sandy. (Plus, I admit, I also was perversely becoming curious to see what would happen if I did nothing.)

A third memo arrived. (All communications were by memo—to the same mailbox to which access had become so difficult.) Now the gloves were coming off. Either I got verification of my high school graduation turned in pronto or they would remove me from admitted student status and I would not be allowed to re-enroll in the future. I filed this memo with the others.

They weren't bluffing. A fourth memo arrived. It informed me I was no longer in the junior class at Ambassador College, Pasadena, and was busted to "special student" status. (This was a category for non-fulltime students taking single classes.) I could forget about graduating or, for that matter, further enrollment at all, until I learned to cooperate better (loosely paraphrased).

Many students from Ambassador College, Big Sandy, have experienced difficulties in the outside world with their academic credentials. I found my 2-1/2 years of Big Sandy work to be of no academic value—at Ambassador College, Pasadena.

On this note my final semester ended at Ambassador College. I walked out the door into the world outside, and the story of this book of my Ambassador College years comes to a close.

Ambassador College, Pasadena: 1976

The editor of *Ambassador Review* (which later became *Ambassador Report*) mentioned earlier in this chapter published this exchange in one of his newsletters which about says it all:

> *With all your smarts, how in _____ did you ever get mixed up with the WCG in the first place?*
>
> Editor: I was once very young and foolish. I am also reminded of this scene from the movie *Casablanca*:
>
> > RENAULT (Claude Rains): And what in Heaven's name brought you to Casablanca?
> > RICK (Humphrey Bogart): My health. I came to Casablanca for the waters.
> > RENAULT: Waters? What waters? We are in the desert.
> > RICK: I was misinformed.

~ ~ ~

It was like returning from outer space. I had seen strange creatures and exotic sights. I had explored new terrains of belief and synchronisms in many-splendored worlds of eschatological reality. I had reached out, until the exploration, like some Laingian inner odyssey, began to collapse as the journey became understood.

CHAPTER 23

THE RETURN HOME

It is 1984 …
It is August, and I am one of about three hundred camped near the Pantex nuclear bomb assembly plant in the hot, desolate, endless prairie outside Amarillo, Texas.

Pantex is the site of final assembly of all U.S. nuclear weapons. From this plant these nuclear warheads are then transported by train and truck, at the rate of about three per day, to points east and west for deployment and perhaps eventual use.

A giant American Indian drum is set up on its side. Every thirty seconds or so, around the clock, someone hits that drum with a giant mallet, swung full force with both arms. Like thunder the deep drumbeat rolls out and reverbates for miles across the flat prairie, including within the factory of death in the distance where the weapons of mass destruction are being assembled. The drum is carrying out a native American ritual expressing the Great Spirit's displeasure. We pray for the seemingly impossible: the day to come when this factory will forever end its deadly business of assembling nuclear weapons.

An outside observer might say (and plenty did) that it was one hundred percent futile. What possible difference could three hundred ragtag Americans and a drum make in the face of an abyss of that scale, involving powers of money and might extending worldwide that can scarcely be grasped in magnitude? I wondered would the time ever come when not 300 but 30,000 or 300,000 or 3 million Americans might blockade such sites, and the same in other lands. (For a factory producing weapons of mass destruction has no more business existing than Auschwitz.)

The Return Home

But that wasn't the case. We were only a tiny three hundred. I wrote in my journal:

> August 5, 1984. My thirtieth birthday. As I watch the shimmering complex in the distance while staying up most of the night, it looks awesome, frightening, yet strangely entrancing at the same time. The cool night air is a welcome relief from nearly 100 degree temperatures by day with no cloud or tree for shade. Heat lightning strikes the flat prairie all around for hours during the night, creating a dazzling light and sound show as backdrop to the sprawling castle in the distance. The castle is separated from the roadside of our encampment by a fence, then a huge expanse of plowed dirt field on all sides of multiple square miles surface area which like some giant moat is rumored to be planted with mines as deterrent to invasion of the complex by land, then a patrolling armed truck circling the plant without letup, twenty-four hours a day, then the inner fence, barbed wire, guard towers and searchlights. These all protect the deadly wares inside from the sight and knowledge and interference of the humans outside. It is a time for much reflection.

As I stared into the face of this source from which I imagined might issue forth the destruction of earthly creation, this preparation of man for hell, this basis for our nation's economy, this evidence of our spiritual desolation ... I longed for another world, another time, another land of clear skies, lakes and mountains and oceans, peaceful people ... and where there is no knowledge of war. As the paradise I knew at Big Sandy had been lost, so in that moment the larger paradise which was the dream of America seemed to me also lost.

And the solemn drumbeat continued the wordless, timeless sighing of the Great Spirit.[214]

~ ~ ~

---

[214] In 1991 Pantex of Amarillo stopped assembling nuclear weapons completely. Since then it has only dismantled nuclear weapons. Since 1991 Pantex has disarmed some 30,000 nuclear warheads.

The Return Home

That experience provided a stark contrast to my visit just days later to the quiet, pastoral setting of the yearly meeting of Conservative Friends (Quakers) in Barnesville, Ohio.

There, among these simple Friends of plain dress, on the grounds of the Friends Boarding School where my grandfather had met my grandmother, I felt rest. I had seen, in a night show down in Texas, an ocean of darkness, vast and overwhelming. But now, to quote a Quaker metaphor, I saw an even vaster ocean of light shining over that darkness. From my journal again, a meditation from that experience.

> August 20, 1984. As Quaker action and business are practical application of the Quaker mysticism within, so mysticism is not apart from practical life, nor action from contemplation. Resurrection comes not from death, but from the void. The void is not death, any more than the silence and stillness of a gathered Quaker meeting is nothing. The void is living. It must produce forms, just as the gathered Quaker silence will produce words of God without advance knowledge of when, where, or through whom.

As I brushed the hair off my forehead on a bright summer day in rural Ohio, I reflected that it had been a long journey from former days. Yet I saw that seeds of this return had been present all along.

I reflected that Herbert Armstrong had been raised a Quaker. But, like another famous American whom he believed to be both a relative of his and America's greatest President, Richard Nixon, Herbert Armstrong fell away from the Quaker foundation of his youth. These two distant cousins each made their mark on the world. Both in their adult lives betrayed their Quaker heritage and behaved, in the view of Quakers, in ways that lead to perdition. One became a prophet, an acclaimed head of a religious following with designs on ruling the earth. He "taught for the fleece and made a prey of the people" as the early Quakers characterized those who took tithes. He urged the world to give homage to the other apostate Quaker (his distant cousin), who had become the most powerful military commander in the world's history. This American President's defining theory of military policy was what he called "the Madman Theory"—the attempt to make those who would make war with him fear that he was mad—like a wild animal.[215]

I thought of the irony that the person who first greeted my father, my brother, and me at our first Worldwide Church of God Sabbath services in Akron, Ohio in 1968, Walter Warrington (1920-2005), was from these very Conservative Friends. He was the door-greeter that day. In his youth he had graduated from the Friends boarding school on whose grounds I was then standing. Walter Warrington and my father compared times past that first Sabbath in Akron, even remembering each other from long ago, as he welcomed us across the threshold into the new world.

I looked across the Ohio fields and pastures. I thought on the role Quakers played in America's First Amendment guarantee of religious freedom. I thought of Pennsylvania and the "peaceable kingdom" built by William Penn and the Quaker settlers with him. I thought of the Liberty Bell in Philadelphia. I thought of Quaker schools and colleges, teachers and nurses and librarians, from frontier days to now, building a peaceable culture one child, one brick, one book at a time. I thought of Quaker lobbying activities working to build a world in which disputes are settled in court instead of by war. I thought of Quaker refusal to pay "war taxes."

I thought of the stories of Quaker men and women of old coming before kings and sultans. These Quakers did not come bearing expensive gifts and arriving in limousines. They came in plain dress speaking plain words. They addressed kings directly by name, without title, as was the Quaker manner. They came

---

[215] "I call it the Madman Theory, Bob. I want the North Vietnamese to believe I've reached the point where I might do anything to stop the war. We'll just slip the word to them that, 'for God's sake, you know Nixon is obsessed about Communism. We can't restrain him when he's angry—and he has his hand on the nuclear button'—and Ho Chi Minh himself will be in Paris in two days begging for peace" (Richard M. Nixon, quoted in H.R. Haldeman, *The Ends of Power*).

The Return Home

speaking truth to power, calling on rulers to release prisoners wrongly held and cease oppression of the defenseless.

I thought how Quakers from the beginning practiced equality of men and women in speech and decision-making (for Quakers believed that male dominion over women entered as a result of sin).

I thought of the way Quakers speak the language of holding persons "in the light." I thought how that expression warmed me—so simple, so sincere, so beautiful.

I thought how easy it is to be drawn to systems with answers taught authoritatively. But Quakers chose a different path. Quaker ways were built on probing questions for examination from listening to the Teacher within ("the Light of Christ that shines to every person"). Quakers read the Bible and quoted its words but did not believe it was sufficient or inerrant. They would say to their interlocuters: "You will say, Christ saith this, and the apostles say this; but what canst *thou* say?"

I looked at the cemetery next to the old meeting house with the gravestones of John and Sarah Doudna, "ancestor of all the Doudnas," side by side, at rest forever.

It had been a long journey, this return to my roots. But, I reflected, sometimes it takes a long journey to discover truths which were always close at hand, all along.

~ ~ ~

I wrote an article describing my visit to the Conservative Friends. It was published in the May 15, 1985 issue of *Friends Journal* and is reprinted here by permission.

The Return Home

"Returning to Quaker Roots. A Visit with Conservative Friends"
Greg Doudna
© 1985, *Friends Journal*

Conservative Friends may be the purest surviving form of early American Quakerism.

Outwardly, they continue many of the traditions and customs of Friends of earlier days in their use of the "plain" language and the plain or near-plain dress of some older members. Inwardly, meeting for worship is held on the basis of silence, without music or hired ministers. And their peculiar combination of conservative values—refusal to participate in war, deep dependence on the sober leading of the inner Light, and the use of scriptural texts from memory when speaking—mark them as both Universalist and evangelical—and yet neither. They are not quite at home with any but their own.

As I attended unprogrammed Friends meetings over the past four years in Eugene, Oregon; Arcata, California; and Tulsa, Oklahoma, where I now live, my encounters with Friends deepened my interest both in Quakerism and in the conservative Quaker origins of my father and the Doudnas before him. All of us trace our origins to Barnesville, Ohio, where Doudnas have been part of Ohio Yearly Meeting (conservative) since its beginnings in the early 1800s.

And so to widen my encounters with Friends and learn more about my Doudna origins, I went to Barnesville this past August to attend Ohio Yearly Meeting.

It is one of only three conservative yearly meetings still in existence, and I am told it is more "conservative" than either Iowa or North Carolina—that is, least adapted to the worldly ways of the larger body of Quakerism.

Yearly meeting members gather each year at the meetinghouse constructed for that purpose in 1878 on the campus of Olney Friends Boarding School in Barnesville. Because of the school's 108-year history, because it represents the greatest financial outlay of the Yearly Meeting, and because most of the yearly meeting's members were graduated from it, the boarding school occupies a very high place in the hearts and concerns of yearly meeting.

The campus has a special history for me. The graveyard immediately adjacent to the Barnesville meetinghouse contains the graves of "John Doudna—ancestor of all the Doudnas," and that of Sarah Doudna, his wife. It was at the boarding school that my grandfather, Willis Doudna, who was working on the school farm, met my grandmother, Hannah Hoyt, who was working in the school kitchen. The nearby Somerset (or "Ridge") Meetinghouse, where

The Return Home

Doudnas (all old now) still predominate, is where my grandfather attended meeting in his childhood.

My visit introduced me to some of the lasting values of Ohio Yearly Meeting. Its predominant strength is in its elders, and the awareness of this brings real sadness to some of its older members.

They recognize that there are few young members to carry on the traditional ways which mark conservative Friends. It brings a sadness to me, too—given this recent return to my roots—to think of Ohio Yearly Meeting being absorbed into the larger body of Quakerism and the distinctive Wilburite ways lost.

During my visit, I learned that attendance at the meetings for business averaged between 60 and 100, with perhaps 150 on the final First-day meeting for worship. The decline in membership is clear when comparing these numbers with the following newspaper account in 1878, the first year of the meetinghouse.

> "By careful estimate, it is believed the house will seat 1,200 people comfortably; but its crowded condition Sunday morning and afternoon, when public services were held, leaves no doubt that at least 1,500 were present, the afternoon meeting being rather the larger one. But through the kindness of the ushers, all—with a few exceptions—were provided with seats, every available space being occupied, even the steps leading to the galleries. The order and quiet were remarkable—not a single instance of disorder occurring."

Every Friends meeting in the country would do well to observe Ohio Yearly Meeting business sessions. The ones I attended began with from 20 to 30 minutes of silent, unprogrammed worship; then, out of the silence, the clerk rose and introduced the first item for consideration.

In a slow, methodical way, items were raised and discussed, and a minute representing the sense of the meeting was composed by the clerk and approved. There was no rush, and much use was made of silence between speaking. Yet business was conducted more effectively than in many other Friends meetings in my experience. This was due in large part to the skilled clerking of William Cope and the decentralized participation of the meeting as a whole.

When a Friend rose to express a thought or an opinion that represented the minds of others present, I heard voices arising from different parts of the room simultaneously: "I approve." "So do I." "I approve, too." A similar response of perhaps a dozen or more voices scattered through the meeting, verbally affirming approval, would follow the clerk's reading of the minute he was composing as the group dealt with a matter. Other times, Friends would suggest corrections of the clerk's minute, or there would be further speaking to the matter until it expressed the true sense of the meeting. Often interspersed with the affairs of business at hand would be simple silence and sometimes a spoken message on a spiritual matter. This is a reflection of all Friends' regard for business meetings as, in fact, "meetings for worship in which business is conducted," and not as if worship and business, with its concern over money and material affairs, are in separate spheres.

I have often thought that for Friends to do business and actually function for 300 years without authority of office or voting to make decisions for the group would be unthinkable for most of society. Yet, Friends have done so. Not without problems, certainly; but it stands as a marked example through the test of time that the seemingly impossible can be made possible and real.

Such a method of corporate decision making—by listening to the voice and leadings of every person who feels called to speak, and letting a gathered sense of the meeting form in its own unpredictable and timely way—must be developed over time with experience. Ohio Yearly Meeting's conservative Friends have had 171 years of experience. This is a resource which newer Friends everywhere would do well to observe and learn from. Even the world at large might do well to consider experientially applying, perhaps in small ways at first, the ways of conservative Friends in business affairs, and, perhaps ultimately, in the affairs of government. [END]

CHAPTER 24

LETTERS AND REFLECTIONS

Entering Ambassador College, Big Sandy, the same time I did in 1972 was a fellow freshman named Earl Smith. Everything I have described in this book at Big Sandy Earl lived through too. After graduating in 1976 Earl worked as a journalist, including a memorable stint as editor of a small-town newspaper in Fort Jones, California. Now, from his land in northern Minnesota near a town called Browerville, Earl took time out from building a house to write reflections on this book and the Big Sandy experience (excerpted here from several letters):

> All of us who got into the WCG originally believed, and then as we began to believe less and less of it, we began to struggle and suffer. Your book is a monument to the struggle, the story of someone who at first believed with more vigor and energy than most of us, in my opinion, and certainly one who did a whole lot more research than most of us during his "believing" phase. Then it's the story of the struggle, a harder struggle than most of us had, to come to terms with our unbelief and to figure out what the WCG really was and what we were going to do about it. It clearly articulates many specific issues that we struggled with, and the effect on me the reader was to find clearly spelled out specific things that I had felt only vaguely. I can't say enough about how helpful this book would be for anyone, particularly ex-WCG of course, but anyone who has struggled with fundamentalism of any stripe, or is struggling with it.
>
> Your paper about the history of British Israelism ... brings back so many memories for me, as it was that book (USBCP [*The United States and British Commonwealth in Prophecy*]) that led me, as so many, into the Church. I remember that for some reason in the

middle of my junior year I got to reading USBCP and noticed all the assumptions and lack of connectivity and wondered, for a minute or two, why I had been so impressed with it. At that stage in my life I wasn't able to consciously question the Church yet, so the moment just flitted away. It was then, too, that I leafed through [Joseph H. Allen's 1902] *Judah's Sceptre* and noticed 1) that it was even more imaginative than USBCP, in places and 2) a lot of it had been yanked out by the roots and then transplanted into USBCP. I loved your explanation of Tea-Tephi.

On the whole thing of British Israel and race identifications, speaking as a former journalist, I know how hard it can be to nail down the facts of what happened last night at the City Council meeting, so I am dubious of anyone's claim to know what happened 5,000 years ago.

I see AC and WCG as places full of the tension caused by contradictions. When something comes along to upset the balance, he gets into difficulty. Your particular role, as a discoverer of new truth, made you very capable of upsetting those balances. By balance I mean here the kind of balance that can make you believe, for example, that Mrs. Adam had children of three different races, because you want to believe that you've been called to rule over 10 cities starting maybe in a couple years and they all fit together some way.

In essence WCG/AC was full of people who wanted it all to be true and were experienced at finding ways to believe things. They didn't want to challenge or analyze, they wanted to believe, yet had to convince themselves that it was all logical and provable, too. Having set up this system where all beliefs either stand or fall together, we found ways to believe that the U.S. was Manasseh because we wanted to be king over part of it someday soon; we found how to believe in Mrs. Noah's fertility and talking snakes because we wanted to believe John 3:16. This required for most of us the construction of rickety logical edifices at which Rube Goldberg would flinch and a learning how not to question them ...

In the fall of 1972 WCG/AC was brewing ... People who'd believed for 15 years against all odds that they were going to [Petra] in January 1972 were being forced, now that nine months had passed since then [to see] that it hadn't happened ... When you arrived, 1972 had come and gone. The 1974 heresy was brewing even then in the hearts of thousands who had planned to be in Petra by then. And your pivotal paper (Ephraim v. Manasseh) appeared around the same time as the 1974 Falling Away. The church at that time was very gunshy of new ideas ...

Letters and Reflections

> I think Pasadena's approach was to ignore you and hope you'd go away. Eventually they were right.
> It takes great courage for any institution, even one as small as a dad and mom and a couple kids, to tolerate, let alone invite, dissent. The powers in the institution must be wise and courageous. Few such powers are, as you know, as we learned. Usually the innovators have to work outside the system and spend a lot of time and energy keeping it off their backs, too. To succeed in a closed bureaucracy you cannot be an innovator, but you rather must be a company man ... These types don't innovate, they sustain and feed the system, so it grows bigger. I think of a quote: "They could not love you/ But still your love was true." That's from a song about Vincent van Gogh called "Vincent." That's how your experience, and to a lesser extent mine, with the WCG, was. The system was suspicious of innovation and destructive of innocence. It couldn't contain us, couldn't get the good we had to offer. But we tried with all our youthful energy to contribute.

Earl added this p.s. to one of his letters:

> Greg! I am amazed at one thing. You left out what I consider to be the most quintessential part of the experience of trying to both inject new ideas into the WCG and get it used to the idea that a new idea need not be a ticking time bomb. It was the contribution that reached by far the widest audience.
> To what am I referring? What John Robinson [editor of the *Worldwide News*] called "the Doudna Controversy"; your attempt via the *WN* to get some of your ideas across ... As I recall there were certain elements of economic thinking involved based on Bible ideas as opposed to simple direct Bible exposition; it involved doing a little thinking about Bible economics; but still the controversy was theological ... [The *WN*] was liberal enough then, by printing letters such as yours, to admit the fact that there might be some room for difference of opinion or at least open airing of positions ... And it's extremely funny, to me, the whole thing.
> You laid out some ideas in the *WN* and the sky didn't fall. You provoked debate. But this was too much for the WCG. Does the *WN* today publish letters like yours? I doubt it.

I had forgotten about that. It concerned a letter I wrote to the *Worldwide News*, the church newspaper for members, in the spring of 1976, while at Pasadena during my last semester as an

Ambassador College student. There was a legal case in the news in which a church member, I think in Tennessee, had been fired for keeping the Sabbath—refusing to work on Saturday. The church member was taking the employer to court to compel reinstatement to his former job. Not surprisingly, this legal action had the moral support of most of the church membership, and Garner Ted Armstrong had spoken in support of the member's case. My letter challenged this prevailing view. My letter raised the question of whether it was right to sue employers to force them to permit sabbath-keeping by employees.

Basically I raised two distinct issues. The first was whether this was a right use of government interference in the affairs of a private business, if no actual agreement or contract had been broken. (This might be called the "libertarian" objection.) The other issue was whether a Christian should make use of state coercion and courts at all, even in just causes. (This might be called the "Christian anarchist" objection.)

The next issue of the *Worldwide News* carried an avalanche of letters both pro and con, but overwhelmingly con, on the question raised by my letter. That is, most of the letters supported sabbatarians' use of the legal system to compel business owners to be religiously tolerant. I was later told (late 1980s) that my letter was one of only two instances in the entire history of the *Worldwide News* in which the editors permitted opposing views from members on a topic to be aired in the letters to the editor column. (The other instance was a debate over whether alcoholism is a disease or a moral failure.)

At least two effective letters that I know of favorable to my views were submitted to the *Worldwide News* after the first onslaught of letters against were published. (I have no idea how many others came in apart from the two I knew about.) But the authors of each of these received letters back saying *The Worldwide News* was not going to publish any more on the

Letters and Reflections

subject, and referred to it as "the Doudna controversy."[216] I never received any feedback about my letter from anyone in official position in the church. The issue just died when the *Worldwide News* quit publishing letters on the subject.

More letters

> I enjoyed myself weighing the new ideas and concepts, and also reliving some of the moments from decades ago. And seeing you merge the concepts of WWC with Quaker values. Really we aren't that far apart when it comes to a value system.
>
> Kenneth C. Herrmann
> Gladewater, Texas

> While I have not read it all yet, I like what I have seen so far. Naturally, I do not come to the same conclusions you do on several subjects, such as interracial marriage. But I appreciate reading well thought out presentations, even though I often disagree. I still wonder why you wrote it because in some sections you use Holy Day terminology to illustrate a point, and obviously you do not keep them nor the Sabbath any longer. Seems like disjointed tales of a precocious, disillusioned Ambassador student, or conehead type (no offense, but you are the thick glasses type). I don't get the feeling

---

[216] A church member in Bridgeville, Pennsylvania named Thomas Goonan sent me a copy of his correspondence with the *Worldwide News*. Goonan received this letter dated May 5, 1976, from *Worldwide News* managing editor John Robinson: "Dear Mr. Goonan: Thank you for your contribution to the 'Letters to the Editor' section. I appreciate the thought and effort that went into your reply to what those of us on the WN staff are now referring to as the 'Doudna Controversy'! Since we have already printed a number of letters on the subject raised by Mr. Doudna, we have decided against devoting further space to the matter, since it appears there may be no end to the response. We are also of the feeling that the decision to enlist legal aids is a purely personal matter and perhaps not worthy of further debate in the pages of the paper. Since your letter supported Mr. Doudna's position, we only wish that you had written earlier so that the letters we selected would have been more balanced between pro and con rather than predominantly con as they were as of the date we last printed. Thank you for taking the time to write and hopefully we will hear from you again in the future. Sincerely, John Robinson, Managing Editor."

that the doctrinal truths which the Worldwide taught ever really sunk in to you, else why would you abandon them once you discovered the fact that the church was morally corrupt? My high level job at church administration in Pasadena made me lose my faith in men yet strengthened my faith in church doctrines which these corrupt men were watering down and failing to live up to.

    Richard Nickels
    St. Charles, Missouri

I'm not surprised that it was Trish [Willhoite] who infiltrated second year speech [chapter 1]. She and I grew up together in the Kansas City church and neither of us was particularly known for our kneejerk compliance. I could go ON and ON about the gender bias at AC. The makeup issue alone during the 70s was a trial: that ruling changed about every six months and when it was "out," if a female student so much as applied mascara, or sported lipgloss with a hint of color, she was considered a real live Jezebel. For reasons long since obscured, powder foundation and Vaseline applied to lips and eyelashes (which most co-eds laboriously curled) was acceptable ...

    I can share numerous tales about being cavalierly presented with lengthy lists describing my "character flaws" or "25 things you will need to change if you are going to be a minister's wife" by well-meaning but hopelessly condescending dates, who themselves aspired for a ministerial calling. The descriptive epithet I heard spat repeatedly in my direction by these Pygmalion advisors was "opinionated"—apparently the unpardonable sin as AC female personality disorders went ...

    Linda Moll Smith (graduated AC Big Sandy 1976)
    Tyler, Texas

I find your writing style absolutely terrific. I have difficulty putting your book down when I start, though I must because of my tight schedule. You *really* should be doing something along the line of paralegal or research-writing work ... I think I know a bit about you as a result of reading your book. I almost feel we are "kindred spirits" in that we both seem to be unconventional in lifestyle and have a strong bent toward fulfilling our natural curiosity.

    John Trechak
    Editor, *Ambassador Report*
    Pasadena, California

Letters and Reflections

Many sincere thanks for the copy of your wonderful book on the WCG: it was hard to put down, as I found it most interesting and often very funny.

>Man
>Sydney, Australia

I'm reading—and digesting it now—very nutritious! I find it erudite and profound, full of surprising epiphanies; it demands at least a second reading. I'm alerting my friends to the treasure in store for them.

>Man
>Oregon

The chapter on Jubilees is another good exposition of a young intellect caught up in a system of belief striving to confirm that system for himself. Personal sidelights on various faculty members contribute to realism. One can envision the person espousing the doctrine ... In the chapter "Afterward on Anglo-Israelism" the reader will certainly be reminded of times when she found herself the "victim" of seeming logic. Your personal exercise in the etymology of your surname is a gem.

>Woman
>Ohio

The institution claimed to be receptive to new ideas, properly submitted. You [went] through all the proper channels, to see what it was really like, to make your sincere intellectual contribution to the Work and see it evaluated, properly considered by the noble upper echelons. Thus the crisis, the conflict, a classic confrontation, the Showdown at Big Sandy. Who would win? Individual vs. bureaucracy. Creativity vs. institutional thought. Innocent faith vs. jaded management. Simple sincerity vs. entrenched power. David vs. Goliath. Bambi vs. Godzilla.

>Man
>Oregon

I see a bittersweet thread running through the story, like a man who falls in and out of love with a beautiful harridan ... Young people who haven't established a pair bond and territory feel very uncomfortable. Instead of accepting that discomfort with the understanding they don't have the equipment for that job yet, they try to transfer those feelings. The safest transference is to an idea. A person can reject you. An idea cannot reject you (after all it has no feelings). But, people who make this transference can never grow. The human mind, and body as well, stays alive only if the person has the courage to accept temporary discomfort while working for problem solutions. You were lucky. For you, transference became more uncomfortable than the discomfort of problem solving. You saw the harridan for what she was and rejected her. Show the reader the joy and triumph that comes from problem solving. I see that joy in the discussion of the Irish annals. Point out clearly the discomfort you felt and the absolute joy in solving it.

> Woman
> Washington

Your story is fascinating. What happened to numbers of highly idealistic young men like yourself with inquiring active minds almost makes me want to weep for what could have been. But we wouldn't listen. Too busy and anyone with a new idea really constituted a threat if they were right. And the cloak of authoritarian infallibility once removed by honest inquiry would have revealed only a shabby and diseased skeleton. Let people like you loose and the first thing you would have found out was that tithing was invalid for the New Testament church and that would have ripped off our $700.00 dollar suits, dried up our daily ration of Dom Perignon champagne and the rest of our bloated lifestyle ...

> Charles Hunting (former WCG evangelist)

I asked Hunting if, in his opinion, Stanley Rader had believed sincerely in the Work at the time he knew him. Hunting's answer:

> Saintly Rader? A very brilliant chap. He believed sincerely in the "Work" as a means of gaining a personal fortune ... I had an admiration for his mental agility and coolness under great pressure. We got along very well and I enjoyed the company of both him and his wife Niki.

Letters and Reflections

I asked Hunting how Herbert Armstrong's emphasis upon a united Europe as the coming "Beast" power was explained to Belgian ex-King Leopold III, one of Herbert Armstrong's friends from the 1960s. Hunting's answer:

> As for King Leopold, he was only interested in what he could get out of Herbert in order to maintain his own personal life style. But then those European kings were experts at lifting money from the wealthy who basked in their reflected glory and who paid prodigious amounts for the privilege. It was all a big game. Herbert got what he wanted—tongs to extract the money from the wallets of the church members who thought he was preaching the gospel—what a gigantic sham that man carried on!—and the ex-king got money and free rides on a jet airplane for himself and wife. The Beast Power? King Loophold couldn't have cared less and the subject never came up. At least not while I was around.

Response from Ronald Dart

Ronald Dart (1934-) was the resident administrator, the deputy chancellor of Ambassador College, Big Sandy (under the absent chancellor Herbert Armstrong), starting from the spring of 1973 near the end of my freshman year through the rest of my time at Big Sandy.

> November 24, 1987
> Dear Greg,
>   It's very difficult for me, after all these years, to recall any specifics, but I can say that your account seems true to the spirit of the times, and that nothing you say strikes a false note with me. Unfortunately, I'm just not in a position to confirm much that you say because of a lack of recollection.
>   I'm not sure what audience you're writing for, but I'm wondering if they will find what you say particularly remarkable. Let me explain. The Worldwide Church of God of those years suffered from a surfeit of inputs. Apart from the theology and religion faculty of three colleges, the church had in excess of 500 field ministers dealing constantly with biblical topics. The year in question, 1974-75, was right at the pivotal point of some of the most intense doctrinal discussion the church had ever experienced. Much of the work of the

intervening years culminated in the production of the STP [Systematic Theology Project] in 1978. It's possible that your readers might consider it remarkable if a college sophomore was able to have a paper seriously considered by the church's hierarchy. This is not in any way to question the integrity or even the truth of the papers considered, merely the likelihood of anything coming from a college sophomore being seriously considered by *any* religious organization. Normally, such papers are dealt with by the instructor of the classes to which they are submitted.

I think most of us generated our share of "new truth" during our college careers. The problem was not the truth or error of what we were submitting, but with being heard from our position way back in the pack.

Nothing I am saying should be construed as a defense of the Worldwide Church of God's obtuseness and obstructionism. It was definitely there. But the fact that a church organization—any church organization—ignores a lot of doctrinal papers submitted to it is hardly significant. There are a lot of reasons for this, not the least of which is a phenomenon called information overload. I have very little doubt that a lot of papers were submitted to us in those years which were never considered, not because they didn't contain truth, but because the truth was buried in so much verbosity that it was never discovered. Your papers were at least coherent, but many are not.

Another factor bearing on the acceptance of a paper is whether its time has come. In an organization like the Worldwide Church of God with its history, momentum, inertia, etc., asking it to make too radical a change is an exercise in futility. When the church finally changed Pentecost from Monday to Sunday, it was not because of a newly-discovered concept—although HWA tried to present it as such. All the arguments that finally were decisive in making that change had been around for years. The reason it was finally changed was that enough other factors had fallen into place to make it acceptable. Unfortunately, politics are a fact of life in any *organizational* search for truth. This is why the *personal* nature of the Christian religion is so important. The scriptures tell us that we are held accountable for what we know, not what our organization teaches. That doesn't mean you abandon the organization the first time it fails to accept what you see as "new truth." It does mean that you begin to obey it as soon as you see it ...

The segments in your paper on race relations are an interesting illustration of the problem of change in any organization. There were many of us who were uncomfortable with the college's policy, but

Letters and Reflections

not even Herbert W. Armstrong could change that policy by fiat—amazing as that sounds. Racial feelings were too deeply rooted in everyone concerned, and there are some changes that have to be made over time as people grow and learn. They cannot be forced. I believe this is one of those questions ...

Please don't construe anything I've said in this letter as a putdown of your work. It is not intended that way at all. I appreciate what you are trying to do, and I assume you want me to be honest with you in my response.

All the best to you. I hope you are successful in telling your story.
Sincerely,
Ronald L. Dart

Report from inside the Black Hole (headquarters): Charles Dorothy

Many of my papers written at Big Sandy were submitted to the headquarters Theological Research Project at Pasadena. Dr. Charles Dorothy (1933-1996) headed the Theological Research Project in the years 1973-77. Throughout my time at Big Sandy, I had no idea what was happening on the other end of my submissions. Here is Dr. Dorothy's story, told to me by a gracious Dr. Dorothy by telephone in 1988 (after I told him the nature of my book).

In late 1973 Dr. Dorothy had been assigned to do the Theological Research Project. He was given offices and a budget and he hired staff members. Along the way, Dr. Dorothy started computerizing the doctrines and the papers. Besides the mass of material the church had already produced, several zealous persons were submitting material, "including papers coming in from you and your friend Russ [Gmirkin]." The idea was to compile and organize the doctrines and get the material that was on paper and in their heads into the computer.

This was a period when doctrinal changes were being made. Dr. Dorothy stalled the Project in order to get new truths included. "This was not authorized," he says. "I knew I was going out on a limb doing this. I felt I was high enough up in the organization and knew Herbert Armstrong well enough to know what should be done, and what he would want done once he knew the facts. So I did it."

But Dr. Dorothy was removed from his job in 1977. The Project was renamed "Systematic Theology Project" and was now headed by Robert Kuhn. Dr. Dorothy was shoved out of his offices and given a tiny cubicle somewhere else in which to work. He had difficulty finding a desk. Finally he was able to scrounge one up. He said, "I had read *The Peter Principle*. When someone who was as well-placed as I was has trouble finding a desk, then you know you're in trouble."

At this point, with his past years of work shot out from under him, Dr. Dorothy said, "I'm dying inside." "By now," he said, "I realize that the problem *is* the top. It isn't just people below Herbert Armstrong blocking things from him. Herbert Armstrong himself is the screw-up." Dr. Dorothy contributed a little more to the Systematic Theology Project but his heart was no longer in it. "I could see the handwriting on the wall. I knew the time would come when I would either be forced out altogether, or else a matter of conscience would come up and I would have to take a stand and be kicked out."

Under the new direction of Robert Kuhn, the troubled Systematic Theology Project was finally completed about a year later. A lot of Dr. Dorothy's earlier work was in it. The "STP," as it was known, was compiled in notebook folder form to be distributed to the ministry. Kuhn took it to Tucson and showed it to the 86-year old Herbert Armstrong at his home. For several hours Kuhn went over the whole thing with Herbert Armstrong, carefully showing and explaining every page to him, walking him through everything it said, and received approval. But when the document was issued, an outraged Herbert Armstrong had forgotten this had ever happened and said he had never been told.

The real truth was something no one wanted to admit. Herbert Armstrong was going senile. For hours Herbert Armstrong would be totally out of it, in a stupor, acting like he was half brain-dead. People would have to nudge him to get his attention, shout at him: "Mr. Armstrong!" Herbert Armstrong would then come to with a start for a moment, then drop back into never-never land. But then, without warning, Herbert Armstrong could come alive and be as bright and alert as ever. It was these times which toadying headquarters ministers would report to the members. "Why, he almost wore *us* out!" the members would hear. As happens in senility, Herbert Armstrong just "popped back and forth," bobbing in and out. Dr. Dorothy himself saw Herbert Armstrong in these stupor situations and knew that he was losing it.

The Systematic Theology Project was recalled and Herbert Armstrong ordered Robert Kuhn fired. Dr. Dorothy's association with the Project resulted in his too being fired. (The actual firing occurred a couple months later when Dr. Dorothy refused to support Stanley Rader in the receivership action and do things like go down to the Los Angeles courthouse to demonstrate in support of Rader.)

Part of what led to Dr. Dorothy's disaster on the Theological Research Project was his participation on the Doctrinal Committee. The Doctrinal Committee was composed of leading headquarters ministers and researchers charged with recommending doctrinal positions and changes to Herbert Armstrong. Dr. Dorothy was the key person instrumental in changing Pentecost from Monday to Sunday (March 1974). Then, divorce and remarriage was changed, and Dr. Dorothy was one of the key persons involved in that (May 1974). The third thing was makeup. Dr. Dorothy was personally responsible for Herbert Armstrong's change on that (October 1974). Here is Dr. Dorothy's account—the inside story of how the daily morning rituals of tens of thousands of grown women worldwide got decided by an edict of an 86-year old man in Pasadena, California. Dr. Dorothy:

> I and others knew the biblical basis for forbidding makeup on women was baseless. I wrote a one page letter to Herbert Armstrong explaining this. Actually this was a condensation of a fourteen page paper Lester Grabbe had written. I condensed it to one page. That was the

way you had to do it with Mr. Armstrong. If it was a ten page article he'd never get through it.

Wayne Cole and Robert Kuhn set up a lunch meeting with Herbert Armstrong and me. We all went out to lunch, then returned to his office. Then they turned to me to give my letter to Mr. Armstrong. I thought, "I'm going to get fired right now, on the spot. If Mr. Armstrong gets mad and blows up, this is the end for me."

Dr. Dorothy handed the one page letter to Herbert Armstrong. Herbert Armstrong read it and did not blow up.

After he had read my letter, Mr. Armstrong simply replied, "Well, you mean the teaching against makeup isn't in the Bible?" I said, "No, sir, it isn't." Mr. Armstrong thought for a long time and was silent. Finally he said, "Well, let's change it."

So there were three successes—Pentecost, divorce and remarriage, and makeup. Next was tithing. Dr. Dorothy continued, "There would have been a change on tithing if the process had not been stopped." Most of the researchers on the Doctrinal Committee thought tithing needed to be changed. The various scriptures and relevant subtopics were divided up and everyone submitted papers on their assigned topics.

But then Dr. Hoeh came to a Doctrinal Committee meeting one day and announced in a formal voice: "Mr. Garner Ted Armstrong has read your papers. We have discussed it and Mr. Ted Armstrong has decided that there is no need to change the tithing doctrine. Therefore all of your papers will be edited in accordance with this policy." Dr. Dorothy refused to permit his paper to be used in this way. Those papers that were edited resulted in the collection of study papers on tithing that were distributed to the ministry.

It was when the Doctrinal Committee got into tithing that everything blew up. The Doctrinal Committee was summarily disbanded. Herbert Armstrong took back personal control with the attitude, "Who do they think they are talking to me this way?"

Letters and Reflections

Through all of these Doctrinal Committee meetings and issues, Dr. Dorothy expressed his opinions. This contributed to his removal from the Theological Research Project. Dr. Dorothy said he walked out of a couple of Doctrinal Committee meetings. One meeting on racial matters involved a shouting match between long-time evangelist Roderick Meredith and a lesser ranked black minister named Tom Hall. Dr. Dorothy said, "Even though we were supposed to uphold the higher rank, I couldn't bring myself to see that Tom Hall was in the wrong."

I asked Dr. Dorothy about Herbert Armstrong's claim that he never knew of the existence of the Theological Research Project. Dr. Dorothy said:

> Well, Ted got it going. Herbert Armstrong was out meeting world leaders. But Herbert Armstrong would have had to have approved it somewhere. He kept up with what was printed in the Ministerial Bulletin [where the Theological Research Project was discussed]. He may have forgotten. No one wanted to admit he was going senile.

This was the maelstrom into which my humble papers, from my setting at Ambassador College, Big Sandy in east Texas, typed, prepared, carefully folded into envelopes, and stamped, were mailed to God's Headquarters. This was what was happening on the other end.

In memorium: Howard A. Clark (1930-2002)

The colorful, charismatic speech instructor at Ambassador College, Big Sandy, Howard Clark, who did so much to inspire students to think for themselves, was known throughout the college and church for an extraordinary healing he had experienced in 1958. From his home in Gasquet, California in 1988 Clark recounted to me more of the story.

For eight years Clark had been confined to a wheelchair after having been badly shot up in Chosin Reservoir, Korea, in December 1950. The left side of his face, his left arm, and his whole body from the chest down were paralyzed. He suffered paresis (partial paralysis) on the right side of his face and right arm. His paralysis and paresis were caused by multiple injuries including contusions of the brain and spinal cord (neuro-encephalopathy). A wartime friend persuaded a woman to have one date with Clark as an act of mercy to a dying man. To everyone's surprise Clark lived. The woman became his wife, Beverly Clark, and they went on to have six children. The medical prognosis was that Clark could expect to be confined to a wheelchair for the rest of his life. But in 1958, after Richard David Armstrong anointed and prayed for him, Clark experienced what doctors called a "dramatic accelerated remission" of his paralysis. It was not a complete restoration to full body mobility (at Big Sandy he required a walking stick and his movements were slower than normal), but it was an extremely dramatic improvement. Such "accelerated remissions" in persons with Clark's specific condition have occurred in other cases, though Clark's was unusual in happening after that much delay. In retrospect, how did Clark interpret the events of 1958? Was it a miracle? Did faith play a role? "Yes, faith played a role, but it wasn't the doing of the organization," Clark told me. "They didn't play a role except for commercializing it. True faith is not meant to be Disneyland and all sunshine, but to work through the rain and snow of life. True faith is not a bubble-gum type of atmosphere or carnival show."

As for his non-use of ministers' perks like chief seats and chief parking lots, Clark said: "I tried to live and teach what I understood Jesus did, e.g. a minister was to serve a congregation. He was to be generous, hospitable, loving, etc. It was his job to teach by example, living what he believed. That was plenty hard for some of those who lived like royalty. They didn't like it much. But what I was I was, and I wished I could be more like the true example."

As for Herbert Armstrong, Clark said psychologists with whom he had talked had diagnosed Herbert Armstrong as an "authoritarian paranoid reactive" personality. Clark explained, "That means he was the nut around whom the shell was built.

Letters and Reflections

The church was the shell. He captured a bunch of innocents and created his own universe within the shell to isolate himself from the realities of the world." Clark added, speaking of those days, "I never met a church member I didn't love dearly."

CHAPTER 25

BIG SANDY VOICES: THE SONG OF THE QUEST

I close this book with a poem by a fellow student from Big Sandy days. The author, Minnesotan Peter Leschak, was a Big Sandy student 1970-74, two years ahead of me. A long-distance runner, journalist, photographer, sewage treatment expert, alligator caretaker, logger, and poet, Leschak was one of the most well-liked and respected students at Big Sandy by both students and faculty. I spent hours at his dorm's fireside, spellbound, listening to him and his upperclassmen friends tell tales and discuss exhilarating ideas. After Big Sandy Leschak returned to rural northern Minnesota with his wife, fellow Big Sandy alumnus Pam Cope. Leschak became a leader of a professional forest fire fighting crew flying in helicopters, battling the elements and, as he put it, making up for the Vietnam combat experience he missed out on except this is saving lives. Leschak has also written a number of well-received books with true-life adventure themes which remind me of the writings of Jack London. These range from his first, *Letters from Side Lake: A Chronicle of Life in the North Woods* (1987), to his more recent *Ghosts of the Fireground* (2002), which includes flashback reminiscences to Ambassador College and stories of Howard Clark, whom Leschak presents as a sort of Christ-figure at Big Sandy. Leschak sided with the dissidents in the 1974 dissident uprising and wrote the following poem soon after, which he has never otherwise published. He has kindly agreed to its appearance here.

Song of the Quest

THE SONG OF THE QUEST

a loose and rambling parody
sung by a traveling minstrel at the
Broken Sceptre Tavern

discovered and edited
by
Peter M. Leschak

© Peter M. Leschak 1975

I. The Royal Deliverance

In fiery dread of wrathful days
The rituals ensued,
In prophecies of golden times
My spirit warmed and brewed.
With sabbaths weighed and counted,
Lost kingdoms gleaned from time,
I forsook the Holy Grail
With repentance vast, sublime.

I rose from dungeon darkness
And one set of chains were cut,
I slew a mad magician
Who had me in his clutch.
With fealty by water rites
I died and then returned
To fall in homage at the feet
Of one whom I had spurned.

This one had come on air waves
His words had bit and stung,
He flew a thunderous silver bird
And called magicians dung.
He spoke of joyful men he knew
In places west and south,

511
Song of the Quest

He spoke of learned scholars,
Of feasts and smiling mouths.

He told of happy laborers
Of altruistic saints,
He mentioned seekers of the truth
He offered peace and grace.
In gratitude I drew my sword
And added to his coffers,
From the north I journeyed to the south
To accept his glorious offers.

II. A Squire in the Land of Dreams

His palace sat in rustic land,
Was beautiful and vast,
I stood, a squire, overcome
By what he had amassed.
His arm was strong, he'd garnered much
But only a son was he,
His father ruled him from the west
In a palace by the sea.

The father was a patriarch
His son the leading king,
Below them other kings and knights
And several squires like me.
The loyal peasants of the realm
Brought honor, gifts, and gold
To aid the kings and scattered knights
(They called themselves a "fold")

So at the palace of the south
I practiced with my sword
To be a knight and speak with kings,
To rule and guide the fold.
The learned scholars opened books
(Many were even knights)
They told me of a dove with claws,
They made the dull seem bright.

They preached of faith and love and grace
But still they sentenced death,

Song of the Quest

They cornered freedom for all men
Then in the next drawn breath,
The laws and rules and rituals
The patriarch's own whims,
Came rushing from their mouths to say,
"To not agree is sin!"

III. The Dawn of the Jesters

I chafed at growing tyranny
I perceived a chain remained,
I rattled swords at midnight
And saw spiders in the rain.
While drinking wine with jesters
(The kings had thought them fools)
I learned that some were knighthood
Tarnished by misrule.

I listened to the jesters long
And likewise other squires,
We thought and searched and argued
And found some knights were liars.
We hunted snakes and spiders
Yes, in the Hall of Books,
We hacked at them with sharpened swords
And cornered them in nooks.

But word had reached a lesser king
Of the palace of the south,
It whispered of a secret group
Who opened much to doubt.
The lesser king was many years
With the palace and its law
(His orations were as sleeping pills)
On his shield was a saw

He rose in indignation
And railed at jester's light,
He drew his sword to challenge doubt
But warped it in the fight.
But even as the skies grew black
And webs began to form,

Song of the Quest

This king was sent across the sea
And another quelled the storm.

Now this man seemed an easier man
(A dart was on his shield)
He promised to hear the jesters,
Perhaps to even yield.
I wrote upon a parchment,
Well-meaning to advise
And sent it to the royal court,
It spoke of sin and lies.

IV. Advisor to the King

I saw a spider down in hell
Or was he in my hand?
I peered beneath the cover
And my eyes were filled with sand.
A seagull flitted through the air
He blessed the purple sun,
I staggered on the barren beach
And dropped my rusted gun.

I listened to the royal horn
(I wish I had the tape)
In a poem to the new-crowned king
I accused his court of rape.
While bearing gifts unknown to them
The royal members came,
Their faces spoke of mutant men
But their robes were still the same.

I knelt upon the barren beach
The spider in my hand,
The king has closed the cover
But my eyes are cleansed of sand.

V. In the Days of Bloody Thunder

And so the jesters lived in scorn
Their words, though keen, unheard,
The patriarch was in the clouds
With sea below his bird.

Song of the Quest

The king of kings his son, though bright,
Had dwindled love and trust
More knights grew restless in the realm
And peasants ate more dust.

Till then a knight and all his fief
Rose up and cast a glove,
With swords like polished silver
They stabbed the taloned dove,
But not alone in all the land
More fiefs of serfs gave cry
And severed from the palace grand
(The best that money could buy)

The son and many lesser kings
Came rushing from the sky
With crooked swords and cursing words
(They let the old shit fly)
Thousands swirled with clanging swords
As I fled the palace door,
A dozen fiefs were all in flames,
The father was down for war.

To quench the heated, fervent fire
The kings all met and said:
"Hold fast you peasants of the realm
It's all as we have said.
The Old Ones spoke of us you know,
They told of falling away
The Spider Lord is in on this
And many under his sway."

And though they changed some unjust laws
It was years and lives too late,
Even one king cast away his crown
And strode from the palace gate.
Two score knights were banished,
Two thousand serfs went free,
But among the noble squires,
Only handfuls chose to flee.

Song of the Quest

VI. The Revelation.

T'was among the cries the rebels heard
"Where can you ever go?"
Beyond the palace gates you're told
Is error, sin, and woe."
"No other sons of men can know
What's proper, right, and good.
No other learned scholars
Can feed you living food."

I journeyed long and narrow roads
Where few had gone before,
Where lonely little towns had sprung
Around the Old Ones' lore.
There in scattered hamlets
Knights and scholars wrote
The peasants never tasted dust,
There were no kings to boast.

I sojourned there among the wise
(Afar from palace bars)
And shared their fires of warmth and light
Beneath new midnight stars.
Celestial men who keep not birds
Nor royal gates and doors,
Who rise not over lesser ones
(And put them all in drawers).

I still can hear the patriarch
In his palace by the sea,
I often see his many kings
And what I sought to be.
I hear them claiming precedence
And how the rest are dearth,
Though even in their confidence
They do not rule the earth.

VII. The Song of the Quest

And so I ride the mountain trails
An ever wary sword
To kill the coiled vipers

516
Song of the Quest

And flush the Spider Lord.
In prophecies of golden times
Like purest snow-fed streams,
My spirit quenches fiery thirst
For real lands of dreams.

The wrathful dogs of desert nights
And shamans by the score
Come tugging at my stirrups
And fall beneath my sword.
But soon from o'er the mountain peaks
A royal horn will ring,
The sun will rise like thunder
And reveal the only King.

Addendum

The Demise and End of Ambassador College, Big Sandy

In 1977 Herbert Armstrong closed the Big Sandy campus of Ambassador College. Then in 1981 Herbert Armstrong decided to reopen the Big Sandy campus. In 1985 he decided to close it again. In January 1986 Herbert Armstrong died and his successor, Joseph Tkach, Sr., decided to keep the Big Sandy campus open again.

In 1990 the campus at Pasadena, California was permanently closed. All Ambassador College operations were moved to Big Sandy.

In 1994 Ambassador College, Big Sandy, became accredited for the first time and the name was changed to Ambassador University.

In 1994 and 1995 the Worldwide Church of God leadership announced changes of its historic doctrines, lost many members and its income declined. In 1995 the Worldwide Church of God announced it would no longer subsidize Ambassador University. In December 1996 the University's regents voted to close it. In May 1997 Ambassador University, Big Sandy, closed its doors for good.

In 2000 the Big Sandy campus was sold for $8.5 million to an arts-and-crafts company called Hobby Lobby, which leased and then sold the campus to the Institute in Basic Life Principles, a ministry of controversial evangelical minister Bill Gothard. Today the Big Sandy campus is the home of the Gothard-affiliated ALERT Academy, a military-like skills and character training program which trains young men in disaster relief and emergency services.

Entering freshman class of 1972-73 at Ambassador College, Big Sandy, Texas (from the college yearbook, the Envoy)

Jennifer Agee
Scott R. Ashley
Glenn K. Bailey
Linda S. Banninger
Kitty S. Beane
Cheryl E. Beattie
Brent R. Blomberg
Patricia M. Bogol
Curtis A. Borman
A. Michael Castro
Sharon S. Catron
Joseph L. Cochran
Thomas Crabb
Paula Jo Crim
William E. Cummings
Catherine Curran
L. Nolan Davis
Mary E. Dean
Greg K. Deily
Guido S. Denzler
Janet J. Domagala
Gregory L. Doudna
Kay F. Duke
Ricky Dykes
Russell S. Edwards
Leslie L. French
David R. Friestad
Joseph H. Garner
J. Edward Glancy
Marsali A. Gordon
Melissa L. Gouker
Deborah A. Graby
Diane C. Grede
Randy L. Gregory
Jan M. Gully
Michael J. Hale
Terry L. Hammer
Clifton L. Handy
Mark L. Hanna
Robert L. Harrison
Allen R. Heckman
Rebecca A. Henson
James I. Hepper
Diana L. Hill
Tony K. Hill
Dennis R. Houglum
Jesse L. Howell
Faith M. Hull
Faye S. Hull
Cindy R. Jackson
Valerie A. Jaros
Jolinda J. Jenkins
Melba J. Jenison
Stephanie A. Johnson
Margarethe Kardos
Ronald L. Kelley
Dyle R. Koch
Julia A. Lane
Linda M. Link
Mark L. Littleton
Vera D. Mahone
Rebecca E. Marshall
Linda C. Martin
Kathy R. Mathews
Dale A. McCloud
Joel J. McCormick
Marilyn A. McGee
L. Elaine McMillan
E. Lu McSpadden
Thomas P. Melzer
Leslie F. Mooneyham
Kimberly A. McCullough
Creighton N. Miller
Angela M. Mohler
Larry F. Moluf
William O. Murray
Peggy J. Neal
S. Myles Newman
Dorothy, A. Niekamp
Faith E. Olmstead
Timothy M. O'Connor
Robert S. Overstreet
Terry A. Pair
Kenneth D. Pearson
Keith A. Perrin
Linda M. Peyton
Robert G. Robinson
Norman R. Rowe
B. Jamie Rush
Gary R. Ruxton
Stephanie R. Saracino
Tom W. Sash
Rex I. Sexton
James D. Share
Maxine Skaggs
Mary A. Slider
Danny L. Smith
Earl W. Smith
Gary M. Smith
L. Gregory Smith
Ronald O. Smith
Timothy Sobitz
David M. Sutton
Rebecca A. Sutton
David Swaim
Guy C. Swenson
Paul W. Syltie
Mark S. Thomas
Ada M. Travis
Marilyn L. Wade
Laurie R. Wagner
Daniel R. White
Wayne R. Whitman
Patricia L. Willhoite
Evelyn J. Wilson
Tom D. Wilson
Gary H. Woodring
Charlene B. Workman
James T. Worthen

INDEX OF PERSONS

A

Adali, Selim F., 228
Adams, Tom, 156
Adenauer, Konrad, 34
Allen, J.H., 202
Allen, Joseph H., 175, 202, 206, 212, 213-14, 492
Ames, Richard, 14, 22, 71-72, 75-76, 195-97, 263-64, 462
Anderson (Big Sandy faculty), 419
Anne, Queen (of England), 192
Antion, David L., 45, 52-53, 150, 429, 438
Apartian, Dibar, 226, 429
Arfons, Art, 164
Armstrong, Dwight, 54
Armstrong, Eva, 36-37
Armstrong, Garner Ted, 4, 13, 44, 52-53, 56, 58-60, 64-66, 113, 135-36, 145-54, 164, 255, 336, 339, 347, 349, 356, 361, 366, 383, 409-410, 427, 431-32, 437-39, 442-43, 464, 475-77, 494, 504-505, 510-511, 514
Armstrong, Herbert W., v-vii, 4-7, 10-13, 17, 19-20, 26-27, 30-32, 34-57, 64-70, 82, 89, 94, 109-110, 115, 123, 132, 134-35, 137, 140, 145, 147-52, 154-59, 162-63, 167, 173-79, 193, 195, 199-207, 211, 213-14, 217, 220, 226, 244-46, 251, 256-57, 260, 263, 268, 271, 274-75, 279, 282-85, 289, 291-92, 295, 299, 310, 321-24, 330, 335, 338-42, 344-52, 360-67, 370, 383, 385-87, 389-94, 396-99, 409, 412, 425-27, 431, 434-38, 442-43, 455, 460, 464, 469-73, 485, 499-507, 511, 515, 517

Armstrong, Horace, 36-37
Armstrong, Loma, 37-38, 42, 385, 387-89, 392
Armstrong, Ramona, 53
Armstrong, Richard David, 18, 282, 506
Armstrong, Sarah Emily, 32
Armstrong, Shirley, 4, 60, 65
Arvidson, Gary, 272-76
Asimov, Isaac, 72

B

Bacchiocchi, Samuele, 378
Bach, Richard, 18
Bacon, Margaret Hope, 30
Baebler, B., 237
Bailey, Vance, 124
Baldwin, James, 143
Balmer, Randall, 254
Barth, Karl, 296
Bauckham, R.J., 378
Becker, Hans Albert, 243
Billingsley, Michael, 15
Bin Laden, Osama, 175
Bivens, Don, 84-85
Blackwell, Dean, 24, 130, 170, 456, 458
Bogart, Humphrey, 481
Boraker, Robert, 231-32
Borchardt, Frank L., 243
Borman, Curtis, 84
Bowden, Henry Warner, 254, 288
Bradescu, 52
Brezhnev, Leonid, vi, 461
Brothers, Richard, 200-201, 204, 242, 289
Brown, Clyde, 272-76
Brown, Dee, 254
Brown, John, 143
Brunt, John, 315

Index of Persons

Bryant, Paul William "Bear", 5
Buchman, Frank, 34
Bunker, Ellsworth, 57

C

Cabot, John, 88
Callahan, Virginia Woods, 287
Cantleberry, Lillian, viii
Carozzo, Al, 149
Carson, D.A., 378
Cartwright, Dixon, 273, 276
Catron, Sharon, 163
Charles, Prince (of England), 174
Cheung, Alex, 314-15
Chodos, Hillel, 363
Chomsky, Noam, 277
Clark, Beverly, 19, 506
Clark, Bobby, viii, ix, 316-17
Clark, Bryce, 53, 65, 254, 427, 439
Clark, Howard A., 17-20, 22-23, 153-56, 356, 395, 505-507, 509
Clifton, Howard, 4
Clover, R., 377
Cochran, Joe, 5
Cohen, Leonard, 363
Colby, Chris, 410
Cole, Raymond, 282
Cole, Wayne, 504
Collins, Steven M., 276
Condon, Richard C., 294
Cope, Pamela, 509
Cope, William, 489
Cornwall, Henry, 361-62
Coston, Woody, 15
Cowan, Richard, 10
Crotzer, Tom, 419
Cullmann, Oscar, 376
Curley, Harry, 269-70, 273

D

Dankenbring, William F., 134-35, 139, 259-62, 264-66, 268-70, 274-76
Dart, Ronald, 10, 14, 17, 76, 78-79, 87, 90, 115, 121-22, 124, 126, 128, 135-36, 146, 151-53, 155, 168, 180-82, 275, 327-29, 396, 429, 431, 438, 440-44, 499-501, 513
Davidy, Yair, 272
Deakins, Donald, 14, 413-14
Denzler, Brenda, 395
Diakonoff, Igor M., 230
Dickerson (Dean, Pasadena), 95
Dietz, Dennis, 73-4, 76, 77-81, 83, 86, 88-91, 412-14, 419
Dornbert, John, 243
Dorothy, Charles V., 167, 322-24, 371-72, 374, 396-97, 501-505
Doudna, Anne Caroline, viii, 517
Doudna, David, vii, 14, 32-36, 45-46, 54, 58, 66, 220, 385
Doudna, Ephraim, 220
Doudna, Hosea, 220
Doudna, John, 219-20, 487-88
Doudna, Paul, 21, 35
Doudna, Phyllis, 34-36, 46, 48, 66, 385, 436
Doudna, Sarah, 487-88
Doudna, Shawn, 35, 45-46, 58, 66, 385
Doudna, Willis, 33, 488
DuBois, W.E.B., 143
Dugger, Andrew, 40, 203
Dugmore, C.W., 376, 378

E

Earle, Neil, 32
Eash, Mike, 453-54
Eccles, Wes, 419
Edelman, Diana, 98
Edward I, King (of England), 204, 216
Edward VIII, King (of England), 202
Edwards, Norman, 269-72
Edwards, Russ, 269
Eisenberg, Harry, 412, 437
Elizabeth I, Queen (of England), 192
Elizabeth II, Queen (of England), 174, 192, 205, 274, 426
Ellett, Briscoe, 22
Ervin, John W., 363
Eshelman, M.M., 202

Index of Persons

F

Fahey, Robert, 47
Falwell, Jerry, 135-36
Filmer, W.E., 216
Finlayson, John, 242
Fischer, Bobby, 163
Flaherty, Roderick, 209
Foland, C.A., 137
Foland, Doreen, 137
Ford, Henry, 202
Fotopoulos, John, 315
Fox, John, 214
Fredkin, Edward, 423

G

Gager, M.H., 240
Galileo, Galilei, 264
Gandhi, Indira, 339
Gandhi, Mahatma, 34
Gardner, Martin, 354
Geiger, Peter, 52
George III, King (of England), 200
Geraty, Lawrence, 376-77
Germano, Michael, 275-76
Gerson (law partner of Rader), 361
Gibbs, Murdock, 128-32, 136
Gilreath, Fred, 475-76
Giulini, Carlo Giulini, 157
Glover, F.R.A., 213, 216
Gmirkin, Russell, viii, 92-98, 167-68, 328-32, 370-73, 377, 453-54, 501
Godbey, Allen, 228, 240, 250
Gödel, Kurt, 333, 354
Gogh, Vincent van, 493
Goldman, Henry, 361
Goldman, Shalom L., 240
Goonan, Thomas, 495
Gordon, John, 270
Gothard, Bill, 517
Gotoh, Osamu, 363-64
Goudoever, J. van, 377
Grabbe, Lester, 503
Grant, Asahel, 239
Green, Carlton, 9
Gregg, Robert C., 281

Gregory, Randy, 5
Griffin, John James, 113, 122, 124-28, 139, 141
Groh, Dennis E., 281
Guillory, Berlin, 14

H

Haines, Larry, 11
Haldeman, H.R., 486
Halhed, Nathanael, 200
Hall, Richard, 216
Hall, Tammy, 15
Hall, Tom, 505
Hammer, Buck, 4
Hannay, Bruce, 232
Hanisko, Jerry, 21
Hanson, Thomas, 131
Hatch, Nathan O., 253-54
Heath, Alan, 14
Heffley, Mike, viii
Hegvold, Sidney, 14
Helge, Ralph, 361
Herrmann, Kenneth, 14, 90, 99-105, 282-83, 337-38, 419, 455, 495
Heschel, Abraham Joshua, 108
Hill, David Jon, 292
Hirohito, Emperor (of Japan), 363
Hitler, Adolf, 177-79
Hoag, Perry, 160-61
Hobbs, G.A., 203
Hoeh, Herman L., 43, 55, 74, 79, 81-82, 85-92, 94-97, 99-103, 106, 167-68, 208-212, 218, 224, 226-27, 238, 242-43, 252, 259-60, 282, 335, 417-22, 437-39, 442, 461, 504
Hoffer, Eric, 18
Hogeterp, A.L.A., 98
Hoover, Herbert, 32
Hoover, J. Edgar, 35
Hopkins, Joseph, 131-32
Houglum, Dennis, 156
Hoyt, Hannah, 488
Hunt, Keith, 214
Hunting, Charles, 340, 383, 498-99
Hussein, King (of Jordan), 69, 339

Index of Persons

I

Ignatiev, Noel, 142
Israel, Manasseh ben, 239
Ivantchik, Askold, 230, 236-37

J

James, William, 20
Janes, Wayne, 126
Jessup, W. Edgar, Jr., 363

K

Kackos, George, 166, 168-69
Kackos, Merry, 168
Kaplan, Mark, 14, 107, 126, 161, 194-95, 346, 419
Kelly, Ronald, 13-14, 111, 127, 153, 290, 434
Kennedy, John F., 255-56
Kennedy, Robert F., 45, 256
Kenyatta, Jomo, 34, 339
Kessler, Jack, 361-62
Keyser, John, 266-67
Khrushchev, Nikita, 256, 460-61
Knauf, Al, 419
Knowles, Brian, 438
Koehler, Dean, 60-61
Koestler, Arthur, 354
Koo, Eddie, 159
Korzybski, Alfred, 18
Kristensen, Anne, 228-38
Kuhn, Robert, 351, 397, 502-504

L

Laessoe, Joergen, 228
Laing, R.D., 481
Lanfranchi, G.B., 230
Larson, Bob, 284
Lash, Symeon, 288
Lee, Albert, 202
Leopold III, King (of Belgium), 340, 499
Le Sage, Georges-Louis, 93
Leschak, Peter, 124-26, 509-516
Lienhard, Joseph T., 281

Loma Armstrong, 386
London, Jack, 509

M

Mackay, Charles, 253
MacKendrick, W.G., 203, 240
MacManus, Seasmus, 210-11
Manteufel, Allen, 14, 224-25, 419
Marcos, Ferdinand, 339
Marsden, George, 253-54
Martin, Ernest, 147, 275, 352, 437, 439-40, 442
Martin, Ramona, 53
Martin, Walter, 285
Mary I, Queen (of England), 192
Mary II, Queen (of England), 192
May, Ross, 137
Mazar, Benjamin, 68-69, 418
McBride, Bob, 126
McCann, Kathleen, 273
McCann, Lewis, 273
McCarthy, Eugene, 161
McCullough, Les, 12-13, 512-513
McDowell, Josh, 284-85
McGough, Hugh, 215
McNab, Jamie, 387
McNair, Raymond F., 148, 226, 246-50, 260, 268-70, 321
McReynolds, Dr. (Adventist), 383
Melton, J. Gordon, 39, 200
Melzer, Tom, 11
Meredith, C. Paul, 282, 421
Meredith, Roderick C., 148, 255, 282-83, 464, 505
Meyer, Jacob O., 300
Meyer, William, 23
Mikasa, Prince (of Japan), 341, 363
Milhous, Franklin, 32
Miller, Alice, 63
Miller, Creighton, 11
Minh, Ho Chi, 486
Mitchell, John, 145-46, 514
Moll, Linda, 17, 496
Moluf, Larry, 11
Montagu, Ashley, 113, 116
Moore, A.D., 354

Index of Persons

Moore, Bill, 217
Mussolini, Benito, 177-78

N

Napoleon Bonaparte, 201
Neilson, Geoff, 274
"Neotherm," 16
Nicholas II, Czar (of Russia), 426
Nickels, Richard, 41, 132, 387, 430-31, 495-96
Nilsson, Martin P., 289
Nithsdale, F.M., 216
Nixon, Richard M., 31-32, 338, 485-86
Noll, Mark, 253-54

O

O'Connor, Timothy, 156, 169
O'Curry, Eugene, 207-209
O'Donovan, John, 217
O'Flannery, Roderick, 212
O'Lochain, Cuan, 217-18
Odie, Faye, 45
Orr, Ralph, 203
Orwell, George, 89, 277, 439, 457
Overstreet, Bob, 11
Overton, Mac, 419

P

Pallazo (accounting partner with Rader), 361
Parpola, S., 230, 251
Pavlik, Dan, 454
Pavlov, Ivan P., 410
Peat, F. David, 353
Penn, William, 36
Phillips, E.C., 124
Pinchas, Theophilus G., 232
Pius XII, Pope, 177
Plache, Richard, 429
Portune, Albert, 150
Prettyman, Anthony, 15
Price, George McCready, 418
Price, T.A., 216
Prociw, Steve, 10

Pyle, Norvel, 130

R

Rader, Niki, 498
Rader, Stanley R., 7, 27, 37, 148-49, 163-65, 339, 349-52, 360-63, 498, 503
Rains, Claude, 481
Rand, Ayn, 454
Reedy, Daryl, 14
Regtien, Martin, 160
Reier, Jim, 260
Reipas, A., 241
Reser, Brenda, 395
Riak, Jordan, 63
Ribb, James Olof, 21
Richardson, Alan, 288
Rigdon, Mary, 169
Rigdon, Russ, 169-70, 453
Rivers, Johnny, 15
Robinson, David, 11-12, 130, 148
Robinson, John, 42, 493, 495
Robinson, Robert, 11
Rohan, Dennis, 45
Ronish (Big Sandy faculty), 419
Rordorf, Willy, 378
Roth, Cecil, 200-201
Royer, Paul, 427, 439
Rucker, Rudy, 353-54
Rumney, Gavin, 275
Runcorn, Ora, 38
Rush, Jamie, 113

S

Sadat, Anwar, 339
Sagan, Carl, 394
Salomaa, R., 241
Salyer, Larry, 260
Sartre, Jean-Paul, 333
Sato, Bunsei, 472
Sauter, Hermann, 230
Sayce, Archibald Henry, 248-50
Schonfield, Hugh, 21
Schultz, Roy, 95
Schumacher, E.F., 77

Index of Persons

Schurter, Dale, 80
Schwarzschild, Karl, 333
Segall, Marc, 42
Selassie, Haile, 339
Sexton, Rex, 113, 454
Share, James, 11
Shepard, Sam, 3
Sheppherd, Steve, 271
Sherrod, Rick, 271-72
Simpson, Richard, 244
Skene, William, 217-18
Slider, Mary, 5
Smith, Earl, viii, 247-48, 491-93
Smith, Gary, 126
Smith, Joseph, 240
Smith, Linda Moll, 17, 496
Smith, Ron, 11
Smyth, Alfred P., 217
Sneider, Harry, 163
Sobitz, Timothy, Jr., 11, 163-65
Sobitz, Timothy, Sr., 164
Spencer-Brown, G., 353
Spillane, Mickey, 55
Stalin, Joseph, 460
Stevens, Karen, viii
Stewart, Don, 284-85
Stough, H.E., 216
Strand, Kenneth, 376, 378
Strauss, Franz Josef, 179
Strommen, Marjean, 6
Sturcke, Henry, 378
Swenson, Guy, 156, 181-82

T

Tabor, James, 289
Taylor, Gordon Rattray, 72
Thiele, Edwin, 106
Timmins, Lyle, 269-70
Tkach, Joseph Jr., 15, 139, 366
Tkach, Joseph, Sr., 49, 134, 137, 139, 203, 260, 366, 398-99, 517

Tkach, Tammy, 15
Torrance, Lynn, 111, 162, 164, 167-68, 341-42, 344-45, 356-58, 360-61, 363-65, 455-56
Trechak, John, 383, 426, 428-29, 481, 496
Treybig, David, 310
Tuit, John, 361
Turner, Sharon, 225-26

V

Vespucci, Amerigo, 272
Victoria, Queen (of England), 192, 274

W

Wakefield, J. Richard, 410
Wakefield, Richard, 14, 410
Walker, Frank, 41
Wallace, George, 128
Ward, Donald, 14
Warrington, Walter, 486
Waterhouse, Gerald, 56, 138, 463
Webster, Wesley, 132-33
Westby, Kenneth, 150, 272-76
Wharton, James Allen, 107-108
White, Craig, 106, 420
White, Ellen G., 39
Whitman, Walt, 454
Wild, Joseph, 201-202
Willhoite, Patricia ("Trish"), 16-17, 496
William III, King (of England), 192
Wilson, Bryan, 240
Wilson, John, 201, 203, 240, 242
Wlodyga, Ronald, 260
Wolverton, Basil, 55

Z

Zuse, Konrad, 423

About the author

Greg Doudna, originally from Akron, Ohio, attended Ambassador College, Big Sandy, Texas, from 1972 to 1975. In 1989 he entered the University of Oregon as a freshman, graduating with a B.A. in linguistics in 1991, an M.A. in Near Eastern studies from Cornell in 1992, and Dr. Theology from the University of Copenhagen in 2002, with a focus on study of the Hebrew Bible/ Dead Sea Scrolls. He lives with his wife Anne Caroline in Bellingham, Washington, where he writes, teaches, and cleans windows.

www.scrollery.com

www.ingramcontent.com/pod-product-compliance
Lightning Source LLC
Chambersburg PA
CBHW020300010526
44108CB00037B/168